SUNSPOTS AND THE SUN KING

the
humanities
laboratory

Sunspots and the Sun King

SOVEREIGNTY

AND MEDIATION IN

SEVENTEENTH-CENTURY

FRANCE

ELLEN M. MCCLURE

UNIVERSITY OF
ILLINOIS PRESS

URBANA AND
CHICAGO

Publication of this volume was made possible in
part by support from the Humanities Laboratory
at the University of Illinois at Chicago.

⊗ This book is printed on acid-free paper.

Library of Congress
Cataloging-in-Publication Data

McClure, Ellen M., 1968-
Sunspots and the Sun King : sovereignty and
mediation in seventeenth-century France /
Ellen M. McClure.
p. cm. – (The humanities laboratory)
Includes bibliographical references and index.
ISBN-13: 978-0-252-03056-7 (cloth : alk. paper)
ISBN-10: 0-252-03056-7 (cloth : alk. paper)
1. Monarchy–France–History–17th century.
2. Louis XIV, King of France, 1638-1715.
3. Mediation–France–History–17th century.
4. France–Politics and government–1643-1715.
I. Title. II. Series.
JN2358.M37 2006
320.94409'032–dc22
2005034478

Contents

Acknowledgments

In writing this book, I have benefited enormously from the generosity of several institutions and individuals. At the University of Michigan, a Rackham Predissertation Fellowship allowed me to begin a process of research and writing that ultimately led me to a much different place. Domna C. Stanton supervised that first project with patience, skill, and generosity; without her encouragement and that of Jim Porter, I would never have begun to explore the rich world of seventeenth-century France.

A Mellon Postdoctoral Fellowship at the Newberry Library allowed me to accomplish much of the research and writing of this book. James Grossman, Sara Austin, and the rest of the staff at the Newberry helped make that year both productive and enjoyable. The other fellows were inspiring models of discipline and scholarship. I would especially like to thank Rebecca Bach for her friendship and intellectual generosity. At the University of Illinois at Chicago, I received research and travel assistance from the Office of the Vice-Chancellor for Research and the Institute for the Humanities. I would also like to recognize the staff of the Archives of the Ministère des Affaires Etrangères (Quai d'Orsay) for their helpfulness.

I am also indebted to the many audiences to whom I presented parts of this work. They provided invaluable support and suggestions, and I take full responsibility for all errors of fact or judgment that may have survived their careful critiques. The 2004 NEH summer institute, "The Intersection of Philosophy, Science and Theology in the Seventeenth Century," led by Stephen Nadler and Donald Rutherford, was extremely helpful to me in revising the introduction; I would particularly like to thank Christia Mercer for her encouragement and suggestions. Part of chapter 1 was presented at the Renaissance Workshop at the University of Chicago; the Modern France Workshop, also at the University of Chicago, allowed me to present part of chapter 4. I would like to thank David Armitage and the other members of the 2002 Folger seminar "The Foundations of Modern International Thought (1494–1713)" for allowing me to present parts of chapter 3 and for welcoming a literary scholar into their midst. Bob Bucholz encouraged me to present parts of chapter 4 at the Newberry Library Seminar on Courts, Households and Lineages and has provided good-humored and unfailing support for this project. I would also like to thank Renaud Morieux, Pascal Dupuy, and the Université de Rouen for inviting me to participate in a *journée d'études* on seventeenth- and eighteenth-century Anglo-French treaties. The Society for Interdisciplinary Seventeenth-Century French Studies (SE17), founded and led by Francis Assaf, deserves much credit not only for providing an invaluable home for work such as my own but also for welcoming me into its warm community. Many of the colleagues I have met there have become good friends, and I thank all of them, especially Didier Course, for their encouragement and advice.

Part of chapter 5 appears in my article "Lieu Tenant: Diplomacy and Dementia in Racine's *Andromaque*," forthcoming in *Actes de Dartmouth*, to be published by Gunter Narr Verlag (Biblio 17). I am grateful to Wolfgang Leiner and the press for permission to republish this material.

I am particularly indebted to Sander Gilman, Dawn Marlan, and the UIC Humanities Laboratory's First Book Series for assisting in this book's publication. The two anonymous readers for the University of Illinois Press provided valuable suggestions and corrections, and I thank them for their careful reading of the manuscript. Willis Regier, my editor at the University of Illinois Press, has guided me expertly through the entire process. I would also like to thank Yvonne Ramsey for her careful editing of the manuscript.

On a more personal note, I would like to thank the many friends and families who have supported me during the long process of research and writing. The Lagier family first introduced me to the delights of France and has always welcomed me warmly into their home. I am honored and privileged to know them. The Arslanguls and Yagoubians also provided me with ample moral and material support during my long stays in France. My mother, Paula Dziminski, and father, Richard McClure, have patiently, proudly, and lovingly encouraged all of my endeavors. Michael Arslangul has added the key ingredients of laughter and a sense of perspective to the virtues of patience, pride, and love that he has expressed in often undeserved abundance, and for that I can never thank him enough.

Note on Translations

With the significant exception of Paul Sonnino's translation of Louis XIV's *Mémoires pour l'instruction du dauphin*, in order to preserve the signification of the original wording all translations are my own. I have also preserved the original spelling and punctuation of the texts, except where there were clear typographical errors.

SUNSPOTS AND THE SUN KING

In 1610, Henri IV was assassinated by the fanatic François Ravaillac, who claimed to be acting in the larger interests of the Catholic faith. During the same year, Galileo began observing spots on the sun with his telescope; he would publish his findings in 1613. Both events represented a disquieting challenge to order and hierarchy. Henri IV's murder renewed lingering questions about his legitimacy; Galileo's sunspots brought the celestial sun into the realm of terrestrial corruption. Against both of these developments, the restoration of faith in an order grounded in permanence and transcendence was more urgent than ever before. Efforts to effect this restoration resulted in the creation of the Sun King, whose authority and monarchical identity was constructed at least in part to counter the destructive implications of the sunspots.

This is not to say, however, that the Sun King was an unproblematic symbol of hierarchy and absolutism. The creation of a satisfactory model of royal authority in seventeenth-century France was neither an entirely mystical and mythical enterprise nor a wholly cynical and rational expression of reason of

1

state. Rather, these two currents of thought responded to and influenced one another, each pointing out the other's inconsistencies and vulnerabilities. The duality present in seventeenth-century French monarchy is therefore not the duality identified by Ernst Kantorowicz of "the king's two bodies." As Hélène Merlin-Kajman has argued, it is, rather, a conceptual duality that is symbolized by the differing approaches of Kantorowicz and Carl Schmitt to the state; Kantorowicz emphasizes the institutions and continuity of kingship, while Schmitt is concerned with the suddenness and amorality of the coup d'état, or political act.[1] Yet while Merlin-Kajman is correct that to fully appreciate the complexity of seventeenth-century French theories of political authority these approaches must be read together, or at least against one another, her concern is largely with the expression of this duality in the theater of Pierre Corneille, and therefore she does not address the ways in which this tension is a symptom of a widespread and urgent preoccupation during this period with reconciling two incommensurable ways of thinking about power and the relation of God to the universe. Considering sunspots and the Sun King together not only reminds us that they belong to the same period; it also reminds us of the cosmic stakes involved in restoring and recasting political authority.

The ongoing tension between a worldview that stressed the interrelatedness of God and the world and one that stressed the independence of the parts composing the universe provided the century's basic intellectual framework and dynamism. Throughout Europe, seventeenth-century scientists and philosophers such as Galileo were discarding the magical subtleties of scholasticism in favor of logic and definition. In France, Descartes was working to strip the physical world of innate and imaginary qualities and to reconstruct it on principles of clarity and simplicity.[2] While this method was both revolutionary and attractive, it was also seen as threatening to a larger hierarchy of the world based upon a continuity supplied by the dynamic and intimate relation between God and creation. Descartes' successors, most notably Malebranche, therefore worked to modify his philosophy to accommodate this vision. The preface to the *Recherche de la vérité* announces Malebranche's commitment to the union and connection between the disparate realms of the universe: "L'esprit de l'homme se trouve par sa nature comme situé entre son Créateur, et les créatures corporelles; car selon saint Augustin, il n'y a rien au-dessus de lui que Dieu, ni rien au-dessous que des corps. Mais comme la grande élévation où il est au-dessus de toutes les choses matérielles, n'empêche pas qu'il ne leur soit uni, et qu'il ne dépende même en quelque façon d'une portion de la matière, aussi la distance infinie, qui se trouve entre l'Etre souverain et l'esprit de l'homme, n'empêche pas qu'il ne lui soit uni immédiatement, et d'une manière très intime."[3] (The human mind by its nature finds itself as if situated between its Creator and the corporal creatures; for according to Saint Augustine, there is nothing above it but God, and nothing below it but bodies. But just as its great elevation above all material things does not prevent it from being united with them, nor from being in some fashion dependent upon matter, so also the infinite distance which is between the Sovereign Being and the human mind does not prevent it from being united to Him immediately and in a very intimate manner.) Descartes' philosophy, of course, does include the divine, but valorizes human attempts to approximate the divine position, as in the sixth part of the *Discours de la méthode* where he famously asserts that the knowledge obtained by his method "[peut] nous rendre comme maîtres et possesseurs de la nature" ([can] make us as if masters and possessors of nature).[4] In addition, he emphasizes the individual effort to search for truth, unfettered by human authority, including his own: "on ne saurait si bien concevoir une chose, et la rendre sienne, lorsqu'on l'apprend de quelque autre, que lorsqu'on l'invente soi-même" (one cannot conceive something and make it one's own quite as well when one learns it from someone else than when one invents it oneself).[5] Malebranche's approach is strikingly different in that it de-emphasizes the godlike qualities of humanity in order to stress humanity's essential *dependence* on the divine. His citation of Augustine in the first lines of his own search for truth is only one demonstration of his fundamentally different attitude toward authority.

Malebranche's effort to modify Descartes is typical of the ongoing dialogue between the discrete and the continuous during the seventeenth century. It is important to note that for the participants in this debate, the ultimate victory of the discrete and the individual was by no means assured or foreseen.[6] The idea that the world was grounded in (and, for Malebranche, authored by) the divine can seem quite strange to the modern reader, but it needs to be taken very seriously if we are to fully appreciate the uniqueness of the period. Efforts to square the circle by reconciling independence and continuity extended beyond pure philosophy to reach almost every area of seventeenth-century French thought. The two seemingly incompatible doctrines appeared in full force in attempts to redefine the monarchy after the chaotic events of the sixteenth century. In the wake of the religious wars and the troubled succession of the Protestant Henri IV to the French throne, a veritable deluge of treatises offered different accounts of the origin and proper structure of the French state. Protestant writers such as François Hotman asserted that the ultimate authority behind the state had always lain with the French people, who temporarily delegated their sovereignty to the king. Writers of the Catholic League sought to minimize the power of the Crown in relation to the supreme authority of the pope. Both sides marshaled historical texts and examples in their defense, each presenting themselves as the true representatives of French tradition.[7] Faced with what was becoming a cacophony of political theories and voices, Jean Bodin, sought to strip government to its essential core. The result was a tightly defined, independent, and self-sufficient entity called sovereignty–a new idea that appealed to the emerging ideals of simplicity and clarity and that Bodin, importantly, declared true precisely because it was both simple and clear.

In a move that resembles Malebranche's efforts to adjust Cartesianism several decades later, Bodin's successors found his innovative concept and method appealing but in need of modification. In the first chapter of this book, I argue that the theory of divine right monarchy was elaborated in part to correct a perceived overemphasis on the independence of the sovereign in Bodin. This reading asserts that divine right was no more a "return" to age-old principles of government than were the alternatives proposed during the sixteenth century; rather, it should be regarded as highly dependent on the particular needs of the French state at the time.[8] Divine right theorists asserted that royal authority and action were underwritten, and even initiated, by God. This theory had the singular advantage of erasing all human influence from the origin or exercise of royal power; neither subjects nor *parlement* has any role in its elaboration–something quite important given the events of the sixteenth century and, later, the Fronde. The king's status as human, yet somehow and ineffably superior to his human subjects, is secured; in the terms outlined by Malebranche above, he is the equivalent of the human mind, united yet superior to his corporeal subjects. This qualified model of royal authority, wherein the king is less an independent actor than an instrument for the expression of divine will, owes a considerable debt to the resurgence of Neoplatonism in early seventeenth-century France. Indeed, Cardin Le Bret's decision to cite Philo Judaeus on the first page of his treatise on monarchy only makes sense in this context.[9] Neoplatonism, present in almost all of the treatises I discuss, has largely been overlooked as a source for seventeenth-century French political theory. Yet it offered a means of conceptualizing the king as the *singular* meeting point of the divine and the human. The prominence of Neoplatonist language offers the interesting possibility that theorists of the time were adjusting their vision of monarchy: less the heart or the head of the state, the king becomes something like its soul.

The distance of this model of the state, wherein power, creation, and initiative begin in the divine and filter through the king to his subjects, from the model of what we think of as representative government cannot be overstated. If any representation is occurring in the former model, it is of an entity–the divine–who remains visible only through its effects. Moreover, the king and his subjects are thought of as recipients of authority and not its source. Indeed, establishing the citizenry of the republic as the source of political authority was, to a certain extent, the goal of the French Revolution. Of course, this effort to redefine authority and its agents was not without its own difficulties. These difficulties are eloquently described by Paul Friedland, who recounts the debates surrounding questions such as the precise role of the deputies to the new National Assembly. Did they represent immediately and transparently the citizens who sent them, or did they achieve a certain independence from popular authority by virtue of their status? Yet even in such questions, the role of the people as the source of authority was unquestioned. If representation differs from what I call mediation in what it identifies as the source of authority, it also differs from it in its valorization of self-interest. In her landmark study *The Concept of Representation*, Hannah Fenichel Pitkin argues—correctly, I believe—that one cannot speak of representation until the eighteenth century, when the language of self-interest emerged in the work of philosophers such as Burke, Mill, Madison, and Bentham.

Pitkin's statement begs the question of what, exactly, preceded representation. An alternate term is needed that takes into account the overwhelmingly negative opinion of self-interest during the seventeenth century and offers a model that accounts for the *disinterestedness* that was invariably held up as a model for figures in authority. For writers such as La Rochefoucauld, self-interest was inescapable but also and unfortunately contributed to an unruly world dominated by passion, where true and false become inoperable concepts.[10] Such a disordered state of affairs only made the ideal of the disinterested prince more attractive and necessary. The legitimate prince has no self to speak of; rather, his interest is equated with the larger interest of the state. This is the proper meaning of the apocryphal "l'état, c'est moi": it is not a triumphant celebration of ego but the expression of the identity of the royal self with the larger community he both serves and embodies. As Bossuet, the most eloquent advocate for divine right, states, "le prince n'est pas né pour lui-même, mais pour le public" (the prince is not born for himself, but for the public).[11] While the king's royal birth and hereditary right to the Crown retained their importance in establishing his superiority, writers of the time also emphasized the monarch's ability to overcome the self-directed interests and passions that characterize his subjects. A prince consumed by self-interest was universally described and denounced as a tyrant. But what ensures or guarantees this elevated disinterestedness on the part of the king? Theoreticians of divine right found the solution by asserting that royal power originated in God and was only temporarily delegated to the monarch. To cite Bossuet once again, "Que [les rois] respectent donc leur puissance, parce que ce n'est pas leur puissance, mais la puissance de Dieu, dont il faut user saintement et religieusement" (Kings should respect their power, for it is not their own power, but that of God, which should be used in a saintly and religious manner).[12] Establishing the divine as the anchor of royal power was therefore seen as a means not of absolving the king of responsibility for his actions but rather of moderating his power.[13] This image of the king as the quasi-transparent instrument of a power that originated and ended well beyond his own person was intended to counter and soften the solid, discrete, and independent sovereign described by Bodin.

Given the vast philosophical differences underpinning the seventeenth- and eighteenth-century models of political authority and its delegation, it seems entirely inappropriate to use the term "representation" to describe divine right monarchy and its delegation. Although the word was widely used during the seventeenth century, including in many of the texts that I examine in this book, its meaning, especially in politics and diplomacy, was quite different. A survey of the diplomatic use of "représenter" during the seventeenth, eighteenth, and nineteenth centuries illustrates the shift toward self-interest that Pitkin describes. The Académie Française's *Dictionnaire* from 1694 gives the following example of its governmental use: "On dit, que *Les Ambassadeurs représentent les Souverains qui les envoyent,* pour dire, que Par leur caractere, ils sont revestus en quelque façon de la dignité & des prerogatives de ceux de la part desquels ils sont envoyez" (One says that *Ambassadors represent the sovereigns who send them,* to say that through their character, they are clothed in some fashion with the dignity and prerogatives of those on whose part they are sent). In 1762, the definition shifts slightly: "On dit, que *Les Ambassadeurs représentent les Souverains qui les envoient,* pour dire, qu'Ils tiennent en quelque façon la place des Puissances qui les envoient" (One says that *Ambassadors represent the sovereigns who send them,* to say that they hold in some fashion the place of the powers that send them). Already, the quasi-mystical language of dignity and character has disappeared, and the personalized "ceux" has been replaced with "puissances." In the sixth edition of the dictionary, from the period 1832–35, the legal use of the term has made inroads: "REPRÉSENTER signifie aussi, Tenir la place d'une ou de plusieurs personnes, en vertu du droit qu'on a reçu d'elles. Il se dit particulièrement des délégués à certaines assemblées délibérantes, des envoyés d'un souverain, et de quelques hauts fonctionnaires" (To represent also signifies to hold the place of one or several persons, by virtue of the legal authority that one has received from them. It is particularly said of delegates to certain deliberative assemblies, of envoys of a sovereign, and of certain highly placed government workers). It should of course be noted that none of the definitions from the ancien régime use "représentatif" to describe governments.

If it goes without saying that the seventeenth-century king does not represent the people, he was nonetheless often described in terms closely resembling those of the ambassadors in the examples cited above. As I point out in chapters 3 and 4, the language of place-holding and of the transfer of dignity and power from its source to its instrument in diplomacy closely resembles the language used by theorists of divine right, and diplomacy therefore becomes a useful way of further exploring the contradictions and implications of seventeenth-century theories of kingship. A lieutenant (literally, place-holder) of God, the king represents the divine in much the same way as the ambassador in the first example represents his sovereign. It should be clear by this point that this idea of representation is quite different from the one that we are accustomed to; our idea of representation is to a large extent formed by the very victory of the individual and the self that this model of kingship was elaborated to counteract or control. For this reason, I have replaced the term representation with that of "mediation" in order to signify the movement of power and authority from the divine *through* its royal instrument. My use of the term is not entirely arbitrary; writers such as Bellarmino devoted much attention to the issue of whether the relation of temporal power to the divine was *immediate,* which is to say, direct, or *mediated* by, for example, the Catholic Church and the pope. In fact, the 1694 edition of the Académie Française's *Dictionnaire* offers the following example for *immediatement:* "Le Roy tient immediatement de Dieu son autorité" (The king holds his authority immediately from God). He therefore occupies the position of mediator between God and the kingdom, and this language preserves the Neoplatonist framework of divine right treatises, wherein, like the soul or Malebranche's human mind, the king participates equally in the transcendent and the material spheres, holding the two together. In discussing diplomacy, I have retained the term "representation," in keeping with the language of the texts themselves, but it should be understood as an extension of mediation, even though the appearance of the term in the diplomatic context can and should be read as a symptom of the difficulty writers of the time had in characterizing the precise relation of the ambassador to the king who sent him and to the powers to which he was sent.

Using the term "mediation" to describe this configuration of authority and legitimacy also serves to mark its strangeness for the twenty-first-century reader. Part of the argument of this book is that in failing to grasp the widespread influence of this way of thinking, we risk misreading the French seventeenth century. Much more scholarly attention has been paid to the idea of "reason of state" or to exceptional and atypical writers such as Pascal than to the articulation and establishment of divine right, although this is beginning to change, especially in France.[14] The treatises that I examine in this book demonstrate, through their variety, the extent to which certain presuppositions and concerns dominated the period's thought on monarchy and social order. If divine right is correctly and most commonly associated with Bossuet, it should be recognized that the Bishop of Meaux was building on a foundation carefully laid by his predecessors. From the jurist Cardin Le Bret to the Oratorian Senault to the Jesuit Le Moyne, writers considering monarchy and the state were faced with the task of elaborating a system that avoided the dual dangers of tyranny and popular sovereignty. The results often lacked the logical clarity and rigor of Bodin, and their somewhat contradictory conclusions led less to an alternative "reason of state" than to a quasi-religious "mystery of state" whose fundamental principles should remain shrouded in secrecy. Jacques Truchet, discussing Bossuet's political thought, reminds the reader of the bishop's statement that truths should not be reconciled, but rather that one should hold strongly to "les deux bouts de la chaîne, quoiqu'on ne voie pas toujours le milieu par où l'enchaînement se continue" (the two ends of the chain, even though one cannot always see the middle through which the chain continues).[15] Faced with two incompatible truths, Truchet notes that Bossuet "met son zèle et son honneur à essayer d'entrevoir quelque chose du mystère que constitue leur double réalité, mais il n'espère pas l'élucider totalement" (uses his zeal and honor to try to perceive something of the mystery that their double reality constitutes, but he does not hope to elucidate it entirely).[16] While this is unsatisfactory political philosophy, it provides an important testimony that, for many in the period, the mystery of state was at least as significant as its rationality.

Eliminating divine right and the concept of mediation from considerations of early modern political thought therefore deprives the century of its inherent dynamism. As Joël Cornette asserts, Louis XIV appears at the center of a contradiction between the sacred monarchy of divine essence described by Bossuet and the terrestrial, rational, and active monarchy that is evidenced in the work of Vauban.[17] The age-old platitude that the king is "the image of God on earth" in fact obscures an important debate that is in many ways specific to the seventeenth century. Is the king, like Descartes' philosopher, godlike insofar as he shares the divine attributes of independence, self-sufficiency, and free will? If so, the divine referent is only of minimal usefulness, a cover to protect the monarch from charges of tyranny. Is the king, like Malebranche's mind or the Neoplatonic soul, godlike insofar as he channels divine will through his person to the state? If so, we have the paradox that the more legitimate the monarch, the more invisible he becomes; he is reduced (or elevated) to the status of a selfless, transparent instrument of the divine. The conflict is less between two separate bodies of the monarch than between two rival visions of political, and divine, power.

Seventeenth-century political theorists were fully conscious of the shortcomings of each of these models considered alone. Chapter 1 examines how the early architects of divine right tried to establish a hierarchy that elevated the sovereign while avoiding the perils of tyranny. A close reading of their texts demonstrates that they were not always able to conserve the specificity of the individual monarch–his creative power or his will–intact. In this context, Louis XIV's decision to write memoirs for the education of his son and heir becomes no less significant than the content of this extraordinary text. Chapter 2 shows that the memoirs, which simultaneously celebrate the "mystery of state" and the active, independent self of the king, take on new meaning when considered against the backdrop of divine right. The text is less a strict application of divine right and its ideal of pure mediation than a response to its shortcomings, even though the secretaries' struggle to strike the appropriate tone when adopting the king's point of view demonstrates the continuing difficulty in identifying the precise nature of monarchical power and identity.

The elevation of the monarchy beyond the critical examination of the king's subjects, whether through reason or mystery of state, can tend, however, to render debates concerning the finer points of divine right and the source of royal authority of limited practical import. How is one to prove whether the king is godlike in his independence, or if he is truly the selfless servant of a larger design? Answering this question is even more difficult during a century that had a sharpened appreciation for the value of scientific proof, an appreciation that led, for example, to the critical challenge of miracles and of natural occurrences such as comets. Yet there is one figure whose identity and whose exception from the laws normally governing human society provide an opportunity to assess the influence of divine right and mediation on a public and practical stage: the ambassador. In chapter 3, I provide an overview of European attempts, from the sixteenth century through the seventeenth century, to recategorize the diplomat. In this period of intense international contact and conflict, the ambassador assumed a new importance; however, the sacrality that guaranteed his age-old inviolability no longer corresponded to the divergent demands and interests of post–Westphalian Europe. From a sacred envoy promising Christian peace, the diplomat was recast as the representative of his sending sovereign. This redefinition was, in turn, continually adjusted to meet the practical issues of exterritoriality, inviolability, and the need for continual correspondence between the ambassador and his home court. In many ways, the difficulties involved in defining the diplomat, whose entire official identity is contextual and relational, parallels those encountered by French writers attempting to define royal power and legitimacy. Treatises on diplomacy shift between emphasizing the ambassador's role as stand-in for his absent prince (a function that implies a certain invisibility of the actual diplomat) and his role as someone possessing instead the judgment and actual point of view of his sovereign (a function that elevates the ambassador while obscuring, or, more dangerously, duplicating, the source of his authority).

The problem of appropriately characterizing the ambassador's status and power was particularly acute in France. Louis XIV was quite interested and involved in diplomacy, especially during the first years of his personal reign in the early 1660s. The French king and his *secrétaires d'état* seized upon the new representational justification for diplomatic immunity. Defining the diplomat as place-holder of the king's person reinforced the structure of mediation underlying divine right, all the while affording the monarch a visibility and personal agency that divine right had a tendency to obscure. In other words, if, in the relation between God and the king, the monarch occupied the rather impersonal role of instrument executing actions ultimately attributable to the divine, in the relation between king and diplomat, the monarch occupied the position of God, with the ambassador reduced to the function of instrumental executor of his will. In chapter 4, I provide an overview of how the new characterization of the diplomat resonated particularly well in the framework of divine right as well as an examination of two diplomatic incidents—one in London in 1661, the other in Rome in 1662—that were engineered and managed in such a way as to establish Louis XIV's status as the preeminent ruler in Europe. The symbolic and ceremonial aspects of these incidents and their resolution demonstrate their role in proving the unprovable—that Louis XIV enjoyed an unmediated relation, unique in Europe and rivaling even that of the pope, with the divine source of his authority.

During the process of recasting diplomatic inviolability, theorists turned from comparing the ambassador to the angel to drawing parallels between the ambassador and the actor. This move seems strange unless we realize the extent to which seventeenth-century theories of acting were radically different from those of the eighteenth century or our own. The comparison also implicitly recognizes that issues of mediation and its crisis resonate especially deeply in theater. In chapter 5, I show how d'Aubignac's theory of theater demonstrates the problems inherent in properly describing theatrical authorship. The complex and nuanced status of the playwright is further revealed through the issues raised during the *querelle du Cid*, which was provoked by Corneille's declaration of authorial sovereignty. Not unlike the "absolute" monarch, the playwright seeking complete originality and credit for his creation is limited by the fundamental laws of *vraisemblance* and the expectations of spectators, not to mention an often vexed relation to his source texts. Furthermore, the need to employ actors raises the possibility that any particular success might be attributed as much, if not more, to them than to the writer supplying their lines. In this sense, the comparison between the ambassador and the actor that several theorists of the time deploy raises more issues than it solves, pointing to the dangers inherent in the delegation of authority and control.

My consideration of these theoretical and historical issues prepares my readings of three of the period's best-known plays through the lens of mediation. I show that Rotrou's *Véritable Saint Genest* can be read as a reflection on the essential difference between a tyranny divorced from the divine and the pure mediation of the actor. I then consider Racine's recasting of Orestes as the ambassador of the Greeks in *Andromaque* as a particularly acute, albeit often overlooked, means of intensifying the problems of mediation, authority, and legitimacy that run throughout the play as a whole. Finally, I return to Corneille, whose last play, *Suréna*, presents an ambassador as the title character. Suréna's quest for recognition and autonomy tragically conflicts with his proper role in the state and indicates both the necessity and limitations of mediation as a framework for governance.

My account of sovereignty and mediation in seventeenth-century France is necessarily partial and incomplete. It is meant less as an exhaustive account of the deployment of the language of mediation in this period than as a suggestion for reassessing the dominant discourse of legitimacy and our larger approach to seventeenth-century politics and literature. Kingship, along with its relation to religion, was not a stable and uncontested backdrop to the active, and often turbulent, life of seventeenth-century French letters and science; rather, I hope to convince the reader that it participated intimately in some of the period's most vexing questions. This in no way, however, implies a weakening of the monarchy. Central to my analysis of the passages and treatises that I have chosen is the implication that the presence of the fundamental contradiction between agency and dependency at the very heart of state power and its delegation and centralization lent a certain dynamism to the state that was lost when, toward the end of Louis XIV's reign, the identification of royal intention and divine will was taken for granted, not least by the king himself.

WHAT IS A KING?

In his *De l'institution du prince*, published in 1516, Guillaume Budé describes the monarch's role as distributor of justice in the kingdom as follows:

> Et pour ceste cause, les Roys sont exaltés en honneur, & ont souveraine puissance, & dons de prerogatives: & prennent profict & emolument sur le populaire, par dessus touts aultres, en telle & si raisonnable portion qu'il leur plaist: & s'ilz ne sont subjects aux Loix, ny aux Ordonnances de leur Royaulme, comme les aultres, si bon ne leur semble. Car il est à presumer, qu'ilz sont si perfaicts en prudence, si eminens & elevés par noblesse, si imbuts & proveus de Justice & de Equité, qu'il ne leur fault point de reigle, ny de forme escripte, pour les estreindre par creinctes de peines, ou de mulctes, qu'on appelle condemnations pecuniaires, ou par arrests de leurs biens ou personnes, ou aultre correction, ou necessité d'obeïssance, comme il fault aux aultres subjects. Et doibt suffire pour leur commander la Loy divine seulement, qui a authorité de DIEU legislateur souverain, & non pas des hommes, selon laquelle, touts hommes sont egaulx, sans distinction ou preéminence, quant à l'obeïssance qu'on doibt porter à icelle Loy.[1]

[And for this reason, kings are exalted in honor, and have sovereign power, and gifts of prerogatives: and take profit and recognition over the people, over and above all others, in such reasonable portion as they please: and they, unlike others, are subject neither to the laws or the ordinances of their kingdom unless they choose otherwise. For it is to be presumed, that they are so perfect in prudence, so eminent and elevated by nobility, so imbued and provided with justice and equity, that they need no rule, nor written form, to limit them by fear of punishment or monetary damage, or by arrests of their goods or persons, or any other correction or necessity of obedience, unlike their subjects. And they need for their command divine law alone, which has its authority from God, sovereign legislator, and not from men, and according to which all men are equal, without distinction or preeminence, with regard to the obedience they need to show to this law.]

Spelling aside, Budé's description could come from the second half of the seventeenth century. His advocacy of the king's freedom from any human constraint marks Budé as an early advocate of what we have come to label, however problematically, absolutism.[2] Yet Budé's text is less a carefully argued political treatise than a plea for increased recognition of the humanities by the French king. As such, it presents two contradictory perspectives that do not challenge each other but are instead allowed to coexist. On the one hand, the king is indisputably and essentially superior to all other subjects of the kingdom. On the other hand, from the vantage point of divine law, all men are equal. Budé is able to describe such self-canceling descriptions of the monarchy because his goal is not to *prove* the king's superiority; such superiority is instead taken as given, as presumed. By the end of the sixteenth century, however, the confidence and tranquility evinced in this willfully logic-defying passage would become impossible. The incompatibility between the city of man, where the king possesses self-evident superiority, and the City of God, where all of humanity is equal, would no longer be allowed to persist without violent dispute and debate.

It is difficult to underestimate the impact of the Protestant Reformation on the early modern French articulation of kingship and sovereignty; unfortunately, recent studies that make the connection between the intellectual underpinnings of Calvinism and the redefinition of the state rarely extend their analyses beyond the sixteenth century.[3] When dealing with seventeenth-century French kingship, even the most subtle theorists have demonstrated a tendency to adopt Kantorowicz's English, medieval model of "the king's two bodies" instead of considering the profound effects of the Reformation on French political thought.[4] This is particularly troubling given not only the almost entire recasting of the relation between king and God (and indeed, God and man) that Protestantism introduced at the heart of French political life during the succession crisis of Henri IV but also the complete absence of explicit references to "the king's two bodies" in treatises on monarchy of the time.[5] Although many accounts of political theory during this period point to its incoherence (with the advent of Henri IV, Protestants who were against monarchy suddenly became its most ardent supporters, while the Catholic League began looking antimonarchical), in their haste to dismiss such changes as political opportunism they fail to see the intense damage done to traditional ways of representing royal mediation. Theorists of monarchy during the period following the accession of Henri IV had to decide whether a close link between God and king was necessary or even desirable and, if so, what form it would take. Veiled references to the king's Christlike attributes, common in the Middle Ages, implied a submission, humility, and readiness for self-sacrifice at odds with the increasing demands of royal administration.[6] Likewise, the traditional reliance on Eucharistic imagery to bolster the king's image as terrestrial God was out of the question. Almost no issue was as hotly debated during this period as the precise nature of Eucharistic transformation, and the increasingly obscure and technical language that the Catholic church used to defend it was ill-suited to a royal propaganda that needed more than ever to be accessible to all. Despite all of this, however, we still read in the first pages of Louis Marin's seminal *Le portrait du roi* that Louis XIV's (apocryphal) statement "l'état, c'est moi" bears a close resemblance to the Eucharistic "ceci est mon corps."[7] This may be so, but given the then recent ravages of the religious wars and the ensuing philosophical debates, anyone picking up the similarity during Louis XIV's reign would receive a far different impression of its meaning than someone hearing it one hundred years before. To understand the stakes involved in seventeenth-century efforts to theorize the monarchy, we must first appreciate the forces ripping at the traditional links among God, king, and country.

GIVE TO GOD THAT WHICH IS GOD'S

Although Jean Calvin himself never advocated disobedience to secular authority, his religious writings—especially, as Christopher Elwood points out, his writings on the Eucharist—contributed substantially to a fundamental rethinking of the earthly king's proper place in the universe. In the *Institution de la réligion chrétienne*, Calvin outlines a worldview characterized by the complete separation of human and divine, body and soul, temporal and spiritual. Man, irrevocably fallen from his first glory, can do nothing to reestablish communication with the divine. Only God can initiate contact between the two spheres, and the means that he has instituted for doing so can be found in Scripture alone. The points of mediation between the human and the divine are therefore few and far between, but where they exist, they are to be valued not in themselves but only as conduits. To elevate the objects of mediation, whether the water of baptism or the bread of the Eucharist, to objects of worship or even undue attention in their own right is to fall victim to the innate human tendency toward idolatry. These objects are of no use whatsoever unless animated by the Holy Spirit and by faith.

The overall effect of this philosophy is to place much more of an emphasis on the processes of communication and mediation than on their actual instruments. For Calvin, the intangible, airy breath of the spirit or of God's word in Scripture is of primary concern, and only Christ is the perfect mediator. All other objects or entities must be handled with extreme caution, in that according importance to them in and of themselves turns human attention away from the godly life and blocks the paths of communication between God and humanity. In light of this structure, where divine presence and intent is not implicated in all of creation but only in those objects specified by God, Calvin's views on monarchy, however moderate, invited divergent interpretations. In the chapter of the *Institutes* dealing with civil government, Calvin strongly chastises those who would see monarchy and civil government only as punishment for man's sinful ways. To answer those who would advance such an interpretation, Calvin cites Scripture to justify the respect due to kings as representatives of the divine on earth, who are to be obeyed no matter how tyrannical they might appear. Yet if we place Calvin's description of monarchy against that of sacramental objects, or even of Christ, a strong difference between the former and the latter begins to emerge. Kings may represent God's power on earth, but they are in no way useful mediators between God and man. God never speaks *through* kings, and respect of kings does not, in itself, bring humanity closer to God. The individual king is suffused with the thickness of temporality and historical contingency, as if to remind the subject that the true goal of human existence is attainment of the kingdom of God, a kingdom that remains completely separate from the community of men. As Christopher Elwood has argued, Calvinism implicitly displaces the traditional emphasis on the religious grounding of the French king's superiority and legitimacy. What had been described as the good fortune of the French to be ruled by monarchs so clearly chosen and favored by God becomes in Calvin a question of indifference as to whether the king is just or tyrannical. The connection between the French king and the Eucharist, evident in festivals and parades throughout French history, is uncoupled in the *Institutes*.[8]

As a result, French Protestants were able to view Calvin's pronouncements on the need to respect royal authority as rather incidental to the larger theological structure he outlined in this work. As many of them pointed out, Calvin's advocation of civil obedience was in many ways inconsistent with his teachings regarding the Eucharist and Scripture.

The results of Protestant questioning of royal power were considerable and should not be underestimated, since they opened questions and issues that had been unthinkable before. At worst, the king was a man like any other, and all respect shown him amounted to idolatry. At best, the king was absolute on earth, but only in response to the sins of his people. In what is often presented as a Protestant defense of monarchy, Elie Merlat, in his *Du pouvoir absolu des souverains*, repeated the argument that God has given the French an absolute monarch because of their sinfulness and tendency to rebel. He accompanied this position, explicitly condemned by Calvin himself, with a detailed extrapolation of how this belief is in accordance with Calvinist faith. The Calvinist challenge to the legitimacy of monarchy and its inherent connection to the divine, combined with the turbulent events of the end of the sixteenth century, led to a fundamental reconsideration of royal power, all the while demanding a more logically consistent defense of monarchy as a system—a political counterreformation of sorts, with no Council of Trent to support it. In order to appreciate the devastating nature of the Calvinist challenge once applied to the political sphere, it is worth examining in some detail the monarchomachic *Vindiciae, contra tyrannos*, which summarizes the more extreme religious-based arguments for popular rule.

The *Vindiciae* was written either by Duplessis-Mornay or by Nicolas Lambert as a response to the Saint Bartholomew's Day massacre of 1572, but it summed up ideas that had been circulating in Protestant circles well before this event.[9] In a gesture that with one blow strikes at the heart of recent efforts to extend royal power outside of the city of man and into the City of God, the authors emphasize the idea that with regard to divine law, "all men are equal, without distinction or preeminence." Unlike Budé, however, who had accompanied this assertion of human equality with the qualification that, in human terms, the prince enjoyed undisputed (and deserved) superiority, the writer of the *Vindiciae* extends this equality into the political sphere itself. By asserting that even in the political sphere *all* men enjoy an unmediated relation to God, untrammeled by the interpretations of the Church, the *Vindiciae*'s author is able to minimize, if not eliminate entirely, the prince's importance in the kingdom. The relation between king and people, the author argues, is far subordinate to the contractual relation between God and his people, on the one hand, and between God and the king, on the other. If one of these contracts is broken or if its limits are transgressed, organized opposition to the monarch is justified:

> Man is made up of body and soul: God formed the body and also infused the soul. Therefore He alone could use both of them with absolute right . . . kings have jurisdiction over bodies, God over souls. . . . These two tributes are so different and distinct that neither impedes the other; the fisc of God deprives Caesar's fisc of nothing, but each one keeps its right. In short, anyone who confuses these mixes up heaven and earth and wants to reduce everything to primordial Chaos. . . . But if a king claims for himself both types of tribute—as if he were trying to reach and scale the heavens after the manner of Giants—he is guilty of attempting to seize the kingdom; and just like a vassal who usurps regalian rights, he forfeits his fief and is most wisely deprived of it.[10]

What stands out clearly in this passage is not only its strong justification for opposition to the state but also the fact that this opposition is based on a clear-cut delineation of the rights of the king and those of God. This delineation is in turn reflected in the very nature of man, who is characterized by an absolute split between body and soul that can only find meaningful reconciliation in the divine. The state is utterly displaced as a potential source of unity. Instead, through its very existence, meant to be seen as transitory against the permanence of divine Scripture, it attests to the riven nature of fallen man. What the author of the *Vindiciae* sets out to accomplish in his treatise is the strict identification of *limits,* of definition, a goal he sets forth in the opening pages: "Therefore, from this manner of discussing our investigations, it clearly and necessarily follows what the duty of the prince is toward the people, what the right and office of the people is toward the prince; and that these obligations are distinct from one another, although they are mutual and reciprocal. Further, it follows that certain limits (*termini*) are constituted both by God and nature, and by the customs of nations; whoever crosses his own bounds (*metae*) gravely offends God, the laws, and the law of nations."[11] "Clear," "necessarily," "limits," "bounds," even "own"; all of these terms announce the radical nature not only of the break between the human and the divine, between the historical and the scriptural, but of the author's project itself. This rhetoric of boundaries and transgression has deep roots in Protestant theology, but its implications for articulations of secular sovereignty and legitimacy are exceptionally profound.[12] For although the *Vindiciae* ostensibly places the human in the middle of a continuity bounded on one side by the "profound chaos" occasioned by the mixing of heaven and earth and on the other side by the productive unity to be found in God, the creator of all things, the delineation and definition ascribed to the human undermines the very possibility of such a continuity, which in fact turns out to be only apparent. In other words, precisely because of man's fallen nature, unity and continuity cannot be achieved except from the point of view of the divine as revealed in Scripture. Due to the sharp distinction between God and humanity outlined in the text, this unity is invisible to humans, who can never place themselves in the divine position. Therefore, humanity's role in the community is limited to one of defining, of identifying the limits that cannot be transgressed; reason becomes a testament to human deficiencies rather than a reflection of divine origins. Whereas (only) God sees purposes and links between the various parts of his creation, and between various events in time, humanity can only see gaps. Any effort to take over this divine role in the universe, to see things from God's perspective, will be most severely punished.

This articulation leads to a radical break between God and humanity, a break from which the king is not only not exempt but of which he is the principal manifestation. The author of the *Vindiciae* does not fail to cite the biblical origin of kingship in the dissatisfaction of the Jews with the direct rule of God.[13] Accordingly, the king becomes not God's privileged vehicle of expressing his will to his people–this role is reserved for Scripture–but a sign of human insufficiency and vanity. In case the message is still unclear, the author of the *Vindiciae* states plainly, correcting his metaphor in the first passage cited above, that "This is all the more fair because there is some proportion between a vassal and a superior lord, but there can be none between a king and God, *between some simple man and the Almighty*."[14]

This characterization of humanity as irrevocably *other* to the divine, as operating on a plane of consciousness that is not only different than that of God but that has the potential to undermine divine order completely, has, as the *Vindiciae* amply illustrates, severe consequences for the definition and defense of royalty. Any proponent of monarchy writing after the confused and confusing events of the second half of the sixteenth century would have to acknowledge and counter the damage done by such a radical questioning of the legitimacy and origins of secular authority. This would entail a deep reflection on political matters as well as a judgment of the human capacity to describe the special powers held by the monarch. The means of articulating the royal position through language and logic would come into play as never before.

BELLARMINO AND THE TEMPORAL AUTHORITY OF THE POPE

To counter the quasi destruction of hierarchy, continuity, and, indeed, order that theories such as those articulated in the *Vindiciae* seemed to represent and advocate, Catholic theorists seized upon the writings of Roberto Bellarmino to advance a restored chain of mediation, but one in which the French monarch was ultimately subject to the authority of the pope. In the system of mediation outlined by Bellarmino, God expresses himself primarily through the Catholic Church and therefore through its spiritual leader, the heir to Saint Peter. For Bellarmino, the state was in the church, and not the church in the state, and as long as the king was going to ground his legitimacy in a divine mandate, this mandate would have to pass first and foremost through the hierarchy of Catholicism. The language used by Bellarmino and his French opponents is worth examining, since, anticipating more elaborate arguments for Gallicanism at the end of the seventeenth century, it provides further evidence of the ways in which mediation provided the framework within which the political implications of the religious wars were worked out.

Bellarmino intervened personally in the succession crisis of Henri IV, arguing that the then-Protestant heir was unfit to occupy the throne. Such an argument was consistent with Bellarmino's general picture of the world, one in which the pope retained spiritual authority over all secular princes. While Bellarmino also challenged the French claim of freedom from the Council of Trent (which had not been officially registered in the kingdom), he reserved his strongest arguments for the suggestion, eloquently advanced in texts such as De Belloy's *Apologie Catholique, pour la succession de Henry Roy de Navarre à la couronne de France,* that kings hold their authority directly from God and are thus even spiritually free from the orbit of papal control. Bellarmino repeats De Belloy's statement that "Les Empires & Royaumes ne peuvent estre ostez des mains des seigneurs legitimes, soit pour l'heresie, soit pour quelque autre cause que ce soit: pour autant qu'ils les tiennent immediatement du Dieu eternel, & non par la force humaine" (Empires and Kingdoms cannot be taken from the hands of legitimate lords, not for heresy, nor for any other reason: because they hold their authority immediately from eternal God, and not from human force).[15] Against this argument for the *immediacy* of divine involvement in French government, Bellarmino offers the following:

> Davantage que l'institution des Roiaumes aye prins son origine par les eslections des hommes, & appartienne au droit des gens, est jusques icy, si notoire à tout le monde: que mesme iceluy Apologetique ne le pourroit nier: car ny du droit naturel, qui est immediatement de Dieu, peut-on faire que les hommes regnent plustost par Monarchie; que Aristocratie, & Democratie, ou par autre forme de regir & gouverner: autrement toutes les Republiques seroient injustes & illicites, beaucoup desquelles nous voyons estre en l'Eglise Catholique florissantes avec grand honneur & loüanges. Et ou les Royaumes sont ordonnez &

instituez, cela n'est pas immediatement de Dieu, que ceste famille, plustost que ceste-là occupe le Royaume: mais par le consentement & volonté de tout le peuple, les Rois sont instituez.[16]

[Moreover, the institution of kingdoms took its origin from human election, and belongs to the law of nations, a fact that is well known to everybody, and that even this apologist cannot deny: for natural law, which comes immediately from God, cannot determine that men reign by monarchy rather than aristocracy or democracy, or any other form of reigning and governing: otherwise all republics would be injust and illicit, many of which we see flourishing in the Catholic Church with great honor and praise. And where Kingdoms are ordered and instituted, this is not immediately from God, that this family, rather than another, occupies the throne, but rather from the consent and will of all the people that instate Kings.]

As we see, Bellarmino's idea that temporal states have a human, rather than divine, origin closely resembles that of the most violent monarchomachic Protestant treatises of the time. Against the Protestant claim that only those methods and figures of mediation described *as such* in Scripture (a figure they would almost limit only to Christ) are legitimate or valid, Bellarmino holds the equally constrictive view that only the pope can provide ongoing mediation between God and humanity.

Furthermore, of singular interest to our discussion here, Bellarmino points to the touchiest area of the argument for direct royal mediation: that of the law. As we will see, legal minds such as Cardin Le Bret will founder in their attempt to reconcile divine right monarchy with the right of the ruler to make, or create, civil law. Bellarmino anticipates this difficulty: "Mais [les rois] n'ont pas de Dieu immediatement qu'ils puissent establir de bonnes loix, comme si en dormant (ainsi comme autresfois à Salomon) il leur donnast la sapience infuse ou dictée les loix: mais par conseil, prudence, industrie & par labeur, Dieu toutesfois y aydant, les Legislateurs decernent de justes loix; d'où vient que l'on ne les nomme pas divines, mais humaines" [But kings do not obtain their ability to establish good laws from God immediately, as if in sleeping (like Salomon) God gives them wisdom or dictates their laws; but rather by counsel, prudence, industry and work, with God's help, legislators discern just laws, and this is why we call them not divine, but human].[17] As will soon become apparent in our discussion of Bodin, there is, rather counterintuitively, a way in which the claim for direct divine involvement in the process of government *takes away* from the monarch's authority. Without identifying the monarch as representative of the divine, writers could give more credit to this "conseil, prudence, industrie & labeur" shown by a particularly skillful ruler.

For those asserting the superiority of the French Crown, especially during the succession crisis of Henri IV, opening the door for direct involvement of the papacy in French government, which is precisely what Bellarmino would have liked to see happen, represented a significant risk. Bellarmino's ideas remained widely diffused throughout Henri IV's reign. In 1610, the year of Henri IV's assassination by the would-be Jesuit Ravaillac, an act that did nothing to endear Bellarmino's order to the French, the Parlement of Paris condemned Bellarmino's *Tractatus de Potestate Summi Pontificis in temporalibus adversus Guillelmum Barlaium,* arguing that the possession, printing, or selling of this book was tantamount to lèse-majesté. Soon afterward, an anonymous author dedicated a treatise to the regent queen that simply compared Bellarmino's statements with those of the Bible itself. Among the biblical passages cited to confront Bellarmino's argument for papal primacy *in temporalibus* was Romans 13:2–6, which included the statement that "les puissances qui sont, sont ordonnées de Dieu" (the powers that be are ordained by God).[18] Yet as the rest of this chapter will show, this small phrase gave rise to enormous difficulties as writers moved beyond its polemical uses and into its implications for the business of government itself.

THE TWO FACES OF HERCULES

Both radical Protestantism and radical Catholicism had, as many correctly perceived, disastrous implications for the efforts to ground the legitimacy of the French state upon a transcendent, yet independent, source. Into this apparent impasse of impossible mediation versus a mediation controlled by the Church stepped Jean Bodin, with his attempt to define monarchy independently of the terms so vehemently defended by the two sides.[19] The damage done to mediation and the various claims on its control during the last half of the sixteenth century appears with particular force when one contrasts passages dealing with an identical topic–eloquence–from Guillaume Budé and Jean Bodin. For eloquence is one of the more salient manifestations of the holistic connection, relation, and continuity that theorists such as Michel Foucault and Timothy Reiss view as characteristic of the Renaissance. Bodin's contempt for eloquence demonstrates his will to define sovereignty as a perfectly self-referential concept, yet as I will show later in the chapter, many writers following Bodin deeply felt that such continuity could not be so readily abandoned.

That both Budé and Bodin would choose to treat the subject of eloquence in treatises ultimately concerned with the nature of states and their governance is, of course, of paramount importance, since what is at stake is both the ability of the prince to tie the disparate elements of the state together and the writers' own ability to use language to describe the monarch. In his *De l'institution du prince*, Budé makes reference to the unique French practice, noted by Lucan, of embodying eloquence not in Mercury but in Hercules, who was represented as an old man whose mouth was attached to his followers' ears with gold and silver chains. Lucan's Gallic interlocutor explains this representation as follows:

> Et pource, nous Celtes entendons Eloquence, par Hercules, lequel fut homme non pas fort & vaillant de corps, comme lon croit communément: mais fut sça-vant, saige, si bien & si deuëment parlant en bon ordre, & de bonne grace que de toutes grandes entreprinses, il venoit à fin, par la prudence singuliere, qu'il demonstroit en son langaige sententieux, & delectable, avec la persuasion qui s'en ensuivoit, laquelle les Rommains appellent Suada, pource qu'elle persuade ce, qu'elle veult : & les Grecs la surnomment Psitagogè, & les Latins semblable-ment, flexanime: signifians par ces vocables dessusdicts, qu'elle meut les coeurs & couraiges des hommes, gouverne & modere à son plaisir leur affection, comme la bride & le frein faict le cheval. Laquelle contourne de toutes parts la pensée des Auditeurs, incite & donne des esguillons, pour arrester & contrein-dre le vouloir & le liberal arbitre, selon ce, qu'il vient à poinct ou à plaisir à cel-luy, qui parle ou escript : à fin de persuader, que les petites chennes d'or & d'argent signifient l'Eloquence fondée en science. . . . Car quand le parler est fondé en science & congnoissance de toutes choses: c'est la grande & profonde mer, & qui ne se peult espuiser. Et parler aultrement de soy, sans naturelle pru-dence, ou sans grand sçavoir acquis, est une chose superficiaire, & sans aulcun fond: en laquelle n'y a aulcune solidité, & d'ou il ne peult proceder, que reso-nance vaine & inutile, avec superfluité de langaige (non pas Eloquence) sans aulcun fruict, effect, ou vigueur, tout ainsy que d'une trousse vuyde, & d'un arc sans traict desempenné.[20]

[And since we Celts understand Eloquence through Hercules, who was not, as commonly thought, a man strong and valiant of body, but who was wise and who spoke so well and with such grace that he was able to succeed in any enter-prise through the singular prudence that he demonstrated in his sentencious and delectable language, with the persuasion that followed from it that the Romans called Suada, because she persuaded people of anything she wanted; and the Greeks named her Psitagogè, and the Latins, similarly, flexanime: sig-nifying by these words that she moves the hearts and courage of men and gov-erns and moderates their affection at will, just as the bridle and bit manage the horse. This it is which surrounds the Listeners' thoughts on all sides, inciting them and spurring them on to fix and constrain desire and free will, according to the pleasure of he who writes or speaks. This signifies that the small chains of gold and silver signify Eloquence founded in science. . . . For when speech is founded in science and the knowledge of all things it is a great and deep sea that cannot be exhausted. And speaking of oneself otherwise, without natural prudence or the acquisition of wisdom, is something superficial and without ground, in which there is no solidity and from which can only result a vain and useless resonance, with superfluity of language (not Eloquence) without any fruit, effect, or vigor, like an empty bag or a bow without a string.]

Of course, it is quite natural for Budé the humanist to characterize the government of men in terms of accomplished eloquence; his treatise, after all, contains a call for the prince (whose superior nature, again, is never placed in question) to instruct himself in Greek, Latin, and history. Yet the vastly different tone taken by Bodin in describing the same image goes far in demonstrating the profundity of the crisis in legitimacy, sovereignty, and language of the later sixteenth century. Unlike Budé, who sees in eloquence a unique means of tying knowledge, its expression, and even society together, Bodin places eloquence firmly in the camp of sedition, stating that

> Mais outre les causes des seditions que j'ay dit cy dessus, il y en a une qui depend de la licence qu'on donne aux harangueurs, qui guident les coeurs & volontés du peuple où bon leur semble. Car il n'y a rien qui plus ayt de force sur les ames que la grace de bien dire: comme nos peres anciens figuroyent Hercules Celtique en vieillard qui trainoit apres soy les peuples enchaisnés, & pendus par les aureilles avec chaisnes qui sortoyent de sa bouche: pour monstrer que les armees & puissance des Rois & Monarques, ne sont pas si fortes que la vehemence & ardeur d'un homme eloquent, qui brusle & enflamme les plus lasches à vaincre les plus vaillants, qui fait tomber les armes des mains aux plus fiers, qui tourne la cruauté en douceur, la barbarie en humanité, qui change les Republiques, & se jouë des peuples à son plaisir. Ce que je ne dy pas pour la louange d'eloquence, mais pour la force qu'elle a, qu'on employe plus souvent à mal qu'à bien. Car puis que ce n'est autre chose qu'un desguisement de la verité, & un artifice de faire trouver bon ce qui est mauvais, & droit ce qui est tort, & faire une chose grande de rien & du formi faire un elephant, c'est à dire l'art de bien mentir: il ne faut pas douter, que pour un qui use bien de cest art, cinquante en abusent: aussi est-il malaisé entre cinquante Orateurs en remarquer un homme de bien: car ce seroit chose contraire à la profession qu'ils font, qui voudroit suyvre la verité.[21]

[But aside from the cause of seditions that I have named above, there is one that depends upon the freedom that we give to speechifiers, who guide the hearts and wills of people where they wish. For nothing exerts more force over souls than the grace of speaking well, as our ancient fathers figured Celtic Hercules as an old man who dragged people chained behind him, hanging from their ears by chains that came out of his mouth, to show that the armies and strength of

Kings and Monarchs, are not as strong as the vehemence and ardor of an eloquent man, who burns and incites the most cowardly to vanquish the most valiant, who makes arms fall from the hands of the most prideful, who turns cruelty to sweetness, barbarism to humanity, who changes Republics, and who toys with people at his whim. I do not say this to praise eloquence, but to describe the force it has, when it is employed more often for ill than for good. For since it is nothing but a disguising of truth, and an artifice to find good that which is bad, and straight that which is bent, and to make a great thing out of nothing, and an elephant out of an ant, which is to say the art of lying well, we must not doubt, that for someone who uses this art well, fifty abuse it; thus is it hard to find one good man among fifty Orators, since it should be counter to their own profession, that one of them should wish to follow truth.]

Bodin's characterization of the Celtic Hercules could not be farther from Budé's. Writing after the bloody events that were, in large part, provoked by the wildly differing interpretations of Scripture that were diffused in Protestant predication and Catholic sermons, Bodin feels that eloquence must be viewed with suspicion if power is to be placed back into the hands of the prince. For while Budé also recognizes the tendency of language to mislead, he counters this possibility by tying eloquence to science, to a "connaissance des choses." Bodin rejects this option, opposing linguistic seduction, however well founded, to the deployment of physical strength and violence by the king. This, not the knowledge of science, is the ground zero of the republic, as Bodin confirms in his stark statement that "La raison & lumiere naturelle nous conduit à cela, de croire que la force & violence ont donné source & origine aux Republiques" (Reason and natural light cause us to believe that force and violence have given the source and origin to Republics).[22]

If behind Budé's thought lies a sort of classical symposium, characterized by the free and humane exchange of ideas and *exempla*, and behind the *Vindiciae* stands the authenticity of Scripture and the City of God, then behind Bodin's treatise one can discern the ever-possible, and always legitimate, deployment of violence by the state. In all three texts this practice of referring to something beyond the text itself leaves the treatises open to difficulty or contradiction. Budé's constant references to classical models, it may be argued, leave him vulnerable to the historically contingent (a category just becoming recognizable at the time that he was writing),[23] while the *Vindiciae*'s practice of employing Scripture as the only authoritative text implicitly raises the thorny question of the proper interpretation of the will of God. Yet Bodin's text, by founding both its language and the republic in violence, raises the fundamental question of legitimacy—of the possibility that leadership may be arbitrary rather than fixed in a classical or scriptural beyond. This possibility in some sense accounts for

Bodin's insistence upon the importance of definition, itself a kind of rhetorical violence, in his methodology and in his object of study.

"*IL EST ICI BESOIN DE FORMER LA DÉFINITION DE SOUVERAINETÉ . . .*"

Jean Bodin's *Six livres de la république,* first published in 1576, can be read as an attempt to provide a rational analysis and defense of sovereignty and as an implicit response to the intellectual challenges that Protestantism posed to the kingdom. By applying the same standards of clarity and necessity appealed to by the *Vindiciae,* yet by refusing to privilege biblical precedent in his account of the development of republics, Bodin tries to establish sovereignty largely outside of the contentious domain of scriptural interpretation, so much so that later writers almost justifiably accused him of atheism.[24] Yet is it entirely possible to define sovereignty on its own terms?

Bodin announces the close association between sovereignty and definition in terms as strong as those found in the *Vindiciae,* albeit without the language of transgression and its consequences found in the Protestant work. His purpose in the treatise is to filter out from sovereignty all extraneous considerations, including, it would seem, Scripture:[25] "Or la nature de la definition, ne reçoit jamais division, & ne faut pas qu'il y ayt ny plus ny moins d'un seul poinct en la definition, qu'en la chose definie, autrement tout n'en vaut rien" (The nature of definition can never receive division, and there must not be more or less than one sole point in the definition, as in the thing defined, otherwise it is useless).[26] Unlike Budé, for whom language, eloquence, and representation served as a mediating and connecting force between divine and human, past and present, Bodin dreams of an authoritative treatise whose language would mirror the object described. By establishing a one-to-one relation between "la définition et la chose définie," Bodin anticipates the classical ideal of a perfectly transparent language shorn of rhetorical flourish, wherein the highest praise consists of saying that someone "dit plus des choses que des paroles" (says more things than words).[27] For Bodin, the inability of his predecessors to understand the republic stems from their failure to work from clear definitions. On the opening page, he declares that "la definition n'est autre chose que la fin du subject qui se presente: & si elle n'est bien fondee, tout ce qui sera basti sur icelle se ruïnera bien tost apres" (definition is nothing but the end of the subject which is presented: and if it is not well founded, everything built upon it will soon be ruined). He therefore opens his treatise with a definition of the republic: "Republique est un droit gouvernement de plusieurs mesnages, & de ce qui leur est commun, avec

puissance souveraine" (A republic is the right government of several households, and of what they have in common, with sovereign power).[28] The following chapters of his work proceed to define, in turn, each element of this
definition, moving from the family to the city to the republic, but it soon
becomes clear that the centerpiece of his work is the idea of "puissance souveraine" and what it might mean.

Indeed, the importance of this concept and its proper definition is evident
in the opening lines of the eighth chapter of the first book, "De la souveraineté," which not only define sovereignty—"la puissance absolue et perpetuelle d'une Republique"—but justify the method of definition once again:
"Il est icy besoin de former la definition de souveraineté, par ce qu'il n'y a
ny Jurisconsulte, ny philosophe politique, qui l'ayt definie: jaçoit que c'est
le poinct principal, & le plus necessaire d'estre entendu au traitté de la
Republique" (Here, we need to form the definition of sovereignty, since there
have been neither jurisconsults nor political philosophers who have defined
it, even though it is the principal and most necessary point to understand in
a treatise on the Republic).[29] While Bodin implies that the lack of existing definitions of sovereignty can be attributed to his predecessors' lack of rigor, this
explanation hides the fundamental novelty of his own project. Sovereignty
had never been defined, in part because no one had viewed it in quite the same
way as Bodin.[30] As Marcel David argues, the medieval separation of what theorists following Bodin term "souveraineté" into "auctoritas" and "potestas,"
with the former meaning the aura of majesty surrounding the pope and the
latter suggesting the temporal powers of the prince regarding *administratio*
or "puissance publique," avoided much of the confusion occasioned by the
adoption of the term "sovereignty." The new concept of sovereignty therefore
blurs spheres of power that medieval thought and terminology had main-
tained as distinct, albeit intimately linked. Accordingly (and ironically, given
Bodin's penchant for definition), David holds Bodin responsible not for
increased clarity in the idea of sovereignty but for its increased fuzziness. Part
of this confusion can be attributed to the progressive historical tendency of
kings to appropriate papal *auctoritas,* but much of it can also be explained by
the French term's tendency to slip in meaning from "puissance" itself to the
person holding this power, the "souverain."

Evidence of this slippage is evident in the lines following Bodin's definition
of sovereignty, where he traces the Latin (*maiestatem*), Greek, Hebrew, and
Italian equivalents of the French term. Noting that the Italians use the term
segnoria, he notes that the word is used "aussi envers les particuliers, et
envers ceux-là qui manient toutes les affaires d'état d'une République" (also
in reference to individuals and those who are in charge of all of a Republic's

affairs of state).[31] In the pages that follow, I will argue that this slippage is essential to upholding the rational definition of monarchy that Bodin seeks to provide, since the unitary nature of the monarch mirrors, and renders comprehensible, the fundamental singularity of the concept of sovereignty itself. But first, I would like to explore how the need to tie sovereignty to the sovereign can be viewed as the result of a fundamental tension between sovereignty and the very ideal of definition.

In both of his calls for improved definition cited above, Bodin characterizes the properly defined object, and the definition itself, as a "point." In the first case, he refers to the "ni plus ni moins d'un seul point";[32] in the second, he calls sovereignty the "point principal" of his treatise on the republic. The language in the first quotation indicates that Bodin envisions the word "point" not merely in its rhetorical meaning but as a geometric entity—the smallest entity possible, completely consistent with itself. According to this implicit metaphor, the defined object, like the definition, would have no parts that could be alienated from it without its ceasing to be what it is.[33] Bodin's effort to define sovereignty therefore rests upon the belief that there is something, some real object, to be defined. Yet if we look again at his actual definition of sovereignty, as well as at the chapter that follows, we find that sovereignty is a strange object indeed, one that is corralled only with difficulty into the image of a self-consistent point.

Bodin states that sovereignty is "la puissance absolue et perpétuelle d'une République." This definition is the first revelation that sovereignty may prove more resistant to definition than Bodin would have the reader believe. We should remind ourselves that the republic itself is defined in the treatises' first lines as being comprised not merely of distinct entities, the "plusieurs ménages," but also of what these households hold in common. Sovereignty would seem to be what ensures the definition and commonality of these entities. But sovereignty itself is not an entity or object; it is instead a "puissance," that is to say, a relation *between* objects. Indeed, Furetière's dictionary defines *puissance* first as *souveraineté* or *pouvoir absolu,* but the rest of the definitions reveal the problematic nature of the idea by characterizing *puissance* as a force, therefore not merely a relation but as the potentiality for a relation. Yet to turn back to Bodin, what is noteworthy about this "puissance" is that it is defined, or limited, precisely by its very lack of limits, either in potentiality or in time: "la souveraineté n'est limitée, ny en puissance, ny en charge, ny à certain temps" (sovereignty is not limited in power, or in charge, or in a certain time).[34] Both of these aspects render the definition of *sovereignty* exceedingly problematic, since definition implies, as Bodin himself recognizes, the "ni plus ni moins" that gives shape, form, and meaning to the object defined.

As a result, Bodin's effort to elaborate upon his definition moves imperceptibly from a characterization of sovereignty as such to a description of those holding it (the *souverains*) or to a description of its outward manifestations (the *marques de souveraineté*), since these actualizations of *puissance* are more accessible to the status of objects than sovereignty itself. Bodin's illustration of *puissance perpétuelle* may serve as an example of the difficulty of defining this power on its own terms: "J'ay dit que ceste puissance est perpetuelle: parce qu'il se peut faire qu'on donne puissance absolue à un ou plusieurs à certain temps, lequel expiré, ils ne sont plus rien que subjects: & tant qu'ils sont en puissance, ils ne se peuvent appeller Princes souverains, veu qu'ils ne sont que depositaires, & gardes de ceste puissance, jusques à ce qu'il plaise au peuple ou au Prince la revoquer: qui en demeure tousjours saisi" (I have said that this power is perpetual because it is possible to give absolute power to one or many for a certain time, who, after it expires, are nothing more than subjects; and as long as they are in power, they cannot be called sovereign princes, given that they are only depositaries and guardians of this power, until it pleases the people or the prince, to whom this power belongs, to revoke it).[35] This statement does little to further Bodin's goal "d'éclaircir ce que signifie puissance souveraine" (to explain what is meant by sovereign power);[36] rather, like so much of what follows, it describes what perpetual power is not. In a move that prefigures the methodology of Descartes, wherein the perfection of God is proved through the imperfection of man, Bodin proves that sovereign power must be perpetual because it can be taken away. Someone somewhere must hold the power that is given on a temporary basis to those who exercise it, and Bodin's sentence mirrors the manner in which this holder of perpetual power is generated by the process of limitation. Indeed, the entity that gives absolute power is first identified as the abstract, impersonal "on," and those who receive it are "un ou plusieurs." Only upon having this power revoked do the recipients take on a firm political identity as "subjects," and only in retrospect can one say that they had no right to refer to themselves as sovereign princes. This quality belongs to those who hold the power, who are now referred to not as the mysterious "on" of the first clause but as the people or the prince.

Bodin's difficulties in defining sovereignty rest in part upon the close alliance between sovereignty and the very process of division and definition. If sovereignty is what enables definition—in this case, the separation of the "on" into people and princes, or the "un ou plusieurs" into subjects—then it may well be that sovereignty as such cannot be defined without reference to what it is not. Many seventeenth-century treatises on monarchy follow Bodin in their attempts to reduce sovereignty and *puissance* to the clarity of definition. For as

Budé's praise of eloquence demonstrates, before Bodin there was if not a certain comfort then a certain language with which to describe (not define) sovereignty as that which makes language and definition possible. The Bible provides the example of Adam, whose sovereignty over the animals is established and expressed by his dividing, defining, and naming them. Yet it is perhaps Guillaume Budé, citing Ovid, who provides the most helpful way to see the problem that Bodin is trying to confront and conquer: "Ovide dict, que Majesté fut produicte & procreée de Chaös, avec les elements: & qu'elle feist la discretion des ordres, & des dignités tant celestielles, comme elementaires. Et que sans son ordonnance, les choses inferieures n'eussent porté reverence aux superieures: mais eussent voulu occuper le lieu d'icelles" (Ovid says, that Majesty was produced and procreated from Chaos, with the elements: and that it makes the distinction of orders and dignities both celestial and elemental. And that without its orders, inferior things would not have shown reverence to their superiors, but would have wanted to occupy their place).[37] This description characterizes majesty as the force of separation itself, as that which transforms chaos into order and works to prevent this order from collapse. As such, it is not so much something to be defined as it is a force to be protected, a potentiality that, Budé states, does not need to be manifested continually through acts of war but that can be evident in the admiration with which the prince and his authority are viewed.

FROM SOVEREIGNTY TO SOVEREIGN

As Bodin's sharp critique of the political use of eloquence implies, such poetic renderings of majesty and sovereignty are insufficient for a society that has begun placing the mysteries of the state under the same scrutiny as those of religion. In light of Protestant critics of monarchy demanding a clear, rational definition of the state and its precise relation to the people, and against the just as tightly defined hierarchy of the Catholic Church defended by Bellarmino, Bodin must counter with a justification of sovereignty that is no less persuasive, that confers solidity and reality upon something whose existence Bellarmino and the Protestants minimize or deny: temporal power. After following his effort to define "puissance perpetuelle" with more negative definition, this time expressed in a list of those—dictators, the Athenian archon, or the "lieutenant général et perpétuel d'un Prince avec puissance absolue" (general and perpetual lieutenant of a prince holding absolute power)[38]—who are *not* sovereign, Bodin revises the problem by considering "ce qu'est la puissance absolue" (what is absolute power).[39]

Here, Bodin encounters less difficulty than with his definition of sovereignty, stating famously that sovereign and absolute *puissance* is that which is bound to no laws other than those of God and nature. Although many critics have read this definition as proof of Bodin's limitations on sovereignty or absolutism, the sudden entrance of God into the equation of sovereignty, which up until now has been defined in strictly secular terms, should give the reader pause. Introducing divine and natural law into the definition of sovereignty would seem to run against Bodin's earlier statement that a definition should include neither more nor less than the thing defined. Why, then, is this principle evoked at this point?

The beginnings of an answer may emerge from an analysis of Bodin's imperceptible slippage from "sovereignty" as *puissance* to "sovereignty" as that which is held by the *souverain*. We have seen that sovereignty as force remains almost impossible to define on its own terms, since, strictly interpreted, it is that which enables the very process of definition. To be properly identified or made manifest, sovereignty must be tied to the conditions of its exercise, the most obvious of which consists in the identification of its holders and deployers. Bodin, in his typical thoroughness, considers a variety of configurations involving sovereignty and those who have it—the one (monarchy), the few (aristocracy), and all (democracy). His concern for the indivisibility of sovereignty, which he views as essential to its existence, leads him to correct Aristotle's opinion that mixed states are possible. Since sovereignty cannot be divided without ceasing to be sovereignty (just as the best definition is one that cannot be further divided into constitutive parts that need, in their own turn, to be defined), it is impossible to have concurrent holders of sovereignty. Only these three models are possible, although the ultimate holder of sovereignty may temporarily delegate governmental functions to the few or the many.

Bodin's rebuttal of Aristotle further demonstrates how essential the principle of the indivisibility of sovereignty, and, by extension, that of definition itself, is to his overall project. We should therefore not be surprised when he uses this principle to cast doubt upon the possibility of democratic government. If all hold sovereignty, Bodin argues, sovereignty ceases to exist as such, since there is no one upon whom this power may be exercised.[40] In a description evocative of the *Vindiciae*'s *chaos perpetuel,* no one is sovereign, and therefore no one is subject. Bodin then entertains the argument that the best form of republic would be one that reconciles the extremes of democracy and monarchy, mixing the best of both: "Car s'il est ainsi qu'en toutes choses la mediocrité est louable, & qu'il faut fuïr les extremités vicieuses, il s'ensuit bien que ces deux extremités vicieuses estans rejectees, il se faudra tenir au moyen, qui est l'Aristocratie, où certain nombre des plus apparents entre un & tous, a la seigneurie souveraine: comme s'il y a dix mil citoyens, qu'on face chois de cent: qui sera justement le nombre proportionné entre un & dix mil, & croistre ou diminuer le nombre selon la multitude des subjects: en quoy faisant on tiendra la mediocrité louable & desiree entre la monarchie & la Democratie" (For if it is true that in all things mediocrity is praiseworthy, and that one must flee the vicious extremities, it follows that these two extremities having been rejected, one must hold to the middle, which is Aristocracy, wherein a certain notable number between one and all has sovereign lordship, as if there being ten thousand citizens, one chooses one hundred of them, which would justly be the proportional number between one and ten thousand, and the number would be augmented or diminished according to the multitude of subjects. In so doing, one would hold the praiseworthy and desirable mediocrity between Monarchy and Democracy).[41] Yet this application of Aristotle's golden mean to the political sphere ignores the specificity of sovereignty. If sovereignty's essence is its indivisibility and independence, it cannot be held within the continuity between the many and the one; rather, it escapes this model by its very nature. It therefore follows, from the definition of sovereignty that Bodin has advanced, that the best form of republic is a monarchy:

> Mais le principal poinct de la Republique, qui est le droit de souveraineté, ne peut estre ny subsister, à parler proprement, sinon en la Monarchie: car nul ne peut estre souverain en une Republique qu'un seul: s'ils sont deux, ou trois, ou plusieurs, pas un n'est souverain, d'autant que pas un seul ne peut donner, ny recevoir loy de son compagnon: combien qu'on imagine un corps de plusieurs seigneurs, ou d'un peuple tenir la souveraineté, si est-ce qu'elle n'a point de vray subject, ny d'appuy, s'il n'y a un chef avec puissance souveraine, pour unir les uns avec les autres: ce que ne peut faire un simple Magistrat sans puissance souveraine.[42]

> [But the principal point of the Republic, which is the right of sovereignty, cannot subsist, speaking properly, other than in Monarchy: for no one can be sovereign in a Republic but one person; if there are two or three or many, not one is sovereign, especially since none of them can give or receive the law from his companion; and as much as we imagine a body of several nobles or a people holding sovereignty, there can be no subject or support of sovereignty unless there is a chief with sovereign power to unite the ones with the others, which a simple Magistrate without sovereign power cannot do.]

Here, the alliance between monarchy and sovereignty is sealed, based upon these entities' similar essences. Yet here also, the revolutionary nature of

Bodin's thought becomes apparent, as the monarch, by virtue of the sovereignty he holds, becomes absolutely separate from the state he governs. Bodin replaces the linear continuity between the one and the many (comprised, one might suppose, of several "ones") with continuity between the singular, discrete nature of sovereignty and the singular, individual nature of the monarch. Only by positing this entity *outside* of the assemblage of people comprising the republic can the republic exist as such; as Bodin states above, without sovereignty held by the "chef," society dissolves into the coexistence of individuals. Ironically, through a process of definition that threatened to bring sovereignty into the world of objects susceptible to definition, Bodin finishes by establishing a unified object that may then, because of its possession of sovereignty, be separated from the world over which it presides.

THE IMAGE OF GOD ON EARTH?

This model, while ensuring the exceptional nature of a sovereignty that founds the state without existing within it, does little to quell the persistent question of legitimacy. In creating an individual who commands the law and has the ultimate power of life or death over his subjects but to whom human laws, and indeed philosophical models, are inapplicable (because it is precisely this sovereignty that founds these laws and models), Bodin has conjured up the potential for an extraordinary abuse of power. This is all the more so in that Bodin's model, which accords sovereignty to the monarch without considering the process through which the monarch becomes a monarch in the first place, is incapable of accounting for the origin of sovereignty. Indeed, since sovereignty is perpetual, its origin is beside the point. Yet if the monarch is grounded in the sovereignty he possesses, sovereignty must in turn be founded in something beyond itself, or it slips immediately toward tyranny. For Bodin, the question becomes one of how to tie sovereignty to something outside of itself without compromising the integrity that not only makes sovereignty what it is but enables it to determine all else in the realm. Bodin's solution to this problem by invoking God may appear unsurprising, but the way in which he does so is unique and will mark efforts to define the king well into the seventeenth century.

For once again, Bodin eschews the model that links different concepts through either contiguity or the relation of part to whole. Just as the monarch becomes the best holder of sovereignty because he, like the concept itself, is singular and whole, so the monarch, in his unity, reflects the unity of the divine. As Bodin states at the beginning of his chapter on the marks of sovereignty: "Puis qu'il n'y a rien plus grand en terre apres Dieu, que les Princes souverains, & qu'ils sont establis de luy comme ses lieutenans, pour commander aux autres hommes, il est besoin de prendre garde à leur qualité, à fin de respecter & reverer leur majesté en toute obeïssance, sentir & parler d'eux en tout honneur; car qui mesprise son Prince souverain, il mesprise Dieu, duquel il est l'image en terre" (Since there is nothing greater on earth, after God, than sovereign Princes, and they are established by him as his lieutenants to command men, we need to pay attention to their quality, in order to respect and revere their majesty in all obedience, speaking and feeling about them in all honor, for who scorns his sovereign Prince scorns God, of whom the prince is the image on earth).[43]

Although this formulation of the relation of God to the king is highly traditional, its placement in Bodin's treatise inflects the meaning to be accorded to the phrase "the image of God on earth." It is noteworthy that Bodin does not begin his definition of sovereignty with this well-worn formulation; rather, it occurs *after* sovereignty as such has been defined. The reader must therefore consider this passage while bearing in mind the indivisibility and incommunicability that form sovereignty's essence. If, then, there is a relation between the king and God (a relation that must exist in order to prevent the state from sliding into tyranny), this relation must be viewed in terms that describe not so much a dependence, or even a privileged communication between one and the other, but rather a similarity in their potential force and their unaccountability to human laws. Bodin's insistence throughout his text that sovereignty can never be communicated or delegated reinforces this position. While Bodin acknowledges, as many critics have noted, that the king is subject to divine and natural law, this acknowledgment does nothing to establish royal *dependence* upon the divine; rather, it underscores the fundamental similarity between the king and God himself, who, Bodin notes, is also subject to his promises and to the laws established by his creation.[44] The king is to be respected not so much because he submits himself visibly to God but because he rules the kingdom with the same authority with which God rules the universe—an authority that cannot be challenged or transferred. In short, sovereignty for Bodin can never be a mere delegation of divine authority; it is complete in its own right. The relation of the king to God is therefore much different than the relation between the monarch and his delegated representatives or magistrates, whose authority can be removed at any time. It is a relation of similarity in independence, and Gérard Mairet is therefore correct in concluding, in his introduction to his edition of the *Six livres,* that "On voit que la doctrine de la soumission du prince à la loi naturelle et divine bien loin de limiter la puissance du prince sert au *contraire* à justifier qu'elle soit sans limites" (We see that the doctrine of the prince's submission to natural and divine law, far from limiting the prince's power in fact justifies that this power is limitless).[45] In linguistic terms, one can say that the relation between God and king is not one of signified and signifier but one of two unique signifieds, whose similarity justifies their comparison one with the other.

By articulating a system in which sovereignty, the king, and God are linked only by their fundamental *independence* from all else, Bodin fails to resolve the potential problem of tyranny—despite his eloquent delineation of the difference between the king and the tyrant in the fourth chapter of the second book. Here, Bodin provides a long list of characteristics opposing the two sorts of monarchs. For example, "le roi se conforme aux lois de nature, et le tyran les foule aux pieds. L'un entretient la piété, la justice, et la foi; l'autre n'a ny Dieu, ny foi, ny loi" (The king complies with the laws of nature, and the tyrant mocks them. One entertains piety, justice, and faith; the other has neither God nor faith nor law).[46] Indeed, argues Bodin, the difference between king and tyrant is so obvious that everyone can see it: "Il n'est pas besoin de vérifier cecy par beaucoup d'exemples, qui sont en veue d'un chacun" (There is no need to verify this by many examples, which can be seen by everyone).[47] Yet this traditionalist definition of tyranny, wherein the tyrant is the king who has forgotten his faith and his dependent relation to God, would completely undermine the system of well-defined, independent entities that Bodin has gone to such lengths to construct. At a time in which opinions regarding the nature of piety, faith, and the involvement of the divine in human society are being wildly contested, almost anyone disagreeing with the king's actions could accuse the king of tyranny. Bodin therefore moves quickly away from his rather perfunctory, largely historical (and rhetorical) description of tyranny to the subject of whether tyranny can be resisted. In arguing that the only possible resistance to tyranny should be passive, Bodin concludes with a striking passage that puts the existence of tyranny as a clear-cut category in serious doubt. "O qu'il y auroit de tyrans s'il estoit licite de les tuer: celuy qui tire trop de subsides seroit tyran, comme le vulgaire l'entend: celuy qui commande contre le gré du peuple seroit tyran, ainsi qu'Aristote le definit és Politiques: celuy qui auroit gardes pour la seurté de sa vie seroit tyran: celuy qui feroit mourir les conjurés contre son estat seroit tyran. Et comment seroyent les bons Princes asseurés de leur vie?" (O there would be so many tyrants if it were licit to kill them: he who takes too many taxes would be a tyrant, as the people understand it; he who commands against popular will would be a tyrant, as Aristotle defines tyranny in the *Politics;* he who employs bodyguards would be a tyrant; he who puts to death conspirators against the state would be a tyrant. And how would good Princes be assured of their lives?).[48] This description of tyranny, which reinvokes the seditious nature of eloquence that can transform a fly into an elephant, anticipates, and is hardly different from, the argument of Hobbes that "they that are discontented under *Monarchy*, call it *Tyranny*."[49] Those of Bodin's contemporaries who accused him of atheism noted the weakness of the tie between prince and God as well.

Yet to fully appreciate Bodin's originality, we must consider the way in which he defused the Protestant challenge to kingship. By basing his defense of sovereignty on the principle of clear definition adopted by texts such as the *Vindiciae*, Bodin managed to transform definition from a liability of the human condition into a proof of self-evidence and superiority. Bodin speaks not in terms of boundaries that must be transgressed but in terms of definitions that are so clear that they support no adulteration from outside concerns. As such, the objects defined—God, the king, sovereignty—are absolutely independent from both the trickery of rhetoric and its corollary of sedition. Once established, these entities are no longer open to discussion or negotiation, and it is Bodin's genius to have suggested that their self-contained consistency is precisely what endows them with limitless power.

However, the abandonment of mediation implied in this elevation of definition and pure, irreducible entities creates serious problems for the articulation of the legitimacy of royal power. As Bodin himself implies, there really is no difference between the king and the tyrant under his system. Seventeenth-century treatises on monarchy would be characterized by their attempts to reestablish and rearticulate the links between God, the king, and the people all while preserving the unity and uniqueness of the monarch. As I will show in the following pages, these efforts ultimately led to the near-disappearance of the monarch as an identifiable element in the system, as it were—a signifier (no longer a signified) fading quickly from the page.

DESCRIBING THE KING

The *Vindiciae* and the *Six livres de la république* are worth exploring at such length because they set firm yet divergent parameters for the definition of sovereignty and the specificity of the king. The *Vindiciae*'s monarch is merely one man among others, with no privileged access to God's will, while Bodin's monarch is so godlike in his independence of will that, paradoxically, any link to the divine is threatened. Seventeenth-century French writers on sovereignty and monarchy needed to reestablish this link in order to eliminate the possibility of government by popular election and to ground the elaborate hierarchy of French society in the transcendental and the permanent. A privileged link between God and the French king would go a long way toward "proving" the fundamental *difference* between the monarch and his subjects, a difference that would establish a mystique surrounding the ruler that could not be easily questioned or penetrated. Yet given the need, in many ways introduced by Bodin himself, for logical proof and examination of sovereignty and the monarchy, these writers had to explain both the origins of this link and its practical implications for government. The result is an often startling mix of theology and political science; my contention in this chapter is that it is a mistake to try to view them as separate. Perhaps no idea concerning monarchy was more widespread during this time than the view that good monarchy was rooted in the divine and that tyranny was a form of idolatry where this divine source has become obscured. However, the seventeenth-century writers addressing these quite traditional definitions had to contend, at least implicitly and quite often directly, with the ideas introduced by Protestant rebels, the Catholic League, and Bodin himself. Therefore, the question posed by these writers was whether the absolute, godlike independence that Bodin had uncovered in his efforts to define sovereignty could be reconciled with the need for the monarch to connect the disparate parts of his kingdom to himself and to God.

To illustrate this dilemma, I have chosen three texts: Cardin Le Bret's *De la souveraineté du roy* (1632), Jean-François Senault's *Le monarque, ou les devoirs du souverain* (1662), and Pierre Le Moyne's *De l'art de regner* (1665). This selection offers an overview of how similar problems and ideas were treated by quite disparate figures. As an accomplished jurist who participated in Louis XIII's administration, Le Bret tries to resolve the tension between princely independence and royal submission by invoking the power of the law. Senault, a prominent member of the Oratory—the order founded by Pierre Bérulle, who himself tried mightily to reconcile the glory of the French monarchy with the idea that the state should be located in the Church and not the other way around—offers, not surprisingly, an approach grounded in religion and the monarch's ties to God. Despite the intervening years and events (the quasi-miraculous birth of Louis XIV, the Fronde, the death of Mazarin) as well as their differing backgrounds, Senault's treatise closely resembles that of Le Bret, less in its language than in the problems that it both addresses and evokes. This similarity reveals the persistence of certain issues in the theorizing of sovereignty during the entire seventeenth century, issues that can only be partially treated using the model of the "king's two bodies." Finally, the Jesuit rhetorician Le Moyne's treatise demonstrates the theoretical need for the shift to what we might call propaganda in dealing with the king. If both Le Bret and Senault demonstrate, despite themselves, the impossibility of successfully describing sovereignty using only the terms of God and man, Le Moyne's creative use of solar imagery—although it runs into its own problems—represents an attempt to escape the theoretical frustrations of the other two and should be taken just as seriously.

One of Jean Bodin's first major successors was the jurist Cardin Le Bret. The title of Le Bret's work, written in 1632 under Louis XIII, is itself a testimony to the influence of the concept of sovereignty introduced by Bodin. The content of the work, however, demonstrates a sharp divergence from Bodin's methods and priorities, which is apparent from the text's first lines. *De la souveraineté du roy* begins with an elucidation of royalty: "M'estant proposé de representer en cet Ouvrage en quoi consiste la Souveraineté du Roy: il me semble que je ne le puis commencer plus à propos que par la description de la Roïauté. Il seroit mal-aisé d'en rapporter une plus acomplie que celle que nous donne Philon Juif en ses Livres de la vie de Moïse, quand il dit, qu'elle est une suprême & perpetuelle puissance déferée à un seul, qui luy donne le droit de commander absolument, & qui n'a pour but que le repos & l'utilité publique" (Having proposed in this work to represent what royal sovereignty consists of, it seems that I could not start better than with a description of royalty. It would be difficult to find a better description than that which Philo Judaeus gives us in his Books of the life of Moses, where he says, that it is a supreme and perpetual power deferred on one person, which gives him the right to command absolutely, and whose only goal is public usefulness and repose).[50] If we compare this opening to that of Bodin—"République est un droit gouvernement de plusieurs ménages, et de ce qui leur est commun, avec puissance souveraine" ("A republic is the right government of several households, and of what they have in common with sovereign power.")[51]—the contrast between the two writers is striking. Bodin's terseness and generality mark his desire to establish a (universal) definition of all of the parts composing any republic; only later does it emerge, precisely from these definitions, that monarchy is the ideal government. Le Bret, however, turns Bodin's methods around, beginning with a *description* (not a definition) of royalty that in turn is based not on the pure logical consistency of definition but rather on a text from Philo Judaeus. If we look at Philo Judaeus's observations, we see that the elements familiar to us from Bodin, *perpétuelle puissance* and *un seul,* are paired with the condition of such a power's legitimacy: the goal of public repose and utility.

By reversing Bodin's order of argument, Le Bret is able to take as a given what Bodin leaves disturbingly open—the legitimacy of the king and his essential *difference* from the rest of his subjects. For while Bodin's system of definitions leads almost organically to the conclusion that monarchy is the only suitable government for a republic, this rulership is ultimately founded in acts of violence and war; almost anyone (perhaps one of the fathers of the families that are the ultimate ground of patriarchal government) could lay claim to the right to rule–if he could defend that right properly. Le Bret's restorative appreciation of the *specificity* of the monarchy in general, and the French monarchy in particular, needed to prove that the king was completely different from his subjects, just as he was from other European rulers.[52] Yet as we shall see, while Le Bret's effort to single the French monarch out as exceptional restores the close bond between the French king and God, it also endangers the connection between the king and his subjects. At the same time, his emphasis on the king's identity as a *link* between the various components of the realm endangers the exceptional nature of the monarch. *De la souveraineté du roy* can therefore be seen as an elaborate yet self-contradictory attempt to rebuild the bridges that the events of the past half century had destroyed. As the citation of Philo Judaeus demonstrates, for Le Bret royalty is only legitimate and useful if it reaches beyond itself. This is a far cry from Bodin's insistence on the absolute independence of the sovereign.

By viewing sovereignty more as an instrument than as an object of logical perfection, Le Bret, unlike Bodin, must offer an explanation or justification of sovereignty's origin. Why, Le Bret seems to ask himself, is it necessary to redefine the "souveraineté du roi"? The need for active government, for the exercise of sovereignty, is, unfortunately, intimately tied to disorder; if the kingdom were perfectly tranquil, government would fall away. However, the source of this disorder needs to be carefully identified. If human, it would imply that, as the Protestants argued, God instituted monarchy as a punishment to man (we may recall Elie Merlat's sly argument, proposed much later in the century, that France has a strong monarchy precisely because it is the most sinful of nations). In addition, the idea that flawed humanity is itself the source and origin of monarchical government would, of course, imply that monarchy itself is much less than perfect. Although Le Bret later repeatedly invokes the French populace's seemingly infinite capacity for disorder and sinfulness as the motivating reason for royal intervention in human affairs, here he avoids this problem by attributing disorder to the randomness of fortune: "La suite du discours m'oblige de traiter maintenant de la Souveraineté. Car bien que de sa nature elle soit à la Roïauté ce que la lumière est au Soleil, & sa compagne inséparable: Toutesfois depuis que la fortune s'est mêlée des afaires humaines, elle a par ses continuelles revolutions tellement perverti l'ordre des grandeurs & des puissances de la terre, qu'il est maintenant bien dificile de connoître qui sont celles que l'on peut dire proprement souveraines" (The flow of my discourse obliges me to treat sovereignty now. For although by its nature it is to royalty what light is to the sun, and its inseparable companion: since fortune has mixed herself in human affairs she has, by her continual revolutions, so perverted the order of the grandeurs and powers of this earth, that it is now very difficult to know which are those which can properly be called sovereign).[53] Fortune is responsible for the need not just for government itself but also for Le Bret's treatise, since her meddling has obscured the tight link between God, sovereignty, and the king that enables government to exempt itself from (and control) fortune's activities.

Yet how can one prove this formidable alliance, and does the introduction of God and France into sovereignty compromise its independence and indivisibility? A look at Le Bret's justification of God's special interest in the French state and its monarch may begin to provide a response:

> il n'y a point eu de Princes en l'Univers, qui aïent traité plus doucement leurs peuples, que nos Rois. Aussi certes ils ont pour ce sujet merité du Ciel des graces si particulieres, que S. Gregoire avoit acoûtumé de dire en leur loüange qu'ils surmontoient d'autant plus les autres Princes Chrétiens, que les Chrétiens surpassoient en probité de vie tous les infideles. Ce qui a donné sujet à plusieurs graves Auteurs, de dire, que la Majesté Divine avoit établi ce Roïaume, au lieu de celui de Juda, suivant cette Profetie de Daniel, *Suscitabit regnum aliud, quod in aeternum non dissipabitur.* Et de fait, il n'y a jamais eu de Monarchie, qui ait duré si long-tems en sa splendeur, ni qui dans l'état où elle est à present, se puisse promettre à l'avenir plus de gloire & de felicité, que celle de la France. Car bien que sa fortune ait été souvent agitée par de furieuses tempêtes qui lui ont été souvent suscitées, ou par l'envie de ses voisins, ou par la propre malice de ses peuples: Toutesfois Dieu l'a toûjours relevée au dessus de l'orage, & l'a renduë plus puissante qu'elle n'étoit auparavant. . . . Et nous devons esperer qu'elle ne pourra jamais être ébranlée, tandis que nos Rois continuëront de maintenir en son lustre la Religion, de cherir leur peuple, & de leur faire part de la felicité que Dieu leur donne.[54]

[there are no princes in the universe, who have treated their subjects more gently than our kings. Consequently, they have earned from Heaven such particular graces, that Saint Gregory used to praise them by saying that they surpassed all other Christian kings as much as Christians surpassed all the infidels. This has led several serious authors to say that divine majesty has established this kingdom, rather than that of Judah, following Daniel's prophecy. . . . And in fact, there has never been a monarchy that has lasted so long in its splendor, nor which, in the state in which it finds itself at present, can hope for more glory and happiness in the future, than that of France. For although her fortune has often been agitated either by furious storms or the jealousy of her neighbors, or by her own people's malice, God has always picked her up from the storm and has made her stronger than she was before. . . . And we should hope that she will never be shaken as long as our kings continue to maintain the Religion, to prize their subjects, and to share with them the happiness that God has given them.]

Here, the need to establish a clear link between God and the French kings—a link so clear that France, not Judah, might be the kingdom established by God in the Bible—in order to ward off the storms of fortune is evident. But the question of how this alliance between God and the French kings came to be raises sticky questions about royal agency, questions that plague the entirety of Le Bret's treatise. On the one hand, the French kings have *earned* divine favor through their devotion to their subjects. On the other hand, at some point this singular merit provides the means for God to intervene directly in French affairs. While this difficulty mirrors the larger debate opposing free will to predestination that penetrated almost all of seventeenth-century French thought, Le Bret's desire to assert the presence of both leaves one question disturbingly open. Who, precisely, the kings or God, is responsible for the glory of the kingdom? Any answer to this question is intimately related to how the state should be governed as well as to how the role of the king in this state should be understood.

Le Bret's treatise must therefore address, however implicitly, the question of the significance and, indeed, authorship of royal acts. Beyond the question of whether the kingdom's tranquility is attributable to God or the king (or whether a choice between the two ever really exists), Le Bret considers the following problem, one more in line with his own concerns as a jurist. Does the king's ability to make law establish him as the parallel image of the creative God, in a model similar to that of Bodin, or should the monarch's role be restricted to preserving order in the kingdom, upholding laws made in a distant past?[55] While this issue arises explicitly concerning the question of instituting new currency in the kingdom (Le Bret recommends, unsurprisingly, that caution be used), it and its implications are perhaps better illustrated in the following passage concerning the age at which French kings achieve majority: "Le Roi Charles V, dit le Sage, fit cette célébre Ordonnance en l'année 1375, touchant la Majorité des Rois, par laquelle il les déclare Majeurs, hors de tutelle, & capables de gouverner leur Roïaume, si-tôt qu'ils auroient ateint l'âge de quatorze ans, ce qu'il fit prudemment & avec juste raison. Car l'on a souvent remarqué, que ces personnes sacrées, par une faveur particulière du Ciel, sont dés leur jeune âge ordinairement enrichies de plusieurs vertus & belles qualitez qui ne se rencontrent point aux autres de plus basse condition" (King Charles V, called the Wise, made this famous edict in 1375, on the subject of the majority of the kings, through which he declared them major, out of tutelage, and able to govern the kingdom as soon as they had reached the age of fourteen, which he did prudently and with just reason. For it has often been noted, that these sacred persons, through a special favor from Heaven, are from an early age ordinarily enriched with several virtues and good qualities that are not found in those of lesser condition).[56] This passage clearly illustrates Le Bret's struggle to reconcile the historicity of royal actions (indicated by the precision of the date) with the intemporality of legitimacy.[57] By altering the conditions for acceding to full monarchy, Charles V would seem to have usurped a right that is God's alone. Yet, as is implied by Le Bret's reminder that he was called "the wise," it is possible to view Charles's action as mere confirmation of a status that everyone was already aware of, thereby subsuming his intervention into French history of God's plan for these "personnes sacrées."

Le Bret's difficulty in dealing with the proper status of the king and of royal action–the fact that the monarch's special status accords him the potential to disrupt the kingdom through his decrees as much as, if not more than, the constant revolutions of fortune–is inseparable from the question, hotly debated throughout the French seventeenth century, of the place and role of God in the natural world. We should remember that the period saw the scientific *deus absconditus* coexist uneasily with a vision (articulated by, among others, Pierre Jurieu later in the century) of a divinity intimately involved in human affairs through miracle and disaster. Once again, the source of this debate may be traced to the religious conflicts of the sixteenth century. On the one hand, Protestants and Catholics, increasingly suspicious of politicizing claims of miracles on behalf of their believers, chose to do battle on the grounds of tradition. Competing claims to represent the true nature of the Church as it was originally intended to operate opposed the Protestant view that all human attempts to interpret divine intervention were suspect to the Catholic view that the priesthood could and did apply God's will correctly to changing circumstances. If this was the tenor of the argument on an intellectual and elite level, belief in miracles and the constant interpretation of events such as the Saint Bartholomew's Day massacre in terms of divine intent persisted among members of both faiths. A writer such as Le Bret trying to provide a divinely grounded model for the relation between the king and his state had to come to terms with the implications of this debate. Startling changes in the government could be seen as much as could Machiavellian expressions of self-interest (this was, in fact, the argument put forth by Gabriel Naudé in his *Considérations sur les coups d'état*) as justifiable, miracle-like interventions in the order of things. In such a climate of mutual suspicion, it is far more sensible to emphasize, as Le Bret in fact does, the essential conservatism of the throne–its distance from the turbulence of "fortune."

Accordingly, the monarch that results from this reconfiguration of the relation between God and the world becomes the benevolent overseer of a well-designed machine.[58] The king's intent is to be found not in any one sudden or glorious action but in the continued organization and motion of the parts comprising his state. In such a vision of monarchy, the king becomes the equivalent of the spirit of the law, the force underlying the workings and coordination of the separate aspects of his realm, rather than a singular, acting deity. This, indeed, is what we find in Le Bret. The middle of the work illustrates as much as it describes this process. A multitude of articles, each dealing with a separate aspect of the state from nobility, to the church, to the coining of money, to rivers and forests is presented in relation to the king's power, often expressed by the phrase "il n'apartient qu'au Roi de" (only the king can).[59] The uniqueness of the king is no longer viewed in terms of an acting, active subject but rather in terms of a unifying *force*, almost a phantom object projected from the diversity of the kingdom and its need for union. For Le Bret's treatise, despite its title, does not spend much time describing the monarch himself, especially when compared to the time he spends describing—and defining, in the sense of circumscribing—the different elements of the kingdom. Take, for example, his description of why rivers seem to be particularly suited to sovereign control: "Ce n'est pas sans raison que les Fleuves & les Rivieres navigables, ont merité d'être mises en particuliere protection des Rois; car c'est par ce moïen que les Provinces se communiquent les unes aux autres les biens qu'elles recueillent avec abondance dans leur étendue; ce sont elles qui facilitent le commerce, qui comblent de toutes sortes de richesses les païs par où elles passent, qui animent la terre pour produire les foins, les blez & les fruits qui servent de nouriture & d'aliment aux hommes & à tous les animaux" (It is not without reason that Rivers and navigable streams have earned the special protection of kings, for it is through this means that Provinces communicate with each other the goods that they produce in abundance; the rivers and streams facilitate commerce, bestow their riches upon the countries through which they pass, animate the earth to produce hay, wheat and fruit that serve to nourish all men and animals).[60]

In describing the rivers in this fashion, Le Bret marks a clear distinction between the separate units of the kingdom (in this case, provinces) and the force that joins them. This passage is representative of the special attention that Le Bret accords, throughout his text, to what may be termed points of mediation or connection between the discrete entities that constitute the country. Indeed, there would seem to be a close association between these units—rivers, roads, the postal service, embassies, letters, and money—and the king himself. The ultimate mediator between these discrete units of the state is, of course, the law, and it should not surprise the reader when Le Bret notes that the king is both the law and that which makes the law possible: "le Prince . . . est la Loi de son Etat, & donne l'être & l'autorité à toutes les autres loix" (the Prince is the Law of his state and gives being and authority to all other laws).[61] I demonstrated earlier how Bodin's insistence on the unity and indivisibility of sovereignty led directly to his opinion that monarchy could be the only true embodiment of this principle. In compromising this vision, Le Bret moves back to an idea of sovereignty as more of a spirit than an idea in need of embodiment, but this conception is no less unique, and no less problematic. Le Bret embraces Bodin's implied idea of sovereignty as that which underlies all divisions and definitions but ultimately resists definition itself. In so doing, Le Bret manages to exclude the monarch from the rules of self-interest that governed most of his subjects and that made good government necessary in the first place, whereas Bodin could only ultimately admit that there was no essential difference between the independence of paternity and that of the monarch. As that which joins independent entities, Le Bret's king cannot be seen as one of these entities in his own right, and therefore he cannot divert his attentions from the kingdom to a self that does not, properly speaking, exist.

This rather ingenious reconfiguration of the monarch does not lead to his invulnerability, however. Although Le Bret never treats tyranny as a possibility in his text, he does consider, at length, the threat of counterfeiting to the commerce of the kingdom. Great attention is given to "faux-monnoïeurs" as well as to the specificity of the king's marks that guarantee the authenticity of his letters. Le Bret justifies this attention through the inherent perfidy of fallen humanity:

> Tandis que les hommes ont vécu dans leur premiere innocence, comme l'usage des Signatures & des Cachets n'étoit point dans le monde, la seule parole ou le simple écrit, étoit le seul lien de leurs promesses & de leurs obligations. Mais depuis que les parjures & la perfidie ont banni de la terre la candeur, la franchise, & la fidelité; la défiance s'est tellement rendue maîtresse des esprits, que l'on a été contraint d'inventer les Seaux, de créer les Notaires, & d'introduire plusieurs autres moïens pour afermir les traitez & les conventions, & pour s'assûrer de la foi & de la loïauté des uns des autres.[62]

> [When men were living in their first innocence, the use of Signatures and seals was not known in the world, and one's word or a simple written note furnished the only tie of their promises and their obligations. But since perjury and perfidy have banished from the earth candor, frankness, and loyalty, suspicion has made itself so much the master of men's minds that they were forced to invent seals, to

create notaries, and to introduce several other means to hold up treaties and conventions, and to assure themselves of each other's good faith and loyalty.]

The fact that one could easily add the invention of kings to this list demonstrates once again Le Bret's need to draw a complete line between the world of subjects and the world of their rulers. Kings *must* be exempted from the human condition and tied rather closely to God; otherwise, the entire system would be incapable of order or redemption.

Yet Le Bret's attention to the destructive possibility of counterfeiting in the kingdom may be read as more than just another example of the human tendency toward dishonesty. In choosing to emphasize the importance of the king's position rather than the actual identity of the current occupant of the throne, Le Bret introduces the distressing possibility that anyone, provided they are anointed with the *chrême* and can claim privileged access to God's will, may serve as the uniting mediator of the kingdom; no personal skill is involved in upholding an impersonal law. By placing the king outside of the temporal realm occupied by his subjects, Le Bret has to sacrifice the linkage of time, heredity, and legitimacy that would privilege the royal race over any overzealous, inspired pretender. This is all the more the case given Le Bret's intense suspicion of the importance of authorship to the governing of the kingdom. In Le Bret's strongly legalistic vision of the French state, the king truly becomes a lieutenant, or place-holder, of God in the kingdom. Indeed, the bulk of the body of the text, enumerating at length the king's unique power over the elements of his kingdom, should not distract us from the sentiments expressed in the first and last pages of the treatise, in which the king as such almost disappears. On the first page: "Amien Marcellin dit, que [la royauté] n'est autre chose, que *cura salutis aliena.*, & S. Crysost., un exain de solicitudes & de veilles, pour le salut d'autruy. Afin de montrer que le principal ofice du Prince est de se dépoüiller de ses propres interests, retrancher de ses plaisirs, se dérober à soi-même, pour se donner entierement au public, & faire en sort que, *Omnium domos, illius labor; omnium delicias, illius industria, omnium vacationem, illus occupatio défendat:* dit le Philosophe Sénéque" (Amien Marcellin says, that royalty is nothing but the care of others' well-being, and Saint Crysostome, a mass of solicitude and worry for the well-being of others. In order to show that the main responsibility of the prince is to rid himself of his own interests, to rein in his pleasure, to take himself away from himself, in order to give himself entirely to the public and to do in sort that he works for the good of all).[63]
And on the last page:

[Les rois] doivent être soigneux de domter cette inclination vicieuse des hommes, qui les porte insensiblement dans la licence & la tirannie, lorsqu'ils voïent que toutes choses obéissent à leurs volontez, & d'avoir toûjours en la pensée ce sérieux Precepte d'un ancien Pere de l'Eglise, *Regis norma Deus est,* voulant dire que les Rois étans les images vivantes de ce grand Modérateur de l'Univers, ils doivent prendre peine de l'imiter en toutes leurs actions; & que comme cette souveraine Bonté semble n'avoir point d'autre objet, que d'épandre continuellement sur les hommes ses graces & ses faveurs: que de même les Rois ne doivent point avoir d'autre but ni d'autres desseins en l'esprit, que de rendre leurs Peuples heureux, & de les faire jouir de toutes sortes de felicitez. Ils peuvent s'assûrer que s'ils sont curieux d'observer tous ces conseils, Dieu sera toûjours de leur côté, qu'il fera prosperer toutes leurs entreprises, & qu'il les rendra toûjours victorieux & toûjours triomphans.[64]

[Kings must take care to conquer the natural inclination of men toward licentiousness and tyranny when they see that all things obey their will, and to always keep in mind the serious precept of one of the Church Fathers, *The norm of kings is God*, meaning that kings, as the living images of the great Moderator of the Universe, should take care to imitate him in all of their actions, and that as this sovereign Good seems to have no other object than to pour continuously upon men its graces and its favors, that similarly kings should not have any other goal or plans in mind than to make their peoples happy, and to allow them to enjoy all sorts of felicities. They can assure themselves that if they take care to observe this advice, God will always be on their side, and that He will make all of their plans prosper and will make them always victorious and triumphant.]

That these passages, with their emphasis on continuity over action and on God's authority rather than the king's, support a vision in which the identity or contributions of the individual monarch is obscured is reinforced by what follows. In the description of Louis XIII's praiseworthy actions, such as the "réduction du Bearn, la subite déroute de Soubize aux Isles d'Oleron, etc." (the reduction of the Béarn, the sudden defeat of Soubise in the Oleron Islands, etc.),[65] Louis XIII is never named once. Rather, he is merely described as "le roi qui régne à present sur nous" (the king reigning over us at present).[66] Moreover, and perhaps more significantly, his acts are not seen as original— as breaks in the tradition of "la royauté" and God's defense of it—but rather as fulfillment of scripture: "ces paroles prophétiques de Salomon au Ch. 30 des Prov. ont été acomplies en sa personne. *Gallus succinctus lumbos suos: Non est Rex qui resistat ei;* car s'ils considerent toutes les guerres qu'il a genereusement entreprises, ils reconnoîtront que le Dieu des armées, le Dieu fort, & le Dieu tout-puissant l'a visiblement acompagné aux plus dangereuses ocasions, a combatu pour sa défense, lui a fait remporter de signalées victoires, & l'a fait enfin glorieusement triompher de tous ses ennemis" (These prophetic words of Salomon in Chapter 30 of the Proverbs have been accomplished in his person. If people consider all of the wars that he has generously undertaken, they will recognize that the God of armies, the strong God, the omnipotent God has visibly accompanied him in the most dangerous occasions, has fought in his defense, and has made him win significant victories, and finally, has led him to triumph over all of his enemies).[67]

Le Bret's monarch has a tendency to disappear from the page, caught between an all-powerful God and a sinful nation. His exemption from the rules of self-interest sets him off from his people and ties him to the continuity and generosity of the divine, yet this same exemption also makes it difficult to see how he can attain any kind of individual glory or reputation—how, in short, he could make a name for himself. The state as described by Le Bret has made significant steps toward ensuring the legitimacy of its ruler but remains vulnerable to a counterfeit king, a prophet who could claim God's favor and inspiration for himself. Although Le Bret himself was instrumental in furthering the centralization of the kingdom, serving as prosecutor of Leonora Concini, as an *intendant,* and as a lawyer in the trials of Marillac and the Duc de la Valette,[68] it remains difficult to see how what we have come to call absolutism could arise out of this web of limitations and precedent.

LOUIS XIV

The future Louis XIV was born in 1638 after many long years of waiting for an heir to the Crown. His quasi-miraculous appearance, exemplified by the name of "Dieudonné" given to him, seemed less to signal the prowess of his father than to provide concrete proof of God's direct intervention in the affairs of the French state, encouraging the move away from a strictly hereditary view of monarchical succession and toward divine legitimization that was, as we have seen, already under way.[69] If 1638 marked the literal entrance of Louis onto the world stage, however, in 1661 Louis XIV made a second entrance, this time entirely of his own invention. Having reigned since 1643 under the aegis of the problematic Jules Mazarin, the French king took advantage of his first minister's death in March 1661 to announce that henceforth he would rule without a *premier ministre.* Both events were widely celebrated in the kingdom; taken together, they appear to offer the possibility of reconciling the idea, exemplified by Louis's birth, that only God can be the true agent of French history with the idea, inherent in Louis's 1661 declaration of independent authority, that inalienable sovereignty can be held by the monarch alone. In this context, it is important to understand that the proliferation of images and panegyrics surrounding Louis XIV's reign is a manifestation not of some sort of popular naïveté but rather of intense relief that the profound tension among sovereignty, legitimacy, and agency (problematized earlier by Richelieu's active involvement in state decisions, and more recently by the actions of Mazarin) would seem to have been resolved once and for all. The unity of the royal person provided a cover of sorts for the merging of two incompatible accounts of agency and governance and therefore needed to be celebrated.

This appears at first glance to be the tone of Jean-François Senault's *Le monarque, ou les devoirs du souverain*, published in 1662 shortly after Louis XIV's accession to full personal power in 1661. Patriotic and religious (he would become general superior of Bérulle's Oratory the year after his treatise appeared), Senault produced a text that attempts to glorify the French monarch while steering clear of blasphemy or idolatry. His treatise is therefore a fascinating negotiation between the royal and the divine, a constant oscillation between the merging of the two and their separation. *Le monarque, ou les devoirs du souverain* therefore illustrates, once again, the difficulty of thinking of mediation in a consistent manner in seventeenth-century France.

The fundamental tension in Senault's work—between Bodin's model of the monarch as godlike and Le Bret's idea of the monarch as pure connectivity between God and his subjects—is evident in both its title and its structure. By calling his text *Le monarque, ou les devoirs du souverain*, Senault reveals the impossibility of joining the semantic and sovereign independent entity—the monarch—to his reason for being, which is to serve the state and God alike. The phrase "les devoirs du souverain" should shock us and may have shocked readers of the time familiar with Bodin's insistence on the absolute independence of sovereignty. That Senault's title is possible at all reveals the extent to which the slide from *souveraineté* to sovereign that I noted in Bodin has become, in the intervening years, complete. "Monarch" becomes the marker of independence, the object to be defined on its own terms, and Senault does this in the first section. "Sovereign" appears merely as a synonym of "monarch," watered down from Bodin to the extent that the second half of Senault's treatise is devoted to describing the obligations and duties of the king toward God, his subjects, and the Church. As may be expected, Senault's observations in the "devoirs" section of the treatise enter into direct contradiction with those in the section on "le monarque."

Senault begins his treatise by discussing the supremacy of monarchy as a mode of government, based not upon its logical superiority (as in Bodin) but rather upon its founding in the Bible. Senault's account of the origin of monarchy is interesting, since it provides a variation on a story alluded to by almost all writers on the subject—that of the movement, in Judea, from direct government by God to government by kings. If for Protestant writers this story provides proof of the fallen status of man, perpetually tainting monarchy with the nostalgia for a direct rule by God that was foolishly rejected, the Oratorian Senault avoids this interpretation by eliding the people's envy of other states ruled by kings: "Mais disons que quand Dieu a voulu fonder un Estat dans la Judée, il en fut luy-mesme le Roy, ou qu'il luy donna des Rois pour le gouverner. Le peuple Juif aprés sa sortie d'Egypte relevoit immediatement de Dieu: Les Juges n'étoient que ses Lieutenans; Ils commandoient en son nom; Ils le consultoient dans la Guerre & dans la Paix, & ne donnoient que les ordres qu'ils avoient receüs de luy: Si bien que l'on pouvoit dire que Dieu estoit un Roy invisible qui conduisoit ce Peuple par les Juges, comme par des ministres visibles" (But let us say that when God wanted to found a state in Judea, he was himself its king, and he gave it kings to govern it. The Jewish people after leaving Egypt depended immediately upon God: the Judges were only his Lieutenants; they commanded in his name; they consulted him in War and in Peace, and gave only orders they received from him: So much that one could say that God was an invisible King who directed this People by Judges, as if by visible ministers).[70] By describing God as an invisible King, Senault reverses the order of the Bible, where monarchy as such finds its origin in man's falling away from direct rule by God. If the Jews were already subjects of a monarchy, no such fall could take place. Kingship is thereby naturalized and seen to be of divine, rather than human, creation. This tight connection between God and the king that confers divinity upon the monarchy serves Senault's goal, which he shares with Le Bret, of separating the king absolutely and essentially from his subjects:

Il faut pourtant avoüer que la verité a plus de part que la flatterie aux Eloges qu'ont receüs les Rois, & que leur grandeur est si élevée au dessus de toutes les autres, qu'il est assez difficile de trouver des termes pour en bien exprimer les avantages. Car si nous separons leur dignité de leur personne, & que nous considerions le rang & la puissance qu'elle leur donne sur les autres hommes, nous serons contraints de reconnoistre que Dieu n'a rien fait de plus excellent ni de plus auguste que les Rois. L'Ecriture qui ne sçait flatter personne, les appelle Dieux, & la juste crainte qu'elle a, que leur grandeur ne les enfle, l'oblige a leur declarer aussitost qu'ils sont mortels comme les hommes: Et de peur que cet Antidote ne soit pas assez puissant pour les preserver du poison de la vanité, elle ajoute qu'ils sont plus mortels que les autres hommes, et que Dieu qui prend plaisir à humilier les orgueilleux, semble choisir les testes couronnées pour la bute de ses foudres.[71]

[We must admit, however, that truth has more of a role than flattery in the praise that kings have received, and that their grandeur is so elevated above all else, that it is rather difficult to find the terms to express its advantages well. For if we separate their dignity from their person, and if we consider the rank and power that this dignity gives them over other men, we will be forced to recognize that God has not made anything more excellent or more august than Kings. Scripture, which does not flatter anyone, calls them Gods, and the just fear that it has, that their grandeur will inflate them beyond measure, obliges it to declare immediately afterwards that they are mortal like men. And from fear that this antidote will not be strong enough to preserve them from the poison of vanity, Scripture adds that they are more mortal than other men, and that God, who takes pleasure in humiliating the proud, seems to aim his lightning at crowned heads in particular.]

Unlike Protestant writers who hew to the letter of Scripture (where kings are rather suspect), here Senault places royal dignity above the possibilities of language. Kings are not capable of being described or, for that matter, created by human means; rather, their very status imposes the terms used in attempts to evoke their grandeur. That Senault extends this restriction to Scripture itself, which is thereby *obliged* to declare that kings are not only mortal but more mortal than other men, shows that the limits placed upon royal power are not intrinsic to it but instead are reasonable, yet optional, safeguards that protect the king from full realization of his powers.

As a result of this ineffable superiority over men, Senault's king, like Le Bret's, belongs to a time and sphere utterly different from those occupied by his subjects. This is especially true of French kings, whose accession to royalty is marked with unction by the royal *chrême*, originally delivered by the Holy Spirit in the form of a dove. It follows that French kings are the true extension of the biblical kings, Saul and David, who also received this unction, and are thereby direct participants in God's glory and plan for the world. The idea that royal time participates in divine time is reinforced by Senault's parallelism between Louis XIV and Saint Louis: "La Minorité [de Saint Louis] a tant de rapport avec celle de Louis quatorzième à present regnant, qu'il est impossible de la passer sous silence. Ces deux Princes vinrent presque enfans à la Couronne; mais la Providence divine les pourveut l'un & l'autre de deux excellentes Meres & Regentes" ([Saint Louis's] minority is so similar to that of Louis XIV who reigns at present, that it is impossible not to remark upon it. These two princes came to the crown as near-infants; but divine providence granted them both excellent mothers and regents).[72] Senault's text, unencumbered by the legal considerations of Le Bret and written after Louis XIV's seizure of personal power, demonstrates that royal decision and action can rightfully be viewed as miracles, as the direct intervention of divine providence into the lives of French subjects. This capacity for direct intervention, strongly different from Le Bret's ideal of a conservative law-upholding (rather than law-making) monarchy, allows Senault to name the monarch in his text. The king "à présent regnant" is not an individual temporarily invested with the power of the Crown but himself participates in divine time.[73]

Or so it would seem. When Senault begins to describe the monarch's duties toward God, a change in rhetoric takes place. The very idea of duty implies a separation and, perhaps even more important, a hierarchy between the king and the divinity he embodies. If the merger between king and God described in the first quotation—in which the difference between the two was so slight as to escape language—were perfect, the king would have duties only toward his subjects. Here, once again, I must take issue with the idea that Protestant influence on ideas of sovereignty and its incarnation ceases with the advent of Louis XIV to the throne, if not before.[74] Senault's language, in following his rather pre-Reformation praise of the godlike king with an enumeration of the king's duties to God, reads as a clear attempt to avoid charges—first brought and developed by the sixteenth-century Protestant monarchomachs, although later adopted by the Catholic League—that excessive divinization of the monarch is tantamount to idolatry. As I have shown above, the wars of religion and the iconoclastic agitation of the sixteenth century subjected the status of objects seen as manifestations of the divine to sustained questioning. This questioning was all the more urgent when attempts were made to ascribe the role of divine mediator to a human being, insofar as Protestantism viewed all men as equally subject to divine election or damnation. We have seen how this dilemma affected Le Bret's description of the king's precise relation to God, wherein, on the one hand, he is born to divine favor, and on the other hand, he has earned (or must earn) this favor through good governance. Senault must therefore include the following in his introduction to the subject of the king's piety: "Encore que tous les hommes se puissent vanter qu'ils sont alliez à Dieu par leur Creation, & que dans la misere de leur nature ils se puissent glorifier, qu'ils ont l'honneur d'estre ses images; Il faut pourtant avoüer, que les Princes possedent bien plus hautement ce glorieux avantage, & que par leur condition ils sont bien de plus nobles portraits de Dieu que les autres hommes. Ils representent sa Majesté à leurs Sujets, ils tiennent sa place dans leur Estat, ils parlent en son nom par leurs Edits, & il semble que Dieu se rende visible en leur personne sacrée" (Even though all men can boast that they are allied with God through Creation, and that in the misery of their nature they can glorify themselves as God's images; we must admit that princes possess this glorious advantage to a much greater extent, and that by their condition they are more noble portraits of God than other men. They represent his Majesty to their subjects, they take his place in their state, they speak in his name through their edicts, and it seems that God makes himself visible in their sacred person).[75]

This passage demonstrates Senault's difficulty in articulating the precise position of the king in the state and in God's universe. What is happening here is the breaking apart of any sense of continuity, of interpenetration, between the spheres of subject, king, and God. The God that suffuses all of his creation, that extends his grace and power indiscriminately to all men made in his image, is replaced by a circumscribed, localized entity, who has pulled so far back from the world that he needs the king to run it *in his place*. The idea of the divine needing some sort of human representation is problematic enough, as it assigns a certain limit to God's powers.[76] But even more troubling than the increasingly contentious role of God in the universe is the precise status of God's *lieutenant* on earth: the king. Like Le Bret, Senault finds himself confronted with the problem of attributing qualities to the monarch that may be removed if he loses God's favor, thereby undermining the historic emphasis on the glory of royal lineage and the importance of hereditary succession.[77] This problem does not arise if royalty is seen as an institution of human origin, since this theory (advanced by the *Vindiciae* as well as tentatively by Bodin and later by Hobbes) indelibly marks the king with the signs of man's fall from divine grace even as it justifies his power. By tying royalty directly to divinity, however, both Le Bret and Senault must address the question of what, besides Bodin's unicity and independence, qualifies the king to represent God on earth. Ironically, in asserting the king's legitimacy in such strong terms—terms that separate him both from God and from the subjects he governs—these writers ultimately undermine the strength of the king's position. Nowhere is this problem more evident than in the following, quite curious, passage in Senault:

Le Prince est une Image de Dieu; mais une Image qui doit toute sa beauté à celuy qu'elle represente. Il n'est regardé de ses Sujets qu'autant qu'il est regardé de Dieu. . . . Mais il faut que passant le Souverain plus outre se souvienne qu'il est tellement l'Image de Dieu qu'il cesse de vivre si-tost que Dieu cesse de le regarder, & qu'il ressemble à ces Images de nous-mesmes que nous voyons dans la glace d'un miroir. Elles subsistent par nostre presence, Elles se détruisent par nostre absence, & elles disparoissent aussi-tost que nous cessons de les former en nous regardant. Il en est ainsi du Prince à l'égard de Dieu; Il a l'honneur d'estre son Image, & de le representer à son Peuple; mais s'il s'éloigne de Dieu, ou qu'il oblige Dieu par ses crimes à s'éloigner de luy, cet éloignement cause sa perte, & dés que Dieu détourne son visage de dessus luy, il n'a plus de puissance ni de majesté.[78]

[The Prince is an Image of God; but an Image that owes all of its beauty to that which it represents. The prince is looked upon by his subjects only to the extent that he is looked upon by God. . . . But the sovereign must also remember that he is so much the image of God that he ceases to live as soon as God stops looking at him, and that he resembles one of those images of ourselves that we see in a mirror. These images subsist by our presence, they are destroyed by our absence, and they disappear as soon as we cease to make them by looking at ourselves. Such is the prince with respect to God; he has the honor of being his image, and of representing him to his people, but if he distances himself from God, or if he forces God to distance himself by his crimes, this distance causes his fall, and as soon as God turns his face away from him, he no longer possesses power or majesty.]

Here, Senault puts a fascinating new spin on the time-worn formulation of the king as "image of God on earth." By drawing a parallel between the king's relation to God and the image of ourselves that we view in a mirror, Senault reduces the monarch—elsewhere praised as a terrestrial God—to the ephemeral status of a mirror image, which has no reality in and of itself. The king has no power or authority of his own; all that he has is temporarily on loan to him from God, who can rescind this power just as easily as he gives it simply by turning away. In addition, this image reveals that God, the king, and the king's subjects are separated by such a distance that the relation among them cannot be one of contiguity. It is a relationship of vision, the sense that depends the most on distance between the observer and observed. Senault's repeated use of the verb *s'éloigner* only reinforces this structure. The monarch, as middle term in this relation, thereby becomes a sort of mirage, "qui n'est regardé de ses Sujets qu'autant qu'il est regardé de Dieu." As a result, his decisions for the kingdom can never be his own, but only translations of God's intent: "Mais il y a une troisiéme obligation qui est imposée aux Princes par la Politique, qui leur semblera plus nouvelle, & qui ne leur est pas toutefois moins necessaire; C'est qu'ils doivent consulter Dieu dans leur conduite, & entretenir un commerce avecque luy, afin qu'ils gouvernent en son Esprit, & qu'ils soient plûtost ses Lieutenans, que les Souverains de leurs Sujets" (But there is a third obligation imposed upon Princes by Politics, which will seem new to them, but is no less necessary to them; This is that they must consult God in their conduct, and entertain a commerce with him, in order to govern in his Spirit, so that they will be more God's Lieutenants, than the Sovereigns of their Subjects).[79]

This complete dependence of the monarch's authority on God's will practically invites a return of civil disobedience to the kingdom. Who is to judge that the king is following God's advice, and that he is, therefore, still king? Despite Senault's defense of successive monarchy in the first section of the treatise (even though succession is preferred to election essentially as further proof of the hand of divine providence in government), here, royal power is no longer justified by lineage; only the king's relation to God confers upon him *puissance* and *majesté*. Memories of the religious wars (and the continued presence of Protestants in the kingdom, however curtailed their rights), the Fronde, and the recent events in England render protection against such a powerful objection absolutely necessary in any treatise dealing with royal power and its foundation in the divine. Senault would seem to suggest that the people are so far from God that they are incapable of reading his wishes correctly; for the Oratorian, the king's position as privileged interpreter of God's will for France places him in a position quite similar to that of the Church in spiritual affairs. The interaction between monarch and God would therefore, during this part of the century, become enveloped in the "mystery of state," to which no one other than the king himself—except, perhaps, his council of ministers, whose meeting place Senault compares to a temple—has access. That this mystery occurs daily and that the French king continues to enjoy the special favor of God must ultimately be taken on faith.

This fundamental inscrutability of the center of governance would seem to protect the monarch from criticism, since to question the king's actions is to question God's design. Yet Senault's elaboration of the perfect monarch, incarnated in Louis XIV, has its fault lines, and, as in Bodin's work, these fault lines become apparent in the treatise's treatment of tyranny. If the cornerstone of good government is piety and the correct interpretation of God's will, tyranny is the result of false piety, of superstition and hypocrisy. What makes this distinction at once immensely important and highly problematic, however, is the inability of man—any man, even the king—to see God clearly. Senault's definition of piety announces this problem in advance. Taking piety to consist in "affection" and "action," Senault asserts that if the first, based on faith, is "obscure, mais certaine," the second, since always mediated by God's imperfect creation, is "plus évidente, mais bien moins assurée."[80] Taken together, these two aspects of piety render the distance between God and the king much more difficult to bridge than Senault's pronouncement of the king's need to consult God about all of his actions lets on. In a move that in some ways synthesizes the views of Bodin, who sees the possibility of tyranny in the king's independence, and Le Bret, who displaces the matter by discussing instead the subjects' natural tendency toward counterfeiting, Senault reveals the monarch's own susceptibility, driven by self-interest, to false piety.

> Mais il faut qu'ils prennent garde, qu'en cherchant la veritable pieté, ils n'en rencontrent pas une fausse, dont les effets sont aussi funestes, que ceux de la Pieté

solide & sincere sont utiles. Tous les Philosophes anciens & modernes ont déclamé contre cette fausse Religion, & ont employé toutes leurs raisons pour en éloigner les Princes à qui elle fait souvent commettre de notables fautes, sous pretexte d'exercer d'illustres Vertus. Ce Monstre qui prend les couleurs de la pieté, & qui se glisse dans l'ame des Rois sous cette belle apparence, n'est autre chose que la superstition, qui offense le Ciel en le voulant honorer, & qui l'irrite en le pensant appaiser.[81]

[But they need to make sure that, in looking for true piety, they do not encounter a false one, whose effects are as poisonous as those of solid and sincere Piety are useful. All ancient and modern Philosophers have decried this false Religion, and used all of their reasoning to keep princes from it, since this false Religion often makes them commit notable faults under the pretext of exercising notable Virtues. This Monster that takes on the colors of piety, and that slips into the soul of kings under this beautiful appearance, is nothing other than superstition, which offends Heaven in wishing to honor it, and which irritates it in thinking that it appeases it.]

In the long personification of false piety and her corrosive effects on social cohesion and governance that follows, Senault works to obscure the fact that false piety is, in some sense, built into his system, as the necessary outcome of his attempt to attach the king's legitimacy to his privileged intercourse with God. On the one hand, the king's authority depends upon the inability of his subjects to fathom God's plans for the universe and human history; this protects royal decisions from scrutiny. On the other hand, since the king is also human, God's word is equally inscrutable to him; to pretend otherwise would be to make God in the king's image, rather than the other way around, and either to slide into tyranny through the monarch's claim to enjoy quasi-divine status or to invite his subjects to idolatry. Both options, of course, obscure legitimacy. In either case, Senault's text, much like Le Bret's, clearly demonstrates that positioning the king between God and the royal subjects is almost impossible to do without sacrificing the monarch's unique identity as well as the authorship of his actions.

The fact that both Le Bret and Senault encounter similar difficulties when attempting to articulate the precise relation of the king and God—and, by extension, the king's ineffable legitimacy—may be attributed to their adherence to similar models. Both authors take as their point of departure the tripartite division of God, king, and the French subjects. The latter's need for a monarch must be explained by their lack of direct contact with the divine in the temporal sphere (and here, once again, we see the political threat posed at least indirectly by Protestantism, which poses all men either as equally distant or equally close to the divine), while the uniqueness of the king must be explained by his essential difference from his people, which is founded in part upon his privileged relation with God. Yet if the king is too different from his people, his rule will be compromised; communication, not to mention legislation, cannot pass between two mutually incomprehensible entities. Hence the frequent allusions to the king as a man, yet more than a man, and as a God, but less than a God. Both sovereign over his people and subject to God (indeed, often described as more subject to God than his subjects themselves), this Janus-faced monarch can almost be viewed as a miragelike excrescence of the increasingly fraught relation between the human and the divine, as Senault's evocative image of the mirror seems to indicate. The solidity that was accorded the monarch by previous models such as Budé's, which confidently asserted the superiority of the royal race and the weight of French history, becomes undermined by the pressure of recent events and by the inroads of logic and rationalism, which demanded, as Bodin understood, a defense of monarchy on its own terms.

LE ROI-SOLEIL

Senault's work, with its awkward characterizations of the tensions between *le monarque*, in all his independence, and the *devoirs du souverain*, which reduce the king to miragelike evanescence, marks a transitional point between the fraught efforts to redefine royalty from Henri IV through the Fronde and the purely admirative and descriptive accounts of Louis XIV as the ideal embodiment of a sovereignty whose workings were celebrated as mysteries. Despite the optimism of Bodin and his followers, logic had repeatedly failed to grasp and explain the contradictions inherent in the reconciliation of sovereignty and legitimacy. Any effort to link these two concepts closely only led, on the one hand, to the obscuring of the individual monarch or, on the other, to the placement of his actions and authority under suspicion of tyranny.

Gradually, then, logic gave way to a mysticism that, if it could not resolve these problems, at least preserved them from sustained examination by the public. This movement toward what could be called a religion of state is perceptible in Le Bret, and even more so in Senault, who describes the king's council as a temple closed to outsiders. Yet it is most overt in Père Le Moyne's massive treatise, *De l'art de regner*, published in 1665. In the rhetorically gifted Jesuit's opening pages, the king's superiority and legitimacy is as evident as it was for Budé; it is almost as if the intervening decades and difficulties had never happened:[82]

On a toûjours veu, & on verra toûjours de l'or & des pierreries, des peintures & des machines. Mais quand a-t-on veu, & quand verra-t-on un Prince de si grande mine, & si bien fait; de si bonne grace, & si adroit en tout ce qu'il fait?

Cette mine & cette grace, SIRE, viennent d'aussi haut, & sont d'aussi bon lieu que l'Esprit & l'Intelligence. Elles sont le premier assortiment & le plus naturel apannage de l'Empire. Et le Fils de Dieu venant regner parmy les Hommes, n'apporta point de plus visibles marques de sa Royauté, & n'en prit point d'autres sur la Terre. Ces marques-là, SIRE, qui ne consistent pas en dorures ny en pierreries, qui sont de l'impression du doigt de Dieu, & sont inherentes à vostre Personne, ne sçauroient vous estre ostées. Et quand V.M. pour mettre nos yeux à l'épreuve, & pour faire essay de ce qu'elle est, se seroit cachée dans la foule de ses Gardes, nos yeux ne laisseroient pas d'aller droit à elle: & toute la pompe, toute la magnificence qui se montreroit ailleurs, ne détourneroit point ailleurs nostre veneration & nostre culte.[83]

[We have always seen, and will always see, gold and jewels, paintings and machines. But when have we seen, when will we see, a Prince of such high mien and so well made, of such good grace, and so skilled in all he does?

This mien and grace, SIRE, come from a place as high and as well situated as Reason and Intelligence. They are the first ornament and the most natural accompaniment to the Empire. And the Son of God coming to reign amid Men, did not bring any more visible marks of his royalty, and did not take any others while on Earth. These marks, SIRE, which do not consist in gold or jewels, which are the impression of the finger of God and are inherent to your Person, cannot be taken away. And even if Your Majesty, to test our eyes and to experience what he is, hides himself in the crowd of his guards, our eyes will not fail to go directly to him, and all of the pomp, all the magnificence that are shown elsewhere will not turn our reverence and our faith elsewhere.]

Granted, these lines are from the preface to the work, where praise for the monarch to whom the treatise is dedicated is de rigueur. Yet it would be difficult to imagine any of the writers previously discussed expressing themselves in these terms. Even Senault, writing at the beginning of Louis XIV's personal reign, carefully adds the expression "si nous separons leur dignité de leur personne" to his description of kings as Gods on earth. Le Moyne, however, makes no such qualification. Rather, he emphasizes the physicality of the monarch in order to link him to God by the "impression" that the divinity has made on him. This impression is not only permanent but is associated with the king—and with him alone. Unlike jewels or gold, it cannot be removed or, one might add after reading Le Bret and Senault, counterfeited. This emphasis on the monarch's physical relation to God invites the comparison with Jesus Christ that, in fact, Le Moyne supplies. As the difference between the king and Christ is minimized, the result is a new "culte," or civic religion.

What has happened here? Le Moyne's startling equation of king and God allows him to dodge the problems that the more cautious writers could not avoid. He is able to valorize the individual king's specificity while affirming his divinely anchored legitimacy. By treating the proof of the alliance between God and Louis XIV as so evident that even a king in disguise cannot obscure it, Le Moyne removes any threat of idolatry or tyranny from the outset of his work. What follows will be less a proof of this link than a celebration of it, since the link itself is never in question. Yet this very position of ineffable superiority leads to danger, not so much for the subjects, who can never worship their monarch too much, but for the monarch, who may become stuck in a narcissistic mode of self-admiration.

In the body of his text, then, Le Moyne develops the idea, already voiced by Le Bret and especially Senault, that the king's uniqueness, indeed, even his identity as king, lies in his disregard for his own person. Arguing that tyrants can be as prudent and valiant as legitimate kings, Le Moyne describes the essential difference between the two in terms of justice, which tyrants never exercise. This discussion of justice and tyranny brings Le Moyne to the conclusion that

de tous les membres dont se forme le Corps Politique, il n'y en a point qui soit moins à luy, & moins pour luy que le Prince. Qu'on le traite de Souverain & d'absolu tant que l'on voudra: qu'on luy donne de l'Independance à pleine bouche: & si l'encens n'est assez fort, que les Flateurs doublent la dose, & ajoustent la Divinité à l'Independance: il est certain que comme le Tyran ne croit estre que pour luy, le vray Prince aussi ne croit estre que pour son Peuple. Le Droit des Gens sur lequel est fondée l'institution des Princes, le veut ainsi: & la nature de la Justice, qui est leur propre caractere, le demande. . . . Et Saint Ambroise nous apprend, que n'estant pas née pour soy-mesme, & ayant sa fin hors de soy, toute sa gloire est de s'abandonner, & de resigner tous ses interests au Public: de mettre son bien, & d'établir son repos dans l'ordre, dans le calme, dans l'harmonie de la Société civile. Cela presupposé, qui ne voit que si la Justice, qui est comme la forme du Prince, n'est pas pour soy, & se doit toute entiere à autruy; le Prince estably Prince, & distingué du Tyran par la Justice, se doit aussi tout entier & sans reserve à ses Sujets: & ne se peut reflechir sur soy, ne peut rien donner à ses interests, que ce qui luy reste des effusions qu'il doit aux necessitez de ses Peuples.[84]

[of all the members which form the Political body, none are less their own than the Prince. We may call him absolute as much as we want, we can give him independence, and if the incense is not strong enough, flatterers can double the dose and add divinity to independence—it is certain that just as the Tyrant thinks he is only for himself, the true Prince believes himself to be only for his people. The law of nations (*ius gentium*) on which the institution of princes is founded wants it that way, and the nature of Justice, which is their proper characteristic, demands it . . . And Saint Ambrose tells us, that not being born for himself and having his goal outside of himself, all of his glory is to abandon himself, and to sign all of his interests over to the public: to put his good and repose in the order, calm, and harmony of civil society. This assumed, who cannot see that if Justice, which is like the form of the prince, is not for itself, and owes itself completely to others, the Prince established as Prince and distinguished from the Tyrant through Justice owes himself entirely and without reserve to his subjects, and cannot reflect upon himself, can give nothing to his own interests but what remains after he has given everything necessary to his people.]

This passage, whose basic sentiments reflect a long tradition of writing on kings and also recur throughout Le Moyne's treatise, seems a bit shocking coming after Le Moyne's own flattery in the *epistre*. Yet it is precisely this juxtaposition of views that indicates the intense difficulty surrounding any attempt to speak to or of the monarch in seventeenth-century France. On the one hand, the king himself is lauded for physical qualities such as his grace, appearance, and majesty; on the other hand, he is reminded that "il n'est que le Substitut de Dieu" (he is only the substitute of God)[85] and is prevented not merely from taking pride in his position or appearance but from considering his grandeur at all. This model of kingship runs against Louis Marin's famous reading of the king's portrait; the king is in fact the one person in the state who is *not* allowed to look at himself. Rather, when he looks around him, he sees either his people, united by his gaze, or God, in whose regard he is nothing. Ironically, the gaze that unites and organizes the kingdom can never look upon itself.

The presence, in Le Moyne's text, of such strikingly opposite attributes of the monarch reveals the Jesuit's desire to evoke and celebrate such surface contradictions rather than to explain them away. As a result, obliquity, rather than pure logic, will be the tool that Le Moyne uses to investigate the fundamentally mysterious (and undoubtedly divine) essence of kingship. Le Moyne finds the ideal vehicle to treat the king's nature in the magic of the *devise*—an emblem consisting of image, slogan, and explanatory text to which Le Moyne would devote his next treatise, *De l'art des devises,* a year later in 1666. In this later work, Le Moyne praises royal medals that combine word and image, and, in so doing, transcend them both. Stating that "La Devise . . . est la propre diction des Empereurs, des Roys, des Generaux d'Armée, & de semblables gens, qui ne font pas autrement profession d'Eloquence" (the devise is the means of expression unique to Emperors, Kings, Generals of the Army, and people like that, who do not otherwise make a profession of eloquence),[86] Le Moyne identifies the terseness of the *devise*'s expression and its potential universality as the artistic equivalent of royalty itself–an interesting variation on the radically different views of eloquence held by Budé and Bodin.

Yet although kings and emperors might express themselves naturally in *devises*, in Le Moyne's view, not all symbols are equivalent. Although any naturally occurring object may serve as the object of a *devise*, one object stands out in particular: the sun. In *De l'art des devises*, Le Moyne calls it a "corps universel . . . qu'on ne sçauroit trop alleguer" (a universal body that cannot be overused). Through its very universality and omnipresence, the sun calls upon its human admirers to supplement its glory with a text explaining precisely the meaning that should be attributed to it: "le Soleil . . . estant comme il est, le plus clair & le plus connu de tous les exemples, ne verse pas plus d'influences differentes, qu'il a de differentes proprietez; & qu'il peut fournir ou d'expressions, ou de similitudes Politiques, Morales & Chrestiennes, fondées sur ces proprietez. Mais elles ne se presentent pas d'elles mesmes avec ses rayons, & la parole ne leur est pas moins necessaire pour sortir de cette confusion de lumiere, qu'elle le fut aux Elemens & aux Astres, pour sortir de la confusion du premier Chaos" (The Sun . . . being the clearest and best known of all examples, gives forth as many influences as it has different properties; and can furnish expressions or political, moral, and Christian similarities based on these properties. But they do not present themselves with the sun's rays, and the word is no less necessary for them to emerge from this confusion of light, than it was for the elements and stars to emerge from the first Chaos).[87] Le Moyne's likening of the creation of *devises* to the divine creation of the world demonstrates just what is at stake in the elevation of this art form. The *devise* becomes the ideal mixture of divine and human, of created and creating. And no object brings forth the demiurgical nature of the author–and, by extension, of the person described, a monarch whose natural mode of expression is the *devise*–than the sun, whose intense light and power need only be channeled to their proper destination.

Le Moyne's treatise on *devises* was meant, in part, as a justification of his procedure in the earlier *De l'art de regner*. Each section of this treatise on royalty introduced its topics with a *devise* and an explanatory poem. Not surprisingly, each image used to describe royalty included the sun, and most of the *devises* exploited the sun's ability to express royal qualities (both created and creating, divine and human, glorious yet self-ignorant) in their contradictory nature.[88] In one example, Le Moyne praises the sun's ability to keep moving without straying from its course, thereby marrying action and continuity and solving the problem of legitimizing the king's intervention in the lives of his subjects: "Mais si le Prince est l'image & le Lieutenant de Dieu dans son Estat; s'il y doit regner comme Dieu regne dans le Monde; prendra-t-il pour modele de son regne, le regne du Dieu d'Epicure, qui estoit un regne d'assoupissement & d'oisiveté? ou celuy des Dieux des Fables, qui estoit un regne d'Adulteres, d'Incestes, de Parricides? . . . Le Prince Chrestien s'en éloignera donc le plus qu'il pourra: il aura la veuë tousjours arrestée, & l'intention tousjours fixe & immobile, sur le regne du vray Dieu, qui tourne toutes ses pensées, & dresse tous ses desseins aux besoins, aux commoditez, aux plaisirs mesmes des hommes" (But if the Prince is the image and lieutenant of God in his State, if he should reign like God in the world, will he take for his model the reign of Epicurus' God, which was a reign of laziness and inattention? Or that of the Gods of the fables, which was a reign of adulteries, incests, and parricides? . . . The Christian Prince will thus remove himself as far as he can from such models: he will always fix his vision and attention on the reign of the true God, who turns all of his thoughts and adjusts all of his plans to the needs, comforts, and pleasures of men).[89]

Even this delicate matter of the Janus-like king, whose gaze is at once fixed upon God and upon his subjects, lends itself to characterization by the sun, whose glory reflects that of its creator, all the while granting its beneficial rays to the people below. Many more examples follow, from the moderation inherent in the solar monarch to his authority, which is without rival.

By directing attention away from the king's human similarity to his subjects, as well as away from any possible resemblance between him and the divine, Le Moyne's solar *devises* provide him with a means not only of providing unity to his text but also of evading most of the problems faced by earlier writers. The *devise*, with its carefully constructed equivalencies between monarch, sun, and artistic expression, celebrates the harmony that Le Moyne views as essential to the successful state: "Cette Foy donc qui n'est ny Divine, ny Historique, mais civile, est une juste & perpetuelle harmonie entre le penser, le dire, & le faire. Ou s'il est plus intelligible en ces termes, c'est une constante & parfaite correspondance entre l'intention, la parole, & l'action. Je l'appelle harmonie & correspondance, parce qu'elle se fait du concert & de la liaison, qui doivent estre entre l'intention & la parole, & entre la parole & l'action. Et ce concert doit estre si juste & si uniforme; cette liaison demande une telle jointure & une si parfaite union, qu'il n'y ait point de difference entre l'intention & la parole, point de dislocation ny de rupture entre la parole & l'action" (This faith, which is neither divine nor historical, but civil, is a just and perpetual harmony between thinking, speaking, and doing. Or if we can understand it better this way, it is a constant and perfect correspondence between intention, speech, and action. I call it harmony and correspondence, because it is made from the concert and liaison that should exist between intention and word, word and action. And this concert should be so just and uniform, this liaison demands such a perfect link and union, that there should be no difference between intention and speech, no dislocation or rupture between speech and action).[90]

This civil faith firmly occupies the position of mediator—between divine and human, between human individuals as well as aspects of the state, and finally between intention and action. It is, as Le Moyne shows, pure harmony. As such, it mirrors the perfect *devise*, which happily combines the human, specific word with the naturally occurring, created object. It also resembles the attributes accorded to the anchor of the civil faith, the king himself, whose ability to transform voiced intent into immediate action was often evoked.[91]

The smooth correspondence that Le Moyne wills as a reflection of the king, and of the *devise*, does, however, break down in places, and to his credit, Le Moyne attempts to deal with these difficulties as they arise: "Je sçay bien que toutes choses ne sont pas semblables entre le Soleil & le Prince. Celuy là ne va, pour ainsi dire, que par autruy: tous ses mouvemens sont d'impression: le principe qui les luy donne, est hors de luy: l'Intelligence qui le gouverne, par quelque endroit qu'elle luy applique sa vertu, ne luy est pas propre. Mais tout cela est hors du dessein de la Devise: & il suffit pour en verifier la justesse, que la ressemblance soit des choses exprimées par le Mot, qui est comme l'esprit & la forme de la Figure" (I am well aware that not all things are similar between the Sun and the Prince. The former only moves, as it were, through another: all of its movements come from elsewhere: the principle that gives it motion comes from outside of it, the intelligence which governs it is not its own. But all of this falls outside of the devise's intention: it is enough to see that the resemblance is one of things expressed by the word, which is like the spirit and form of the Figure).[92] Like Le Bret before him, Le Moyne is confronted with the problem of royal action, of how to reconcile the king's freedom to do as he pleases—to create, rather than merely enforce, the law—and his unshakable legitimacy. Here, once again, the quality that resists easy integration into the symbolic network is the king's capacity for action—his possession of a will that is his own. As I have shown, this aspect of royalty is one of the qualities that undermine a perfect model of mediation between God and the chosen kingdom of France. At some point the king moves from maintaining order to creating it and, in so doing, weakens any divine basis for his action, which Le Moyne, to his credit, avoids describing in Senault's rather convenient language of mystical and constant intercourse between God and the monarch.

While Le Moyne recognizes this difficulty, this inherent *difference* between the king and the sun, he does little to try to solve it. His acknowledgment of the monarch's problematic yet necessary free will is never fully developed in his theory, beyond repeated exhortations that the God whom the king should emulate is not the idle God of Epicurus. The resistance to transparent mediation constituted by the king's free will is instead evoked obliquely in Le Moyne's repeated references to new theories concerning sunspots. If true, these theories, which posit the spots as part of the sun itself rather than as extraneous objects, would corrupt not only the solar model that Le Moyne privileges throughout the text but, more important, the entire network of transparency and clarity that anchors this model to the king and anchors the king, in turn, to his kingdom and to God.[93] In the first of these references, Le Moyne's attempt to preserve the sun's purity is evident: "Bien davantage, [le soleil] ne prend aucune part aux corruptions qui se font sous luy: son innocence ne s'altere point par la veuë des mauvaix exemples. Les exhalaisons & les vapeurs, la boüe & les ordures ne salissent point sa pureté: & par quelque lieu qu'il passe, à quoy que ce soit qu'il touche, il ne soüille point sa lumiere. Les taches que luy trouvent les Astrologues, sont de l'illusion de leur veüe, ou de la tromperie de leurs lunettes" (Even more, the sun does not take part in the corruptions that occur under it; its innocence is not changed by the sight of bad examples. The exhalations and vapors, the mud and the trash do not dirty its purity: and by whatever place it passes, whatever it touches, they cannot sully its light. The spots that Astronomers have found in the sun, are either the illusion of their sight, or a mistake of their telescopes).[94] What is at stake for Le Moyne is the correct reading of the monarch's relation to the messy "exhalaisons" of history and its contingencies, that which Le Bret chose to refer to under the guise of fortune. The ingenious model of the sun, which affects every living creature without ever becoming affected in return, provides a means for Le Moyne to explain this difficult relation between an entity at once of this world and beyond it. Yet this model is irrevocably compromised if the theory regarding sunspots as intrinsic to the sun holds true. The materiality that Le Moyne flees, as a general rule, would emerge as part and parcel of the idealism upon which his universe is based. Indeed, Le Moyne's second invocation of sunspots occurs as he is trying to compare the king and the sun in terms of consistency and transparency, in terms of a perfect correspondence between interior and exterior: "Ajoustons, qu'il n'est jamais autre au dedans, qu'on ne le voit au dehors. Comme son interieur est lumineux, aussi l'est son exterieur: son centre & son cercle ont une mesme teinture: & ce qui se voit de ses rayons, n'est pas different de ce qu'il en cache. Les taches qu'on remarque en luy, ne sont pas de luy: elles sont, ou de nos yeux que sa lumiere éblouït;

ou de quelque corps jaloux qui luy fait ombre: & c'est bien à tort qu'on l'en charge, en estant aussi éloigné qu'il est" (Let us add, that the sun is never other on the inside than it is on the outside. As its interior is luminous, so is its exterior: its center and circle have the same tint: and what is seen of its rays is no different from what it hides. The spots that others have seen, are not part of it: they come either from our eyes that have been blinded by the light, or from some jealous object that imposes its shade: and it is without reason that we attribute spots to the sun, given its distance from us).[95]

The sunspots in this case symbolize a radical lessening of the distance between heaven and earth, between, as it were, king and people. In a variation on the theme of the mystery of state, Le Moyne implies that the sinful French nation is incapable of truly seeing the monarch's grandeur. If there are imperfections, they are the people's, not the king's. Denying the reality of sunspots shows that the distance between monarch and subjects must be preserved, and the monarch kept from corruption, if the sun/king is to impose order on the world. The final reference to sunspots occurs in relation to the sun (king)'s almost incomprehensible benevolence, in ignoring those who would accuse it/him of impurity: "Que les Astrologues luy reprochent des taches qu'il n'a point: qu'ils l'accusent des sterilitez dont il est innocent: que les Poëtes fassent de contes de ses amours & de ses galanteries: qu'ils luy donnent des Maistresses & des Bastars: que d'autres le chargent de la naissance des serpens & des poisons; il ne s'éloignera pas d'eux pour cela: il ne sera pas moins prompt à les éclairer" (Let Astrologers reproach it for having spots that it does not have: let them accuse it of sterilities of which it is innocent: let Poets make up stories of its loves and its gallantries: let them give it Mistresses and Bastards: let others charge it with the birth of serpents and poisons, the sun will not distance itself for all that: it will not fail to shine on them).[96]

Le Moyne's clear interest in sunspots could surprise the reader, given the tendency to dismiss treatises such as his as flowery shows of rhetoric. Certainly, Le Moyne is a less serious observer of the state than a Bodin or a Le Bret, and anyone would be surprised to see his writings in a collection of seventeenth-century political theory. Yet his inclusion of sunspots into an otherwise idealized portrait of the monarch demonstrates his investment in a substantial comparison between the king and the sun that reaches beyond rhetorical convenience. The sun of which he speaks is not the poet's abstract sun but the real one, material proof of the miracle of God's creation and of a concrete entity that mirrors the actual king's functioning in the world. The symbol's status as that which allows Le Moyne to avoid the pitfalls of earlier works, works starting from the premise that the king's humanity is common with his subjects, must be shown to be founded in hard fact. Despite appearances to the contrary, Le Moyne's treatise is just as influenced by the need to ground kingship in reality as that of Le Bret, which compares the king to a river, or that of Bodin, which approaches monarchy through pure reason.

The king's reign, and the contradictions it presents, must therefore stand up to recent advances in scientific inquiry; they cannot just remain poetic fantasy. Le Moyne addresses the king's relation to science specifically in the following: "Que le Prince appelle donc à son conseil, des gens de science & de probité, quand il voudra s'instruire de la justice de ses Armes. Et afin que le mot de Science n'abuse personne: je repete encore icy, que je ne parle pas de ces Sciences oisives & inutiles, qui passent les journées entieres, ou à disputer pour des atomes avec Epicure; ou à pointiller sur des lignes avec Euclide; ou à rêver sur des nombres ou sur des chiffres avec Diophante. Je parle de la Science qui juge des Droits & des Devoirs; qui distingue les bornes du Bien & du Mal; qui donne des regles à l'Honneste, & des mesures à l'Utile; qui dirige la Morale par l'Evangile, & la Politique par le Christianisme" (The Prince should call to his council men of science and probity when he wants to learn of the justice of his armies. And so that this word of science misleads no one: I repeat here once again, that I am not talking about these lazy and useless Sciences that spend days either fighting about atoms with Epicurus, or nitpicking about lines with Euclid or dreaming of numbers with Diophantus. I am speaking of the Science which judges rights and duties; which distinguishes the limits between Good and Evil, which gives rules to the Honest and measures to the Useful, which directs Morals by Scripture, and Politics through Christianity).[97]

Le Moyne's science, and that of the prince, is the science of judgment, of applying the universal to the particulars of the reign. The rule for such applications remains, of course, Christianity, and this implies some sort of smooth mediation between God and the human subjects of the realm. This science, administered through the king's arms and decisions, endows the chaos of the particular with form. Yet it is contrasted with another kind of science, a science dismissed by Le Moyne as "oisive" and "inutile"; this science is worth mentioning since is it not without links to the science that postulated the existence of sunspots.

This other science focuses on atoms, numbers, and lines. Le Moyne's phrasing "pointiller sur des lignes" evokes a long-standing debate that continued to elicit scientific opinion throughout the seventeenth century.[98] This debate revolved around the question of how it could be possible to obtain lines by combining Euclid's dimensionless, discrete mathematical points. Like atoms, and like numbers themselves, this question raised the troubling issue of cohesion—of how material nature could stick together and communicate amongst its various particles. Needless to say, this issue of cohesion was of utmost importance to theories of the state. Just as sunspots would irrevocably compromise the transparent nature of God's communication with the French through the king, so atomism, with its insistence on discrete particles and its troubling problematization (if not abolition) of cohesion, would render the king useless as mediator between the elements of his state. This is of particular concern given the ongoing attempts to reconcile independent sovereignty with legitimacy. (Le Bret famously claimed that sovereignty was no less divisible than a point in geometry, although the dominant image of his monarch resembles some sort of Stoic *pneuma* much more closely.)

But are sunspots and atoms at all related? Although Le Moyne names his philosophical enemy as Epicurus—a move all too common during this period, especially among Jesuits—the twin concerns of sunspots and atoms that he reveals in his treatise would seem to suggest that his unnamed enemy is Galileo, or at least the science that Galileo and his French supporters represent. Galileo, of course, famously wrote the "Letter on Sunspots," in which he argued that sunspots were neither illusions nor extraneous objects to the sun but rather were part of its essence. The redrawing of traditional Aristotelian boundaries between substance and accident that such a theory implied became even more explicit in his later work, the *Assayer*. In this work, Galileo advanced an atomist theory of physics that had the potential to explode Aristotelian notions of matter as well as Catholic explanations of the Eucharist. In a controversial work, Pietro Redondi argues that this atomism, not Copernicanism, lay at the heart of Galileo's condemnation by Rome, precisely because it would make transubstantiation impossible.[99] As such, Redondi contends, this theory presents problems much more serious to Catholicism than any hypothesis regarding the position of the distant sun in relation to the earth, since it strikes at the heart of the privileged means of mediation between the human and the divine. By problematizing transubstantiation, atomism would threaten the identity of Counter-Reformation Catholicism, whose major (indeed, at times, whose only) difference with Protestantism rested on the real substitution of Christ's body under the aspect of the bread.

Le Moyne's decision to single out this new science for criticism marks to what extent it replaced Protestantism as the major threat to the Catholic Church, and, by extension, to the state. Even if the king's status as mediator between God and the kingdom was no longer expressed in Eucharistic terms, atomism posed a serious challenge to efforts to elaborate an alternative theory of legitimacy, which would have to rest on some sort of cohesion and possible communication between the ideal and the real. Gassendi's revival of Epicurus worked hard to reconcile atomism with Christianity, but arguably at the price of placing in question the entire relevancy of universals, whether

mathematical or philosophical, to human experience. Descartes, while respect-
ful of Galileo, famously refused to advance any hypotheses whatsoever regarding transubstantiation, which was to be treated exclusively as a matter of
faith. Géraud de Cordemoy, who tried to reconcile atomism with Cartesianism, also implicitly illustrated the problems the theory posed for transubstantiation by addressing the question of how bread becomes man uniquely
through the process of-digestion.[100]

Le Moyne's dismissal of sunspots and atoms is therefore of a piece. It may
be fair to say that atomism, much like Protestantism at the beginning and end
of the century, remains the hidden scandal of mid-seventeenth-century
France and that its influence reached far beyond physics into the most central tenets of faith and, as Le Moyne shows, monarchy. Much like the Protestant challenges to royalty during the sixteenth century, atomism proposed a
universe made of interchangeable components, with none to be privileged
over any others, a direct refutation of Louis XIV's official *devise, nec pluribus
impar.* Yet atomism conveyed a danger even greater than Protestantism by
insisting that each particle of matter was self-contained, separated from its
neighbors by a void that flew in the face of dominant theories of God's creation of the world. This could also be viewed as a radicalization of the Protestant emphasis on limits shown at the beginning of this chapter. Unlike
Calvinism, however, it placed in real doubt all possibilities of mediation
between the divine and the human, the king and his subjects, in a great equal-
ization of separateness that accompanied the emergence of the modern, bourgeois, economic subject.

The new science, with its sunspots and epicurean atomism, becomes for Le
Moyne what Protestantism represented for Le Bret and Senault—a menacing
figure behind his treatise that threatened to reduce its elaborate hierarchies and
correspondences to a series of words divorced from reality. As seventeenth-
century writers tried to strengthen the ties of duty and legitimacy surrounding the monarch, they retreated increasingly from the marriage of reason and
kingship that Bodin had so incisively operated. Sovereignty and monarchy
were placed firmly beyond rational scrutiny, evoked more and more by the
mystery of state or the *je ne sais quoi.* Accompanying this movement was a
progressive evaporation of attempts to describe the essence of royalty. Treatises were replaced by panegyrics, and it was almost generally agreed that the
only person who could understand or transmit the meaning of sovereignty
was the king himself.

2

THE ABSOLUTE AUTHOR:
LOUIS XIV'S MÉMOIRES POUR L'INSTRUCTION DU DAUPHIN

THE RECEPTION OF THE *MÉMOIRES POUR L'INSTRUCTION DU DAUPHIN*

The idea that the secrets and mysteries of state were excluded from the scrutiny of a king's subjects explains the public reaction to Louis XIV's decision to contribute to the education of his son, the dauphin, by writing his memoirs. Although the king had been keeping journals with the memoirs in mind since the beginning of his personal reign in 1661, the first public knowledge of the royal project came ten years later, when Paul Pellisson alluded to it in a panegyric delivered to the Académie Française. Pellisson praises the king's care for his son's education, which is not limited to the selection of the best tutors but goes so far as to "mettre par écrit, pour ce cher fils, et de sa main, les secrets de la royauté et les leçons éternelles de ce qu'il faut éviter ou suivre" (write down in his own hand, for his dear son, the secrets of royalty and the eternal lessons of what should be avoided or followed).[1]

Yet a closer look at the context of Pellisson's remarks reveals the complex problems that the memoirs' very possibility introduces. As with Bodin, these problems turn on the question of the origins of sovereignty and royal power. All discourse concerning royal education introduces the suggestion that kings are not so much born as made.[2] To eliminate the listeners' temptation to apply this possibility to Louis XIV himself, Pellisson prefaces his remarks on the memoirs with a passage that begins by asserting that the great monarch is never unfaithful to his role as king: "De près plus que de loin on découvre à tous momens davantage sa véritable grandeur. Jamais que des sentimens, jamais que des expressions de Roy" (From up close even more than from afar one discovers at every moment his veritable grandeur. [One sees] only the feelings and expressions of a king). It is impossible to imagine such a king ever being less than he is at present; he is as constant as Le Moyne's sun. Pellisson draws the obvious conclusion from such consistency; in the sentence immediately following the remarks above, he asserts that "J'ay cru mille fois qu'il n'étoit pas né; mais qu'il avoit été fait nôtre Maître, comme sans comparaison, plus raisonnable que pas un de ses sujets" (I have thought a thousand times that he was not born, but that he was made our master, as someone without comparison more reasonable than any of his subjects).[3] Complete in himself, without the passions or defaults that mark his subjects, the king is therefore exempt from what would otherwise be an understandable jealousy toward his successor, "un Prince en qui la nature luy representât déja d'elle-même tous les premier traits de ses propres vertus" (a Prince in whom nature already shows the king the first traits of his own virtues).[4] Through his persistent feeling that Louis XIV was not born so much as made, and made less through human intervention and education than through divine fiat, Pellisson is able to transform the effort to educate the dauphin from a worrying reminder of royal imperfection into further proof of Louis XIV's own generosity and exceptional nature. He transcends humanity as "non seulement pere de cet aimable Prince, ni pere des peuples même; mais pere de tous les Rois à venir" (not only father of this lovable prince, nor father of the people, but the father of all kings to come).[5] Pellisson skillfully sublimates the question of the king's humanity as well as that of the very possibility of royal authorship both through rhetorical alchemy and through avoidance of the issue of Louis XIV's own birth and education.

The image Pellisson puts forth of an ideal, secret text in which the mysteries of state are divulged *in the king's own hand* must have made his audience in the Académie Française, a body composed in part to defend and create such visions of plentitude, shudder with delight at the thought of this text's existence.

Indeed, this delight was evident in the entries, submitted six years later, for a poetry prize awarded by the academy. The subject for the 1677 prize, bestowed on the king's feast day, was Louis XIV's decision to educate his son himself by writing the memoirs. One of the entries emphasizes the almost mystical power of the image of the king's hand penning the text: "Toy-mesme, pour l'instruire aux sublimes projects,/Pour luy mieux assurer le coeur de tes sujets,/Tu veux, de cette main qui sçait domter le Tage,/Luy tracer de ton Regne une fidelle image" (Yourself, to instruct him in these sublime project,/ To better assure him of your subjects' hearts,/You wish, with the same hand that conquered the Tagus,/ To trace for him a faithful image of your reign).[6] Another entry echoes this emphasis on the royal hand, evoking, a few lines later, the profundity of the royal "secret":

> Peuples le croirez-vous? de cette mesme main
> Dont le foudre vengeur ne part jamais en vain,
> Sous qui l'audace tremble et l'orgueil s'humilie,
> Il trace pour ce Fils l'Histoire de sa vie,
> Ce long enchainement, ce tissu de hauts faits
> Qu'aucuns momens oisifs n'interrompent jamais. . . .
> Mais les profonds secrets de sa haute sagesse
> Ce n'est qu'à son DAUPHIN que ce Heros les laisse.
> Tous ces vastes desseins qu'execute un instant,
> Et dont il ne nous vient que le bruit éclatant,
> Les yeux seuls de son Fils découvrent leur naissance.[7]

> [Peoples, will you believe? With that same hand
> From which the vengeful thunder never parts in vain,
> Under which the audacious tremble and the prideful submit,
> He traces for his son the history of his life,
> This long chain, this fabric of high deeds,
> That no idle moments have interrupted. . . .
> But the profound secrets of his high wisdom
> Are left by this hero to the Dauphin alone,
> All these projects executed in an instant
> And conveyed to us by their brilliant noise alone,
> Only his son's eyes can discover their birth.]

This poem's insistence on the dauphin as the memoirs' only reader manifests the sentiment that only those occupying the center of power can know the secrets of state. Restricting the memoirs to the dauphin's eyes reinforces the idea that kingship should not be subjected to rational scrutiny. Made under a shroud of solitude and mystery, the monarch's decisions are an indescribable combination of rationalist calculation and interpretation of the will of God. Any attempt to demystify this central alchemy–such as those made by Bodin, Le Bret, and Senault–would be, under Louis XIV's careful regulation of access to the inner circles of power, tantamount to lèse-majesté. The seduction that this mystery operated on the king's subjects is evident in yet another of the entries for the 1677 poetry prize:

> Sous l'éclatant fardeau d'un sacré diadesme,
> Chargé de tant d'illustres soins,
> Ce grand Prince souvent se dérobe à luy-mesme,
> S'enfermant en secret, travaille sans témoins:
> C'est là que rappellant ses combats, ses victoires,
> Ses peines, ses travaux, ses veilles, ses progres,
> Les dessins que le Ciel comble d'heureux succés,
> Il en fait de rares mémoires
> Pour servir de conduite au doux espoir des Lys,
> Et sur une étude si belle,
> Rendre ce DAUPHIN un modele
> Des Heros les plus accomplis.[8]

> [Under the brilliant weight of the sacred diadem,
> Charged with such illustrious duties,
> This great prince often reveals himself,
> Closing himself up in secret, working without witnesses,
> It is here that, recalling his combats, his victories,
> His troubles, his works, his sleepless nights, his projects,
> His ideas to which the heavens have granted happy success,
> He transforms them into rare memoirs
> To guide the conduct of the sweet hope of the lys,
> And upon such a beautiful study,
> To render the dauphin a model of the most accomplished heroes.]

It would be far too easy to dismiss these poems, of dubious literary value, as shameless examples of carefully orchestrated royal propaganda, written solely to advance the writers' careers. Rather, the fact that the works were submitted anonymously in response to a suggested theme demonstrates important aspects of absolutism as understood by its contemporary admirers. The themes of secrecy, of the king's hand, of the almost miraculous conjunction of reflection and action in the same person, recur in each of the entries. This recurrence is more than coincidence; it reflects a deep-seated belief in the uniqueness of the French king and a conscious refusal to scrutinize the inner workings of the monarchy. This refusal was not new; its appearance repeats, to a certain extent, the similar procedure of philosophers who refused to extend their skepticism or reasoning to the central mysteries of the Catholic faith. For as the treatises discussed earlier have shown, the marriage of reason and religion was no less difficult for the monarchy to effect than it was for Descartes, who famously refused to discuss the intricacies of transubstantiation. That there are as many modern studies investigating Louis XIV's assumption of a godlike position in his state–along with the accompanying "propaganda"–as there are works disputing his "absolutism" and pointing to the limitations of his power demonstrates both the success of his reign in confusing reason and religion in the "mystery of state" and the enduring tension between the two. In light of the variety of interpretation of the reign that has persisted until the present day, one can hardly fault seventeenth-century writers for their refusal to analyze the deeper nature of Louis XIV's monarchy.

The case of Paul Pellisson himself supports the theory that the refusal of the king's contemporaries to contemplate the mysteries of state was not an admission of lack of access to a text that would not be published until after the king's death but was, rather, quite calculated. For when Pellisson proclaimed, in his 1671 panegyric, the profoundly secret and personal nature of the king's decision to write the memoirs, he was lying. While the king himself was intimately involved in the writing of the memoirs,[9] he did not pen the entire text himself. Rather, the work was the result of a complicated collaboration, a collaboration detailed with great care by Charles Louis Dreyss in the introduction to his nineteenth-century edition of the work. Dreyss proves that the king worked closely with the dauphin's then *gouverneur,* Périgny, to establish the memoirs for 1666 and 1667. Once Périgny had been replaced in his position of *gouverneur* by Bossuet, Pellisson himself was assigned the duty of transforming the notes for 1661 and 1662 into a cohesive text. Why, then, would Pellisson allege that the king was writing the document on his own? It is not impossible that Pellisson, obliquely referring to a collaboration that he could not, with *bienséance,* admit, was inviting his fellow academicians to unearth, and subsequently reward, his collaboration in such an esteemed project. This did not happen. A much more probable explanation is that, as the entries for the poetry prize reveal, the mystique surrounding the throne was so great–and critics' attempts to seize this mystique directly so inadequate–that historical accuracy was sacrificed for ideological consistency. Pellisson's refusal to divulge either the contents of the memoirs or his own participation in their composition marks the profound nature of the complicity of Louis XIV's contemporaries in the construction of the absolutist state–a state that, like the memoirs themselves, could only admit of one author.

As the public reaction to the king's decision to undertake his son's education personally shows, the *Mémoires pour l'instruction du dauphin* held out the promise of the essence of royalty distilled and transmitted in a quasi-magical text. This text, like the battles won so decisively, was further proof of Louis XIV's unique enjoyment of God's favors. The tight relation between God and the French monarch traditionally expressed in the *sacre* had become, it seemed, living truth. For although the panegyrics and poems erred in attributing to the monarch sole authorship of the text, they were correct in positing the king's efforts as unprecedented in French history. While the *Mémoires pour l'instruction du dauphin* certainly had models both in kingship treatises and in manuals for educating the royal successor, never before—with the significant yet historically distant exception of Saint Louis—had a king of France undertaken this task himself. As the unprecedented nature of the memoirs becomes apparent through a careful look at possible inspirations, the question of *why* Louis XIV viewed himself as the only possible instructor for his son becomes more pressing. This question will lead us in turn to an examination of the memoirs' contents to see if, and how, the king's ambitions—abandoned after the onset of the Dutch war in 1672—were realized.

In some sense the memoirs fall into the well-established category of mirrors for princes (which were, however, never written by the king himself). In his own study of the memoirs' composition, Charles Louis Dreyss suggests various sources for the king's project. Specifically, he names the Abbé de Brianville's *Abrégé méthodique de l'histoire de France*—a difficult work, written in French, Latin, and Greek, that offered profiles of past monarchs for the dauphin's consideration—as well as La Rochefoucauld's *Maximes,* a contemporary model of universal *morales,* albeit hardly destined for future kings. Dreyss's choice of possible sources demonstrates his own dream of the perfect memoirs: a text that would ideally synthesize moral tenets with Louis XIV's own experiences to form a perfect blend of particular and universal, upholding the maxims of monarchy with a vivid depiction of events appropriate for a young reader. According to Dreyss, however, the failure of this ideal was mainly due to the contributing secretaries' immersion in the treatises of Senault and Le Moyne, both of which Dreyss dismisses as flowery rhetoric with no possible practical applications.

All of these sources, along with Claude Joly's anti-Mazarin *Recueil des maximes veritables et importantes pour l'instruction du roi,* which Dreyss cites as a sort of negative inspiration for the king, may indeed have played a part in the genesis of the royal memoirs. Yet Dreyss can be faulted for his failure to look for models beyond the 1660s or outside of the frontiers of France. Within France, throughout the seventeenth century, memoirs were multiplying. Almost everyone, male or female, nobleman or persecuted Protestant, was setting on paper their personal experience of the events around them. The meaning of this textual proliferation has proved elusive, however, for historians and literary critics alike. "At the crossroads of prose genres,"[10] memoirs escape easy categorization, as the intentions of their authors vary almost as widely as the texts themselves. This diversity must have represented a certain danger for a monarch intent on mastering his kingdom and the events inside and outside of it.[11] For the Louis XIV who proudly announced to Parlement in 1661 that there would never again be a *premier ministre* in France and who destroyed all of Parlement's records from the years of the Fronde, the most troubling memoirs would have been those of *frondeurs* such as Retz or La Rochefoucauld, or even those of ministers such as Richelieu and Colbert. Dreyss does note the importance of Colbert's notes and memoirs in the construction of the *Mémoires pour l'instruction du dauphin,* but more as a source of verification than of (possibly negative) inspiration. Given Louis XIV's assertion in the opening paragraphs of his own text that "ne doutant pas que les choses assez grandes et assez considérables où j'ai eu part, soit au dedans, soit au dehors de mon royaume, n'exercent un jour diversement le génie et la passion des écrivains, je ne serai pas fâché que vous ayez ici de quoi redresser l'histoire, si elle vient à s'écarter ou à se méprendre, faute de rapporter fidèlement ou d'avoir bien pénétré mes projets et leurs motifs" (and having no doubt that the rather great and important things in which I have participated both within and outside my kingdom will one day stimulate the intelligence and the passions of writers in various ways, I shall not be displeased for you to have here the means to correct history if it should go astray and misunderstand, from not having fully penetrated into my plans and into my motives),[12] one may certainly assume that the idea that Colbert's lists of numbers could one day be transformed into a text with the minister, not the king, as protagonist contributed to the monarch's decision to produce his own record of his reign. The public would certainly have applauded the king's efforts; already, a pamphlet had been produced soon after the death of Henri IV that purported to be the former king's ghost speaking to his young son, Louis XIII.[13] Likewise, toward the end of Louis XIV's reign, in the early 1700s, a long, rather strange text appeared, titled *Codicilles de Louis XIII . . . à son très cher fils aîné.*[14] The appearance of such impostors (as well as other "official texts," such as those by Bussy-Rabutin) speaks to the public curiosity regarding the secrets of monarchy and must have further encouraged Louis XIV to set the record straight in his own publicized, but not published, work.

Other possible sources for the *Mémoires* can be found beyond the frontiers of France. It is entirely possible that Louis XIV was thinking of Julius Caesar's *Commentaries* when he decided to write of events soon after their completion, rather than waiting for old age. As Georges Lacour-Gayet points out in his excellent *L'Education politique de Louis XIV,* the *Commentaries* were one of the key texts in Louis XIV's education, and the young king was rumored (almost certainly falsely) to have translated them himself.[15] What better gift could the king offer for his own son's education than a replacement of the *Commentaries* by a narrative of his own actions? The parallels between the two works did not go unnoticed by Louis XIV's contemporaries, whose awe that a soldier and hero could also take up a pen–in the same hand!–was a direct echo of the widespread fascination with Caesar's literary productions. Louis XIV's possible desire to surpass the *Commentaries* is evident in his replacement of Caesar's third-person narrative by the first person, although as we shall see, the royal "je" is by no means an easy pronoun to articulate.

The text that most closely resembles Louis XIV's *Mémoires pour l'instruction du dauphin* was written soon before the French king's reign, and by a monarch who had similar aspirations to divine right–"absolute"–kingship. James VI of Scotland wrote the *Basilikon Doron* during the last years of the sixteenth century; the first widely available edition was published in 1603, the same year that, upon the death of Elizabeth I, he became James I, king of England. Like Louis XIV, James initially meant the work to be read only by his son and heir and other members of his family; unlike Louis XIV, who initiated the project in the first years of his personal reign, James wrote the *Basilikon Doron* at a time when he believed himself near death.[16] The similarities of purpose between the *Basilikon Doron* and the *Mémoires pour l'instruction du dauphin,* as well as the great possibility that Louis XIV would have either read or heard of James's text, invite a comparison between the two works.

However, the reader expecting to find a precursor of Louis XIV in the pages of the *Basilikon Doron* is soon disappointed. James's belief that his kingship was firmly rooted in God's authority alone leads less to a celebration of his own powers than to an admonition to his son to follow God and religion in all things. This attitude is summarized in the sonnet presenting the argument of the book:

> God giues not Kings the stile of *Gods* in vaine,
> For on his Throne his Scepter doe they swey:
> And as their subiects ought them to obey,
> So Kings should feare and serue their God againe:
> If then ye would enioy a happie raigne,
> Obserue the Statutes of your heauenly King,

And from his Law, make all your Lawes to spring:
Since his Lieutenant here ye should remaine,
Reward the iust, be stedfast, true, and plaine,
Represse the proud, maintayning aye the right,
Walke alwayes so, as euer in his sight,
Who guardes the godly, plaguing the prophane:
And so ye shall in Princely vertues shine,
Resembling right your mightie King Diuine.[17]

Indeed, according to James I's advice to his son that the ideal guide to good government can be found in Scripture, his own text is almost bereft of accounts of events that he faced during his reign in Scotland. Such detail would be a concession to the need to interpret human history on its own terms, whereas the Protestant James placed his trust in God's plan for his kingdom. Good governance will be rewarded, and tyranny will be punished–if not in this world, then certainly in the next. This interpenetration of divine and human through the king leads James I to advise his son to practice a moderation in his behavior and dress that has direct echoes in the Aristotelian golden mean: "[I]n your garments be proper, cleanely, comely and honest, wearing your clothes in a carelesse, yet comely forme: keeping in them a middle forme, *inter Togatos & Paludatos,* betwixt the grauitie of the one and lightnesse of the other: thereby to signifie, that by your calling yee are mixed of both the professions; *Togatus,* as a Iudge making and pronouncing the Law; *Paludatus,* by the power of the sword: as your office is likewise mixed, betwixt the Ecclesi- asticall and ciuill estate: For a King is not *mere laicus,* as both the Papists and Anabaptists would haue him, to the which error also the Puritanes incline ouer farre."[18]

What a contrast between the "absolutisms" on either side of the Channel! The harmony evoked by James, wherein the attributes of various roles merge and intermingle in the king's person, is quite far from the concentrated unity of power advocated by Bodin (who, we should recall, hated all sorts of mix- tures) and evident even in Le Bret's famous assertion that "la souveraineté n'est non plus divisible que le point en la Geometrie" (sovereignty is no less divisible than a point in geometry).[19] Part of this difference in imagery may be explained by the mixed nature of British government. In addition to need- ing to find a way to speak of and shore up his authority against that of Parlia- ment, the Scottish James needed to embody successfully both the Scottish and English nations. This situation stands in stark contrast to that of post-Fronde France, where the Parlement of Paris had been denied any representative or governmental role in the kingdom. The strong difference between the two countries and their ideas of royal authority during the seventeenth century recalls Kantorowicz's warning against applying his theory of "the king's two bodies" outside of England.[20] While English monarchs were keenly aware that theirs was not the only established authority in the state, on the other side of the Channel the rapidly developing French doctrine of mystery of state attested in part to the inability of the subjects to call the king's actions or motivations into account. James I's vision of the monarchy as carrying out a divinely authored script is therefore grounded not only in his Protestantism but also in his need to firmly assert both his legitimacy and authority to Parliament. God, not the king, becomes the ultimate agent of his monarchy.

If James presented himself as the privileged yet ultimately passive vehicle through which God's will expressed itself, Louis XIV occupied the more Bodinian position of asserting his God-given legitimacy through his similarity with God. Godlike, rather than godly, the French monarch embodied the singularity, the will, and the creative power of the supreme being much more than the humility of Christ or of a passive believer. Perhaps the single most repeated word in the memoirs is the first-person *je*. The pages of the memoirs often offer a dizzying sequence of royal actions and decisions. Locutions such as "je fis commander," "j'ordonnai," "je mandai," "je dépêchai," and finally "je fis faire"—all in a single paragraph—attest to the king's awareness of his power to command. As I have argued above, even the decision to undertake his son's education himself reveals a strong reluctance to have the events and actions of his reign interpreted by others. Louis XIV's celebration of his own ability to wield power is what most commentators have detected in the memoirs, and it is unquestionably there.[21] Yet, by abstracting this remarkable text from the debate that had surrounded the question of kingship since the end of the sixteenth century, these commentators fail to see its importance and indeed, its scandal.

SOLE AUTHOR OF THE KINGDOM

The treatises on kingship examined in chapter 1 demonstrate the difficulty in reconciling authority and legitimacy. By privileging the latter, Le Bret and Senault were both faced with a subsequent fading of the king's role, as his actions were more divine than royal in inspiration. I agree with Dreyss that the works of these writers had a direct influence on the project of the *Mémoires pour l'instruction du dauphin* but would argue that the memoirs seek less to apply the precepts inherent in such treatises than to counter the royal disappearance that application of those precepts implies. Against the nameless king inhabiting the last pages of Le Bret, the memoirs seek to articulate the king's voice, actions, and positions as his own, yet this articulation is anything but simple. One of the reasons that identifying possible sources and inspirations for the king's decision to write is an ongoing task is that the text itself fails to mention any specific precursors or influences. Indeed, as Dreyss himself noted, "Quel accueil Louis XIV eut-il fait à un étalage de documents d'où n'auraient pu se produire sa pensée et sa personnalité? Que lui importaient les théories du monde ancien, ou les doctrines d'un âge pendant lequel la royauté n'était pas une souveraineté absolue et incontestée? Richelieu même, qui a mis la dernière pierre à l'imposant édifice, n'est jamais cité" (What would Louis XIV have done with a stack of documents where his thought and personality could not have expressed themselves? What importance could the theories of the ancient world, or the doctrines of a period during which royalty was not an absolute and uncontested sovereignty, have had for him? Richelieu himself, who placed the last stone on this imposing edifice, is never cited).[22] Richelieu is not the only striking absence from the text; the considerable works of Lionne, the minister of foreign affairs, and of Colbert himself are given short shrift. Perhaps most important, no other king of France is named specifically; rather, Louis XIV generically refers to them as "mes prédécesseurs." The overall impression of sole authorship and responsibility for the monarchy is in line with the Bodinian principle that only the king can administer the state; all other power is possessed, temporarily, only with his permission. To a large extent, the story of the memoirs is that of a king reestablishing his rightful primordial place in his state, thereby countering the ongoing disappearance of the monarch displayed by the earlier treatises. Louis XIV's desire to make himself visible, to assert himself as sole author of his reign, is evident not just in the decision to write the memoirs but also in several other initiatives described throughout the text. In 1661, this desire for authorship and authority appears in his explanation of his decision to curb the rights of the *parlements:* "de réduire toutes choses dans leur ordre légitime et naturel, quand même, ce que j'ai évité néanmoins, il eût fallu ôter à ces corps ce qui leur avait été donné autrefois, comme le peintre ne fait aucune difficulté d'effacer lui-même ce qu'il aura fait de plus hardi et de plus beau, toutes les fois qu'il le trouve plus grand qu'il ne faut, et dans quelque disproportion visible avec le reste de l'ouvrage" (to reduce all things to their natural and legitimate order, even if it had been necessary—although I have avoided it—to deprive these bodies of part of what they had been given, just as the painter has no hesitation about softening what is most striking and most beautiful in his own work whenever he finds that it is bigger than it should be and clearly out of proportion with the rest of it).[23] This passage demonstrates the mixture of conservatism and innovation with which Louis XIV regards his role in the state. Although his actions are presented as merely restoring an "ordre légitime et naturel," thereby righting the wrongs of the past just as his memoirs are written to right the wrongs of the future, they are no less radical and no less his own, as the comparison of himself to a painter demonstrates. In 1662, the same pride in his originality and work would come to the surface in his description of the king of Spain's decision not to replace Don Luis de Haro as prime minister: "[Le Roi d'Espagne] me témoigna son estime d'une manière dont j'avoue que je fus agréablement flatté, quand, après la mort de don Louis de Haro, il dit publiquement, devant tous les ambassadeurs des princes étrangers, que c'était à mon exemple qu'il ne voulait plus avoir de premier ministre. Car il me semblait tout ensemble bien généreux pour lui, et bien glorieux pour moi, qu'après une si longue expérience des affaires, il reconnût que je lui avais servi de guide dans le chemin de la royauté; et sans me donner trop de vanité, j'ai lieu de croire qu'en cela même plusieurs autres princes ont regardé ma conduite pour régler la leur" (The King of Spain displayed his esteem for me in a manner that I confess flattered me pleasantly when, after the death of Don Luis de Haro, he stated publicly in front of all the foreign ambassadors that he wanted to follow my example in not having a prime minister any longer; for it seemed to me both very generous of him and very glorious for me that, after so much experience in affairs, he acknowledged that I had been his guide in the path of royalty; and without being too presumptious, I have reason to believe that many other princes have also imitated my conduct in this).[24] From his assertion that war on land is preferable to a naval war—because in the latter, "le bien de l'Etat ne permettant pas qu'un roi s'expose aux caprices de la mer, je serais obligé de commettre à mes lieutenants tout le destin de mes armes, sans jamais pouvoir agir de mon chef" (the good of the kingdom not permitting me to expose myself to the caprices of the sea, I would be obliged to commit everything to my lieutenants without ever being able to act in person)[25]—to his recognition of the people's desire to see the king during *carrousels* and other such entertainment, Louis XIV and his secretaries demonstrate an acute awareness of the need to establish the king firmly as the central point of the kingdom. All initiative, all decisions, emanate from him, and even if this vision runs counter to what we know about the administration of the state during this period and beforehand, it must be preserved.

Of course, this very initiative and visibility can, as Le Bret and Senault had foreseen, serve to obscure royal legitimacy. Louis XIV's approach to monarchy would seem to conflict with earlier treatises' descriptions of the legitimate king. Nowhere does Louis XIV portray himself engaging in the ongoing conversation with God that Senault evokes as the special prerogative, if not the duty, of the monarch. Nor does Louis XIV submit himself completely to the rule of French law—on the contrary, as we have seen, he proudly describes his curtailing of the rights of *parlements*. The passage of the memoirs that comes closest to the language of these treatises is far from unambiguous: "Exerçant ici-bas une fonction toute divine, nous devons paraître incapable des agitations qui pourraient la ravaler. Ou s'il est vrai que notre coeur, ne pouvant démentir la faiblesse de sa nature, sente encore naître malgré lui ces vulgaires émotions, notre raison doit du moins les cacher sitôt qu'elles nuisent au bien public pour qui seul nous sommes nés" (Exercising a divine function here below, we must try to appear incapable of the agitations that could belittle it, or if our heart not being able to belie the weakness of its nature feels the rise of these vulgar emotions in spite of itself, our reason must be extremely careful to hide them if they are harmful to the good of the state, for which alone we are born).[26] Here, what is remarkable is Louis XIV's strange distance to his divine mandate, a distance underscored by his assertion that he (and again, the pronouns here turn to "nous," making the lesson applicable as much, or more, to his son than to himself) should *appear* to be incapable of shaking the divine foundations of his power. God himself is not mentioned as an agent but rather as an adjective. Moreover, reason's task is to *hide* the vulgar emotions of the heart—not completely, but only when they affect the public good. The language of dissimulation penetrating this passage is a long way from the complete transparency (and corresponding passivity) recommended by Senault. By positioning himself as author not only of the memoirs but of all administrative action, Louis XIV risks violating the subordination to God's plan that writers such as Bossuet would continue to deem essential for distinguishing between legitimate king and tyrant, a subordination that James I's scripture-thick writings, in contrast, illustrate so well.

Louis XIV's awareness of this difficulty emerges in a passage that comes just before his description of his influence on the other kings of Europe cited above:

> Pour voir, mon fils, comme vous devez reconnaître avec soumission une puissance supérieure à la vôtre et capable de renverser, quand il lui plaira, vos desseins les mieux concertés, soyez toujours persuadé, d'un autre côté, qu'ayant établi elle-même l'ordre naturel des choses, elle ne les violera pas aisément ni à toutes les heures, ni à votre préjudice, ni en votre faveur. Elle peut nous assurer dans les périls, nous fortifier dans les travaux, nous éclairer dans les doutes, *mais elle ne fait guère nos affaires sans nous,* et quand elle veut rendre un roi heureux, puissant, autorisé, respecté, son chemin le plus ordinaire est de le rendre sage, clairvoyant, équitable, vigilant et laborieux."[27]

[As much, my son, as you must acknowledge your submission to a Superior Power capable of upsetting your best-laid plans whenever It pleases, always rest assured, on the other hand, that having Itself established the natural order of things, It will not easily or constantly violate it, either in your favor or to your prejudice. It can assure us in time of peril, strengthen us in our labors, enlighten us in our doubts, but *It hardly does our work without us,* and when It wants to make a king fortunate, powerful, supported and respected, Its most normal course is to make him wise, clear-sighted, fair, vigilant, and industrious.][28]

In this passage, the roles of king and God that the treatises of Le Bret, Senault, and Le Moyne describe seem to have been reversed. The God to which Louis XIV refers is no longer the God of miracles, of spectacular intervention into the human world. Rather, he is the God of stability and of laws, a God who provides the background against which human initiative may assert itself. Therefore, for a king to attribute his failures to divine intervention is for him to manifest the laziness of the people, "[qui] leur permet d'appeler leurs fautes du nom de malheur, et l'industrie d'autrui du nom de bonne fortune" (which permits them to call their errors misfortune and the industry of others good fortune).[29] In other words, as Louis XIV indicates in the final sentence, what God confers upon the monarch is not so much the latter's acts or their outcome but rather the *power,* the potentiality, to accomplish them. The relation of God and the king is less one of dependence than of emulation, and it is often unclear, throughout the reign of Louis XIV, who is imitating whom.[30]

Indeed, in another passage from the text, Louis XIV tries to explain to his son the precise relation that a king should maintain with God:

Et à vous dire la vérité, mon fils, nous ne manquons pas seulement de reconnaissance et de justice, mais de prudence et de bon sens, quand nous manquons de vénération pour celui dont nous ne sommes que les lieutenants. Notre soumission pour lui est la règle et l'exemple de celle qui nous est due. Les armées, les conseils, toute l'industrie humaine seraient de faibles moyens pour nous maintenir sur le trône, si chacun y croyait avoir même droit que nous, et ne révérait pas une puissance supérieure, dont la nôtre est une partie. Les respects publics que nous rendons à cette puissance invisible, pourraient enfin être nommés justement la première et la plus importante partie de notre politique, s'ils ne devaient avoir un motif plus noble et plus désintéressé.[31]

[And to tell you the truth, my son, we are lacking not merely in justice but also in prudence when we are lacking in veneration for Him whose lieutenants we are. Our submission to Him is the rule and the example for that which is due to us. Armies, councils, all human industry would be feeble means for maintaining us on the throne if everyone believed he had as much right to it as we and did not revere a superior power, of which ours is a part. The public respects that we pay to this invisible power could indeed justly be considered the first and most important part of our entire policy if they did not require a more noble and more disinterested motive.][52]

Although this paragraph is followed directly by an admonition to the dauphin to never regard God with interested hypocrisy, the cynicism of the above passage—where God is, in fact, never named—is striking and has been noted by many commentators. In it, Louis XIV makes the Machiavellian argument that religion is one of the primary tools of a successful monarch. Not only does religion capture the imagination of the people, it also provides a transcendental grounding for the monarch's power. In fact, as the passage seems to indicate, it is the *only* grounding for the king's power. This awareness of the fragility of command, almost certainly a result of the Fronde, is striking. By attributing the sole separation between monarchy and anarchy to a "puissance invisible," Louis XIV implicitly argues for the importance of his own visibility, in both power and prayer. If the "vulgaire" has trouble grasping the abstraction of an invisible (and, as we have seen in the passage previously cited, essentially inactive) divinity, it can bolster its religious faith through obedience to its monarch, and vice versa—its faith in God serves as a model for its respect for his visible representative, the king.

The ongoing game between visible and invisible structures the entire text, even as it raises serious religious issues. If the memoirs present the monarch as visibly as possible, engaged in warfare, treaties, and play, they likewise hide the source of his power, God, from view. Yet as we lapse into pictorial language, something that seems to happen almost irresistibly when discussing the royal text,[33] we should try to keep in mind the ambiguities of the memoirs as a written record. That other methods of depicting Louis XIV's reign were available is evidenced in the production, later in the century, of the series of medals commemorating great events. As Louis Marin has demonstrated, this metallic history *shows* the monarch much in the same way as his portraits, transforming the king into icon, and perhaps even idol.[34] Yet the production of the Académie des Inscriptions, much like the *devises* favored by Le Moyne, fails to capture the dynamism that Louis XIV viewed as essential to his reign and that, paradoxically, marks the ultimate impossibility of the royal persona.

"WE HARDLY NOTICE THE REGULATED AND USEFUL COURSE OF THE SUN"

For what the memoirs ultimately reveal is not a king securely occupying the central place of power in his kingdom but rather an individual constantly attempting to inhabit this position. The *je*s that pepper the text with their action reinforce the impression that the king's endless activity aims to occupy a space that may never be filled. Louis XIV acknowledges this space, calling it most often "gloire" or "renommée," as in the following passage: "C'est aux hommes du commun à borner leur application dans ce qui leur est utile et agréable; mais les princes, dans tous leurs conseils, doivent avoir pour première vue d'examiner ce qui peut leur donner ou leur ôter l'applaudissment public. Les rois, qui sont nés pour posséder tout et commander à tout, ne doivent jamais être honteux de s'assujettir à la renommée: c'est un bien qu'il faut désirer sans cesse avec plus d'avidité, et qui seul, en effet, est plus capable que tous les autres de servir au succès de nos desseins" (It is for ordinary men to limit themselves only to what they find useful and pleasant, but the first thought of kings in all their councils must be for what may or may not win them the acclaim of the public. Kings, who are born to possess everything and to command over everything, must not be ashamed to accede to renown. It is a possession that is avidly to be desired, that indeed can contribute more than any other to the success of our plans).[35] Significant here is not merely the contrast between the king and the "common man" but rather the striking contrast evinced in the sentence that follows. On the one hand, kings are born into their position, a position that leads them to possess and command everything. Countering this static image of plenitude is the king's subjection to reputation, a "bien" that inspires endless desire in the monarch. Considering that Le Moyne went so far as to treat, quite seriously, the problem of whether the monarch could allow himself to enjoy either love or friendship without compromising his sovereignty, the stark appearance of desire in this passage should give the reader pause. Although it is, admittedly, desire for glory, it raises anew old questions regarding the role of the legitimate monarch in his kingdom. Should he content himself, like Le Bret's ideal king, with restoring order and the rule of law, repairing the infractions and alienations of the past? Or rather, should he risk the role of tyrant through innovation and initiative? Louis XIV's answer to this question may be found in a passage treating his handling of a food crisis in 1662 as well as the subsequent affection shown him by his subjects:

> A peine remarquons-nous l'ordre admirable du monde, et le cours si réglé et si utile du soleil, jusqu'à ce que quelque dérèglement des saisons, ou quelque désordre apparent dans la machine, nous y fasse faire un peu plus de réflexions. Tant que tout prospère dans un Etat, on peut oublier les biens infinis que produit la royauté, et envier seulement ceux qu'elle possède: l'homme naturellement ambitieux et orgueilleux ne trouve jamais en lui-même pourquoi un autre lui doit commander, jusqu'à ce que son besoin propre le lui fasse sentir. Mais ce

besoin même, aussitôt qu'il a un remède constant et réglé, la coutume le lui rend insensible. Ce sont les accidents extraordinaires qui lui font considérer ce qu'il en retire ordinairement d'utilité, et que, sans le commandement, il serait lui-même la proie du plus fort, il ne trouverait dans le monde ni justice, ni raison, ni assurance pour ce qu'il possède, ni ressource pour ce qu'il avait perdu: et c'est par là qu'il vient à aimer l'obéissance, autant qu'il aime sa propre vie et sa propre tranquillité.[36]

[We hardly note the admirable order of the world and the regular and useful course of the sun until some disturbance in the seasons or some apparent disorder in the machine makes us give it a little more reflection. As long as everything in a state is prosperous, it is easy to forget the infinite blessings that royalty provides and merely envy those that it possesses. Man, naturally ambitious and proud, can never understand why another should command him until he feels the need for it. But habit makes him insensitive to this very need, as soon as it is constantly and regularly satisfied. It is extraordinary incidents that make him consider what he ordinarily gains from this; and that, without authority, he would himself fall prey to the strongest, finding in the world neither justice, nor reason, nor security for his possessions, nor recourse against his losses; and this is how he comes to love obedience as much as he loves his own life and his own tranquillity.][37]

This passage, with its curious slippage of pronouns and subjects, provides a unique demonstration of Louis XIV's view of his place not just in the kingdom, but in the world. The first sentence introduces the ability of man to forget the benefits of the sun, or the well-ordered machine that is the world, until some unforeseen disaster arises. However, by using "nous" in this first sentence, the king alters the entire tenor of what follows. This tendency of humanity to neglect those responsible for the order of the world can, through the *nous*, be ascribed not only to the subjects' relation to their monarch but also to the king's complicated relation to a God, who, having abandoned miracles, has in a way consigned himself to oblivion. The irrelevance of the divine alluded to here goes a long way toward explaining God's curious absence from the text of the memoirs. But if God no longer visibly intervenes in the world, the king does. The king's actions serve to prove his importance not just to his weary and skeptical subjects but also to himself. This capacity for action, for innovations that can be attributed solely to the monarch acting alone, is what ultimately grounds his power, rather than any mystical link with the divine. In effect, the role of God in the universe has been replaced by that of the monarch in his kingdom. The fear that the king's propensity for action will lead to charges of tyranny has been displaced by the fear that his inaction will lead to his being forgotten.

The memoirs in general, then, become a testimony to the relevance as well as the irreplaceability of Louis XIV as monarch of France. Each event described, in such detail that the *maximes* following the episode seem contrived (indeed, the manuscripts show that they were often moved around the text), marks the effort to fuse Louis XIV the individual, acting in a particular place and time, with the universal transcendence of the French monarchy. Yet as Louis XIV himself seems to realize, this fusion, so desired, would also be fatal to his reign. If accomplished, it would lead to stasis and conceivably to a popular revolt provoked by the forgetting of the importance of the monarchy. Imperfection and incompletion are therefore essential to the king's governance. Perfection renders the monarch obsolete. This concept is not unlike Cardin Le Bret's assumption that the king's role is to repair the damage done to society by human failings. But while Le Bret exempts the monarch from these failings, tying him closely to God and thereby separating him completely from the self-interest that governs those he rules, the memoirs demonstrate, despite themselves, that the imperfections that Louis XIV must work tirelessly to correct exist not just in the kingdom but in the monarchy itself.

This is why the *nous* in the passage cited above represents such a significant slip. For while the memoirs may seek to describe the actions of the reign from a transcendent point of view that, if not God-like, is certainly Caesar-like, the decision to relate these events in the first person and to the king's eventual successor causes serious difficulties for the narrative voice. As we shall see, these problems are only natural for a divine right monarch caught between the choice of emphasizing his legitimacy and thereby losing himself or underlining his power and thereby obscuring the source of his authority. The memoirs pose the fascinating question of how writing from such a difficult position remains possible.

THE ROLE OF THE DAUPHIN

Although Louis XIV manages to minimize not only the role of God in the memoirs (arguably, he must if he is to impose himself as sole author of his actions) but also that of his "prédécesseurs" on the throne, the position of the dauphin as future ruler and reader raises many of the same issues that these omissions seek to obscure. The role of the dauphin as *destinataire* is just as ambiguous as the text's detail-laden content. As I have shown above, each royal action both holds out and refuses the prospect of plenitude, of an elusive final coincidence between Louis XIV as individual and Louis-le-Grand as king. Likewise, the dauphin's presence in the memoirs serves as a justification of the textual project and as a sign of its ultimate futility, and both of these roles contribute to the splitting of the royal self in the narrative. On the one hand, as the king's contemporaries noted and as his reluctance to name any personal influences shows, the memoirs demonstrate simultaneously the singularity and universality of Louis XIV's position as king. We may recall that this coincidence of singularity and universality is precisely how Bodin characterizes sovereignty; the memoirs therefore represent the ultimate achievement of this difficult position in the state. From Louis's assertion that "plus la place est élevée, plus elle a d'objets qu'on ne peut ni voir ni connaître qu'en l'occupant" (the higher one's position, the more it has objects that one cannot see or know without occupying it),[38] to his disgust at the emperor's usurpation of his title from its rightful origin and place in France, the memoirs are filled, as we have seen, with allusions to the king's unique and personal hold on power both within his state and abroad. No one else can or should educate the royal heir, since no one else is capable of knowing what it is like to be king: "ceux qui auront plus de talents et plus d'expérience que moi, n'auront pas régné, et régné en France" (those who could have more talent and experience than I, will not have reigned, and will not have reigned in France).[39]

Yet this very uniqueness raises the difficult question of the dauphin's eventual succession to his father, his replacing of what Louis XIV works so hard to prove as irreplaceable. This problem did not go unnoticed by the commentators who praised the project of the memoirs. In the poems submitted for the Académie Française's poetry prize of 1677, the writers puzzled over how such a succession could be imagined. One of the poems cries: "A moins qu'on ne l'imite, en vain on luy succede/Que le sceptre est penible aprés qu'il l'a portée!" (Unless one imitates him, one succeeds him in vain/How painful is the scepter after he has carried it!).[40] Another poem prays, "Grand Dieu qui soûtiens la puissance/Du vaillant & sage LOUIS,/Fay qu'il vive long-temps pour le bien de la France,/Et qu'il revive dans son Fils" (Great God who upholds the power of the valiant and wise Louis, grant him a long life for the good of France, and grant that he should live again in his son).[41]

Indeed, each address to the dauphin is tantamount to an admission of the transience of Louis XIV's own reign and thereby opens a space between the king as individual and the role of monarch that he endlessly attempts to occupy. But this is where the memoirs' difference with other writings, such as those of James I for his heir, become especially striking. A text composed of terse maxims (such as "respect God") would leave room for the son to follow the father; Louis XIV's awareness of this is evident in the recommendations that he wrote for his grandson upon his accession to the Spanish throne in 1701, which consist of a brief list whose elements vary in specificity. The memoirs written for the dauphin, however, follow a completely different strategy. Although Louis XIV does, from time to time, insert references to his son and to the future reality of his reign (a reality that would be eliminated by the heir's death in 1711), the intense depiction of the events of the reign quite often lead the reader to forget for whom, or why, the text is being composed. The insertion of more general reflections upon these events, occurring about every ten pages in Goubert's edition, often only serves to underscore the difficulty of understanding how, exactly, a precise account of the geopolitical situation of 1662 could possibly educate a dauphin who would never encounter that precise conjunction of particular details, events, and personages in his own life.[42] Louis XIV himself seems to hesitate at times, noting in one passage that

> je viens à douter quelquefois si les discours qu'on fait [de la politique] et ces propres Mémoires ne doivent pas être mis au rang des choses inutiles, puisque l'abrégé de tous les préceptes consiste au bon sens et en l'application que nous ne recevons pas d'autrui, et que nous trouvons plutôt chacun en nous-mêmes. Mais ce dégoût qui nous prend de nos propres raisonnements n'est pas raisonnable; car l'application nous vient principalement de la coutume, et le bon sens ne se forme que par une longue expérience . . . de sorte que nous devons aux règles mêmes et aux exemples l'avantage de nous pouvoir passer des exemples et des règles.[43]

> [I sometimes begin to wonder if its discussion and these very memoirs must not be classed as useless things, since the summary of all its precepts lies in good sense and in dedication, which we do not receive from others, and which we find rather in ourselves. But this disenchantment with our own reasoning is not reasonable, for dedication comes to us primarily through habit, and good sense is developed only through long experience or through repeated and continual meditation on things of a similar nature, so that we owe to rules and to examples themselves the advantage of being able to dispense with examples and with rules.][44]

This observation addresses two difficulties at once. On the one hand, the diversity of circumstances that the monarch must face is such that any maxims covering correct conduct would be so general as to be useless. This idea is expressed even more clearly in a section of the memoirs dealing with the problem of balancing the varying interests and opinions that surround the prince. Here, Louis XIV warns his son that "il serait difficile de vous fournir pour cela des règles certaines dans la diversité des sujets qui se présentent tous les jours" (it would be difficult to give you certain rules, given the diversity of subjects which present themselves daily).[45] However, the longer passage above has another meaning, one that suggests the double nature of this "education" of the French heir. Louis XIV seems to be stating that experience alone can confer the necessary wisdom upon the monarch. In other words, the memoirs are truly useful to the dauphin only insofar as he refuses to read them. For placed against Louis XIV's own intense satisfaction at having more or less reinvented the French monarchy, without help from either his ministers or his predecessors, the memoirs take away with one hand what they give the dauphin with the other. A successor who reads the memoirs and subsequently models his conduct after that of Louis XIV will, the memoirs seem to imply on every page, be a plagiarist rather than a true original. If his legitimacy consists in the application of Louis XIV's reasoning to government rather than his own, the dauphin-successor will renounce the very sovereignty and independence of action in which his father takes so much pride.

While other commentators have noticed this implicit double bind whereby Louis XIV corrupts his heir's monarchy even as he passes it on,[46] few have located it in the larger context of the ongoing crisis of legitimacy in the French state. For the impossible situation that Louis XIV writes out for his son is merely the most recent configuration of the troubled relation between the monarch and the divine source of his power. By displacing the emphasis in the text from God to his son, Louis XIV is able to clear an unconflicted space of independent action for himself—a space that I have shown is anything but uncontroversial. The loss of legitimacy that such independence implies, however, is moved from the king to his heir, as Louis XIV once again assumes the place of God as both guide and conferrer of power to the future reign. If the voice of God is no longer clearly audible in the French kingdom, and if the interpretation of this increasingly silent voice continues to be fraught with controversy, Louis XIV, on the other hand, can provide the dauphin with the privileged communication that Senault had seen as central to legitimate power.

Transferring the difficulties of occupying the position of king from himself to his heir is, therefore, essential to obscuring the complexity of Louis XIV's own legitimacy and troubled relation to the divine. Each action that Louis XIV attributes to his own genius or initiative undermines the proper role of a divine right king, which is to be the interpreter rather than the inventor of God's plan for the kingdom. In chapter 1, I demonstrated how divine right monarchy, in which the king derives his power and legitimacy directly from God, differs from race-based monarchy, whereby the ruler takes his power from his predecessors and the royal line. Both Le Bret and Senault minimize the importance of the royal bloodline for the king's identity and glory, insisting instead on his intimate relation with the divine. This shift in emphasis may rightfully be viewed as a result of the assassination of Henri III and the complicated legitimization of Henri IV at the end of the sixteenth century.

While divine right monarchy protects the throne from rival members of the royal bloodline by minimizing their proximity to the succession, it also weakens the monarchy insofar as it is seen to be based on what Louis XIV rightfully dismissed as a "pouvoir invisible," the favors of which may be claimed by almost anyone, raising the specter of a counterfeit king.[47] Louis XIV's *Mémoires pour l'instruction du dauphin* may be read as an attempt to reconcile the horizontal axis of bloodline with the vertical axis of the divinely granted gift of legitimacy and talent. If this reconciliation can be operated through this text, Louis XIV could establish himself as another Saint Louis—the king-saint who was the last monarch to combine both aspects of royalty perfectly and from whose complicated bloodline all following French monarchs traced their origin.

The complex role of the dauphin in the memoirs as carrier of the contradictions that Louis XIV himself may have been unable to resolve contributes to the strange impression that the text makes on almost all of its readers—that this text is less a manual of instructions and maxims than a sort of autobiography. Charles Louis Dreyss says it best when he states that "Louis XIV, qui n'avait pas songé à son fils dans le premier projet de Mémoires, qui a ensuite inscrit à chaque page le nom du Dauphin, n'a pas été utile à un autre qu'à lui-même" (Louis XIV, who had not thought of his son in the first project of the memoirs, who then inscribed on each page the name of the dauphin, was not useful to anyone but himself).[48] The dauphin is another Louis XIV, not only through his eventual occupation of his father's throne, but also insofar as he provides the memoirs' author with a means of isolating separate aspects of his reign. By dividing himself between the roles of king and heir, Louis XIV illustrates a split that other parts of the text reveal to be internal to the king himself. This split is between the king who acts, the tranquil occupant of the throne, and the king who, throughout the memoirs, watches himself act with fascination and not a little detachment. In the body of the text, this split is illustrated in a famous passage (although almost never cited in its entirety) where Louis XIV describes the carrousel of 1662 and his subsequent adoption of the solar symbol as his *devise:* "Ce fut là que je commençai à prendre [la devise] que j'ai toujours gardée depuis, et que vous voyez en tant de lieux. Je crus que, sans s'arrêter à quelque chose de particulier et de moindre, elle devait représenter en quelque sorte les devoirs d'un prince, et m'exciter éternellement moi-même à les remplir. On choisit pour corps le soleil" (It was then that I [began to adopt] the emblem that I have retained ever since and that you see everywhere. I believed that, rather than dwelling on something private and minor, it should in some ways portray the duties of a prince and always inspire me to fulfill them. Chosen as the symbol was the sun).[49] The transformation of Louis XIV into the Roi-Soleil—a transformation that one would imagine to be effected in one glorious instant of power—thus described is strikingly sloppy. The first sentence begins well, with the decisive "ce fut là"; however, the next words mark the beginnings of an awkward game of initiative and identification. The king does not state "que je pris"; rather, he uses "que je commençai à prendre," a phrasing that suggests process rather than completion. When did the king stop beginning to take the sun as his symbol? Is this time different from the time of "j'ai toujours gardée depuis"? The tension between taking and keeping recalls the perpetual movement needed to remember the king's presence and importance to his subjects and ostensibly prevents the stasis of narcissism from enveloping both monarch and realm. Indeed, this is the advantage of the solar symbol: its "mouvement sans relâche, où il paraît néanmoins toujours tranquille, par cette course constante et invariable, dont il ne s'écarte et ne se détourne jamais" (by its perpetual yet always imperceptible movement, by never departing or deviating from its steady and invariable course).[50] These qualities render the sun "assurément la plus vive et la plus belle image d'un grand monarque" (assuredly the most lively and most beautiful image of a great monarch).[51]

Yet this very principle of movement, of the tension between desire and achievement that characterizes a great reign, is precisely what prevents Louis XIV from fully identifying with his symbol, even if this symbol itself represents this tension. There is a gap between the opening "je" and the closing "un grand monarque," as Louis XIV implies that the convergence of the two will always remain tantalizing close and ultimately impossible. If he himself cannot operate this identification between himself and the sun, perhaps his son can. The dauphin is a figure who is even farther away from the sun than his father; from his perspective, the distance between father and sun is smaller. This perspective explains the addition of "que vous voyez en tant de lieux"—another curious choice of words if one considers the alternatives of the passive voice ("qu'on voit en tant de lieux") or the explanation that the people, another extension of the monarch's self, have erected these symbols in his honor ("qu'on a mis en tant de lieux"). The emphasis on the son—and the son's vision—inherent in this choice begins to explain why the writing of the memoirs coincided with the dauphin's birth. Beneath the stated desire to educate the heir lies the more troubling realization that the reader/son represents the nagging excess, the possibility of "écartement," that the memoirs must simultaneously address and prohibit. The condition of the memoirs is the eventual disappearance of the king.

If the play of pronouns is startling in this passage, where the acting "je" of the monarch is surrounded not only by the "vous" who observes but by the "on" that chooses, it is, as one might expect, even more striking in the opening of the royal text. The first passage of the memoirs for 1661 similarly illustrates the difficulty of the king's ongoing struggle to consolidate his many selves—dauphin, public, eternal, mortal—into a writing-acting whole. How can Louis XIV clear a space from which to write? The legitimization of the memoirs is no less difficult than the legitimization of the monarch himself:

> Mon fils, beaucoup de raisons, et toutes fort importantes, m'ont fait résoudre à vous laisser, avec assez de travail pour moi, parmi mes occupations les plus grandes, ces Mémoires de mon règne et de mes principales actions. Je n'ai jamais cru que les rois, sentant, comme ils font, en eux toutes les tendresses paternelles, fussent dispensés de l'obligation commune des pères, qui est d'instruire leurs enfants par l'exemple et par le conseil. Au contraire, il m'a semblé qu'en ce haut rang où nous sommes, vous et moi, un devoir public se joignait au devoir de particulier, et qu'enfin tous les respects qu'on nous rend, toute l'abondance et tout l'éclat qui nous environne, n'étant que des récompenses attachées par le Ciel même au soin qu'il nous confie des peuples et des états, ce soin n'était pas assez grand s'il ne passait au-delà de nous-mêmes, en nous faisant communiquer toutes nos lumières à celui qui doit régner après nous.[52]

> *[My son, many excellent reasons have prompted me to go to a considerable effort in the midst of my greatest occupations in order to leave you these memoirs of my reign and of my principal actions. I have never believed that kings, feeling as they do all the paternal affections and attachments in themselves, were dispensed from the common and natural obligation of fathers to instruct their children by example and by counsel. On the contrary, it has seemed to me that in this high rank of ours a public duty combined with the private, and that all the respects that are paid to us, all the affluence and brilliance that surround us being nothing but rewards attached by Heaven Itself to the care entrusted in us for people and for states, this care would be insufficient if we did not extend it beyond us by handing down all our insights to our successor.][53]

This passage charts the fascinating emergence, retreat, and reemergence of Louis XIV as he begins the memoirs. Most striking, perhaps, is the delay in articulating the "je" that will become the oft-cited protagonist of the text. The first sentence elides the "je" of royal agency, placing the project under the dual motivators of "mon fils" and "beaucoup de raisons." This first monarch is not a "je" but rather a "moi," in two important senses. First, he is not acting but is being acted upon—even the possibility of emerging in the writing of the memoirs is occluded by the verb "laisser." The memoirs are not written so much as "left" for their reader. Second, as the repeated possessives indicate, the monarch depicted in this first sentence is someone who discovers himself in charge of his kingdom and possessions rather than someone who actively takes part in ordering them. This "moi" is the same fragmented figure, described in the opening pages of the memoirs for 1661, who is dismayed at finding his kingdom in a state of almost complete disorder and who only realizes his identity as monarch when he loses himself in work.[54] But returning to the passage above, the first emergence of the "je" does not occur until the second sentence, which opens, signficantly, with the negative of a verb of contemplation rather than a positive affirmation of action: "je n'ai jamais cru." This timid foray into self-expression vanishes almost as quickly as it appears, since it is followed by an observation concerning "les rois"–a class of people from which the "je" seems to exclude itself, since the third-person plural persists until the end of the sentence. Finally, in the third sentence, Louis XIV seems to operate the crucial identification among self, writer, and monarch as he refers to "le haut rang où nous sommes." Is this finally the royal we? Alas, the specification ("vous et moi") that immediately follows once again tempers the strength of this assertion, since it raises still more questions about who is speaking. If the "nous" contains both the "moi" of the king and the "vous" of the dauphin, then what is the rank of which Louis XIV speaks? It cannot be the rank of "French king," since the wording seems to indicate that both figures occupy it simultaneously. Yet this is what the remainder of this rather lengthy final sentence implies, as the "nous" that had contained two different individuals shades into the royal "we" that is instead comprised of two different *persona:* the "public" and the "particulier." By the end of the sentence, the transformation in this "nous" will be complete, as Louis XIV can refer to his son as "celui qui doit régner après nous."

This pronominal confusion stands in sharp contrast with the more reassured paragraphs that follow and that begin with the very "je" that proved so elusive in the memoirs' opening lines. Any reader trying to find the king, to pinpoint his locus and his voice, in the opening paragraph of the memoirs will almost certainly be frustrated. The switch in perspectives is dizzying, as we are taken from the humble image of the king as a father much like any other to his charge, based in heaven, of serving as king-father to the entirety of the French people. The play around the pronoun "nous" also serves to confuse the issue of where the king's voice is coming from, since Louis XIV seems to oscillate between an individual located in a particular time and place and the embodiment of the truly transcendent and eternal spirit of the French monarchy. The problem of locating the king in the midst of the various forces and roles that fight to claim him echoes the ongoing struggle, outlined in the previous chapter, to define–or even to describe consistently–the French monarch.

The *Mémoires pour l'instruction du dauphin* have to resolve this problem at least temporarily in order to begin.

THE PROBLEM OF THE MANUSCRIPTS

If the confusion of the memoirs' first paragraph is quickly replaced by a more assured voice of agency, a comparison of the edited text with the volumes of manuscript penned by Périgny, Pellisson, and the king himself demonstrates that the struggle to identify the monarch's proper voice continued, in fact, throughout the text's composition. The manuscripts for the final edited versions of the memoirs hold a twofold interest. On the one hand, the care that obviously went into choosing the correct phrasing for the memoirs' final version amply justifies my decision to treat the text as the king's own voice and to read each sentence quite closely. On the other hand, the manuscripts reveal the problematic nature of the text's authorship, but not in the strict sense of whether its words are the king's. Louis XIV's frequent interventions in the margins of the manuscripts demonstrate that each sentence that found itself in the final version had the king's tacit approval.[55] What the manuscripts do show, however, is the intense and ongoing difficulty in writing *from the point of view of the monarch*–of successfully operating the (textual) self-reflection that so many theorists had warned their ideal, legitimate monarchs against.

The manuscripts I will discuss here are catalogued in the Bibliothèque Nationale as Fr-MSS 6732, 6733, and 6734. Another three volumes of manuscripts for the memoirs can be found under Fr-MSS 10329, 10330, and 10331. The manuscripts numbered 6732–34 mainly treat the years of 1666 and 1667; if we endorse Dreyss's identification of the author, they were penned largely by the dauphin's *précepteur*, Périgny. These texts, if only through their sheer volume, illustrate the immense energy that went into formulating the king's intentions and, indeed, his essence, for ultimate transmission to his son and heir. Entire passages are taken up over and over again, with only slight changes to their wording. Lengthy, detailed passages, on the other hand, disappear entirely from the memoirs' final version.

It is not my intention to analyze the editorial decisions made by Dreyss, Longnon, and, most recently, Goubert in their transforming the manuscripts and previous editions into a coherent text. Using the manuscripts for the later years treated by the memoirs but that were, in fact, some of the first texts actually written,[56] I would instead like to point out several instances in which the self-editing of the king's secretaries reveals particular difficulties of expression. These areas, as much as the treatises on monarchy that preceded the memoirs, show that the most fraught debates concerning divine right king-ship persisted even under its most accomplished representative, Louis XIV.

Not least of the difficulties encountered by the king's secretaries was the problem of their own role in the memoirs' composition. In assisting in the writing of a text whose official author was a king who, as I have shown, was quite jealous of his authority and initiative, the secretaries had to balance their own suggestions for the memoirs' ordering and content with obedience to the king's wishes. A passage from the first manuscript volume, Fr-Mss 6732, written perhaps by Périgny (although the hand differs somewhat from that used in the following pages of the memoirs proper), expresses the secretary's hesitancy in suggesting that the king treat the subject of religion and measures that the monarchy could take to improve the clergy:

> Mais la passion que j'ay reconu pour toutes les grandes choses et le zele particulier quelle temoigne continuellement pour ce qui regarde la religion m'ont fait imaginer quelle ne mepriseroit pas cette pensee. C'est un effet de l'oisiveté ou je suis depuis le dernier cayer que jay eû lhoneur de luy présenter car ne pouvant ny continuer ce qui est commancé ny matacher à autre chose jusques a ce qu'elle m'ait fait savoir ses volontez sur ce qu'elle y voie mon esprit se promene indiferement sur tous les objetz qui se presentent, et le zele que S. M. temoigne continuellement pour la religion m'a fait penser que cecy ne luy seroit pas desagreable.[57]

> [But the passion that I recognized for all great things and the particular zeal that (his majesty) continually exhibits in regard to all things religious made me imagine that his majesty would not disdain this thought. It is an effect of my idleness since the last notebook that I had the honor of presenting to his majesty; for being able neither to continue what has been begun nor to attach myself to anything else until his majesty has conveyed his wishes to me my mind travels indifferently to every object that presents itself, and the zeal that his majesty continually exhibits regarding religion made me think that this thought would not be unpleasant to him.]

This suggestion, timidly expressed, is then almost immediately rescinded: "Quelque ardeur que S.M. fasse paroitre pour l'interest de la religion Jay sujet de creindre quelle ne s'estone de me voir parler d'une chose qui n'est point de ma profession mais le zele que jay pour la continuelle augmentation de sa gloire m'a fait passer par desus ce scrupule et ne pouvant poursuivre mon travail ordinaire jusqu'a ce qu'elle mait donné ses ordres sur le dernier cayer que je luy ay presenté, je nay pas voulu rejetter cette pensée que mon oisiveté m'a fournie sans l'exposer a son jugement" (However much ardor his majesty exhibits for the interests of religion I have reason to believe that he is astonished to see me speak of something that is not part of my profession, but the zeal that I have for the continual augmentation of his glory made me vanquish these scruples and not being able to continue my work until I have received his orders on the last notebook that I presented, I did not want to reject this thought that my idleness furnished me without exposing it to his judgment).[58] These passages convey a slightly different message than Paul Pellisson's *projet* for the king's history as analyzed by Louis Marin. If in this latter work Pellisson subtly presents himself as the necessary and indispensable agent of the king's glory, here the secretary is entirely at the mercy of the king's will, since the *Mémoires,* unlike Pellisson's potential history, were a project initially suggested by the king himself. Although the secretary writes to the monarch, first to solicit new ideas for the royal text, and second to express his aggravation at his idleness while awaiting the king's next wishes, the overall effect, bolstered by the repetitive structure, is one of complete abjection. What the secretary must do here is avoid any possible implication that he sees himself, rather than the monarch, as author of the notebooks and the memoirs. All ideas and knowledge must come from Louis XIV; without the king's guidance, the secretary's mind–lacking, as it does, its own judgment–can only move superficially among each and every object that presents itself. This fragment, which is bound with the notes for the memoirs that precede the text proper, demonstrates once again both the extent to which we must consider Louis XIV as ultimate author of the text and the degree of trepidation and uncertainty among the scribes who were asked to carry out his wishes.

The same secretary who so plaintively voiced his hesitations upon taking any sort of initiative in the text's composition did, however, contribute a few works of poetry to the manuscript. These works, which did not survive to be included in more final versions of the text, bear mentioning since, with their heavy insistence on the subordination of the king to the God who grants him power, their eventual rejection from the memoirs demonstrates Louis XIV's reluctance to view himself in these terms. The secretary's first text, titled "Paraphrase sur plusieurs versets tirez de divers psaumes," asserts the primacy of God as creation and insists upon the strict equality of the creatures when seen from God's position:

> Luy seul forma les cieux si brillans et si beaux
> Fit la terre solide et rassembla les eaux . . .
> Qui se peut comparer au monarque immortel
> qui du feste eleve de son trosne eternel
> voit la terre et les cieux presqu'en mesme intervale
> s'accuser devant luy d'une bassesse egale
> Et quel autre que luy croit pouvoir a son chois

couroner les bergers et détrosner les Roix
Vous que l'on reconoit pour les Dieux de la Terre
Vous dont on craint le bras autant que le tonerre
Rois venez adorer ce grand Roy qui sur vous
A luy seul tous les droits qu'il vous donne sur nous[59]

[He alone formed the brilliant and beautiful heavens
Made the earth solid and collected the waters . . .
Who can compare himself to the immortal monarch
Who from the heights of his eternal throne
Sees the earth and the skies almost together
Accuse themselves before him of equal lowness
And who else but he can satisfy his will
Crowning shepherds and dethroning kings
You whom we recognize as gods on earth
You whose arm we fear as much as thunder
Kings come adore this great king who alone possesses
All of the rights that he gives you over us]

The secretary's pious vision of the world recognizes that as significant as the king's rights over his people may be, they are meaningless in the perspective of God, who alone is ultimately responsible for his creation. The secretary's corrections, evident in the manuscript, reinforce his hesitancy to compare the king of France with the King of kings. The line "Qui se peut comparer au monarque immortel" originally read "qui se peut comparer au grand souverain"; this first version almost invites the reader to assert that the king of France, *grand souverain* in his own right, may certainly see himself in this verse. Similarly, the line "Vous que l'on reconoit pour les Dieux de la Terre" originally read, much more dubiously, "Venez vous qui passez pour les Dieux de la Terre," which suggests that the parallel the king's subjects draw between the monarch and God is made out of fear or out of some desire to humor the monarch.

The poem that follows this one is equally fascinating, since it upbraids humanity for its failing faith in God. It warns the sinful people of the consequences of their doubt, exhorting them to fear a God whose wrath is appeased only through the people's love:

Mais helas des humains les ames forcenez
A ne plus croire en luy semblent determines
On ne le veut point voir pour ne le pas servir
Et l'estre qu'on luy doit on le luy veut ravir
Tous les hommes daccord dans leurs desseins coupables
avouloir devant luy nous rendre abominables

et parmi tant d'ingrats qui luy doivent le jour
pas un seul ne pren soin d'aquerir son amour[60]

[But alas the enraged souls of humanity
Seem determined to no longer believe in him
They no longer want to see him so as not to have to serve him
And the being that we owe him we want to steal from him
All men agreed in their guilty plots
To want to render us abominable to him
And among so many ingrates who owe him their life
Not one takes care to acquire his love]

The emphasis on the mixture of fear and love with which the people should view God is a clear analogy to the correct attitude toward the kings that this God has established. Yet the repeated references to humanity's refusal to serve, or even to believe, in this God suggests the inroads made by pleasure and reason against a more traditional and less questioning faith. While the secretary laments this change in sensibilities, it is significant that Louis XIV himself, with his removal of the passages in the notes for the memoirs that subordinate him to strongly to God, seems to be moving to exploit recent developments in his subjects' thinking.

As a result, this volume of manuscripts often resembles a war between the secretary's orthodoxy and the monarch's realpolitik. A representative phrase that did not survive the king's editing is the following description of God: "Il est infiniment jaloux de sa gloire mais il sait mieux que nous discerner en quoy elle consiste; il ne nous a peut estre fais si grans qu'afin que nos respecs l'honorassent davantage et si nous manquons de remplir en cela ses dessins peut estre qu'il nous laissera tomber dans la poussiere, de laquelle il nous a tirez" (He is infinitely jealous of his glory but he knows better than us how to discern in what it consists; he may have made us so great only so that our respect honors him more and if we fail to fulfill his designs in this he may let us fall into the dust from which he made us).[61] This sentiment is quite different from that expressed in the final version of the memoirs, where the respect due to God is merely a model of the respect the subjects owe their king, and where belief in God is based less on personal piety than on a "consentement universel."[62] The above passage not only lessens the grandeur of the monarch as well as the extent of his knowledge but also operates the collapse of any distinction between the king and his subjects when seen from the point of view of the divine. From God's lofty perspective, not just the king but all men are created from dust and may be quickly restored to this status.

Other passages that were later omitted seem to commit the fault of clouding royal agency. At the beginning of the memoirs for 1666, Louis XIV justifies his decision to start a European war in the following manner: "j'envisageais avec plaisir le dessein de ces deux guerres comme un vaste champ où pouvaient naître à toute heure de grandes occasions de me signaler. Tant de braves gens que je voyais animés pour mon service semblaient à toute heure me solliciter de fournir quelque matière à leur valeur, plus avantageuse que la guerre maritime dans laquelle les plus vaillants n'ont presque jamais lieu de se distinguer des plus faibles" (I envisaged with pleasure the prospect of these two wars as a vast field that could create great opportunities for me to distinguish myself and to fulfill the great expectations that I had for some time inspired in the public. So many fine men whom I saw enthusiastic for my service seemed to be constantly urging me to furnish some scope for their valor, and it would not have been satisfied through a maritime war in which the most valiant hardly ever have the opportunity to distinguish themselves).[63] This passage is interesting enough, as it demonstrates Louis XIV's pattern of using alternate selves–in this case the "braves gens," who, as subjects, are extensions of the king's person, much as the dauphin is–to voice sentiments that would be unseemly coming from himself. The view of the war as a chance for the king to draw attention to himself is quickly displaced by his subjects' strong desire to do the same. Yet in the first version of the manuscripts, this movement of desire from the king to his soldiers is much less smoothly operated, as the soldiers' understandable wish for distinction is elided in favor of the monarch's own complicated motivations. One version of this sentence reads, "Lattente que le monde avoit conceue de moy dans cette situation et les bruits qui setoient publiez des entreprises que je devois faire aprez la mort du Roy d'Espagne sembloient mengager a ne pas" (The expectation which the world had conceived of me in this situation and the published rumors of the enterprises that I was supposed to undertake after the King of Spain's death seemed to engage me to not).[64]

This version is replaced by the following: "Voyant que depuis longtemps le monde sestoit persuadé qu'à la mort du Roy d'Espagne on verroit eclater de grands desseins et sachant combien par mes autres actions javois excite lattente (et lopinion) publique. . . . Il me sembloit facheux de n'y repondre pas" (Seeing as how for a long time the world was persuaded that after the King of Spain's death they would see great projects emerge and knowing how much my other actions had excited public opinion and expectation. . . . It seemed difficult for me not to respond).[65] The evolution between these two drafts and the final formulation is evident. In the first draft, the king is almost entirely passive, responding to the world's expectations of his actions after the death of the Spanish king. His subsequent decision to go ahead with war seems, if not reluctant, at least curiously defensive. The second draft moderates this tone slightly through the addition that the world's expectations of Louis XIV have been conditioned not through some vague international code of etiquette and war but rather through the king's own actions. Here, the king himself is ultimately responsible for the world's view of his intentions. In the final version, however, all hint of reference to "le monde" has disappeared. Rather, the king takes advantage of the Spanish king's fortuitous death to fulfill a long-standing wish to show himself to the world through action. He views the open fields of possibility that war presents "avec plaisir," and, as I have shown, all sense of defensive response or of having something to prove is transferred onto his eager army.

Yet just as these passages mark a troubling tendency to underestimate the monarch's power and initiative, others, while seeking to define what, precisely, differentiates the king from the rest of his kingdom, seem to go too far in the direction of glorification. The following passage was adjusted several times before finally being excluded from the text altogether:

> Comme il est important au public[66] de nestre gouverné que par un seul, il luy est important aussy que celuy qui fait cette fonction soit elevé de telle sorte au dessus des autres quil n'y ait personne qui ne puisse ny confondre ny comparer avec luy, et lon ne peut sans faire tort a tout le corps de l'estat, oster a son chef les moindres marques de Superiorité qui le distinguent des autres membres. Mais souvenez vous pourtant mon fils que de touttes les preeminences celles que vous devez le plus rechercher, et celles qui vous feront distinguer le plus avantageusement, ce seront celles qui viendront de vos qualitez propres et personelles. L'elevation du Rang n'est jamais plus sollide ny plus assurée que quand elle est soutenue par la singularité du merite, et cest sans doute ce qui a fait croire a quelques uns qu'il pouvoit etre avantageux a celuy qui regne de voir ceux qui le touchent de plus pres par leur naissance beaucoup eloignez de luy par leur conduitte.[67]

[As it is important to the public to be governed by only one person, it is also important to the public that he who occupies this function be elevated so far above the others that there should be no one who can be confused or compared with him, and one cannot take away any distinguishing characteristics of the head's superiority without doing damage to the entire social body. But remember my son that out of all of these preeminences those that you should seek the most, and those that distinguish you the most advantageously, are those that come from your own personal qualities. The elevation of rank is never more solid or assured than when it is supported by the singularity of merit, and this is doubtless what convinced some that it could be advantageous to he that reigns to see those who come closest to him by birth held at a distance from him by their actions.]

As the interesting phrase "L'elevation du Rang n'est jamais plus sollide ny plus assurée" seems to indicate, the secretaries' effort to transmit the precise nature of the essence of monarchy from Louis XIV to his son encounters difficulty in reducing this essence to traditional sources such as birth or outer ceremony. Indeed, the last sentence of this passage shows that birth alone is insufficient to distinguish the king from those around him, since members of the state such as the king's younger brother "touch" the monarch through their close contiguity to him through birth. This passage, in fact, is inserted in the manuscripts immediately after a passage relating the attempts of the king's brother, Monsieur, to elevate his own status and that of his wife after the death of the Queen Mother. Louis XIV's refusal of his brother's requests has survived the editing in a passage where he explains that governorships of provinces, in this case, the Languedoc, are too important to entrust to members of the royal family. To eliminate even the shadow of criticism from hereditary monarchy, the secretaries place the emphasis instead on personal merit, but they must be quite careful that such an emphasis does not reopen the specter of counterfeit kingship identified so shrewdly (yet indirectly) by Le Bret and Senault. Personality should be combined with birth, not be in competition with it, but this mix of qualities runs counter to the desire, evident in this passage, to reduce the essence of sovereignty to its most important aspect.

Yet the relative restraint of this passage is followed, in the manuscripts, by another in which the king's satisfaction with his own qualities (or, rather, the secretaries' adoration of their employer) runs wild:

Ce grand intervalle que sa vertu met entre eux et luy lexpose en plus beau jour et avec plus d'eclat aux yeux de toutte la terre. Ce qu'il y a dans l'esprit dellevation, et de sollidité tire un lustre tout nouveau de la mediocrité de ceux qui l'approchent. Ce qu'on voit de grandeur et de fermeté dans son ame est relevé par l'opposition de la molesse que lon trouve en eux, et ce quil fait paroitre d'amour pour le travail et pour la veritable gloire est infiniment plus brillant lorsquon ne decouvre ailleurs qu'une pesante oisiveté ou des attachements de bagatelle. Dans cette difference tous les yeux sont attaches sur luy seul. C'est a luy seul que s'adressent tous les yeux, luy seul est l'objet de touttes les esperances, on ne poursuit, on nattend on ne fait rien que par luy seul. On regarde ses bonnes graces comme la seulle source de tous les biens, on ne croit s'eslever qu'a mesure qu'on s'approche de sa personne ou de son estime tout le reste est rempant, tout le reste est impuissant, tout le reste est sterilité, et lon peut dire meme que l'Eclat qu'il a dans ses propres estats passe comme par communication dans les provinces etrangers.[68]

[This great interval that his virtue places between him and them exposes him in the greatest light to the eyes of all the earth. What elevation and solidity he has in his mind attains a new glow from the mediocrity of those that approach him. What grandeur and firmness we see in his soul is placed in relief by its opposition to the softness we find in them, and what love for work and true glory he makes appear is infinitely more brilliant once we discover elsewhere only weighty idleness and attachment to pettiness. In this difference all eyes are attached to him alone. It is to him alone that all eyes address themselves, and he alone is the object of all hopes, no one pursues, waits for, or does anything that is not through him. His good graces are regarded as the source of all goods, and one believes one is elevated only insofar as one approaches his person or esteem; all the rest is abject, all the rest is impotent, all the rest is sterile, and one could even say that the brilliance he possesses in his own states is transferred as if through communication to foreign provinces.]

The decision to write this text in the third person reflects, perhaps, the secretaries' realization that its language would be too strong to survive final editing. Once again, we see the sentiment (toned down elsewhere) that imperfection, mediocrity, and error are essential to the elevation of the monarchy, whose perfections would otherwise go unnoticed or underappreciated. Against the backdrop of "cette différence," the absolute uniqueness of the monarch shines back upon the people, however, and the king's power in turn reveals the inadequacy of everything that is not the king. Echoing a sentiment that Dominique Bouhours would express in his *Entretiens d'Ariste et d'Eugene* at around the same time (1671), the secretaries maintain that this reputation, much stronger than weaponry, is able to lead foreign countries to subject themselves voluntarily to Louis XIV's rule.

These missing passages—those that can be found in the manuscripts but are progressively deleted or modified over the drafts—demonstrate a remarkable fragility and anxiety behind the outward appearance of the absolute king. The secretaries struggle to find the right point on the continuum between absolute independence of action and complete submission to God's will, a point that proves elusive throughout their efforts. As I have shown, these difficulties persist somewhat in the final text, despite the relatively successful method of splitting the monarch into father and son, king and people, in order to minimize the contradictions inherent in divine right kingship. Placing themselves between the third-person narration of events deployed in Caesar's *Commentaries* and the self-effacing, God-fearing royal narrator of the *Basilikon Doron,* the *Mémoires pour l'instruction du dauphin* is a hybrid text, one that amply illustrates why the repeated warnings of the theorists that the king can never turn his attention on himself without running the risk of tyranny are ultimately quite well founded.

The fate of the memoirs—never published, yet never quite forgotten—itself reflects their hybrid nature. The project of the memoirs was abandoned when the king focused his attentions on war with Holland in 1672. During the remainder of his long reign, various successors to the throne would die, and various wars would be undertaken. The king, however, never seems to have forgotten the memoirs. They were kept in a cabinet with other documents that the king decided to burn, a year before his death, in 1714. The Maréchal de Noailles, the nephew-in-law of Madame de Maintenon and therefore representative of her interests at the scene, requested that some of the memoirs be saved.[69] They remain less the final word on Louis XIV's vision of himself and his reign, as he intended, than a testament to the dynamism and struggle at the heart of "absolutism."

DEFINING THE DIPLOMAT:

IN CONTEXT

The difficult problem of characterizing the precise nature of the king's relation to God was partially occluded during Louis XIV's reign, although traces
of its urgency can be read in the attempts to find a suitable way of alluding to
his power. The efforts of Louis XIV's contemporaries, working with a system
of propaganda constructed in part by the king himself, to put forth a theatrical, pictorial, and mythological image of the monarch worked to efface the
fault lines that the treatises written earlier in the century had, despite themselves, uncovered.[1] The unpublished *Mémoires pour l'instruction du dauphin,*
which testified to the dynamism, if not the instability, generated by the ultimate impossibility of divine right monarchy, remained hidden behind the
glorious facade of Versailles.

Despite the impressive deployment of royal propaganda celebrating the
king's personal glory and the corresponding fusion of "the king's two bodies," however, the problem of mediation did not disappear. Rather, as the
centralization of the state begun under Richelieu proceeded apace, the problem of delegation, already quite pressing for Bodin, who asserted its ultimate

impossibility, became even more urgent. The state became more dependent on figures of mediation, from the *intendants* introduced by Richelieu to the ministers whose subordination to royal will was emphasized as never before. How was the relation of these figures to royal power to be theorized and explained? Do they embody royal authority, and, if so, for how long and to what extent? Such questions were by no means unique to France or to the reign of Louis XIV. They reflect, instead, a Europe-wide crisis in imagining power, the state, and its instruments that lasted, arguably, from the end of the sixteenth century to the beginning of the eighteenth.

While *intendants* and ministers certainly offer ample material for reflection on the question of delegation and mediation, I have chosen to concentrate on the figure of the ambassador, not least because his universal and quasi-international status allows a comparison between Louis XIV's France and the rest of Europe. This comparison is especially important given historians' general consensus that diplomacy took the form that persists largely to this day during the reign of Louis XIV.[2] However, as James der Derian has noted, the studies that speak admirably of Louis XIV's diplomatic "modernism" are made possible through a view of diplomacy that is, if not ahistorical, relatively acritical. They are written in a vein that accepts current diplomacy as the unproblematic end to which earlier forms inevitably lead.[3] In this chapter, I demonstrate that efforts to define diplomacy *throughout* Europe during the late sixteenth century and throughout the seventeenth were singularly marked by their difficulties in treating mediation and the troublesome "personhood"–part fictitious, part "real," part private, part public–of the ambassador. Only by understanding this larger context can we begin to appreciate to what extent Louis XIV's efforts to establish a tight representational link between king and diplomat were unique and were also a means of taking advantage of the relative theoretical weakness of seventeenth-century diplomatic theory.

Diplomacy would seem to be as old as the existence of different communities or groups, and to a certain extent this is true.[4] Homer's *Iliad* contains fascinating examples of diplomacy, as do the histories of Thucydides and Herodotus. Indeed, many Renaissance accounts of diplomacy lean heavily on ancient examples of diplomatic practice to support their observations.[5] Yet in seventeenth-century Europe these ancient models were increasingly viewed as problematic, if not inapplicable.[6] Beyond the general crisis in mediation stemming from the larger, often religious, causes I have already identified, a number of additional factors led to the reconfiguration of diplomatic theory in the seventeenth century. New developments inside and outside of Europe called for new ideas to govern a rapidly evolving state-system. Crises involving the New World and the Far East led to the articulation of a system of international law and a reconsideration of its intersections with the law of nature, particularly in the work of the Dutchman Hugo Grotius, himself a former ambassador from the Netherlands to England and from Sweden to France. Inside Europe, even before the Peace of Westphalia led to the formation of official German states within the empire–states whose sovereignty posed new theoretical questions for thinkers from Pufendorf to Leibniz, who analyzed the extent of these states' sovereignty by discussing whether they had the right to send and receive ambassadors[7]–the political map was under almost constant change. Already at the end of the sixteenth century, Elizabeth's imprisonment of Mary pointed up the inadequacies of diplomatic idealism,[8] while the splitting of the Habsburg Empire into its Austrian and Spanish branches reaffirmed the importance of the other European states. The United Provinces declared themselves an independent Protestant republic, and Portugal slipped in and out of Spanish control. The political, religious, and legal upheavals of the period–all closely intertwined–contributed to an atmosphere in which defining the ambassador and his status under the *droit des gens*[9] clearly was increasingly urgent, and increasingly difficult as well.

WHAT IS AN AMBASSADOR?

On the surface, defining the ambassador would seem easy enough: the ambassador represents the prince in a foreign country. The deceptive ease of this definition perhaps accounts for the fact, often lamented by sixteenth- and seventeenth-century writers of diplomatic treatises, that none of the ancients managed to leave a treatise on the ambassador for the edification of future generations. As early modern writers throughout Europe sought to remedy this absence, they ran up against the near-impossibility of providing an adequate definition of the ambassador. In 1603, Jean Hotman, a French Protestant diplomat who had served Henri IV for more than twenty years, deplored the lack of models for diplomatic conduct, stating that Polybius had written a treatise titled *De legationibus* but that this work is useless for those wishing to treat the *legato*.[10] Hotman's remark indicates his view that if the practice of diplomacy has existed ever since there have been political entities, not enough attention has been paid to the diplomat himself. Hotman's own efforts to provide an adequate definition were seen, in turn, as lacking, for his treatise was followed by other works, most notably Juan Antonio de Vera Zuniga y Figueroa's Neoplatonist *El enbaxador* in 1620, best known under the French translation by Lancelot that was published in 1635. Despite the intervening years, political events, and treatises, more than fifty years later Abraham de Wicquefort renewed Hotman's criticism, complaining that no one had ever written down what, precisely, the ambassador *is:*

> On ne peut douter, que la connoissance de cette partie du Droit Public, qui traitte des *Ambassadeurs & des Ministres estrangers,* ne soit tresnecessaire, & neantmoins il faut advoüer, qu'il n'y a rien de si universellement ignoré. Il ny a point de Roiaume ny d'Estat qui ne s'en serve, & cependant il n'y a presque personne, qui sçache ce que c'est que *l'Ambassadeur:* quelles sont les qualités qui le forment, quels sont les droits & les avantages dont il joüit, quelles civilités on doit à son caractere, & quelles sont les fonctions de son employ. C'est pourquoy je me suis souvent estonné, que jusques icy on n'ait pas encore veu un traitté achevé sur ce sujet, & que parmy tant de sçavants, qui ont fait leur principale estude de la Politique, & que parmy tant de grands hommes, qui ont fait connoistre leur merite dans les Ambassades, il ne s'en trouve pas un seul, qui ait voulu obliger la posterité, en luy faisant present d'un ouvrage d'autant plus utile, que l'Ambassadeur est un Ministre, dont l'Estat ne peut se passer, & que le Droit de l'Ambassade est la plus illustre marque de la Souveraineté.[11]

[Doubtless, the knowledge of this part of public law, which treats ambassadors and foreign ministers, is very necessary, and yet it must be admitted that there is nothing so universally ignored. There is not one kingdom or state that does not make use of them, and yet there is hardly anyone who knows what an ambassador is: what are the qualities that form him, what are the rights and advantages that he enjoys, what civilities are owed to his character, and what are the functions of his employ. This is why I have often been astonished, that until now we have not seen a complete treatise on this subject, and that among so many scholars who have studied politics and among so many great men who have made their merit known as ambassadors, there has not been one who has wanted to oblige posterity by presenting it with a work that is all the more useful in that the ambassador is a minister without which the state cannot function, and that the right of embassy is the most illustrious mark of sovereignty.]

Yet in 1723, Jean Barbeyrac, in his French translation of the Dutch jurist Bynkershoek's treatise on the proper jurisdiction for ambassadors accused of civil or criminal wrongs, added his own critique to what had, by this time, become a veritable palimpsest of theories. Repeating Hotman's regret that Polybius treated the activity of diplomacy without treating the diplomat as well, Barbeyrac added his own critique, citing his predecessors (among them Gentili, Hotman, and Wicquefort) and calling–in terms strikingly similar to those used by Wicquefort almost forty years earlier–for a coherent, rational diplomatic theory: "On peut dire de tous ces Ouvrages en général, qu'ils fournissent bien des matériaux sur un sujet si vaste; mais il faudroit quelcun qui les mît en oeuvre, pour en faire un corps regulier. L'ordre & la méthode y man-quent beaucoup, & ce qui est plus considérable, on raisonne souvent sur des principes ou faux, ou douteux, ou vagues, ou confus & peu liez" (One could say that all of these general works provide much material on a subject so vast, but we need someone to put them together to make a regular corpus. Order and method are singularly lacking in these treatises, and what is more impor-tant, they often reason from false, vague, doubtful, confused, or badly linked principles).[12]

On the one hand, these remarks are comprehensible attempts on the part of their writers to justify their own published interventions into this field. Yet the strange resonance between comments such as Barbeyrac's and Bodin's regret that sovereignty has escaped attention and definition throughout the ages should give the reader pause. For just as Bodin was in fact innovating in his elab-oration of sovereignty as a replacement for the more traditional ideas of *auc-toritas* and *potestas*, so might these writers be grappling with an emerging figure and corresponding concept–the ambassador–that by its very nature raises more difficulties than it solves. Indeed, the call for "scientific" or "rational" accounts of the diplomat inevitably runs up against the fact that the ambassador's author-ity, identity, and agency are almost entirely dependent upon context. The ambassador would seem to be a figure occupying the liminal space not just between two sovereigns but between the universals of rational precepts and the infinite contingencies of international events.

The struggle between simplicity and an accurate reflection of seventeenth-century political reality can be seen in the evolution of the titles given to diplo-matic treatises. The earlier treatises–Alberico Gentili's *De legationibus libri tres*, Hotman's *L'Ambassadeur*, de Vera's *Le parfait ambassadeur*–announce on the title page their hope that an adequate definition of the ambassador in iso-lation as a distinctive figure is possible. As the century moves on, through West-phalia, Nijmegen, and Rijswick and toward Utrecht, the titles become more timid. Wicquefort's *L'Ambassadeur et ses fonctions* (1681) is divided into two books, one for the ambassador and one for his functions–a distinction I will discuss in more detail later in this chapter. Callières's *De la manière de négocier avec les souverains* (1716), the work that remains the most useful for theorists of diplomacy in our own time,[13] leaves the diplomat out of the main title.[14] Although these titles seem to reflect the ebbing of initial optimism regarding the ability of the ambassador to be defined or captured in a text, inside the covers the writers have not quite given up. The challenge facing them is similar to that which faced the French defenders of absolute, divine right king-ship. How can one define, or even describe, a figure whose constitutive qual-ity–whose legitimacy–is based on his dependence upon circumstances and people outside of himself? The various answers given by those who wrote on this subject, often former diplomats themselves, reveal less an obvious yet neglected truth than a slippery, fragile personage working at the margins of, yet somehow central to, international affairs.

The first step in adequately defining the diplomat is agreeing on what he should be called. As international affairs were being overtaken by events that seemed to have no precedence in earlier times, a new vocabulary became necessary, and the terminology designating the agents of sovereignty, both temporal and spiritual, was proliferating. As Jean Hotman realized as early as 1603, distinctions had to be drawn between legates, envoys, nuncios, *internonces, commissaires,* agents, and, of course, ambassadors. Ambassadors themselves were divided between "ordinary" and "extraordinary"–that is, between those who took up residence at a foreign court as a permanent envoy and those sent for exceptional, often ceremonial, reasons. Resident ambassadors were largely the invention of the fifteenth century,[15] and this innovation in international communication (and surveillance) was viewed by the host countries with suspicion for quite some time, as the line between such residents and spies was ill-defined. As will soon become evident, their existence and deployment challenged the increasingly common definition (and idealization) of the diplomat as representative of his prince.

Although de Vera would assert that "un nom vaut autant que l'autre" (one name is as good as any other)[16] when naming the diplomat either legate or ambassador, other writers, responding to the increasing political tensions and contestations of the time, disagreed. Alberico Gentili arrives at his definition of the ambassador only after he carefully delineates the ambassador's specificity. Noting that "the legate whom it is our purpose to discuss is sometimes designated by the broader titles of spokesman or orator, interpreter and messenger,"[17] Gentili proceeds to define the ambassador as such. This acknowledgment of the almost unavoidable slippage of the ambassador's function into that described by other names marks the difficulty in isolating the ambassador. Take, for example, the following pronouncement on the difference between an orator and an ambassador: "[T]he title of orator, in the strict sense of the term, indicates a personal accomplishment, while the meaning of legate connotes service for others. . . . An orator pleads his own and others' cases, among his fellow citizens and among others; but apart from a legate's individual interest in the state, there is no legate or ambassador of private affairs, nor is an ambassador sent to his fellow citizens."[18] Not only does this passage invite difficult questions concerning the precise demarcation of private and public (a theme that is indeed essential to the ambassador's troubling identity), it also—much like definitions of sovereignty—posits a figure whose chief attribute is his lack of self-referentiality. Unlike the orator, the ambassador cannot act in his own interests. As a result, his qualities can never be attributed to himself; rather, they are attributed to the state that he represents. There can be, Gentili seems to imply, no "personal accomplishment" for him.

This effacement of the ambassador before the message that he is sent to transmit could, however, lead the reader to confuse the ambassador and the interpreter. Gentili warns against this confusion: "Yet there is a difference between interpreter and ambassador, for while one speaks of the interpreter of an author, the term ambassador is never so employed. Moreover, the former acts for one who is present, but whose language we do not understand; an ambassador only for one who is absent."[19] Here, Gentili draws a distinction between the representation of a message and the representation of the message's source. The distinction is of paramount importance, since it affects the degree of autonomy and authority accorded to the diplomat. While an interpreter has no status of his own, the ambassador, as representative of the absent person or entity sending the message, is somehow, at least temporarily, imbued with the sender's authority and indeed, personality. In a passage separating the ambassador (*legato*) from the messenger (*nuncius*), Gentili notes that the difference between the two lies not in their identity but in "summus ex mittendi ratione" (the method of sending).[20]

Properly delimiting the ambassador's activities and identity was by no means an empty academic exercise. The stakes involved in distinguishing the ambassador, the orator, the messenger, and the interpreter become evident in a seventeenth-century dispute between Galileo and the Jesuit Grassi. This dispute demonstrates the stakes involved in the careful parsing of the terms applied to ambassadors, interpreters, and messengers. The debate, which continues to this day, revolves around the title of Galileo's *Sidereus nuncius*. This brief treatise, which appeared in 1610, revealed the results of his telescopic observations, including the "Medicean planets," or moons of Jupiter. The title that he gave his pamphlet demonstrates Galileo's wish for the news of his discoveries to spread rapidly, but it would prove to be problematic in the ensuing years. As Edward Rosen points out, the more common meaning of *nuncius* at the time was "messenger," or "ambassador" (specifically, the papal ambassadors, whom the French would continue to refer to as *nonces*).[21] Less common, but equally valid, was the meaning not of "messenger" but of "message." In 1628, the Jesuit Grassi mocked the earlier title in his attack on Galileo's more controversial *Assayer:* "verax astrorum interpres, age, sidereae nuncius aulae" (translated by Rosen as "come, true interpreter of the stars, ambassador from the sidereal court").[22] Galileo, in an unpublished answer to Grassi, responded that he had not meant *nuncius* to mean "messenger" but rather the message itself.

Edward Rosen defends Galileo's assertion, noting that the title has been mistranslated in almost all of its editions. Citing letters in which Galileo refers to the work as an *avviso*, or diplomatic message, Rosen asserts that this meaning was the intended one all along. In 1958, one year after the publication of his edition of the *Discoveries and Opinions of Galileo*, Stillman Drake defended his decision to call the treatise "The Starry Messenger" in the pages of the same journal.[23] Significantly, Drake abstains from the easier argument that this meaning of *nuncius* should be preferred because it was the one traditionally used in (mis)translations. Rather, he counters Rosen by citing letters that Galileo wrote prior to Grassi's denunciation, by arguing that Galileo never corrected anyone about the title before this time, and by suggesting that Galileo's decision to change the meaning of his title could be explained as a defensive measure against increasingly dangerous attacks by the Jesuits.

Drake's defense of the title "The Starry Messenger" alludes to the powerful connotations surrounding the issue of mediation and, specifically, the problem of the ambassador in the seventeenth century. It is indeed significant that Galileo felt the need to answer the Jesuit's attack by resurrecting a lesser-known meaning of the word *nuncius*. This change begs the question of what overtones were contained in the term *nuncius*-ambassador that made the insult so readily apparent and of how changing the meaning of the term to "message" could be seen to defuse this accusation. The efforts of Gentili and others to mark the specificity of the ambassador, whose talents cannot–and should not–be reduced to the mimicry of the message but whose person carries some of the aura of the sender, shows that the Jesuits were perhaps correct in seeing Galileo's title as an appropriation of divine authority. By arguing that his intended meaning of the term *nuncius* was message, not messenger, Galileo was positing himself as mere herald, a passive carrier of objective observations. Conversely, by accusing Galileo of posing as *messenger,* the Jesuit Grassi was arguing that Galileo viewed himself as somehow chosen by the master of the heavens, God himself, as the far from neutral voice through which his message would be revealed. The tension between personal recognition and scientific legitimacy that characterized most of Galileo's career has been admirably documented elsewhere by Mario Biagioli. For our purposes, it is fascinating, though perhaps not surprising, that these issues crystallized, at least for a moment, around diplomatic language and the status of the ambassador.

The complexity of the ambassador's relation to the prince he represents sur-
faces primarily in the evolution of theories concerning the ambassador's inviolability. Early treatises on diplomacy stressed the sacred origins of the
ambassador. Gentili's definition of the ambassador, which emerges only after
he has distinguished the ambassador from the orator, the interpreter, and the
herald, links the diplomat not just to political affairs but to the divine itself: "I
should define the particular type of legate at present before us for discussion
(and by this as you see I mean the ambassador) as *one who in the name of the
state or of person still more sacred has been sent without the right of supreme
command to a state or person still more sacred to say or do something in the
interest of the state or sacred person by whom he has been sent*."[24] Gentili's
placement of the sacred at the center of his definition of the ambassador is
significant and worth taking seriously.[25] First, his phrasing "the state or person still more sacred" implies his belief that the state is endowed with sacred
origins and approval. This is our first, and far from last, indication that diplomacy may be intimately related to divine right sovereignty. Indeed, the Protestant Gentili, an Italian in service to the English Crown, briefly entertains the
argument that France may be ineligible to send ambassadors, since "in religious matters [the king of France] acknowledges the superiority of the Pope."[26]
Gentili's language likewise invites the reader to consider the prototype of the
temporal ambassador, the angels (*angeloi*, or messengers) sent by God to
humanity.[27] Drawing a tight comparison between angels and ambassadors,
however, may run against Gentili's purposes of clarity and definition, since
the persistent argument over the precise nature of angels—human or divine,
mortal or immortal—was no closer to being resolved than it had ever been.
This may account for Gentili's rather rapid abandonment of the divine model
in his treatise, but its presence as the ultimate model of diplomacy demonstrates how the ambassador's allegiances could be compromised when the
sacred and the temporal were at odds. This would not yet seem to be a problem for Gentili, writing in England, where the prince was the head of state
and church and where the "interests" of the "state or sacred person" would
seem to coincide. Yet the events and turmoil just across the Channel during
this period illustrate how fragile the alliance between secular and divine
could be.

This fragility is evident in Juan Antonio de Vera's 1623 treatise, which was
translated into French in 1635 by Lancelot under the title *Le parfait ambassadeur*. De Vera's work, a dialogue between two friends in a country garden,
was published in a small format to allow ambassadors to carry it with them

more easily and was perhaps the most widely read treatise of its time. It is almost the only book cited by Wicquefort in his later study of the subject.[28] Yet like Wicquefort, later writers found de Vera's text unsatisfactory, and a close examination of the work reveals why. If Gentili was able to align the sacred and secular functions of the ambassador without too much difficulty (although he does treat sticky issues such as whether the ambassador should or can lie), in de Vera we see this alliance falling apart, so that the temporal and the sacred do not reinforce each other but merely coexist uneasily.[29] On the surface, de Vera places the diplomat in a strongly Christian context. Not only does he take the ambassador's sacred character as given, he repeatedly asserts that the ambassador's primary goal is that of establishing Christian peace among the nations. Rather than an envoy sent to carry out a prince's interests, the ambassador is "un Conciliateur des affaires des Princes, un homme envoyé de loin, pour traiter des affaires publiques" (a conciliator of princes' affairs, a man sent from far away to treat public affairs).[30] Indeed, de Vera holds that "nul ne peut être vrai Ambassadeur, que celuy qui des le prémier pas qu'il fait dans le Roiaume où il va exercer cette charge, porte le Rameau d'Olive dans la main" (no one can be a true ambassador besides he who, from the first steps he takes in the kingdom where he is going to exercise his function, carries an olive branch in his hand).[31] Even de Vera's allusions to classical mythology, in keeping with the humanist nature of his text, support the ambassador's mission of peace. He cites the first embassy to humans as that sent after the opening of Pandora's box, to restore unity to humanity, and he sees Mercury as the prototype of the diplomat.

This last reference is significant, for it reveals de Vera's belief that the ambassador is not just sacred due to the *origin* of his message (whether God or divinely sanctioned state, as in Gentili) but also sacred in his own right, given his mission "de conserver deux Princes en amitié" (to conserve two princes in friendship).[32] Here, de Vera's status as a former diplomat for, and subject of, Spain may explain his implicit view that furthering both the goals of the state and the goals of the Catholic Church cannot be in conflict.[33] In fact, his position leads him to endorse the use of priests as diplomats. After citing the Athenians' use of actors as ambassadors, he states: "Donc, si ces gens-là, qui estoient Acteurs de ces jeux si agreables aux Dieux, quoy que de basse lignée, estoient dignes des principales charges des Ambassades, pour quelle raison voudroit-on maintenant exclure les Religieux qui sont Ministres du vray & puissant Dieu, d'un si sacré et si venerable ministere?" (Therefore, if such people who were actors in those plays that were so agreeable to the Gods, although they were of humble birth, were worthy of the principal charges of embassies, for what reason could we now want to exclude priests, who are ministers of the true and powerful God, from such a sacred and venerable ministry?).[34] As de Vera acknowledges, this support for the use of the clergy in embassies had become increasingly controversial during this period. Already Gentili qualified his introductory statements with his remark that "at the present time the category of sacred ambassadors would be represented by those who in the interest of religion set out to attend some ecclesiastical convention."[35] While this assertion may not be surprising given Gentili's own Protestantism and suffering at the hands of the Italian inquisition, by implying that churchmen should be concerned with ecclesiastical affairs only, it does indicate a growing rift between the sacred and the secular. Later in the seventeenth century, the opinion that writers had of priests as diplomats turned to outright condemnation. Wicquefort reserves some of his strongest language for the section of his work titled "Si les Gens d'Eglise sont propres pour les Ambassades," directly addressing de Vera:

> L'Auteur de *L'idée du Parfait Ambassadeur* se declare pour l'affirmative, & fortifie son sentiment de plusieurs exemples, qu'il tire de la Bible, & de l'Histoire, laquelle il seroit bien aise de faire entrer toute dans son livre. . . . Il est vray que depuis que la puissance spirituelle se trouve confondue avec la jurisdiction temporelle en la personne du Pape: depuis que les Cardinaux vont du pair avec les Rois, & que les Evesques sont ensemble & Princes & Prelats, tous les gens d'Eglise suivent leur exemple, & imitent la licence qu'ils se donnent, de se mesler de toutes sortes d'affaires indistinctement. . . . Que celuy qui tient la main à la charüe, ne doit pas regarder en arriere, & que celuy qui se dédie au Ministre spirituel, ne se doit plus mesler des affaires du Monde. On ne peut servir deux Maistres, ny partager le coeur, que l'on a donné & consacré tout entier à Dieu.[36]

[The Author of *The Idea of the Perfect Ambassador* declares himself in the affirmative, and fortifies his sentiment with several examples that he takes from the Bible and from history, the entirety of which he would like to fit into his book. . . . It is true that ever since spiritual power has become confounded with temporal jurisdiction in the person of the Pope, ever since Cardinals treat kings as equals and Bishops are simultaneously princes and prelates, all men of the church follow their example and imitate the freedom they have given themselves to interfere with all kinds of affairs. . . . However, he who holds the chariot should not look backwards, and he who dedicates himself to spiritual ministry should not interfere in worldly affairs. One cannot serve two masters, nor share the heart that one has given and consecrated entirely to God.]

Wicquefort, also a Protestant and former diplomat for the United Provinces, raises several issues in this passage. By accusing the pope of contaminating his spiritual realm with temporal concerns, the Dutchman invokes the separability–indeed, the fundamental and originary separation–between the secular and the sacred. Priests as ambassadors violate this separation; one has only to look at Wicquefort's repeated use of the verb "mesler" to note his wish for strict frontiers between church and state. His closing remarks provide a sly reference to the alleged impiety of those priests who would wish to become diplomats, for in so doing they undermine their professed piety and devotion to God.

Yet if Wicquefort's comments can be attributed to his strong suspicion of the Catholic Church as both Protestant and Dutchman, similar assertions can also be found in François de Callières's *De la manière de négocier avec les souverains,* suggesting that the rejection of priests from diplomatic service had, during the seventeenth century, become widespread and almost taken for granted: "Si on examine bien quels sont les veritables devoirs des évêques, on trouvera qu'ils sont peu compatibles avec les ambassades et qu'il leur est malséant de courir le monde, au lieu de satisfaire à leur premieres obligations" (If we examine what the true duties of the bishops are, we will find that they are hardly compatible with embassies and that it is unseemly for them to run around the world instead of satisfying their primary obligations).[37] Callières's oblique reference to the Council of Trent's order that bishops and priests should remain in their dioceses to minister to their faithful echoes Wicquefort's comments. Both Wicquefort and Callières objected to the use of priests as diplomats chiefly on the grounds of their divided loyalty among their sovereign master, the prince, and a pope who always seemed to be finding ways to intervene in temporal affairs. This reaction should not be surprising given Wicquefort's Protestantism (and suspicion, even hatred, of Spain) and Callières's Gallicanism. Yet a look back at de Vera's struggle to insist upon the sacred mission and nature of the diplomat can show us how the effort to dismiss religion from diplomacy introduces new problems of representation and mediation, problems that Gentili's decision to anchor diplomacy in the sacred allowed him to avoid.

As we have seen, de Vera's ambassador would seem to be tied more to the Christian ends of concord and peace *between* princes than to any one prince that he could be seen to represent. This shift in focus away from the political entity or person sending the ambassador allows de Vera to engage in elaborate praise of the diplomat's unique role and function, since he can be seen as performing a role unavailable to a prince hemmed in by personal or state interest and temporal demands. Indeed, as de Vera states, "De toutes les Charges necessaires au maintien d'un Etat, il n'y en a point de plus difficile à exercer que celle d'Ambassadeur. . . . veritablement c'est une Charge qui ne reçoit point de comparaison avec aucune autre de la Republique. . . . En un mot toutes les bonnes qualitez qui se trouvent dans les autres charges, doivent être rassemblées en celle-ci" (Of all of the charges necessary to maintain a state, there is none more difficult to exercise than that of ambassador. . . . truly it is an office that cannot be compared with any other in the republic. . . . Briefly, all of the good things that are found in other charges should be united in this one).[38] The superlatives that de Vera uses to recognize an office all too often forgotten—an office that he himself had occupied—reveal the necessity of diplomacy to government. Circulating among states bearing the symbols that recall their resemblance to Mercury as well as the olive branch of peace, the diplomats ensure, through their diligence, the peaceful coexistence of states under the aegis of Christianity.

This utopic vision of the ambassador, any attack on whom de Vera promises will be answered less by their sovereign than by God,[39] runs directly into the view, expressed with equal vehemence later in the text, of the ambassador as representative of the prince. The shift in emphasis from one model to the other occurs approximately halfway through the treatise, when de Vera speaks of the prince's need to avenge offenses against his ambassadors, "estimant l'injure aussi grande que si elle étoit faite à sa personne" (considering the injury as great as if it had been made against his person).[40] De Vera goes on to assert that princes who do not protect their diplomats commit greater offenses against the *droit des gens* than those who perpetrated the actual injury, and he follows this maxim with several examples of princes and states avenging their representatives. The question remains, however: how do we move from the violation of ambassadors as an offense against God to the same violation as an offense against the state? Does the diplomat represent his state first and foremost, or does he represent the larger interests of peace? The answer is simple if we accept that the kingship in question is divinely sanctioned and that the sovereign represented by the ambassador is indeed the image of God on earth, just as the ambassador can be seen as the image of the prince. This is certainly what is intended by de Vera; his sovereign is, after all, the Most Catholic King, just as Gentili's sovereign was the head both of the state and the church. Indeed, as he explains later when one of the interlocutors raises the possibility that the ambassador's orders and those of religion might be in conflict, a Catholic king's demands will never run counter to those of God.[41]

In this atmosphere of a tight and unquestioned link between the sovereign and God, de Vera's exhortations to the ambassador to represent his master as completely as possible do not contradict the diplomat's divine function. Given that in formal and ceremonial circumstances, "il n'y a que le Prince seul qui puisse decider ces points-là [i.e., ceremonial details and pretensions to sovereignty], & juger de ses secretes intentions, de ses volontés, & de sa puissance" (the Prince alone can decide such points, judging the secret intentions, wills, and power of the other), the author recommends that, on such occasions, the ambassador refrain from questioning his master's orders and that he execute his instructions exactly: "Par consequent l'Ambassadeur doit suivre exactement son Instruction; & ne doit pas se mêler d'adoucir ou d'aigrir les paroles, en ajoûtant ou retranchant; mais s'il lui est possible il doit prendre le son de la voix de son Prince, & imiter ses gestes" (The ambassador must follow exactly his instruction and must not try to soften or harden the words by adding or subtracting from courtesies and compliments, but if he can he should adopt the tone of voice of his prince and imitate his gestures).[42] In such circumstances, the ambassador must fully efface himself in order to protect his sovereign's power and insight. De Vera's articulation of the complete transformation of diplomat into sovereign is therefore problematic in two ways: it effaces the ambassador, rendering his skills unnecessary, and it creates a second sovereign, nearly identical to its model. Deviating from the letter would pollute the chain of authority and the impression of presence that begins in the divine, extends through the prince, and expresses itself ultimately through the person of the diplomat.

Yet, this zero degree of diplomatic representation is restricted to exceptional occasions; de Vera recognizes that "dans les Affaires communes & ordinaires, ce seroit une impertinente & ridicule maniere de proceder dans celles qui ne sont pas entierement rompuës" (in common and ordinary affairs, this would be an impertinent and ridiculous manner of proceeding as long as negotiations continue).[43] Yet the objection is not merely aesthetic; such a limited role for the diplomat enters into direct conflict with de Vera's earlier praise of the specificity of the ambassador's role and his talents as holder of "the most difficult office in the kingdom": "Car outre que l'exercice de cette Charge seroit estimé ridicule, s'il falloit le faire literalement, comme le veulent ceux qui disent qu'il faut reciter les Ambassades à la lettre, dont nous avons parlé ci-devant, on n'auroit pas besoin de choisir un fort habille homme à qui la donner; il ne seroit pas aussi necessaire qu'il eût un grand esprit, qu'il fût prudent, prevoiant, éloquent, constant, noble, riche & bien fait; ce seroit assez de savoir seulement bien lire pour être capable d'exercer cette charge, qui ne peut être dignement remplie que par des hommes distingués" (For besides the fact that the exercise of this charge would be considered ridiculous if it had to be done literally, as those who say that the ambassador should recite his instructions to the letter would have it, one would no longer need to choose an able man to whom to give this charge; it would no longer be necessary for him to have great judgment, to be prudent, gifted with foresight, eloquent, loyal, noble, rich and handsome; it would be enough to know only how to read well in order to be capable of this charge, which can only be exercised with dignity by distinguished men).[44] This passage echoes Gentili's (and later Wicquefort's) wish to differentiate the ambassador, in whom skill is required, from the mere herald or interpreter, who only repeats the words given to him at the outset. The need for such a distinction is due not only to an understandable wish for diplomacy to be appreciated as a unique skill but also to the growing importance of the resident ambassador, whose function cannot be restricted to delivering his message and departing immediately afterward.

Yet this passage also presents de Vera with a larger theological difficulty. If the prince whom the ambassador represents truly reflects the will of God, then ambassadors would not be necessary, since such princes could never enter into conflict. Writing in the midst of the Thirty Years' War, de Vera must have known that one of the chief rivalries in that conflict was between the Most Catholic King of Spain and the Most Christian King of France. In fact, the certainty of each of the two Crowns that it alone embodied the expression of God's will and presence in temporal affairs had been responsible for the near-collapse of the Council of Trent and constituted the source of tensions that would persist through Westphalia and beyond. The extent to which the ambassador's skills and qualities are required in international affairs indicates the lapse of one or more of the countries involved in the negotiation from the ideal of transparently transmitting the will and plan of God on earth.[45] The ambassador becomes a close reflection, a shadow, of the sovereign, appearing only when the latter falls short. Writers can partially remedy this paradox by asserting that the existence of their own country's ambassadors is due to *other* countries' failure to live up to Christian principle, but this argument would weaken the international appeal of their works, which purport to have universal applicability. Additionally, all theorists of diplomacy recognize to this day that their own country depends upon another country's good faith in agreeing to receive their ambassador. We shall see in more detail how the French managed to reconcile the need for diplomacy with their strong belief in divine right sovereignty. For now, it is sufficient to trace de Vera's conflicted notions regarding the always already double role and function of the diplomat as both a sign of the fallen state of temporal affairs and a signifier of the hope for Christian peace.

For the most part, then, de Vera is able to reconcile this inherent doubleness of diplomacy, since the king's allegiance to Christian principles is never questioned. The perfect ambassador of the title would seem to serve the perfect prince as well. De Vera constantly draws parallels between the City of God and the city of man, as in the following example where ambassadors without *lettres de créance* are compared to heretics: "Il est donc besoin qu'un Ambassadeur porte Pouvoir & Lettre, pour assûrer tout ce qu'il negociera au nom de son Prince; autrement, si l'on se servoit d'autres Instruments moins assûrés, les erreurs & les dangers des Ambassades feintes seroient infinis. De cette espece de faux Ambassadeurs, sont les Heretiques et Dogmatistes, qui tâchent de donner des Signes qu'ils sont envoiés de Dieu pour Prêcher & neanmoins ils n'ont point de plus veritable maître que le Diable, et partant il ne les faut ni croire ni écouter" (Therefore, the ambassador needs to carry Power and Letter, to ensure everything that he will negotiate in the name of his Prince; otherwise, if other, less certain instruments were used, the errors and dangers of ambassadors would be infinite. Examples of this false ambassador are heretics and dogmatics, who try to give signs that they are sent by God to preach and yet they have no other master than the Devil, and therefore one must neither listen to them nor believe them).[46] Interestingly, in this example de Vera evokes the possible dangers of a very skilled ambassador. Unanchored by the written proof of his identity, signed and sent by his sovereign, the diplomat is free to use his immense and "rare" talents to deceive and seduce those to whom they say they are sent. The *lettre de créance* becomes a means of reconciling the skill de Vera alludes to above with the concurrent model, however ridiculous, of absolute representational mimesis. We can see here why resident ambassadors could appear so troubling to early modern governments (the kingdom of Poland never did accept them during the seventeenth century). Neither fish nor fowl, these ambassadors were identified as representatives of their sovereign but were rarely given a specific function to perform. Their increased deployment throughout Europe, more than anything else, raised the question of what, precisely, this representational character meant, since obviously the represented sovereign lacked jurisdiction in a kingdom not his own.

Given the dangers of the untethered ambassador, de Vera and Gentili's need to anchor the ambassador to the divine as well as to the prince becomes apparent. In fact, it often seems that the task of de Vera's ideal ambassador is nothing less than the reconciliation of his prince's interests to the larger ones of God and the Catholic Church. This role would liken diplomats to angels much more than to other civil servants, and de Vera's praise of the ambassador's unique talents would be more than justified. Yet once again, it is important to place de Vera in the context of the Thirty Years' War, a war in which the overriding temporal interests of the states involved became clear. His decision to present his treatise as a dialogue between two friends reads less as a revival of some sort of humanist paradise and more as an inherent recognition of the fundamental duality of his subject. Jules's incessant questions to Louis mark the impossibility of containing the diplomat's role within a neat framework that could embrace both temporal and divine interests. Indeed, near the end of the treatise, Jules raises this particularly insightful point: "si tout Ambassadeur se doit gouverner par les regles de son affection, il est certain, qu'il lui semblera que la Préeminence par dessus tous les autres Rois du monde, appartient à son Roi" (if all ambassadors were governed by their own affections, it is certain that it would seem to them that their king, among all other kings, deserves preeminence).[47] Although Louis's answer contains the requisite references to the Church and Holy Empire, it cannot efface the possibility that the ambassador, far from being an angelic mediator between princes' interests and demands (wherein ultimate agreement always remains possible), is rather the representative of the sovereign alone, sent to ferret out secrets and insinuate himself into his host country's court and political system. To a large extent, the complexity of the ambassador's role in Gentili and de Vera reflects the ongoing debate during the late sixteenth and early seventeenth centuries over whether the origin of political order was human or divine.

THE AMBASSADOR AND THE PRINCE

Attempts to define the ambassador run into the same problem that plagued attempts to define the sovereign, and not only because of the close association of the two figures. De Vera's dialogic treatise remains caught between the two models that characterized Le Bret's efforts to capture sovereignty: the one-to-one mimetic representation of the prince on the one hand, and the more spiritual, mobile force that peacefully unites such particulars on the other. One might imagine that later writers' unwillingness to cast the ambassador in overt religious terms could simplify the situation by restricting the diplomat to representing his sovereign and carrying out his specific orders. Yet the increase in emphasis on representation of the prince that occurred throughout the seventeenth century raised as many problems as it solved. It involved a careful consideration of what this representation means, for both the diplomat and the sovereign, and how it can be established (and taken away).

We have already seen that the idea that the ambassador represents his sovereign master was commonplace well before the second half of the seventeenth century. I have cited de Vera's evocation of the ambassador's duty, in restricted circumstances, to follow his instructions so closely as to imitate the tone and gestures of his prince; likewise, Hotman argues for talented diplomats by stating that since the ambassador represents the glory of his state abroad, his defects or faults may cause others to think badly of his master. Yet common to de Vera, Gentili, and Hotman is a regard less for this representational capacity of the ambassador than for his peaceful mission. Their vision remains one of a diplomat circulating *among* independent princes rather than one of a diplomat closely tied to his own prince. Gentili even points out that "in Roman law the technical term for ambassadors is *legati* from *legare* 'to send with a commission,' and so from their very name the function of ambassadors is limited to those to whom they are sent."[48] In other words, for Gentili the ambassador exists for the sovereign or state *to* whom he is sent as much as he does for the prince sending him. I have also shown how this additional, independent "Christian" function of the diplomat gives the writers room to treat the diplomat's necessary qualities—qualities that a strict mimetic relation to the prince and to his instructions would render superfluous.

The puzzle confronting theorists who rejected outright any religious source or referent in diplomacy was therefore how to account for the ambassador's specific qualities without undermining the agency of the sovereign prince who sent him. In order to solve this problem, an elaborate model of the representational relation between prince and ambassador would need to be established—one that reflected the ambassador's freedom of action while firmly tying him to his monarch, and his monarch alone. For the threat of freelancing diplomats to their masters' sovereignty had moved, in fact, far beyond de Vera's rather picturesque warning that false ambassadors were no different than heretics. The explosion of treatises and legal cases dealing with ambassadors' exterritoriality during the sixteenth and seventeenth centuries led to conflicting ideas concerning the source of the diplomat's inviolability.[49] The turn from the sacred during the seventeenth century is reflected in the decreasing foundation of this inviolability in the divine origin of the ambassador (quite common in the sixteenth century) and increasing reference to the quite secular *droit des gens*. Indeed, the growing idea that only sovereigns can send ambassadors is often justified through reference to the sovereign's *droit du glaive*, or ability to punish those who abused his representative, and not to the prince's divinely sanctioned authority.

As writers turned away from the idea that the ambassador might be sacred in himself, due to the nobility of his mission, and toward the idea that his privileges were linked to his representational relation with his sovereign master, they needed to find a new model to express this sort of person. They found a ready model that combined both representation and personal prowess in the figure of the actor. References to the profound similarity between the two—ambassador and actor—were not new to this period; we have already seen how de Vera approvingly cites the Athenians' practice of using actors as diplomats.

Yet a survey of the attitudes of these writers toward this model and its applicability to the diplomatic stage reveals, once again, the problematic nature of defining the diplomat adequately.

On the surface, the actor would seem to offer an easy solution to the need for qualities in the diplomat. Like the actor, the ambassador hewed to the subject or text supplied to him by the author of his instructions, yet the interpretation of these instructions was subject to variation and indeed improvisation. Yet it may be useful to recall here the controversial status of the actor during this period of revived interest in diplomacy. Throughout the early modern period, the ambiguity of the actor and, more specifically, the actor's implication in the role that he played, however temporarily, troubled critics of the theater. As I will explain in more detail in chapter 5, these critics, among them Pierre Nicole, the Prince de Conti, and Bossuet, argued that those (especially women) who portrayed such strong emotions on stage could not possibly escape their contamination.[50] Actors would thus seem to be as problematic as angels as possible models for the diplomat's persona, and evoking the similarities between acting and diplomacy was not liable to reassure the reader. Given the link between religion and criticism of the theater during this period, and also given the tendency of religiously oriented theorists to turn more toward the model of the prophet or angel than to that of the actor, the writers most invested in the sacred nature of diplomacy rejected (all the while evoking) a similarity between ambassador and actor. Hotman vehemently rejects the comparison, stating flatly that "l'ambassade et la comédie sont choses dissemblables" (diplomacy and theater do not resemble each other),[51] a statement whose brevity suggests that the comparison had become commonplace. Gentili likewise takes care to note the differences between the two figures: "If we would hiss off the boards an actor who, when playing the rôle of king, comes on the stage with a shabby retinue and in anything but royal attire, what is to be done to the ambassador, who is not merely taking part in a play for a few hours, but is actually invested with the personality of his sovereign?"[52] Like Hotman, Gentili founds his objection in the seriousness and exclusivity of the diplomat's performance, as opposed to the much more mercurial role of the actor who can perform many roles equally well. Gentili's ambassador has only one role and mission, which is to preserve peace; he cannot put on and take off this duty at will. "For the doctrine seemed vain even to the boor to whom this question is attributed: What will happen to Fabius after the ambassador has been sent down to Hell? The ambassador's personality is mixed, not double; and since in this mixture the right of God is the stronger, the other element should certainly be controlled by it."[53] Unlike the actor, whose temporary adoption of his character does not have profound implications for his very self, the diplomat in performing his role is permanently transformed.[54] Gentili's reference to the ambassador's person as "mixed, not double," should be taken seriously as a new development in attempts to articulate the relation between any individual and the office he is called upon to perform. If we accept the fundamental similarity between the ambassador and the prince, even if it is based less upon the representational relation and more on their common duties to the divine, Gentili's rejection of the double body reflects (in England!) the transformation of Kantorowicz's doctrine of the king's two bodies during the sixteenth and seventeenth centuries. The challenge, once again, is how to demonstrate this model in an easily understandable manner; the answer, even if it is rejected as ultimately inadequate and in need of modification, would seem to be with the figure of the actor.

The move from suspicion to acceptance of this comparison is marked by de Vera, whose treatise, here as in so many other areas, tries to strike a balance between the secular and the religious and ends in interesting ambiguity: "Un Ambassadeur represente deux personnes tout ensemble; la premiere est celle de son Roi & l'autre la sienne propre;[55] & par conséquent il doit avoir deux sortes de mouvement. Et comme dans une Tragedie, il faut que celui qui represente Alexandre, Jason, ou Cyrus, essaie d'imiter par ses paroles & par ses Actions le Personnage qu'il joüe, pendant qu'il est sur le Teatre avec les habits Roiaux; mais quand il s'est retiré derriere la Scene, quoi qu'il ne quitte pas ses ornements, parce qu'il espere de rentrer sur le Teatre, il agit neanmoins & parle comme une personne particuliere" (An Ambassador represents two people together; the first is the person of his king and the other his own; and consequently, he must have two methods of movement. And as in a Tragedy, the person who represents Alexander, Jason, or Cyrus tries to imitate in speech and action the character he plays while he is on the stage in royal clothing; but when he leaves the stage, even though he does not take off his ornaments, since he hopes to reenter the theater, he nonetheless acts and speaks like a private person).[56] Occurring right after de Vera's rejection of the idea of the ambassador as someone who merely parrots his instructions and who therefore needs no real qualities of his own, this passage reveals the immense utility of the theatrical model in reconciling agency and representation. The figure of the actor would seem to clear a certain space for the expression of the diplomat's personal skill and charisma. Yet by presenting this comparison in the context of the metaphorical stage, de Vera seems not so much to acknowledge the diplomat's qualities as to restore the ambassador's dependence on his sovereign model, since his mission is not to improvise but rather to imitate his masters' gestures and speech. This imitation will never be completely successful; de Vera's use of the verb "try" reveals one of the singular differences between the actor and the ambassador–the contemporary existence of the object of representation. In other words, the (tragic) actor almost always represents someone who is dead, while the ambassador figures forth the absent presence of his master, whose physical limitations and duties to his own kingdom are the only obstacles preventing him from appearing at a foreign court.[57] Indeed, if the actor were to represent a living monarch on the stage, he would most likely be charged with lèse-majesté. This significant difference between the two figures perhaps explains why approving discussions of the ambassador's skills as an actor of sorts are accompanied by strong language that ties the ambassador to the king as his authorized representative. Such language, which indeed immediately precedes the passage above in de Vera, serves to limit the use of this metaphor, since the ambassador's (temporary) embodiment of his king is both more real (insofar as he is vested with authority) and less (the spectators witnessing his "performance" are fully aware that the true king is alive and elsewhere) than that of the actor.

In the passage cited above, the comparison is further blurred and complicated when de Vera attempts to account for the diplomat's identity after his official "performance." Hoping for another turn on stage, he remains dressed in royal clothing yet acting and speaking "like" a private individual.[58] Such rather awkward wording demonstrates the complex realities behind his optimistic and terse title (in Spanish), "The Ambassador." For here the ambassador appears more elusive than ever, trapped in a series of roles that render the ambassador as such rather difficult to locate. "Comme" the sovereign, "comme" a private individual, the diplomat is, in fact, neither. Stripped here of his sacred mission, he is betweenness itself, existing only as a (temporary) conduit between two sovereigns. Given this description, Gentili's curious question of what happens to the ambassador when he is buried starts to make sense. Almost all of these treatises seek to "bury" the ambassador–to fix his protean identity and capture his specific persona and gifts once and for all.

The advantages of the theatrical model of diplomacy take on greater clarity in Abraham de Wicquefort's 1681 treatise, *L'Ambassadeur et ses fonctions*. Wicquefort's efforts to give credit and definition to the ambassador and his rights are linked to his own complex and ambiguous role in seventeenth-century European diplomacy. Active for the Dutch under Mazarin, he was eventually found guilty of compromising state secrets and punished until Mazarin, himself an astute diplomat, decided to employ him in Paris. Later in his career, representing the Duke of Luneburg in the Netherlands, his home country, he was again condemned for his practices and imprisoned. It was during his time in confinement that he wrote this treatise, a follow-up to his earlier, and briefer, *Mémoires*. As critics both then and now have noted, the theoretical orientation of the later text reflects his unique personal situation as much as it demonstrates changing principles in international law.[59] Perhaps not surprisingly, then, given his own mercurial career, Wicquefort unambiguously praises the actorlike qualities of the diplomat: *"L'Ambassadeur* represente la personne du Prince son Maistre, & à cause de cela on luy donne la qualité de *representant public,* dans une signification, qui est propre à ce caractere. . . . Les *representantes* des Espagnols, sont toute autre chose, quoy que l'on ne puisse pas nier, qu'un bon Ambassadeur ne soit aussy un grand personnage de theatre, & que pour reussir en cette profession il faut estre un peu Comedien" (The Ambassador represents the person of the prince his master, and because of this he is given the quality of public represener, in a sense that is appropriate to this character. . . . The Spanish *representantes,* are something else entirely, although one cannot deny that a good ambassador must also be a great theatrical character, and that to succeed in this profession one must be something of an actor).[60] Here, Wicquefort uses the actor metaphor to note the differences between the flamboyant Spanish representatives and their European counterparts. In a move that we have already seen in de Vera, the idea of the ambassador as actor is closely and ambiguously related to his representational link to the prince. Although Wicquefort seems to oppose theatrical performance to a strict representation of the sovereign, he goes on to correct this impression by asserting that all successful ambassadors must possess the qualities of a good actor. This passage therefore demonstrates the essential duality of the ambassador's role as well as Wicquefort's efforts to preserve the ambassador's freedom of action alongside his immunity from persecution, an immunity based on the ambassador's status as lieutenant (in the sense of place-holder, of the person who renders the absent present) of the sovereign. The smooth marriage of these two models— of diplomat as actor and diplomat as representative of sovereignty itself—has dangerous implications insofar as it implies something fundamentally theatrical about sovereignty and monarchy itself. The following passage, where this conclusion is more or less explicitly indicated, gives us an idea of why earlier writers, intent on proving the diplomat's sacrality, were careful to distance him from the actor:

L'Ambassadeur ne negotie pas tousjours; c'est à dire, il ne doit pas faire l'Ambassadeur par tout & en toutes les rencontres. J'ay dit ailleurs qu'il doit estre un peu Comedien, & j'y ajoute icy, que peutestre dans tout le commerce du Monde, il n'y a pas un personnage plus Comique que l'Ambassadeur. Il n'y a point de theatre plus illustre que la Cour: il n'y a point de comedie, où les acteurs paroissent moins ce qu'ils sont en effet que les Ambassadeurs font dans la negotiation, & il n'y en a point qui y representent de plus importants personnages. Mais comme le plus habile acteur n'est pas tousjours sur le theatre, & change de maniere d'agir aprés que le rideau est tiré, ainsy l'Ambassadeur, qui a bien joüé son rolle dans les fonctions de son caractere, doit faire l'honneste homme lors qu'il ne joüe plus la comedie. Dans les assemblées de ceremonies il ne peut pas quitter son rang sans crime, & mesmes en tenant table, où il estale un eschantillon de la grandeur & de la magnificence de son Prince, il le peut representer en quelque façon. Mais comme les Rois mesmes se déchargent quelquefois de cette gravité pesante & incommode, & que comme Moyse, ils mettent quelquefois un voile sur la face, afin que leur Majesté n'éblöüisse pas ceux qui en approchent, ainsy l'Ambassadeur ne peut, sans effacer le caractere d'honneste homme, faire paroistre continuellement celuy de Ministre Public.[61]

[The ambassador does not always negotiate; that is to say, he should not play the ambassador everywhere and in all circumstances. I have said elsewhere that he should be something of an actor, and I add here, that perhaps in all worldly commerce, there is not a more actorly personage than the ambassador. There is no theater more illustrious than the Court; there is no play where the actors appear less what they really are than Ambassadors in negotiations, and there are no other people who represent more important figures. But since the most able actor is not always on the theater, and changes his behavior after the curtain comes down, so the ambassador, who has played well his role in the functions of his character must play the gentleman once he is no longer acting in the play. In ceremonial assemblies he cannot quit his rank without committing a crime, and even in hosting a table where he spreads out a bit of the grandeur and the magnificence of his prince, he can represent him in some fashion. But since even kings discharge themselves on occasion of their uncomfortable and weighty gravity, and like Moses, they veil their faces so that their majesty does not blind those who approach, so the Ambassador cannot, without erasing the character of gentleman, appear constantly as a public minister.]

Although the first half of this passage recalls de Vera's evocation of the ambassador as actor, Wicquefort pushes the similarity between the two figures to its limit. By labeling the ambassador as the consummate actor, Wicquefort signals the immense distance between the diplomat "tel qu'il est en effet" and the majesty he is charged with representing. Yet this intriguing hint of the diplomat's humble status when not clothed in representational character is immediately modified, as Wicquefort signals that the ambassador "offstage" should "faire l'honneste homme." A discussion of the trope, frequently evoked during the early modern period by writers throughout Europe, of the "honneste homme" or courtesan as actor exceeds the scope of this study and has, at any rate, been accomplished by other critics. Here, it is sufficient to note that the role of the ambassador who is not "performing" is no less theatrical than that in which he calls forth his absent master. As with de Vera's reference to the ambassador as an actor who never takes off his stage clothing but who acts the part of a private individual when not involved in diplomatic performance, Wicquefort's model, instead of enlightening the reader as to what the ambassador truly "is," blurs the levels of representation to the point that the individual "tel qu'il est en effet" is impossible to locate.

This dizzying hall of mirrors and representational effects is a shaky foundation on which to base the noble objectives of securing peace and the observation of treaties. This is all the more the case when Wicquefort suggests at the end of the passage above that the actorlike qualities of the ambassador, far from detracting from his representation of the monarch, in fact render him that much more effective, since royalty itself engages in the same practices. By pointing out that the king himself cannot sustain his majesty forever but rather must hide it from time to time, not so much for his own relief as for that of his subjects, Wicquefort leads the reader into a double bind, the result of which is increased respect for that neglected international figure, the ambassador. On the one hand, the reader may interpret his passage as revealing the intensely theatrical nature of monarchy and the court ("Il n'y a point de theatre plus illustre que la Cour. . . ."), in which case the ambassador, as consummate actor, is more worthy of praise (and protection and remuneration, concerns that must have been quite acute to Wicquefort in his prison) than any other courtesan. On the other hand, if we read Wicquefort as insisting that the majesty of the monarch can never disappear even though the prince makes an effort to hide it from time to time, we come to the conclusion—one that would no doubt please Wicquefort—that the ambassador, even after his mission is over, remains somehow an ambassador, permanently transformed by his experience embodying his sovereign. This conclusion leads us straight back to Gentili's allusion to the ambassador's person as mixed, not double; the radicality of the ambassador's transformation into the present monarch can only (especially when viewed by former diplomats reflecting on their past glory) lead to some sort of internal change in the person singled out for such an honor.

Wicquefort's fascinating treatise, like his equally fascinating life as a diplomat, illustrates perhaps better than any other the tensions involved in the "caractère représentant" to which he often alludes. The first volume of his work is devoted to the privileges and protections afforded the ambassador because of his tight representational relation to his sovereign—not, as earlier writers would have it, because of some inherent sacrality. Wicquefort goes to great lengths to establish and stabilize the relation between diplomat and monarch, considering such questions as whether usurpers or governors can send ambassadors and whether the secretary of the ambassador has any sort of representational quality. Yet even in this section, Wicquefort realizes that "representation" means different things in different contexts. A "grand seigneur" can perhaps better represent the prince in ceremonial functions, but if "representation" is interpreted more as "acting in place of" instead of "standing in place of," other qualities are needed.[62] The nobleman who reads a script or invites the members of the court that he visits to a sumptuous dinner may be representing his king but is unlikely to gain any honor of his own on such a mission.

The second volume of the treatise, then, discusses less the ambassador's character than his function. Dismissing extraordinary embassies, "où l'Ambassadeur *ne fait que* representer la personne du Prince" (where the Ambassador *only* represents the person of his prince),[63] Wicquefort defends his separation of person and function in the lengthy passage cited above. The ambassador's glory is to be achieved in the gap between himself as "honneste homme" and himself as representative of his prince, where complications and obstacles need to be overcome with the ingenuity of what even previous writers had noted was the most overlooked, yet the most skilled and important, figure of the kingdom.

WHAT IS "REPRESENTATION?"

While historians such as Adair hold that Wicquefort's observations are of little use in tracing the development and codification of international law during this period (unlike Callières, he is rarely cited in modern discussions of diplomacy), his effort to raise the international status of the diplomat by simultaneously alluding to his close representational tie to the sovereign and to his intelligence and freedom of action speaks directly to the crisis in imagining sovereignty during the seventeenth century not only in France but throughout Europe. Wicquefort's dilemma is not unlike those of the theorists of divine right monarchy, who were also concerned with both stabilizing the source of the prince's authority and giving him room to innovate. Wicquefort's statement, cited above, that during *ambassades extraordinaires* the diplomat "ne fait que representer la personne du Prince" reveals both the essence of the problem and its possible, yet troubling, solution. The emphasis in this phrase should perhaps fall rather on the word "personne," for what Wicquefort is suggesting in his division of the ambassador's "caractère" and his "fonction" is the difference between representing *only* the prince's person and representing the sovereignty that is embodied or held by that person.

Of course, the danger in such a Bodinian model of diplomacy, where the diplomat can be said to represent the sovereign inasmuch as he possesses the same (in most cases, even more) knowledge than his master and is better placed to act upon it, is that the ambassador will escape his sovereign's control—a danger that Bodin, with his repeated insistence on the impossibility of delegating sovereignty, seemed to sense. Wicquefort's definition of the "ambassade ordinaire" is quite suggestive in this respect, as it demonstrates a significant distancing from the protective representative language elaborated in the first volume: "L'Ambassadeur Ordinaire a plusieurs objects vagues, que l'on ne peut ranger sous de certains titres. On en peut dire en general, *que sa fonction principale consiste à entretenir la bonne correspondence entre les deux Princes: à rendre les lettres, que son Maistre escrit au Prince, auprès duquel il reside, à en solliciter la réponse: à observer tout ce qui se passe en la Cour où il negotie:* à *proteger les sujets, & à conserver les interests de son maistre.* Il sert de truchement aux deux Princes, & de courrier du commerce qui se fait entre eux" (The Ordinary Ambassador has several vague goals that we cannot classify under certain titles. We can say in general, that his principal function consists in maintaining good communication between the two princes, in giving his own prince's letters to the prince in whose court he resides, and in asking for the response; in observing everything that happens in the court where he is negotiating; in protecting the subjects and preserving the interests of his master. He serves as interpreter between the two princes, and as courier for the commerce that occurs between them).[64] Like Gentili's diplomat, who immediately after his evocation begins to slip toward other roles, Wicquefort's ambassador seems to escape definition. Insofar as Wicquefort does attempt to formulate the "objets vagues" that are the diplomat's concern, he moves imperceptibly from a "tight" idea of the ambassador to one with much more freedom. From transmitting and receiving letters, the diplomat begins to observe everything that happens around him, eventually becoming someone who protects his sovereign's subjects and interests. The final, nonitalicized line of the definition seems to mark Wicquefort's awareness that his ambassador, however briefly, has exceeded his role; here, he is once again "only" an interpreter and courier.

Indeed, in this second volume dedicated to the ambassador's "function," Wicquefort works to combine the two aspects of diplomacy that coexisted uneasily in de Vera's account. Citing a letter from Elizabeth I to her ambassador Walsingham, Wicquefort proclaims that "dans ce peu de lignes vous trouvez les deux premières fonctions de l'Ambassadeur, qui y est representé comme *un messager de paix* d'un costé, & comme *un espion honnorable* de l'autre" (in these few lines you find the two foremost functions of the ambassador, who is represented as, on the one hand, the messenger of peace, and, on the other, as an honorable spy).[65] The inherent duplicity of the ambassador's character, somehow both sacred and secular, peaceful and intriguing, is mirrored in his function. Notably, however, any reference to the diplomat's *representative* function, so lengthily discussed in the first book of the treatise, is absent here. Rather, these two functions describe, as it were, the two models of diplomatic *independence*–a godlike search for peace and an amoral search for information–which the representative character, confined neatly in the first volume of the treatise, is evoked to control and protect.

Where Wicquefort differs significantly from de Vera and earlier writers, however, is in his recognition that Christian peace among nations is only a mirage in a Europe torn by religious differences and the irreconcilable interests of princes. Indeed, Wicquefort offers the following: "il n'y a presque point de Prince, qui hors la rupture & la guerre declarée, ne vueille estre bien avec ses voisins, & j'ose dire qu'il n'y en a point, qui ne vueille sauver les apparences, mesme avec ses faux amis & avec ses ennemis couverts" (there are almost no princes, who outside of rupture and declared war, do not want to get along with their neighbors, and I would dare say that there are none who do not want to save appearances, even with false friends and covert enemies).[66] Wicquefort's "daring" is in fact just that, insofar as it points out the scandal of seventeenth-century diplomacy: that the ambassador arriving as "messenger of peace" is in fact trying to secure as many advantages for his master as possible. This mutation in European affairs–marked explicitly not only in Wicquefort's pointed rejection of de Vera's treatise as useless but also in his refusal to cite any examples that are not contemporary to the sixteenth or seventeenth centuries–renders the task of determining the "real" role of the diplomat impossible. Just as the diplomat offstage is encouraged to "act" the *honnête homme* in phrasing that clouds the real identity of the diplomat, the ambassador coming as a messenger of peace may be involved in more duplicity in that role than in his role as spy. In other words, authenticity–or to speak less anachronistically, grounding in a transcendental purpose ostensibly rooted in God's plans for the European states–is completely absent from Wicquefort's text. In its place arises "interest," a difficult concept at least for Wicquefort, in that the diplomat's interest–displaying his talents and acquiring glory for himself–can be construed in certain instances as counter to the interests of his prince, just as the interests of his own prince can be interpreted as being at odds with those of other princes.

In this environment of pervasive uncertainty, the representational tie between the diplomat and his master—the *caractère représentant*—becomes the only control on the ambassador's actions. Wicquefort's recognition that the successful ambassador must do more than "just" represent the person of the king seems to be an acknowledgment that this representational relation, especially once shorn of its sacred overtones, is fraught with difficulty. I have already shown how de Vera evokes the ambassador as perfect mimic of his prince, only to nuance this description almost immediately, largely because it strips the diplomat of the ownership, or initiative, of his actions. In fact, any treatise on the diplomat must do the same, insofar as recognition of the ambassador's special skills and contributions to international affairs implies an imperfection in the relation between prince and diplomat; if "mere" representation is all that is required, we could call the ambassador a herald and leave it at that. At a time when the ambassador's mission was essentially one of linking sovereigns in the ideal of Christian peace, this gap could be covered over, since the diplomat's most important relation could be seen as with God rather than with the monarch. The lack of such transcendental certitudes opens the way for writers such as Wicquefort to view the diplomat as representative not merely of the sovereign's person but of his sovereignty itself. This troubling development—after all, all writers on sovereignty agree that it is the one thing that cannot be shared and that it can only be delegated with strict caveats as to its usage—is already present in Gentili, who exalts prudence as a virtue in the ambassador in terms that come close to infringing on the properties of the prince: "In regard to prudence, by which I here mean the virtue that manifests itself in a shrewd analysis of the truth, I lay down the principle that it seems to be specially requisite in an ambassador. *For he is not merely thought of as a bearer of messages,* but is also called a judge of affairs, and (as the noble Venetian has advised us) ambassadors are the ears and eyes of their government."[67]

From here, it is a short step to seeing the deployment of ambassadors less as an attribute of sovereignty than as a signifier of its shortcomings. When viewed principally not as "messenger of peace" but as representative of his master's interests, the ambassador emerges as the necessary supplement to the monarch's physical limitations and the frontiers of his power. Wicquefort's description of the need for ambassadors once again demonstrates the profound ambiguity of the diplomat quite eloquently:

Les Princes ont leur commerce entre eux comme les autres hommes; mais ne pouvant se communiquer en personne, sans quelque prejudice de leur dignité ou de leurs affaires, ils se servent de l'entremise de quelques Ministres, à qui ils donnent le caractere d'Ambassadeur, ou une autre qualité publique. C'est sur quoy se fonde la necessité des Ambassades; parce que les Princes ne pouvant

faire eux mesmes leurs affaires avec les autres Souverains, il faut necessairement qu'ils y employent des personnes, qui les representent, & qui par ce moyen
se trouvent dans une dignité relevée, où on leur rend des honneurs qu'ils ne
pourroient pas pretendre sans cette qualité eminente.[68]

[Princes have commerce between themselves just like other men, but not being
able to communicate in person without causing prejudice to their dignity or
their affairs, they use certain ministers, to whom they give the character of
Ambassador, or another public quality. This is why embassies are needed;
because princes being unable to conduct their affairs with other sovereigns
themselves, they must necessarily employ persons who represent them, and
who therefore find themselves in possession of heightened dignity, where they
are accorded certain honors to which they could not otherwise pretend.]

The combination of Wicquefort's repetition of "ne pouvant," a negation that
marks the limitations of sovereignty, with the opening phrase that refers to
the essential similarity between princes and other men is a clear demonstration of the dangers inherent in the exaltation of the ambassador and the
acknowledgment of his centrality to foreign affairs. Indeed, the monarch's act
of appointing ambassadors is less an exercise of one of the inalienable rights
of sovereignty and more a recognition of what he cannot do himself. Wicquefort's "*il faut necessairement*" leads into a discussion of the ambassador's *caractère* that obfuscates the source of this honor. What Wicquefort seems to be
saying is this: monarchs, unable to undertake commerce with other princes
for whatever reason (other writers explain this inability by saying, for example, that the prince who absents himself from his kingdom not only neglects
his own affairs but exposes himself to the dangers of travel), *must* appoint representatives of their sovereignty, who are thereby transformed (for how long?
can this quality ever be rescinded completely, once given?) into something
more than what they were before, especially insofar as foreigners should treat
them as they would treat the king in person. Careful reading of Wicquefort's
treatise thereby confirms the idea that the diplomat is a figure located at the
precise intersection not only of the home country and countries farther away
but of the prince as embodied individual and as political force as well as of
the truth and falsehood of the politics of the time.

THE INFLUENCE OF PRACTICE ON THEORY: EXTERRITORIALITY
AND DIPLOMATIC DISPATCHES

Increasingly, then, theorists found themselves faced with the daunting task of
reconciling the ambassador's representative character with the unheard-of

difficulties and complexities of diplomacy in the sixteenth and seventeenth centuries. The increased role of the resident ambassador, with his implicit challenge to the very foundation of diplomatic function—that of representing the prince—and the secularization of post–Westphalian Europe (a secularization that I have shown was only incompletely accomplished, if not overtly resisted, in France) led the writers seeking to offer practical advice to the new ambassador to alter their idea of the diplomat in response to the problems he faced in carrying out his task. Two of the major issues confronting the ambassador forced theorists to face the inadequacies of the traditional description of diplomacy: that of exterritoriality, a concept directly related to diplomatic inviolability, and that of the diplomatic dispatch, a singular feature of the resident ambassador. Both issues show, in different ways, the breakdown of the ideal of diplomatic representation, and their increased prominence in diplomatic texts of the period attests to their relative novelty as problems needing to be addressed. For unlike the problem of whether the diplomat could, or should, lie while carrying out his duties, these issues are not eternal but rather are linked to innovations in diplomatic practice. In response to the challenge that they posed, theorists could either revise their idea of what a diplomat should be or rework the problem itself in order to buttress a pre-existing ideal.

Exterritoriality

The problem of diplomatic exterritoriality, or the immunity of foreign diplomats from prosecution by the state in which they reside, would seem at first to be fundamentally linked to diplomatic inviolability, an idea that is as old as that of diplomacy itself and that therefore was easily classified as part of the timeless *droit des gens*. As I have shown, all writers agree that diplomats could not be attacked, although the reasons for this protection varied. De Vera and Gentili attributed the sacrality of the ambassador to his link with the divine project of peace, while for Wicquefort it was tied to the ambassador's representative character, since the sovereign right to send ambassadors was accompanied by the sovereign right to use the *droit du glaive* to protect them. Yet this apparent universal agreement regarding the diplomat's special status broke down almost immediately under the pressure of the demands of particular circumstances. Should the diplomat be accorded universal right of passage in neutral states?[69] The stickiness of this question is revealed by Hugo Grotius's opinions on the matter. While the Dutch jurist argued vehemently for the rights of passage of missionaries and tradesmen in his *Mare liberum,* he was, rather surprisingly, much more reluctant to accord the same rights to diplomats.[70] For Grotius, the ambassador is undoubtedly accorded special rights due to the "fiction" by which they "are identified with the persons who sent them," a strict representational doctrine that perhaps explains his hostility to the institution of resident ambassadors, whom, he holds, the receiving state is under no obligation to welcome. Yet he notes that "This law does not apply to a people through whose territory ambassadors pass without a safe conduct. For if they are going to an enemy of that people, or are returning from him, or are otherwise engaged in some hostile activity, they may be slain. . . . But if no such excuse exists, then to maltreat ambassadors is deemed not a violation of the law of nations, which is the subject of our discourse, but an offense against friendship and the dignity of the one who sent them or to whom they are going."[71] Grotius's strange exception of ambassadors from rights accorded to missionaries or to traders can, perhaps, be explained by the nature of the diplomat, who could be said not to fully occupy his role or function until he is properly received by the prince to whom he is sent. An ambassador who has not yet had his official reception and who is located in a third country could be said to be only half a diplomat; it is indeed not inconceivable that any prince could claim diplomatic status for any of his subjects killed during travel. Grotius's view is also consistent with his wish to establish the law of nations as independent from any perceived intervention of divine intent. Unlike missionaries, who could be argued to be in possession of an ultimate rather than consensually determined truth, ambassadors take their identity from *both* the sending prince and the receiving prince. Hotman, in articulating a similar doctrine years earlier, suggests that the third country's lack of obligation to protect a traveling diplomat is related to the unstable status of the diplomat *going to* a mission.[72] "Mesmes un tiers n'est pas tenu de recevoir & recognoistre pour Ambassadeur celuy qui passe par son pays pour aller faire sa charge ailleurs: & s'il le faict ce n'est que de courtoisie & humanité, laquelle se practique à l'endroit des passans, ausquels en temps de paix tous chemins sont ouverts" (Even a third party is not obligated to receive and recognize as an Ambassador someone who is passing through his country to exercise his charge elsewhere: and if he does it is only through courtesy and humanity, which is practiced with regard to all travelers, to whom in peacetime all roads are open).[73] The essential question here, a question that will recur in our discussion of Bynkershoek's ideas concerning exterritoriality articulated early in the eighteenth century, is the precise nature of what renders an ambassador (especially one in such a liminal situation) different from any other person. Without the strong tie to his sovereign accorded him not only by his *lettre de créance* but also by his specific mission, the strictures demanding the ambassador's protection are no different from those prohibiting harm against any other traveler.

The problem of the traveling ambassador is only one of the complexities facing writers confronting a changing diplomatic landscape. Another problem inherent in the doctrines of inviolability and exterritoriality was that of how far into the diplomat's household and property it should extend. Hotman points to the need for a rule on this matter, given the innovations that allow the diplomat to select his own servants, whose names are no longer held on a central list by the sending state. Hotman cites a law from the Digest, "laquelle estend la peine à ceux qui ont excedé les gens de l'Ambassadeur comme s'ils se fussent addressez à sa propre personne" (which extends the penalty to those who have insulted the ambassador's retinue as if they had insulted the ambassador's own person).[74] According to this principle, then, the chain of mediation leading from the prince to the diplomat to his servants is unbroken. To attack the diplomat's domestic staff is to attack the diplomat himself; to attack the diplomat is to attack the sending prince. Yet although it is true that "le privilege d'un Ambassadeur seroit bien maigre s'il ne comprenoit les personnes de ses domestiques" (an ambassador's privilege would be meager indeed if it did not include the persons of his servants),[75] to ascribe the same representational relation between the diplomat and his servants as that which exists between the king and his ambassador is a stretch indeed, especially for writers who argue for the uniqueness of diplomatic representation (as opposed to the delegated, less representational, authority exercised by other ministers in the state). Indeed, as Hotman indicates quite clearly elsewhere, it is precisely in the relation between the diplomat and his servants that the limited nature of diplomatic representation appears: "Icy est le lieu de la question que font aucuns, sçavoir, si de droict des gens l'Ambassadeur a jurisdiction sur ses domestiques? En quoy je ne voy nulle apparence, pour la raison que je viens de dire. Que l'authorité d'un Prince, & toutes marques de souveraineté cessent chez autruy. Or la punition à mort est la souveraine marque de souveraineté, & pour venir du grand au moindre, l'Ambassadeur n'a donc pas plus de droict que son Prince ou autre Souverain" (Here is the place for the question that certain people ask, which is whether the *ius gentium* authorizes the ambassador to hold jurisdiction over his servants. On this subject, I see no reason to assent, for the reason that I have just stated. That the authority of a Prince, and all marks of sovereignty are invalid in another's country. Since capital punishment is the sovereign mark of sovereignty, to go from large to small, the ambassador cannot have more rights than his prince or another sovereign).[76]

Just as the necessity of ambassadors for the prince's conduct of foreign affairs points up the limits of the sovereign's knowledge or control of events beyond his kingdom, the next dependent relation in this chain of representation plays the same role with regard to the diplomat himself. The authority transmitted from the king to the ambassador is carefully limited, explicitly by the instructions or *plein-pouvoir* given to the diplomat and implicitly through the incommunicable nature of sovereignty itself. Yet if it is relatively easy to understand why sovereignty and its marks are never communicated to the ambassador, it is, as we have seen, no easy matter to characterize exactly the kind of agency that the diplomat deploys while in service. Not sovereign, yet somehow a privileged and essential instrument of sovereignty, the diplomat is once again simultaneously highly empowered, as the temporary stand-in for his prince, and quite limited, as staying inside of his instructions or interpreting them literally, which in itself demotes him from ambassador to "mere" herald. The discipline of servants brings out all of these difficulties in a practical level, as the role played by the ambassador at the foreign court ironically does not extend to his own household.

As might be expected, the problems created by ever-expanding lists of servants and also by the theoretical adjustment in thinking about the diplomat, who appeared no longer as a quasi-angelic messenger of peace but rather as an agent for his prince's interests, led to increased attention to the precise legal status that should be given to the diplomat, his house, and his domestic staff. Wicquefort's discussion of the problem further demonstrates the growing view of diplomacy as an increasingly personal representation of the prince (a representation that the treatise argues can be used to the diplomat's advantage if he is clever enough). While Wicquefort acknowledges that protection of the ambassador in a foreign country cannot be extended to foreigners who take refuge in the embassy, his overall picture of diplomatic representation and the protection it affords the diplomat is much stronger than Hotman's: "la Maison de l'Ambassadeur doit estre respectée, comme si c'estoit le Palais du Prince mesme. Elle l'est en effet, ou du moins elle est en sa protection particuliere, aussy bien que sa personne. C'est pourquoy en plusieurs Cours de l'Europe les Ambassadeurs font mettre les armes de leur Maistre au dessus de la porte de leur Palais, & presque par tout ils ont une chaise d'Estat, qui marque la presence du Maistre du logis" (the ambassador's house must be respected as if it is the prince's own palace. In fact, it is, or at least it is in his particular protection, just as is his person. This is why in several European courts the ambassadors place their master's arms above the door of their palace, and almost everywhere they have a state chair which marks the presence of the master on the premises).[77] Once again, we see the discomfort of the theorist in specifying the exact nature of the relation between the diplomat and the sovereign, this time with regard to his house in a foreign country. Wicquefort moves from the looser, simile-based "as if it were the palace of the Prince himself" to the stronger "in fact, it is," before the final qualification that once again restores a certain degree of fiction to the representative relation between diplomat and sovereign. This wavering in language, like theorists' attempts to liken the ambassador and the actor while saving the distinct characteristics and difficulties of each, demonstrates the resistance of diplomacy to inclusion in an on-off model of representation. The palace, like the ambassador himself, is simultaneously a sign of the monarch's *real* presence and of his absence, and the stripped-down logic of the seventeenth century, bereft of the nuances and contradictions of scholasticism, can only embrace this profound ambiguity at the center of state activity with great difficulty. Yet theorists such as Wicquefort are loath to abandon the rhetoric of mediation entirely. Later in this section, Wicquefort notes that Dutch ambassadors, when writing back to the states general, specify that they are writing from their princes' houses "pas tant parce qu'elles [leurs Hautes Puissances, the States General] font la dépense de l'Ambassade, & payent le loyer de la Maison, que principalement parce que c'est leur representant qui y est logé" (not so much because the States General pays for the embassy's rent and its expenditures, but rather because it is their representative who is lodged there).[78] Such a remark indicates the extent to which this older language of representation, which almost completely excludes diplomatic initiative or creativity, is resistant to newer forms of representation and delegation based more upon the payment of fees. The diplomat, like his servant, is seen not as an employee of the monarch (or of the ambassador) but rather as an *instrument* of his power. Ironically, this latter relation, which would seem to emphasize the dependence of the ambassador on the sovereign, could also be interpreted (as Wicquefort did, eagerly) as allowing for a certain mimetic imitation of the prince's authority to an extent that a paid employee could never attain.

If Wicquefort's discussion of the diplomatic residence concludes as to its inviolability but bases this conclusion on a fundamentally ambiguous idea of its "really" being the prince's house (not through ownership, but through representation), his attention to the issue of servants is no less complex. His language concerning the diplomat's obligation to take attacks on his staff personally strongly resembles that of Hotman but with the elision of key markers of ambiguity, most notably Hotman's "comme si": "L'Ambassadeur est d'autant plus particulierement obligé à proteger ses Domestiques, qu'on ne leur sçauroit faire outrage, qu'on ne le fasse à sa personne mesme" (the ambassador is all the more obligated to protect his servants since outrage cannot be done to them without being done to the ambassador's very person).[79] Like his initial pronouncements regarding the ambassador's residence, Wicquefort's words here suggest an *identity* between the diplomat and his servants, a position quite consistent with his wish to establish a strong representational relation between the diplomat and his prince, wherein an offense to the ambassador is clearly and unambiguously an attack on the prince himself (a position quite useful to someone sitting in prison for his diplomatic activities, as Wicquefort's critics pointed out). Wicquefort approvingly cites, in defense of this position, Louis XIV's reaction to the violence inflicted upon the Duc de Créquy in Rome, an event that I will discuss more at length in chapter 4. Yet it is fascinating to note that in discussing the question of whether the ambassador, as representative of his sovereign, can enjoy the right of punishment and justice abroad, Wicquefort states, "Le Souverain mesme *n'est qu'une personne particuliere,* & n'a point de Jurisdiction dans le territoire d'autruy; de sorte qu'il semble que son representant ne la sçauroit pretendre non plus" (The sovereign himself *is only an individual,* and has no jurisdiction in the territory of others, so that it seems that his representative cannot claim it either).[80]

Indeed, it would seem that the question of diplomatic immunity and rights abroad is another one of those issues that confounds the carefully constructed hierarchy of sovereignty and its representatives. As I have already shown, the rights accorded to the ambassador *specifically* demand a firm definition of how the ambassador differs from any other subject of the prince who is abroad. A bit earlier in his text, Wicquefort tries to accomplish this differentiation through a careful discussion of the *droit des gens,* or *ius gentium,* that applies to ambassadors and is separate from the larger *droit naturel* and the more local, state-bound *droit civil.* This deployment of *ius gentium,* defined as comprised of the consent of all the peoples of the earth, with no single sovereign as its author, liberates the diplomat from both his country's civil law (as well as that of the country in which he resides) and the anachronistic sacrality that, according to Wicquefort, limited the observations of earlier theorists. Once this distinction is made between the three levels of law, the questions pertaining to the diplomat's possible punishment are easy to resolve; the ambassador can only be punished if he violates natural law through violence or the *ius gentium* itself through treason, although in the latter case Wicquefort slyly acknowledges some ambiguity as to whether one should punish the diplomat or the prince who sent him. Yet once again, the extension of the protection of the *droit des gens* to the diplomat's entourage, his house, and his property continued to pose problems to theorists well into the eighteenth century.

It is therefore worthwhile to take a quick look at the Dutchman Bynkershoek's treatise on inviolability, even though it lies outside of the period of this study. The French translation, by Jean Barbeyrac, the popularizer of Grotius and Pufendorf, was not published until 1723, well after the Treaty of Utrecht had solidified many changes in diplomatic theory and practice. Yet the content of this treatise shows us what theorists such as Hotman and Wicquefort were trying to protect in their often convoluted and self-contradictory analyses of the subject.

Bynkershoek's treatise, perhaps unsurprisingly given the gap that Adair points out between theory and practice on these matters, was written in response to a sticky legal question. In 1720, an envoy from the Duke of Holstein went into debt in Holland, and his assets were seized. Bynkershoek's work, in the original Dutch, was first published in 1721. Unlike most of the seventeenth-century theorists, Bynkershoek eschews careful distinctions between ambassadors, legates, envoys, and nuncios (as well as between resident and "extraordinary" diplomats), arguing that they are all essentially the same. He follows the representative doctrine of diplomacy in deciding to analyze the difficult question of what happens to sovereigns who travel or reside in other states, with the goal of later applying his conclusions to diplomats themselves. Yet within this discussion, another distinction breaks down. If sovereigns who travel retain their rights over their subjects at home, this is not quantifiably different from anybody else who travels for a short amount of time: "Que si l'on n'a point prétendu changer de domicile, quelque peu de séjour qu'on fait dans un Païs Etranger ne suffit pas pour établir une Jurisdiction compétente, à laquelle on soit soûmis: & c'est le cas où se trouvent ordinairement les Voiageurs & même ceux qui ne sont que simples Particuliers" (That if one has not claimed to have changed residence, any stay that one makes in a foreign country, no matter how small, is not sufficient to establish competent jurisdiction, to which one is obligated; this is the case where, ordinarily, travelers and even those who are simple private citizens find themselves).[81] Indeed, Bynkershoek's treatise soon becomes an argument justifying the seizure and perhaps death—although he does note that "que si l'on en vient jusqu'à lui ôter la vie, je voudrois que ce fût comme dans une espéce de mêlée, plûtôt que par une procédure judiciaire" (if it comes to taking his life, I would prefer that it occur in a fight rather than through judicial proceedings)[82]—of a sovereign engaged in crimes while abroad, an argument that he correctly envisions could lead to a defense of the right of subjects of a tyrant to overthrow their ruler.

If such a sovereign is, in fact, not put to death, it is because of the respect that the people have for his character. Bynkershoek goes on to ask whether the same respect applies to that sovereign's property abroad: "Si quelcun, pour disputer, s'avisoit de dire, que les Chiens, les Chevaux, & autres choses encore moindres, qui appartenoient à un Empereur Romain, étoient par cela seul regardées autrefois comme Sacrées; il s'exposera à la risée, & ne mériteroit pas qu'on lui répondît sérieusement. D'ailleurs ce qu'il y a de *Sacré* dans le caractére des Ambassadeurs, & dont on parle avec tant d'emphase, n'est pas, à mon avis, la raison pourquoi ils sont exemts de toute Jurisdiction du païs où ils exercent leurs fonctions" (If someone, for the sake of argument, tried to say that dogs, horses and other things even smaller that belonged to the Roman Emperor were for that reason alone seen as sacred, he would be laughed at, and would not deserve to be taken seriously. Besides, what is sacred in the ambassadors' character, and which is spoken of with so much gravity, is not, in my opinion, the reason they are exempt from all jurisdiction of the country where they exercise their functions).[83] Indeed, ambassadors might be regarded as sacred, a term that Bynkershoek promptly divorces from the church by finding its origin in Roman law, which defines sacred by "ce qui est mis à couvert de toute injure & toute insulte des Hommes" (that which is protected from all human injury and insult),[84] but this sacrality is meaningless in practice. In any case, Bynkershoek argues, bringing someone before a court is not the same as doing violence to that person. All of this leads to the conclusion that the ambassador is no different from any other subject of a foreign prince, and the privileges he enjoys are in no way specific to his station.

Such a doctrine would have stunned Wicquefort, who spent so much ink defending and defining the unique position and qualities of the diplomat. Yet Bynkershoek defends his position by citing in a footnote the new theories of Stephanus Cassius, who takes the idea of diplomatic representation to its (il)logical conclusion:

Cela est absolument nécessaire, dans les principes même de ce nouvel Auteur, qui étend si loin l'effet de cette représentation, qu'il prétend que l'Ambassadeur, comme tel, & pendant qu'il est revêtu du caractére, ne peut pas même être puni par son Prince; parce, dit-il, qu'en même tems qu'il est devenu Ambassadeur, & Représentant de la Nation, il a cessé d'être Sujet, & est devenu aussi independent que la Nation même, qui peut néanmoins, en le rappellant, & lui ôtant le caractére, le faire rentrer dans son état de sujettion. Je doute que de pareilles idées fassent fortune, avec quelque confiance qu'on les propose.[85]

[This is absolutely necessary, according to the very principles of this new author, who stretches the effects of this representation so far that he claims that the ambassador, as such, and while he carries his character, cannot even be punished by his prince, since, he says, at the same time he becomes ambassador and representative of the nation, he has ceased to be a subject, and has become as independent as the nation itself, which can, nonetheless, recall him, take away his character and make him return to his state of subject. I doubt that such ideas will be very successful, no matter how confidently they are proposed.]

Due in part to the contradictions inherent in theories of mediation at the time, we are left with a situation in which the two alternatives are either an exaggerated representative doctrine, where the "comme si" marking the relation between prince and diplomat is elided and the line between sovereign and diplomat disappears, or a doctrine in which the ambassador's privileges are almost indistinguishable from those of any other foreigner.

Bynkershoek's sympathies for the latter position lead him to condemn repeatedly diplomatic practice under Louis XIV, who, as I will argue in chapter 4, took the idea of diplomatic representation very seriously indeed. The Dutchman condemns Louis XIV's refusal to allow the elector of Brandenburg to send more than one diplomat to the negotiations at Nijmegen. One may presume that Louis XIV's interpretation of the strict representational relation between sovereign and diplomat would preclude the possibility that the unity of the monarch or prince be represented by several ambassadors, a question that Wicquefort treats as well. Bynkershoek also rejects Louis XIV's rule, unique in Europe, that foreigners cannot be used to represent France abroad: "Je ne vois pas non plus, pourquoi on ne pourroit pas être Sujet en même tems de deux Etats distincts, dont chacun est Souverain & indépendant" (I fail to see how one cannot be the subject of two distinct states, each of which is sovereign and independent, simultaneously).[86] Finally, in the last pages of the treatise, he alludes contemptuously to the common French belief that diplomats have the right to punish their servants abroad, a position, as we have seen, that even Wicquefort dismisses (albeit at the cost of equating the sovereign with a "personne particulière").

This survey of doctrines of exterritoriality as they unfolded throughout the seventeenth century and into the eighteenth century demonstrates the pull of practical considerations on the most elaborate theoretical constructions. Exterritoriality invariably leads the theorist to examine precisely how the diplomat differs from any other person, a discussion that leads imperceptibly to the more dangerous question of how sovereigns themselves justify their exemption from the laws that bind their subjects. Moreover, a monarch such as Louis XIV, who wished to impose his interpretation of diplomacy upon the international stage, could do so, but he had to confront the reality that diplomacy is, essentially, a matter of *betweenness,* of dialogue. The strongest interpretations of diplomacy as the representation of the sovereign's will and wishes had to resist the centrifugal force of the other half of diplomacy, which depended upon the sovereign to whom the diplomat was sent. Louis XIV's efforts to do just this form the basis of chapter 4; for now it is enough to note that it is unsurprising that the most fractures in the representational theory of diplomacy appear in discussions of exterritoriality and inviolability, since these issues deal almost exclusively with the rights and role of the ambassador while out of his sovereign's reach.

Diplomatic Dispatches

The role of the diplomat in transmitting information was no less complex and difficult to define adequately than his identity. Indeed, the latter in some sense merely renders manifest the contradictions inherent in the ambassador's representative role. Like the actor, the diplomat is given a script—his instructions—that must be repeated as faithfully as possible. We may recall de Vera's recommendation, albeit nuanced, that the ambassador go so far as to imitate the gestures and tone of voice of the sovereign who sends him; this radical imitation marks both the complete subservience of the diplomat to his master's instructions and the menacing duplication of the sovereign prince— menacing in that the definition of sovereignty rests precisely on its uniqueness and inimitability—through a representation, likened to that performed by the actor, that can carry connotations of idolatry or even blasphemy. Yet the idea that such faithful representations of the prince's instructions represents, as it were, the zero degree of the ambassador's function is present in the frequent recommendations, in these treatises, to stray as little from instructions as possible. Hotman recommends "qu'autant qu'il luy sera possible il employe les paroles, termes, raisons, et conclusions portées par son instruction, buttant tousjours à la volonté de son Maistre" (as much as possible, [the diplomat] should use the words, terms, reasons and conclusions carried in his instruction, hewing always to his master's will).[87] Yet these recommendations, as I have shown regarding de Vera, are almost always immediately followed by recognition of the diplomat's independence, of his fundamental difference from a herald who is charged with delivering a message verbatim and leaving immediately afterward.[88] The significance of the model of the actor is that it permits a characterization of the ambassador that both gives him a script, as it were, and allows him room for an otherwise troubling improvisation. As I will show later in my discussion of the problem of mediation in seventeenth-century French theater, no one ever attributed a play's authorship to the actor.

Whether to follow instructions, then, even for the theorists most concerned with establishing the ambassador's unique skills and, therefore, independence from his sovereign, is not open to debate. Every ambassador leaves his sovereign with script in hand, and this question is thus rather easy to resolve. Instead, it is in these treatises' recommendations concerning the sending of information *from* the foreign court to the sovereign that the profound ambiguity of the ambassador's role begins to emerge. It is not coincidental that such reports, or *dépêches,* became an issue as the institution of the resident ambassador took permanent hold in Europe, since the diplomat sent to live at a foreign court is arguably there precisely to provide such information to the prince (and not primarily to deliver a message from his prince to the state in which he resides). Here, once again, diplomatic practice seems to outstrip theory, since examples of diplomatic dispatches existed independently of the theorists' (and the ministers of the home states') efforts to control and define their content. This was all the more the case given the considerable time that it took for instructions to reach ambassadors in the field; the demands of seventeenth-century travel were such that some improvisation on the part of the diplomat was necessary. The Venetians were (and still are) rightly regarded as the masters of the diplomatic *relazioni,* and the many theorists who would settle on the Frenchmen d'Ossat and Jeannin, both of whom served Henri IV in extremely complex diplomatic negotiations, as the models of letter writing to follow had an almost limitless body of texts from which to construct their canon.

The diplomatic dispatch was of particular interest to the theorists discussed here, however, because it was the terrain upon which the ambassador could insert some sort of his own authorship. Dispatches reveal the diplomat's own interpretation of what details are noteworthy or important to his master back home. If the message delivered in great style and ceremony approached the ambassador to his prince externally, in appearance, the writing of the dispatch represented a moment in which the diplomat literally put himself in the place of the sovereign, judging which details were important enough to note and which were superfluous. To do this, he had to place himself *mentally* in the position of a sovereign who often either had hidden motives in sending him or who was fully aware (as the diplomat was often not) of what was going on in other courts simultaneously.

The ideological sensitivity of the dispatch, then, led theorists to weigh in on the manner in which it should be written and conceived. De Vera notes that the dispatch should contain observations of the foreign king and his character as well as geographical notes. More realistic writers realized the trickiness of the dispatch; Gentili treats its nature in the context of the successful diplomat's need for prudence, "for [the ambassador] is not merely thought of as a bearer of messages, but is also called a *judge of affairs,* and . . . ambassadors are the ears and eyes of their government."[89] Gentili's discomfort with granting the ambassador a certain sovereignty of judgment explains what follows: "we hear of many ambassadors whose instructions included directions to play the part of spy, and find out everything possible about the affairs of the sovereign to whom they were accredited. . . . Why do Venetian ambassadors fail to acknowledge this openly, since it is their custom on returning from an embassy to omit mention of nothing which pertains to the state in which they have been serving as ambassadors?"[90] Gentili's overall discomfort with the still-recent institution of resident ambassadors—an institution of which he approves, as long as residents are used to save time and money in the treating of specific affairs, and not as spies, "who betray international law"[91]—leads him to confront the unsettling nature of the famous Venetian *relazioni*. At what point is careful observation the implementation of the doctrine that ambassadors are the eyes and ears of their government, and at what point is it spying? Gentili resolves this problem not only by exhorting the ambassador to follow the Christian virtues of prudence, temperance, and fidelity and by tracing his origin to the sacred mission of angels but also by severely restricting the ambassador's freedom, denying him the ability to treat matters for which he is unauthorized. His strong terms are worth citing here: "Nevertheless, inasmuch as the understanding on which the ambassador has been admitted does not include recognition of authority to transact other business in addition to that which is to be transacted with him to whom he has come, any hostile act, as I have said, will be not only contrary to his duty, but also contrary to law. Moreover, not having been sent to any person in regard to the other business, he is not an ambassador so far as that business is concerned."[92] This purism regarding the diplomat's representative function and reduced capacity for observation and action undertaken on his own initiative is, as might be expected, modified a bit later, when Gentili states that "he should know also how to do things, the performance of which, although they have not been assigned to him and do not immediately concern his embassy, may still be useful both to himself and his sovereign."[93] Yet this limited acknowledgment of the dictates imposed by the realities of living at a foreign court where modified instructions or assignments arrive much later than needed does not change Gentili's generally idealistic view of diplomacy. We cannot and should not expect him to provide a detailed account of how to write a diplomatic dispatch or of what it should contain; however, the absence of such information is significant in his text.

Jean Hotman does, however, treat the diplomatic dispatch specifically, toward the end of his treatise. For Hotman, the dispatch is the main opportunity for the diplomat to signal his own work and importance. His assertion that "on ne sçait le plus souvent ce que fait un Ambassadeur en sa charge que par ce que luy mesme en escrit" (often one only knows of what the ambassador is doing in his position through what he himself writes)[94] reveals the struggle of the diplomat against a royal court or administration only too willing to attribute the outcome of negotiations to the prince or his ministers. The ambassador's near-invisibility is also alluded to in the sentence that follows: "les choses ne valent que ce qu'on les fait valoir: il fera bien de se faire paroistre par ses depesches, lesquelles sont veuës & considerees par les Secretaires d'Estat, leuës au conseil & representees au Prince selon le merite du sujet" (things being worth only what they are made to seem, one must appear through one's dispatches, which are seen and considered by Secretaries of State, read in council and represented to the prince according to the merit of the subject).[95] The dispatch therefore appears as the chief opening for the diplomat to assert his own style and his responsibility for the events taking place abroad. It should be noted, however, that Hotman's language is in keeping with the relative freedom accorded diplomats during this period by their masters, as well as with the practice of governing through ministers. At the turn of the seventeenth century, ambassadors such as Cardinal d'Ossat and President Jeannin were able to distinguish themselves—and their dispatches, which were deemed models of diplomatic correspondence throughout the seventeenth century—through their service to a king, Henri IV, whose oversight concerning matters of state was largely delegated to figures such as Sully. Indeed, d'Ossat's status as model diplomat, enhanced by his rather humble origins and the fact that at the beginning of negotiations with Rome he was not the ambassador (du Perron was) but only a secretary, lies as much with his role in reconciling Henri IV and the pope, despite the French king's conversion and divorce, as it does with his style. As may be expected, however, the former exploits are never mentioned explicitly. Praising d'Ossat's style (as well as that of Jeannin, who was instrumental in defusing Spanish support for the Catholic League becomes a means of acknowledging these diplomats' roles in the restoration of the French monarchy without attributing to them authorship per se.

In this context, then, roughly contemporaneous with his treatise, Hotman's assertion that the dispatch is the means for the diplomat to "make himself known" or "appear" seems particularly astute. He sees the diplomatic report as almost exclusively positive, restricting further remarks to recommendations on style and method. This is perhaps due to his view of diplomacy as essentially representative rather than residential: the diplomat writes back to his court reports concerning "affaires" instead of sending descriptions of the foreign court, which Gentili rightly viewed as inherently problematic in that they blur the line between diplomat and spy. This representational interpretation of diplomatic function is further supported by Hotman's recommendation that "Mesme si le service du Maistre le peut souffrir, j'aimeroy mieux ne faire nouvelle depesche que je n'eusse response à la precedente" (even if the service of the prince permits it, I would wait for a response to my previous dispatch before composing a new one).[96] Writing only in response to information or letters from his home court, Hotman's ambassador remains firmly tied to specific "affaires" or subjects and less likely to veer off into unsolicited (and therefore politically suspect, to the court in which he resides) observation.

Wicquefort, as might be expected, devotes a section of the second "functions" volume of his treatise to "lettres et depesches." His general eagerness to point out the importance of the ambassador explains this topic's attractiveness to him. Like Hotman, he perceives the dispatch as the essential means by which the diplomat makes his role and presence known to his home court. Wicquefort holds that the most important advice to give the writing diplomat is that "qu'il s'accommode en cela à l'humeur & à la volonté de son Maistre" (he should accommodate himself to the personality and will of his master).[97] By calling this a "universal rule," Wicquefort shows a certain amount of irony; the form of dispatches is far from universal (in fact, their very existence attests to the specificity of events and issues) and will therefore be determined chiefly by the specific character and interests of the sending prince. There follows the by now standard instructions to make dispatches as terse and clear as possible, writing more "choses" than "paroles." Yet once again, Wicquefort asserts that rules are difficult to establish for the ambassador, whose status as a mediator between sovereigns but also between intention and effect renders him an ill-defined personage whose duty it is to respond to contingency and context. On the addressee of the letters and their content, as well as on the question of when to allow the secretary to take care of the correspondence, Wicquefort states, "Sur toutes ces choses il n'y a point de regles à donner; parce que c'est à l'Ambassadeur, qui peut seul juger de l'importance de l'affaire, & de la curiosité ou de l'interest de son Prince, à s'en consulter luy mesme" (In all these matters there are no rules to give, since the ambassador, who alone can judge the importance of the affair and the curiosity or interest of his prince, should follow his own advice).[98]

This statement reveals the way in which the dispatch becomes a signifier of the ambassador's unique role and power. In order to perform his function well, the diplomat must put himself in the place of the monarch in a way that goes well beyond the performance recommended by de Vera, a performance better suited to the extraordinary ambassador who arrives at a foreign court "merely" to deliver a message from his sovereign. Wicquefort's resident ambassador, the writer of dispatches, is the only person capable of weighing the importance of events transpiring at the court at which he resides, and this judgment, combined with an almost unseemly knowledge of his prince's best interests, is what determines the content of the dispatch. In a certain sense, then, the ambassador exercises sovereignty in place of the prince, far beyond what is contained in his instructions. The dispatch, in Wicquefort, represents the slippage of representation from carrying out specific tasks—an essentially dependent model of representation—to the more active, mimetic role of actually filtering the information that the prince receives. Not only should the diplomat maintain correspondence with all of his country's representatives in other states (acting, then, as a de facto minister of state of sorts), but, despite the earlier recommendation to write "things" rather than "words," he continually substitutes his own judgment for that of his master. He is far from a disinterested observer, reporting events for his prince to consider in his council; rather, in the act of writing, in choosing what to write, he is sovereign, council, and diplomat all at the same time: "L'Ambassadeur ne peut pas estre trop reservé à escrire des nouvelles, soit generales ou particulieres. Il doit estre fort ponctuel à mander celles qui parviennent jusques à sa connoissance; mais il doit bien distinguer entre les douteuses & les certaines, de peur que meslant de fausses avec de veritables, la fausseté des unes ne détruise la croyance qu'on doit aux autres" (The ambassador cannot be too reserved in the writing of news, either general or particular. He should be punctual in sending news that comes to his knowledge, but he should distinguish between doubtful and certain information, for fear that in mixing false information with true the falsehood of the ones may destroy the belief that one owes to the others).[99] Realist novelists of the nineteenth century were no less careful in their own construction of objectivity and believability while obscuring their own role in the presentation of their information.

Indeed, one of the reasons Wicquefort holds up the Cardinal d'Ossat as a model for the writing of dispatches is his ability to hide his own role while ingeniously presenting his information. Take, for example, the following illustration of the cardinal's gifts of depiction:

> Le Cardinal Dossat est fort exact a remarquer celles de toutes les audiances, où il a eu des affaires importantes à negotier: jusques à observer les sousris, la mine & les gestes du Pape Clement VIII, afin que le Roy pust d'autant mieux juger des pensées & des intentions de sa Sainteté: le ton de la voix, la chaleur ou l'indifference de son discours & toutes les circonstances qui pouvoient faire juger, si les paroles estoient estudiées, ou naturelles: ce qui marque la sincerité ou découvre l'artifice & fait distinguer les compliments d'avec les expressions sinceres.[100]

[Cardinal d'Ossat is quite precise in noting all of the audiences where he had important affairs to negotiate, going so far as to observe the smiles, the air and the gestures of Pope Clement VIII, so that the king could judge the pope's thoughts and intentions: the tone of voice, the warmth or indifference of his discourse and all other circumstances that can help to indicate whether the words were studied or natural, which marks sincerity or indicates artifice and helps distinguish compliments from sincere expressions.]

On the one hand, this would seem to be high praise of d'Ossat's ability to remain objective, to describe events exactly as he sees or experiences them, especially as this passage is followed by a recommendation to the ambassador to keep his own feelings out of his dispatches. On the other, however, it is further proof of the indispensability of the ambassador, who alone is in a position to observe the things that d'Ossat observes here. Although Wicquefort carefully words this passage so as to give the capacity of judgment to the king rather than to his representative, in the context of Wicquefort's larger goal of gaining recognition for the diplomat's too-often neglected talents it is clear that he is also showing how d'Ossat, while ostensibly keeping his own judgment and emotion out of the scene, in fact conveys it to the prince through the details he chooses to transcribe. When the king receives the dispatch, the judgment of the pope's sincerity or artifice has already been made. It should be noted that Wicquefort also approvingly cites an instance in which d'Ossat accompanies his transcription of a particularly harsh speech by the pope with details that work against the words' sense, thereby mitigating the pope's anger.

The diplomatic dispatch therefore represents particularly well the predicament of the ambassador. It is a practical example of the tensions pulling at any treatise that would discuss the diplomat in and of himself. On the one hand, the diplomat is the representative of his prince, handed a script—the instructions, or a message—that he should read as faithfully as possible. On the other hand, with the prince's natural curiosity regarding the success of the mission, but also with the rise of the institution of the residential ambassador, the diplomat must report back to his home court, and this time without clear guidance as to what to say. Here, his independence, and his fundamental resemblance to his master not in his person but rather in terms of his judgment and ability to weigh the importance of events and determine their truth or falsehood, comes into play. Perhaps more troubling than the adoption of the prince's tone of voice and gestures described by de Vera is the adoption *of the prince's point of view,* which is supposedly unique.[101] Even if the ambassador absents himself emotionally and personally from his report, the mark of the necessity of his presence is evident in each detail chosen for inclusion in the dispatch.

Control of diplomatic dispatches was therefore paramount if the sovereign wished to minimize the importance of the ambassador while portraying himself as the observer and author of international events. While I will present a fuller description of Callières's diplomatic theory as a fundamental break with Louis XIV's diplomatic practice in my conclusion, a few remarks on Callières and his countryman Rousseau de Chamoy, author of *De l'idée du parfait ambassadeur,* are appropriate here insofar as their goals for diplomatic dispatches differ significantly from those of Wicquefort.

Rousseau de Chamoy's *De l'idée du parfait ambassadeur* can hardly be called a treatise; rather, it resembles an instructional pamphlet, written to instruct a general about to be sent as ambassador to London. Its writer served as Pomponne's secretary during his embassy to Sweden. It is one the very few examples of diplomatic theory written during Louis XIV's reign. Callières's *De la manière de négocier avec les souverains* is often accorded status as a shining example of ancien régime diplomatic theory as well as a foundational text for modern diplomacy, although Maurice Keens-Soper finds the latter claim dubious. As I will argue in my conclusion, however, its publication a year after Louis XIV's death (although it was written in the 1690s and presumably revised during the War of the Spanish Succession in the first years of the eighteenth century) as well as certain aspects of its content mark it as a significant *criticism* of much of Louis XIV's diplomatic theory and practice. It is therefore of minimal use in determining the form that Louis XIV's diplomacy often took, especially in the first years of his personal reign, and much more useful as a document of the profound disillusionment of many French officials with the sovereign's foreign policy during the last years of the reign (1690–1715).

That said, certain aspects of its phrasing are quite different from other diplomatic treatises of the period and match well with Rousseau de Chamoy. The main area where this is true concerns diplomatic correspondence. If almost all writers used the section on the dispatch to point up the skills and necessity of the ambassador, the French writers do not. Rather, when speaking of the dispatch, they make more references to the presence of the sovereign than that of the diplomat. Rousseau de Chamoy's instructions to the diplomat read as follows: "Par cette description aussy vive qu'exacte et fidèle, [l'ambassadeur] rendra son Maistre et ses ministes comme présents à tout ce qui y aura esté dit, il les mettra en estat de luy donner des ordres, *comme s'ils y avaient eu part eux-mesmes*" (Through this description as lively as it is exact and just, the ambassador renders his master and his ministers as if present at everything that he recounts, he places them in a position to give him orders *as if they were participating in these events themselves*).[102] Nowhere in this passage is the role of the diplomat in the writing of the dispatch—his necessary skill, judgment, and powers of observation—alluded to. The foreign court emerges as an already-written text that the ambassador must faithfully *transcribe*. Wicquefort's rather sophisticated reading of the trickery needed to establish an objectivity that never really exists is replaced by the alignment of the dispatch with the ambassador's strictly representational capacity. If the diplomat imitating the tone of voice and gestures of his prince is one way of making the sovereign "seem" present at the foreign court, the dispatch is not a contradiction of this principle but merely an extension of it. As such, it becomes a signifier not of the sovereign's absence (and therefore his need for diplomatic representation) but of his presence. The sovereign, not the ambassador, is the participant and observer of the events abroad. Rousseau de Chamoy's opinion, stated almost immediately after the passage cited above, that the diplomat should only rarely state his private opinions, since "les Princes raisonnant souvent sur des principes qui sont inconnus [à l'ambassadeur], ces refléxions ne leur plaisent pas toujours, et ils croyent avec raison qu'on leur doit laisser le soin" (princes, who often reason according to principles that are unknown to the ambassador, do not always like such reflections, and they believe, with reason, that such judgments should be left to themselves),[103] only further marks the diplomat's constant dependence on the higher knowledge and wisdom of his prince. This quotation should be read in direct contrast to Wicquefort's recommendation that the diplomat maintain relations with the prince's representatives in other countries; such advice would be unthinkable to an ambassador serving under Louis XIV.

Although Callierès joins Wicquefort in noting that the ambassador's role is directly linked to what the prince *cannot* do himself, his remarks concerning dispatches are strikingly similar to those of his earlier counterpart, Rousseau de Chamoy. Callières exhorts the ambassador to convey information "d'une manière si claire et si ressemblante que le prince, ou le ministre qui reçoit les dépêches puissent connaître aussi distinctement l'état des choses dont il lui rend compte, *que s'il étoit lui-même sur les lieux*" (in a manner so clear and life-like that the prince, or the minister who receives his dispatches, can know the state of things that is reported as well as *if he himself was there*).[104] Again, the idea that language can perfectly represent the object described appears here, and again the idea that such language can create the illusion of the sovereign's presence on the scene is expressed. Why does such a difference between the members of the French diplomatic corps and their European counterparts exist?

Assuming that we can infer such a difference through the evidence provided by only two treatises, we can attribute it to two factors. On the one hand, the ideal of French classicism often implied that language, especially the French language, was capable of transparency, of the exact and faithful representation of the objects described. Although this ideal was widespread during the seventeenth century, Bouhours's praise of good language, and the French language in particular, is worth citing here: "Le beau langage ressemble à une eau pure et nette qui n'a point de goût, qui coule de source, qui va où sa pente naturelle la porte, et non pas à ces eaux artificielles qu'on fait venir avec violence dans les jardins des grands et qui y font mille différentes figures" (Beautiful language resembles pure and clear water that has no taste, that comes directly from the source, that goes where its natural inclination takes it, and does not resemble those artificial waters that are conveyed with violence in princes' gardens and that take on thousands of different shapes).[105] Bouhours goes on to argue that French is particularly suited to this type of neutral expression: "la langue française est peut-être la seule qui suive exactement l'ordre naturel et qui exprime les pensées en la manière qu'elles naissent dans l'esprit" (the French language is perhaps the only one that follows natural order exactly and that expresses thoughts in the manner that they appear in the mind).[106] Bouhours's picture of perfect language is not at all out of line with Bodin's critical view of Budé's model of eloquence, the *Hercule gaulois*. Simplicity, but mainly the exactitude of representation—either of thoughts or of external details—is placed well above any kind of attention to the means of expression itself. The neutral clarity and purity of water evokes the complete transparency of communication. Boileau said nothing less when he exhorted poets to privilege sense over rhyme in their work, condemning any aspect of language that would draw attention to itself.

It is therefore not surprising that French writers on diplomacy downplayed the activity contributed by the ambassador. Like language itself (and indeed, this is the recommendation for the diplomat's language in his dispatches, which should be more full of things than of words), the ambassador should strive toward transparency and invisibility. His role is merely to facilitate the presence of the monarch at the foreign court, even in residential situations where this representation is less clear-cut. In a situation directly opposed to that aspired to by Wicquefort, the French ambassador is most successful when his contributions are noted the least, a near-impossible situation that I will discuss at length in chapter 4. Callières, a prominent member of the Académie Française who weighed in on the subject of the quarrel of the ancients and the moderns, would have been keenly aware of the official position regarding linguistic representation; it is therefore not so surprising to see a translation of this principle in his recommendations regarding the diplomat's written communications to his sovereign.[107]

Another contributing factor to the distinctive tone of Rousseau de Chamoy's and Callières's diplomatic writing is the actual policy of Louis XIV regarding dispatches. As the next chapter will show, Louis XIV exerted an unheard-of personal control over his diplomats, largely through their correspondence. As Camille-Georges Picavet notes in his masterful study of diplomacy under Louis XIV, in 1661 the monarch instituted the practice of double correspondence, asking his ambassadors to write one letter directly to himself and another to the *secrétaire d'état*. This seeming concession to the diplomat's judgment was in practice a means of controlling the diplomat even more, since the separation of information into that worthy of being communicated to the king directly and that which should instead go to the *secrétaire d'état* invited constant criticism. As Picavet tells us, Jacques-Auguste de Thou, the French ambassador in Holland, was reprimanded for including too many details in his letters, while a few years later, the king reproached his representatives for not writing enough. The resultant difficulty of the diplomat's position, always caught off guard in the seemingly simple assignment of describing all events tersely and clearly, is evident in the following letter sent by Feuquières, the French ambassador to Sweden, to the king: "Pour ce qui est des particularités ... je m'y étendrai désormais davantage sans m'attribuer le discernement de ce qui importera à votre service, espérant que Votre Majesté excusera la superfluité qui se trouvera" (Regarding details . . . I will provide more of them without attributing to myself the judgment of what is important to your service, hoping that Your Majesty will excuse the superfluities that this method entails).[108] French diplomacy, then, was one of the main areas in which the ideal of perfect representation and the mediation of royal authority collided violently with the practical demands of the ambassador's position. To fully understand this collision and its intimate relation with the doctrine of divine right monarchy carefully articulated and practiced throughout the century, we must now turn once again to the theorists discussed at the beginning of this work.

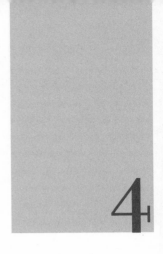

REPRESENTING THE SUN:
DIPLOMATIC THEORY AND
PRACTICE UNDER LOUIS XIV

Although the texts analyzed in the previous chapter show that describing and defining the ambassador adequately was difficult throughout Europe and for some time before the seventeenth century, the treatment of ambassadors under Louis XIV, especially during the first years of his personal reign, merits special attention. If the rest of Europe was proceeding toward a secularized view of diplomacy based on the *droit des gens,* French theory and practice was somewhat different. Having established the monarch as not merely another secular leader but as a divine right sovereign uniquely legitimized through the divine, theorists were able to reconcile sixteenth-century diplomatic sacrality with more recent representational theories. In other words, the French diplomat's status as instrument of his sovereign's authority was seen not as a concession to European practice but as a parallel to the monarch's own status as image of God on earth.

This peculiar characteristic of the diplomat under Louis XIV may go a long way in explaining the relative absence of French theoretical diplomatic texts during the second half of the seventeenth century. Any attention paid to the particular gifts of the ambassador would detract from the king's idealized position as sole agent and engineer of foreign policy. Indeed, to find theoretical reflections on the ambassador, we must return to the treatises on sovereignty analyzed in chapter 1. These treatises demonstrate that the question of the diplomat was often mixed in with the larger question of ministers and that the role of these representatives of the king provided an acute challenge to carefully articulated accounts of the relation between the king and God.

Despite the relative absence of French diplomatic treatises produced during his reign, it is clear, and perhaps not surprising, that diplomacy was one of the areas of government that most preoccupied Louis XIV and in which he took the most pride. Evidence of this can be found not only in the *Mémoires pour l'instruction du dauphin* but also in his rather striking decision to personally read and respond to his diplomats' dispatches from the field.[1] In the fall of 1661, Hugues de Lionne, Louis XIV's minister for foreign affairs, in a letter addressed to the Comte d'Estrades, the king's ambassador to England, expresses his admiration of his sovereign's personal interest in diplomacy as well as his astonishment at its sincerity. The letter is worth quoting at length:

> Ceux qui ont cru que nostre Maistre se lasseroit bien tost des affaires se sont bien abusez, puis que plus nous allons en avant, et plus il prend de plaisir a s'y appliquer, et a s'y donner tout entier. Vous en trouverez une preuve bien convainquante dans la Depesche que je vous adresse cy jointe, ou vous verrez la resolution que S.M. a prise de respondre Ellemesme a toutes les lettres de ses Ambassadeurs sur les Affaires les plus Importantes et les plus secretes: Et de leur escrire mesme directement, quand il naistra icy des occasions de cette nature, comme elle commence aujourdhuy a le faire avec vous. C'est une pensée qui luy est venue de son propre mouvement, et vous jugez bien que personne n'auroit esté asses hardy pour oser luy proposer de se donner une si grande peine. Le motif qu'Elle a eu en cela est digne de beaucoup de louanges, et doit donner a ses sujets fideles et zelez, tels que nous sommes, une consolation infinie. Car il n'est autre, monsieur, que pour s'instruire mieux de toutes les affaires: estre capable de toutes par luy seul, plustost que par le ministere et le service d'autruy, et entrer plus avant dans tout le detail. Voila comme se forment les grands Roys, et je ne scay si depuis que la France est Monarchie, il y a eu aucun Roy, qui ait voulu prendre sur soy un si grand travail, ny plus utile, soit pour la personne du Roy mesme, ou pour le bien et la gloire de ses sujets et de son Estat.[2]

[Those who believed that our master would soon tire of business were sorely mistaken, since the further we progress, the more he takes pleasure in applying himself, and in giving himself up entirely to this business. You will find a convincing proof of this in the dispatch that I am enclosing, where you will see the resolution that His Majesty has taken to respond personally to all of his ambassadors' letters concerning the most important and most secret affairs. He will also write to his ambassadors directly, when occasions of this nature arise, as he has started doing today with you. This idea is entirely his own, as you can imagine that no one would have dared suggest that he trouble himself in this manner. The reason for these resolutions is very praiseworthy, and should give to his loyal and zealous subjects, such as we are, ample consolation. For it is none other, monsieur, than to instruct himself better of all affairs, to be capable of everything by himself alone, instead of through the ministry and service of others, and to penetrate everything in greater detail. This is how great kings are made, and I do not know if during the time that France has been a monarchy there has been any king who has wanted to take such work upon himself, nor more useful, either for the king himself or for the good and the glory of his subjects and his state.]

In this letter, Lionne ascribes the reason for this innovation in diplomatic protocol to the king's desire to take care of foreign affairs personally, without the intervention of ministers or other go-betweens. In so doing, he identifies one of the abiding tensions in Louis XIV's foreign policy, which is the need to assert the king's *authorship* of international events while acknowledging the employment of representatives of his authority—ambassadors—to carry them out. A problem for those writing about sovereignty and, not least, for those to whom these assignments were given, would be how to reconcile the absolute and personal control that the king wished to exert on events and decisions with the need, ever increasing in post–Westphalian Europe, for diplomatic representation.

MINISTERS AND DIPLOMATS IN SEVENTEENTH-CENTURY SOVEREIGNTY TREATISES

Writers who were working to elaborate a strengthened vision of royal sovereignty identified and puzzled over this tension well before Louis XIV's assertion of personal control over the state in 1661. The need for ministers or for diplomatic representation in many respects reveals the incompatibility of theory and practice in the exercise of monarchy, and almost all writers on sovereignty treated the problem in their treatises. Cardin Le Bret, in his *De la souveraineté du roy* (1632), is primarily concerned with the practicalities of administering justice throughout the kingdom; this concern is unsurprising, given his own juristic background and role in Louis XIII's government. If, on the one hand, the chapter headings of his treatise emphasize the king's role as sole source of state justice and administration, on the other hand, the magistracy and the king's ministers are identified as those who allow the king to govern while remaining untainted by the self-interest of his sinful subjects. In discussing the *droit du glaive* that the king enjoys over his subjects (which is one of the most distinctive attributes of sovereignty, but which also lays bare sovereignty's ultimate dependence on force), Le Bret supports the king's delegation of punishment to others: "Or bien que les Rois, & mêmément les nôtres n'assistent que fort rarement au jugement des crimes de leurs Sujets: neanmoins l'on ne doit pas inferer qu'ils se soient dépoüillés pour cela de leur autorité souveraine, non plus qu'on ne peut pas faire grande absurdité que Dieu se soit privé de sa puissance, sous pretexte qu'il emploïe les causes secondes pour le gouvernement & la conduite de cet Univers" (For although kings, and even our own, only rarely participate in the judgment of the crimes of their subjects; nonetheless it should not be inferred that they have, for all that, stripped themselves of their sovereign authority, no more than it can be inferred without absurdity that God has deprived himself of his power just because he employs second causes for the government and direction of this universe).[3]

This formulation clearly demonstrates the similarity between the problem of the relation of the king to those who carry out his orders and that of the relation between God and the world, including the king. If the king's actions are ultimately attributable only to God, in relation to whom the king is a mere instrument, with regard to ministers the same configuration plays out, wherein their actions are really to be seen as those of the monarch. To make the point even clearer, Le Bret moves quickly from this passage to a consideration of whether officers and magistrates may disobey the sovereign: "ce seroit renverser tout l'ordre de la Monarchie, s'il étoit permis aux Oficiers de resister aux Ordonnances du Prince, les rendre ses égaux, & même ses Superieurs: ce seroit aller contre le Precepte de l'Apôtre, qui nous enjoint expressément d'obéïr au Prince, *tanquam praecellenti;* c'est à dire sans aucune exception: si ce n'est pour les choses qui contreviennent directement aux Commandemens de Dieu" (if officers were allowed to resist the orders of the prince, or to make themselves his equal, or even his superiors, it would reverse the entire order of the monarchy and go against the precept of the Apostle, which tells us expressly to obey the prince, without any exception, unless his orders directly contravene God's commandments).[4]

This strong recommendation of obedience shows, however, that ministers and the rest of the populace are equal in their status as subjects. Just as viewing the world from the point of view of God gives the impression that the king is as much a man as the rest of humanity (a point made both by Protestant monarchomachic treatises in the sixteenth century and by Bossuet in the seventeenth century), thereby necessitating a detailed analysis, provided in part by these treatises, of exactly how the king is *different* from everyone else, considering the world from the point of view of the king produces a leveling of the differences between the ministers and the rest of the king's subjects. Such a leveling is impossible for Le Bret, himself a proud member of the government, to tolerate for long, and indeed this passage is quickly followed by one that emphasizes instead the uniqueness of those chosen to serve the king. He does this in a chapter that, unlike the others, which emphasize the powers and rights of the sovereign, marks off those of the ministers, as it is titled "De certains Droits, dont la connoissance n'apartient qu'aux Oficiers du Roi" (Of certain rights, knowledge of which belongs only to the officers of the king). Included in this chapter is the following observation: "Comme la connoissance des choses Saintes n'apartient qu'à ceux qui sont particulierement consacrés à la Divinité; de même l'on ne doit point traiter les questions qui regardent & qui concernent les Droits de la Roïauté, que devant ceux qui ont le caractere de personnes publiques, & qui ont l'honneur d'être Oficiers du Roi" (Since the knowledge of sacred things belongs only to those who are specifically consecrated to the divinity; in the same way one should not treat the questions that concern the rights of royalty in front of anyone except those who have the character of public persons, and who have the honor of being royal officers).[5] These officers, then, incarnate a sort of civil priesthood; no longer mere subjects, they have been invested as "personnes publiques." Yet their special status in turn provokes questions not unrelated to those the Protestants asked of the priesthood. Is the distinction of ministers due, at least in part, to some kind of participation in the king's inalienable power? And if not, how can this distinction be justified? Le Bret leaves the extensive treatment of these questions to others, but they will continue to haunt all efforts to characterize "public persons" during Louis XIV's reign, becoming especially difficult in the case of ambassadors, who must clothe themselves in royal dignity—far from the commanding and controlling gaze of their master—in order to perform their duties properly.

For Le Bret, writing under Louis XIII, a king who placed most of his trust and administration in Richelieu,[6] this problem is not quite as pressing as it would become after the Fronde. This relative tranquility is evident in the sections that treat diplomacy and the right to send ambassadors. While Le Bret's assertion that only sovereign princes and kings can send ambassadors is a clear movement toward the policy of Louis XIV (during the preceding century, the title of ambassador was more liberally granted, as may be seen in the Venetian envoys, who enjoyed the title of ambassador despite representing a republic), his view of the diplomats' mission is still fairly traditional. His language seems to place ambassadors in a different category from other royal officers, since he accords them a fair amount of independence as well as a unique identity: "ils sont employés pour assoupir les dissentions & les inimitiés des hommes, pour terminer les guerres que les Princes souverains se font les uns aux autres, & [. . .] ils sont choisis pour être les arbitres des diferens des Peuples & des Rois, & pour les entretenir en bonne amitié & intelligence. Aussi voïons-nous qu'ils ont été toûjours honorés de tres-grans Privileges, respectés comme Personnes saintes & sacrées" (they are employed to limit the dissentions and enmity of men, to end wars between sovereign princes, and they are chosen to be the arbiters of the disagreements between peoples and kings and to keep them in good friendship and intelligence. Thus we see that they have always been honored with great privileges and respected as saintly and sacred persons).[7] Although this observation is followed by the idea that ambassadors "representent la personne du Prince qui les a envoïés" (represent the person of the Prince who sends them),[8] this representational quality is not the sole, or even the most important, charge of the diplomat. Rather, as indicated above, it is the preservation of international peace. This role implies a certain gap between the prince and his representative, since one may surmise that the preservation of peace or the ending of wars entails a certain sacrifice of the prince's interests or rights—in a word, some sort of compromise. Writing during the final years of the Thirty Years' War, Le Bret, like de Vera, represents a transitional phase between the ideal of the ambassador as missionary of a Christian peace and the ideal of the diplomat as the strict representative or voice of his sovereign. Le Bret endows diplomats with a special status that ministers and magistrates do not enjoy, and his language differs accordingly. This very difference reminds us of the significance of Louis XIV's great innovation in the field of diplomacy, which was to eliminate, as much as possible, any independent role of the ambassador, tying him closely to his own sovereign person.

Jean-François Senault's treatise, *Le monarque, ou les devoirs du souverain* (1662), written before the two international incidents surrounding d'Estrades and Créquy that clearly marked Louis XIV's intent to reformulate diplomacy, bears certain resemblances to that of Le Bret, in that he is much more preoccupied with justifying the figure of the minister than that of the ambassador, but unlike the decidedly secular Le Bret, the religious Senault is faced with different issues, as he tries to preserve the uniqueness not only of the king but also of the divine. Senault is also writing after the Fronde, a period characterized by intense suspicion of ministers, especially the figure of the *premier ministre.* Senault's account of the king's need for ministers marks it, signifi-cantly, as one of the places where the difference between God and king is most perceptible:

> Dieu est si grand qu'il se peut passer de toutes choses: Les Soldats luy sont inutiles pour conserver l'Univers, puis-que d'une seule parole, il a sceu le tirer des abimes du neant. . . . S'il employe les Anges ou les hommes dans la conduite du monde, ce n'est pas pour se soulager, mais pour les associer à son Empire, & pour leur faire part de ce pouvoir absolu qu'il a sur les autres creatures. En mesme temps qu'il s'en sert dans ses ouvrages ou dans ses desseins, il les con-serve par sa Puissance, il les instruit par sa Sagesse, & il les rend capables des emplois qu'il luy a plû de leur donner. *Mais comme les Rois sont des hommes,* & que leur qualité ne les guérit point des miseres qu'ils ont tirées de leur nais-sance, leur force a ses foiblesses, leur connoissance a ses erreurs, & pour se garantir des unes & des autres, ils ont besoin de Soldats pour combattre, & de Conseillers pour deliberer.[9]

> [God is so great that he can do without all things: soldiers are useless to him to conserve the universe, since he created it out of nothingness with a single word. . . . If he uses angels or men in the direction of the world, it is not to unbur-den himself, but to associate them with his empire and to share with them the absolute power that he possesses over the other creatures. At the same time that he uses them in his works or his projects, he conserves them by his power, he instructs them with his wisdom, and he renders them capable of the employ-ment which it has pleased him to give them. *But since kings are men,* and their quality does not cure them of the miseries of their birth, their strength has weak-nesses, their knowledge has errors, and to guard against both, they need sol-diers to combat and councillors to deliberate.]

The king's very humanity necessitates the use of ministers; they are supple-ments to the immense distance between the human monarch and the divin-ity that he in turn represents. If this is a place where the king's role as representative of God on earth breaks down to a certain extent, this gap can be partially repaired by introducing new relations of representation, this time between the councillors and the king. Indeed, it is the very use of ministers–a prerogative of the king's sovereignty–that seems to indicate by inference the limits of that sovereignty by pointing up the king's status as man: "Les Princes bien éloignez d'estre des Dieux, ne sont pas mesme des Geans, & quoy que l'on dise que leur esprit soit plûtost formé que celuy des autres hommes, neanmoins sa grandeur ne répond pas à celle de leur Estat, & comme il est enfermé dans un corps qui n'a que deux yeux, deux oreilles, & deux mains, ils sont obligez d'en emprunter de leurs Ministres, afin qu'ils puissent en mesme temps voir toutes les actions, écouter toutes les plaintes, & subvenir à tous les besoins de leurs Sujets" (Princes, far from being gods, are not even giants, and although it is said that their mind is formed sooner than that of other men, nonetheless its grandeur does not correspond to that of their status, and since it is enclosed in a body that only has two eyes, two ears, and two hands, they are obliged to borrow from their ministers, in order to see at once all actions, to listen to all complaints, and to satisfy all of their subjects' needs).[10] The limits of the king's physicality *force* him to use ministers. Each time a minister acts, the act serves as a reminder of the fact that the king's representation of God is incomplete. But displacing representation onto the minister does not repair this relation; rather, it merely replicates the same problems, as the minister is also human: "Il seroit besoin que le Ministre fust un Ange, ou qu'il eust si peu de commerce avec son corps, que toutes les passions qui s'y forment ne troublassent jamais la tranquillité de son ame. Mais s'il ne peut pas arriver à ce haut degré de perfection, il faut pour le moins, qu'il se défende de ces mouvemens impetueux qu'une fausse generosité nous inspire, & que dans les avis qu'il donne au Prince il regarde toûjours plus le salut que la gloire de l'Estat" (The minister would need to be an angel, or he would need to have so little commerce with his body that all of the passions that are formed there would never trouble the tranquility of his soul. But if he cannot attain this high degree of perfection, he must at least defend himself against those impetuous movements that false generosity inspires in us, and in the advice he gives the prince he must always look more to salvation than to the glory of the state).[11] On the one hand, we have a monarch who can never completely overcome the limitations of his physical body; on the other hand, we have a minister who can never eliminate his bodily passions from his soul. It would appear that the further we delve into the proper government of man, the further we move from the ideal of a monarch transmitting God's will to his people. What is at issue here is the precise and problematic point of contact between universality and contingency, between timeless ideal and history. At some point in the chain that extends from God to the French state, this contact must be located and described; what we see in Le Bret and Senault is the difficulty in doing so. What is needed is the political equivalent of Descartes' pineal gland—an identifiable point that would allow the smooth connection between higher and lower, between history and divine design.[12]

Le Bret and Senault, limited by their twofold language that recognizes God and man (only rhetorically introducing the highly problematic category of angels), struggle to mark off the clear differences between each element in the chain of governance. I have shown elsewhere that there is an inherent danger in advocating a strong similarity between God and the king. That way lies tyranny, or at least idolatry. But in emphasizing the humanity of the monarch, both writers introduce the need for more representational relationships, ones that in turn threaten the uniqueness of the king. It is interesting that Senault warns not against ministers in general but rather against the figure of the *premier ministre,* whose unique status (like that of the king in relation to God, especially in Bodin) makes him all too liable to appropriate his master's identity:

> Un premier Ministre est comme un Mediateur entre le Souverain & ses Sujets: Il reçoit toutes les plaintes, il entend toutes les demandes, il connoist tous les interests des particuliers, & il en fait le rapport au Prince, dont la Majesté ne doit pas estre abordée par tant de personnes differentes en conditions & en humeurs. . . . Disons encore que sa puissance l'oblige à faire un autre luy-mesme, en faisant un premier Ministre: Car il luy communique quelques rayons de sa gloire, il le fait monter sur son Trône, il luy permet de gouverner son Empire, & partageant avec luy son autorité, il partage avec luy sa Couronne. Il semble que Dieu tout jaloux qu'il est de sa grandeur, en use de la façon; il permet aux Anges qui representent sa Majesté, de porter son nom, & de s'appeller Dieux comme luy. . . . Aussi les Jurisconsultes qui sont si soigneux de conserver aux Monarques ces glorieux titres qui les separent si noblement du commun des hommes, n'ont point jugé qu'ils blessassent leur grandeur en traittant leurs premiers ministres de seconde Majesté.[13]

> [A prime minister is like a mediator between the sovereign and his subjects: He receives all complaints, he hears all requests, he knows all private citizens' interests, and he reports them to the prince, whose majesty should not be approached by so many people of such different conditions and humors. . . . We should also say that his power obliges him to make another copy of himself, in making a prime minister: For he communicates to the minister some of the rays of his glory, he allows him to ascend the throne, he allows him to govern his empire, and sharing with him his authority, he shares with him the crown. It seems that God, albeit jealous of his grandeur, does the same thing; he allows angels who represent his majesty to carry his name and to call themselves gods like himself. . . . Thus the jurisconsults who are so careful to conserve the monarchs' glorious titles that separate them so nobly from the common man, have not judged that they injure their grandeur by calling their prime ministers a second majesty.]

The leaking of power down the chain of command must therefore somehow be stopped; one manner of doing so is to employ a council of several ministers, whose multitude in itself signifies their difference and personal insufficiency vis-à-vis the monarch. In language that anticipates Le Moyne's horror of sunspots, Senault calls the use of a *premier ministre* after the king's majority "une tache à sa gloire" ("a stain on his glory").[14] These efforts to limit the powers of ministers leave unanswered, however, God's curious conduct in the passage cited above, wherein he allows angels to take his name. Senault's account of this practice once again demonstrates a potential point of contention in what remains unproblematic in his treatise but would not be so for long–the figure of the ambassador: "Et si Dieu a souffert que l'Ange qui donna la Loy portast son nom, c'est parce qu'il estoit son Ambassadeur, & que representant sa personne il devoit estre revétu de sa Majesté; Ajoûtez aussi qu'il n'y a point d'Ange qui puisse ravir à Dieu sa Couronne, & que Dieu ne puisse aneantir quand il luy plaira" (And if God allowed the angel who gave the law to carry his name, it was because he was his ambassador, and that representing his person he must be clothed in his majesty. We should add that there is no angel who could take God's crown from him and whom God could not destroy when he pleases).[15] This last phrase echoes Louis XIV's observation in his memoirs that one of the great pleasures of kingship is to determine the worth of his subjects. Yet it also, with its strange introduction ("ajoutez aussi"), acknowledges that the explanation given in the previous sentence– that the angels were merely God's ambassadors–may be problematic in its own right and that the ultimate brake on the slippage of authority through representation remains, ultimately, the use of force. Bodin, with his intense suspicion of any delegation of sovereignty, said no less.

The Jesuit Pierre Le Moyne, in his *De l'art de régner* (1666), takes up many of these same themes, although his use of the sun as symbol for the king makes his task a bit easier, allowing him to liken the ministers and magistrates of the kingdom to planets that merely reflect the sun's rays. His tone, however, differs from that of Senault insofar as he depicts the king's need for ministers or councillors only slightly as a sign of royal weakness. Rather, he emphasizes the positive aspects of this representation:

> Les dépendans & les subalternes [du Prince] sont comme ses instrumens & comme ses membres. Il signe les Arrests & les Sentences par leurs mains: il les prononce par leurs bouches: il les execute par leur ministere. Son Nom est à la teste des Edits: les Sceaux portent sa marque & son enseigne: & quelque jugement qui se rende, quelque ordonnance qui se passe, c'est tousjours le Prince qui juge & qui ordonne. Qu'importe que l'Arrest se donne en Bretagne: que l'Edit se publie en Bourgogne: le Prince est par tout où sont ses membres: il agit par tout où ses Officiers agissent pour luy & en son nom.[16]

> [The dependents and subalterns of the prince are like his instruments and his limbs. He signs laws and judgments with their hands: he pronounces them with their mouths: he executes them through their ministry. His name is at the head

of all edicts, the seals carry his mark and his arms: and in any judgment which is rendered, in any declaration which is passed, it is the prince who judges and declares. It is not important if the law is given in Brittany, if the edict is published in Burgundy: the prince is everywhere where his limbs are: he acts everywhere where his officers act for him and in his name.]

This optimism concerning the ability of the prince to be present everywhere in his kingdom is quickly checked, however, since Le Moyne correctly perceives that this effortless extension through representation brings the monarch a bit too close to his divine model, courting idolatry or at least obscuring the reader's memory of the divine source of royal power. Le Moyne catches himself by once again clarifying that the king is in no way the equivalent of God on earth–God can have no such equivalent–and that the limitations of the king with respect to his office necessitate the use of aides: "il n'est point de Prince, & il n'en sera jamais, qui puisse tout seul, & sans le ministere de personne, suffire à des occupations aussi vastes, aussi laborieuses, aussi étendües que sont celles de la Royauté" (there is no prince, and there never will be one, who can alone, without the ministry of anyone, fulfill such vast, difficult and widespread occupations as those of royalty).[17]

As with the other authors, once Le Moyne admits the need for ministers, their status and function must be clearly described and regulated. Le Moyne evokes rather vividly the consequences of a faulty relation between king and minister:

Mais quand cette subordination de rangs est rompüe, & cette dependance d'offices & d'actions n'est pas gardée; quand le Pilote quitte la pouppe aux Matelots, & leur abandonne le Gouvernail & la Boussole: quand les bras se mettent à la place de la teste, & en veulent faire les fonctions, c'est à dire, pour laisser les termes figurez, & m'expliquer en un mot: quand le Prince resigne la conduite de sa Personne & le gouvernement de son Estat à ses Ministres: c'est alors veritablement que l'entredeux de la Souveraineté & du Ministere estant abattu: que les places & les fonctions attachées aux places estant changées, il ne se garde aucune mesure dans l'Estat: & il ne s'y fait rien que hors d'oeuvre & contre les formes.[18]

[But when this subordination of ranks is broken, and this dependence of offices and actions is not kept; when the pilot leaves the deck to the sailors and abandons to them the rudder and the compass: when the arms put themselves in the place of the head and want to fulfill the same functions; that is to say, to leave figured speech behind and to explain myself in a word: when the prince resigns the conduct of his person and the government of his state to his ministers, this is when the gap between sovereignty and ministry closes: and when the places and the functions attached to them have been changed, there is no longer any measure in the state, and everything is done out of order and against form.]

This apocalyptic picture of the risks inherent in any delegation of sovereign authority demonstrates the status of the minister as a problematic symbol of the king's potential weakness. Of course, Le Moyne recovers quickly, citing Louis XIV's own immense authority as a reason for not dwelling on these gloomy possibilities, stating that the Sun King's ministers could never even be imagined as usurpers of his sovereign power.

That said, Le Moyne cannot just leave the topic of ministers and councillors alone. He returns to it in a section on "le conseil," where a comparison between God and the king once again reveals the insufficiencies of princes: "ils ont besoin comme tous les autres de suppleer par le Conseil à leur indigence & à leurs défauts: de s'aider de la prudence d'autruy, où la leur se trouve courte: de fortifier & d'accroistre les lumieres qui leur sont propres, par la jonction d'autres lumieres accessoires & empruntées" (they need, like everyone else, to supplement with counsel their indigence and their defects, to be helped with the prudence of others, where their own is lacking, to fortify and augment their own insights with accessory and borrowed insights).[19] The "comme tous" that haunts this passage, suggesting that the king is a man just like every other man, is, in turn and not surprisingly, corrected later, where Le Moyne replaces his vision of the insufficiency of the king's *lumière* with the use of the solar symbol to characterize the monarch's uniqueness: "Et il ne faut point disputer au Prince cette influence de sagesse, & cette irradiation de conseil, à l'égard de ceux qui le servent. Si ce n'est pas pour rien qu'il porte l'épée, comme le remarque S. Paul; ne croyons pas aussi qu'il porte le Diademe pour rien: & que les rayons qui le couronnent, ne luy doivent servir qu'à la vaine ostentation d'une Majesté superficielle. Il sort de ses rayons, & de la teste qui les porte, des lumieres intellectuelles qui éclairent la Raison, & penetrent l'Esprit des Conseillers qui l'assistent" (And we cannot deny the prince the influence of wisdom and the irradiation of counsel to those who serve him. If it is not for nothing that he carries the sword, as Saint Paul remarks; should we not also believe that it is not for nothing that he wears the diadem, and that the rays which crown him are not merely a vain ostentation of superficial majesty. From his rays, and from the head that carries them, emanate intellectual lights that illuminate reason and that penetrate the minds of the councillors who help him).[20]

What should be evident by this point is the way in which the discussion of ministers, and the prince's undeniable need for them, has an insidious tendency to bring the tensions regarding the king's role as representative of God on earth to the fore. The similes and images surrounding the role of the minister reveal all of the authors' efforts to reconcile this figure with the king's inalienable sovereignty and ultimate independence. Resorting to the model of God's use of angels in no way simplifies the matter, as even Saint Augustine's *City of God* (a model for many writers on monarchy, including Bossuet) tends to break down when considering this problematic figure of mediation between the two realms. This model also implies that God needs angels in order to govern, an implication that is manifestly false. The writer who eschews parallelisms between the situation of the king and that of God ends by emphasizing, instead, the differences between them, entering a slippery slope where the king tends to become undifferentiated from his best ministers. Moreover, when these writers consider ministers directly, they are faced with exactly the same problems of definition that faced them in treating the king. Senault's recommendation that the minister be angelic in his lack of passion and self-interest implicitly acknowledges that the minister, like the ambassador, cannot be defined in his own terms but rather only through his service to others. In a rare admission of a loss for words, Le Moyne also admits the difficulty of defining, or even describing, ministers adequately: "Apres avoir montré comme le Prince doit agir avec ses Conseillers: il me reste, pour couronnement de cette Partie, de montrer comme les Conseillers doivent agir aveque le Prince. La chose n'est pas si facile d'elle-mesme: & d'ailleurs il n'y a pas si peu de mesures à observer, que le hazard y puisse reüssir: & qu'il ne faille qu'y toucher, sans se mettre en peine de quelle main on y touche" (Having shown how the prince should act with his councillors I have only to show how councillors should act with the prince. The subject is not so easy and there are not so few measures to observe that chance can succeed in defining it, and it should not be touched without worrying about what hand is doing the touching).[21] Indeed, all of the impossibility implied in the king's own position—an impossibility that cannot be treated directly, lest it damage the king's sovereignty and legitimacy, the very foundations of the state—emerges dramatically in Le Moyne's treatment of this figure: "L'Homme d'Estat, soit que nous luy donnions le nom de Ministre, ou celuy de Conseiller, est obligé à quelque chose de plus dangereux & de plus rare. Il doit passer juste & sans détour, entre les interests du Prince & ceux du Peuple: & le milieu qui les separe est si mince & si embroüillé, qu'Alfonse Albuquerque ne croyoit pas que personne le pûst tenir, sans heurter les uns ou les autres" (The statesman, whether we give him the name of minister or of counselor, is obligated to something even more dangerous and rare. He must pass directly and precisely between the interests of the prince and those of the people, and the middle which separates them is so narrow and confused that Alfonse Albuquerque believed that no one could navigate it without bumping into one or the other).[22] Just as the king's memoirs try to resolve the difficulty of the monarch's own position by transferring it onto the dauphin, Le Moyne's text–and its attendant solar imagery–seem to have no place for the minister. The metaphor of planets reflecting the sun's light is obviously inadequate, since planets play no role in the diffusion of the sun's rays to parts of the universe that they would otherwise be unable to reach. As the passage above indicates, it is when speaking of the minister, rather than of the king himself, that Le Moyne is forced to consider the idea of mediation and the ultimate inability of containing it in a human figure.

Although both Senault and Le Moyne treat ministers and councillors at length, neither one addresses diplomacy directly, unlike Le Bret, who rightly regarded the sending and receiving of ambassadors as one of the inalienable attributes of sovereignty. It may be argued that they simply did not consider diplomacy to be of direct importance to their topic. Yet this silence occurs precisely at the moment when diplomacy, under Louis XIV, was gaining new prominence and centrality. A hint as to why Le Moyne refuses to address the subject can be found in his recommendations to the king in council:

> N'est-ce pas dans le Conseil que la Royauté a son siege? que l'Art de regner a ses mouvemens & ses ressors? que le Prince doit estre fixe & immobile, pour faire aller avec ordre & de concert toutes les parties de l'Estat? Par tout ailleurs il peut avoir des Substituts & des Lieutenans. Il peut commettre à sa charge & à sa place dans les Armées, & dans les Compagnies de Justice. Il n'y a que la place qu'il doit tenir au Conseil, qui ne se peut remettre à personne: parce que c'est par là principalement qu'il regne. Ce qu'il fait là ne se peut faire par un autre, s'il ne veut remettre à un autre sa Couronne.[23]

> [Is it not in the council that royalty has its seat? that the art of reigning has its movements and springs? that the prince shoud be fixed and immobile in order to make the various parts of the state run in orderly concert? Everywhere else he can have substitutes and lieutenants. He can have others act in his place in the armies and in the bodies of justice. It is only the place he should hold in council that cannot be given to another, since it is here that he primarily reigns. What he does there cannot be done by another, if he does not want to give up his crown to another.]

Le Moyne's emphasis here is on the king's *presence,* so much so that he undermines his repeated recommendations elsewhere to the prince to never stop moving and acting. Here, he is "fixe et immobile," the unmoved mover of all of the state's mechanisms. Although he acts through representatives in the fields of war and of justice, both of those areas comply well with this ideal of a stable center.

Even more than the need for ministers, the need for diplomacy literally points up the insufficiency of the sovereign. To send a diplomatic representative to another sovereign is precisely to recognize that there are other sovereigns. To borrow Le Moyne's language of the solar system, it is to recognize that there are several suns. The doctrine of the sacred independence of the diplomatic corps, in service to Christian peace, that is adopted by Le Bret resolves this dilemma by positioning the world's rulers as planets around the sun of the pope or even God. Yet the Peace of Westphalia, which ended the Thirty Years' War in 1648, put a definitive end to the ideal of Christian internationalism.[24] The years following Westphalia saw the development of the modern state, with its own interests that apologists were no longer able, or even willing, to justify rhetorically as participating in a Europe-wide goal.[25] These changes implied a fundamental adjustment in the practice of diplomacy, whereby ambassadors had to be tied more closely to the princes whom they represented. As the issues confronted by Senault and Le Moyne illustrate, the challenge was to do this without damaging the prince's carefully elaborated sovereignty.

DIPLOMATIC "PROPAGANDA" UNDER LOUIS XIV

If diplomacy remained relatively unexamined in the treatises described above, it emerged as a theme in other forums, treated in a way that transformed it from a sign of weakness or limitation to a sign of power.[26] Dominique Bouhours, in his *Entretiens d'Ariste et d'Eugène*, published in 1671, describes diplomacy under Louis XIV as follows:

> L'esprit de la négociation, auquel on donne la prééminence, et qu'on appelle ordinairement grand esprit et grand génie, ne diffère cependant des autres que par la noblesse de la matière; car on ne peut se rien proposer de plus noble que de traiter des interêts des princes, d'entrer dans leurs desseins les plus secrets, d'accorder leurs différends et de gouverner leurs Etats. C'est l'emploi le plus sublime et le plus glorieux où l'esprit se puisse occuper; rien ne flatte tant l'amour-propre, rien ne remplit davantage l'ambition que ces titres éclatants d'ambassadeur, de plénipotentiaire, et de ministre d'Etat. Ceux qui sont élevés à ces dignités éminentes ont un caractère de grandeur et d'autorité qui les distingue du reste des hommes; ils sont sur la terre ce que sont dans le ciel les anges du premier ordre, qui approchent de plus près du trône de Dieu, qui reçoivent leurs lumières de lui immédiatement et qui sont destinés aux choses les plus importantes.[27]

> [The spirit of negotiation, to which preeminence is accorded and which we ordinarily call great spirit and great genius, differs from the others only by the nobil-

ity of its matter, for nothing more noble can be imagined than to treat the interests of princes, to enter into their most secret plans, to settle their differences
and to govern their states. It is the most glorious and sublime employment of
the mind; nothing flatters the self-image more, nothing fulfills ambition more
completely than these brilliant titles of ambassador, plenipotentiary, and minister of state. Those who have been raised to these eminent dignities possess a
character of grandeur and authority that distinguishes them from the rest of
men, they are on earth what angels of the first order are in the sky, who
approach closest to God's throne, who receive their orders directly from him
and who are destined for the most important things.]

If early treatises attempted to bury the ambassador in the larger category of
government ministers, here the diplomat is valorized on his own terms,
through the "esprit de négotiation." Bouhours mentions ministers only after
ambassadors and plenipotentiaries and valorizes the "esprit de négotiation."
In addition, the function of diplomacy seems to be chiefly that of representing the prince rather than pursuing international peace; the latter function is
quietly mixed in with the others, which have more to do with the prince's own
"interests." Yet perhaps what stands out the most from Bouhours's description
of the ambassador is the comparison of the diplomat to "angels of the first
order." While, as we have seen, the comparison between angels and ambassadors is quite traditional,[28] here the comparison is used less to extol the independent, peace-making role of the ambassador than to support a similarity
between the king and God. Bouhours deftly transforms praise of the ambassador and personal ambition into a panegyric. His emphasis on the prince's
"interests," combined with his enthusiastic descriptions of the French king
elsewhere in his work, leads the reader to conclude that as the angels are to
God, the ambassadors are to Louis XIV. Such proximity to such a divine
monarch is a rare privilege indeed, and Bouhours's eloquence demonstrates,
almost shockingly, how the need for diplomats can be transformed and
redeemed as proof of the king's grandeur.

Further evidence of the inability to discuss the ambassador realistically
under Louis XIV is provided by no less a writer than Racine. In his address to
the Académie Française in January of 1685, Racine famously welcomed
Thomas Corneille into his brother Pierre's academic seat. He also pronounced a panegyric of the diplomat Jean-Louis Bergeret, who was replacing the scientist and historian Géraud de Cordemoy. During this address,
Racine offered what can only be considered as the official interpretation of
the possibilities of diplomacy under so great a king as Louis XIV. Addressing
Bergeret, Racine asks: "Et qui pourra mieux que vous nous aider à parler de

tant de grands événements, dont les motifs et les principaux ressorts ont été si souvent confiés à votre fidélité et à votre sagesse?" (And who can help us more than you to speak of such great events, the motivations and principal components of which have so often been confided to your loyalty and wisdom?).[29] As we have seen in Bouhours, this rhetorical question expresses the idea that ambassadors are indeed privileged, as their representative status affords them a rare access to the jealously guarded mysteries of state. Yet according too much praise and attention to the diplomat, rather than to the king he represents, would obscure the latter's role in international affairs. It would also imply that there are other monarchs in Europe whose will and authority are equal to Louis XIV's, thereby necessitating negotiation by talented diplomats. Racine therefore quickly moves from praise of the Bergeret to royal panegyric: "Toutefois, disons la vérité, Monsieur, la voie de la négociation est bien courte sous un prince qui, ayant toujours de son côté la puissance et la raison, n'a besoin, pour faire exécuter ses volontés, que de les déclarer" (All the same, in truth, Monsieur, the paths of negotiation are quite short under a prince who, having strength and reason always on his side, needs only declare his will to see it executed).[30] This statement reduces the ambassador's role to the passive echoing of the royal voice, to what Gentili would term interpretation and what Wicquefort would call "mere representation." No negotiation can be possible with a monarch who incarnates reason itself and—significantly—who has the power to enforce his will with arms if reason does not work. Racine goes on to cite the public humiliation of the Spanish in 1661 that occurred as a result of the incident involving d'Estrades that I will discuss in the next section. He asks, "Comment s'est fait ce changement? Est-ce par une longue suite de négociations traînées? Est-ce par la dextérité de nos ministres dans les pays étrangers? Eux-mêmes confessent que le Roi fait tout, voit tout dans les cours où il les envoie, et qu'ils n'ont tout au plus que l'embarras d'y faire entendre avec dignité ce qu'il leur a dicté avec sagesse" (How did this change happen? Was it through a long series of tiresome negotiations? Was it through the skill of our ministers in foreign countries? They themselves confess that the king does everything, sees everything in the courts where they are sent, and that their only concern is to express with dignity that which the king has dictated to them with wisdom).[31] As Louis Marin has observed in his study of the awkward role of the royal historian Pellisson,[32] the only suitable subject of history is the king himself. We have seen that even without such a strong view of sovereignty and kingship as the one held under Louis XIV in France, it is exceptionally difficult to define the precise role and function of the ambassador. By pointing out that the only conceivable role of the diplomat under Louis XIV is near-invisibility, Racine implicitly indicates the terrifically complicated position of the ambassador, whose skills may be necessary in practice but who, in theory and ideology, should vanish from the international stage.

PRECEDENCY AND THE SPANISH: THE COMTE D'ESTRADE'S EMBASSY IN LONDON

If theoretical or propagandistic texts written during Louis XIV's reign point to the difficulty involved in accounting for diplomacy in a divine right monarchy that was no less complex, actual events demonstrate the extent to which Louis XIV tried to impose his strongly representational view of diplomacy upon the rest of Europe. In 1661, the Comte d'Estrades was serving as the French ambassador in London when the Swedish diplomat made his official entry into the English capital. As a result of the violent clash between the Spanish and French ambassadors that occurred during this entry, Louis XIV obtained Spanish public recognition of French precedency in all foreign courts. As Jean Racine's discourse to the Académie Française several years later demonstrates, the events in London and their significance persisted in the French memory, and not least in the memory of the king himself. In his *Mémoires pour l'instruction du dauphin,* Louis XIV recounts these events at length[33] for his son's benefit, concluding, "Et je ne sais si depuis le commencement de la monarchie il s'est rien passé de plus glorieux pour elle" (And I do not know if since the beginning of the monarchy anything more glorious has happened).[34] The story of the Spanish apology to the king would find its way into the history of the reign in medals issued by the Académie des Inscriptions in 1702. This incident, therefore, as the first international ceremonial conflict since the death of Mazarin in March of the same year, marks Louis XIV's entry on the diplomatic stage. Louis's handling of the incident demonstrates not only the importance that the king accorded to diplomacy but also the complications involved in attributing credit for the events to himself rather than to d'Estrades. This last point is especially important if we remember that d'Estrades *was* the king when he was in a foreign court, and any injury or insult to him was an insult to the king himself. A closer look at the events of October 1661 and their consequences therefore allows us to see how Louis XIV exploited the representative relationship between his ambassador and himself in order to secure the authorship of the eventually triumphant outcome.

In order to fully understand these events and their importance, one must understand, first, who the Comte d'Estrades was and, second, what exactly was meant in the seventeenth century by *préséance,* or the order of entry accorded to diplomats from various countries at a foreign court. Godefroy, the Comte d'Estrades, was a seasoned ambassador for France, having served as a diplomat between France and the Dutch stadtholder William of Orange during the 1630s and 1640s. He was also named governor of Dunkirk after having defended that city against the Spanish in 1652 and was rewarded by Mazarin for his loyalty during the Fronde with the position of mayor of Bordeaux. He helped negotiate the Treaty of the Pyrenees, the result of which was not only peace between France and Spain but also the marriage of Louis XIV with the infante Marie-Thérèse. Besides his experiences in London in the 1660s, d'Estrades also participated in the negotiations leading to the Treaty of Nijmegen (1678–79), which put an end to the war between Louis XIV and the Netherlands. In sending d'Estrades to London, Louis XIV was employing a distinguished negotiator whose international experience dated far before Louis XIV's rise to personal power in 1661. He had worked under Richelieu and Mazarin, both of whom handled French foreign policy with only minimal involvement from Louis XIII and the young Louis XIV. The letters between Richelieu and d'Estrades from the first years of the diplomat's experience reveal a much different idea of diplomacy than that which would hold under Louis XIV. Richelieu often defers to d'Estrades's judgment; his instructions are merely brief guidelines as to what needed to be accomplished. Perhaps even more significant, during his time in the Netherlands, d'Estrades corresponds often and at length with William of Orange himself. The relation between the two men was so close that William of Orange offered d'Estrades asylum and work after the Frenchman was condemned by the Parlement of Paris for having served as a second in Gaspard de Coligny's duel with the Duc de Guise. Mazarin did not hesitate to use this relationship to his own advantage, for example, in asking d'Estrades to convince William of Orange to break off relations with Spain, but the warmth and tone of the correspondence between the Frenchman and the stadtholder could easily give the impression of divided loyalties. That d'Estrades not only was not suspected of treason but was eventually rewarded for his diplomatic efforts demonstrates the distance traveled in diplomatic theory between this period and the beginning of the personal reign of Louis XIV in 1661. This was the year in which the monarch made the decision, conveyed to d'Estrades by the minister of foreign affairs, Lionne, to handle diplomatic affairs and correspondence himself. Later, as Callières tells us, Louis XIV would act to make the employment briefly envisioned by d'Estrades in the service of William of Orange impossible by prohibiting his subjects from serving as ambassadors of foreign powers.[35] By tying d'Estrades so closely to the representation of his own person and sovereignty abroad, Louis XIV signaled that the laxity of his predecessors had come to an end. Indeed, it would be impossible to imagine the kind of correspondence that existed between d'Estrades and William of Orange ever happening again. Louis XIV's "retraining" of d'Estrades would contribute to the events of October 1661.

A further consequence of the rearticulation of diplomacy around the sovereign, rather than around a more abstract ideal of peace and international community, was increased attention, throughout Europe but especially in France, to the problem of *préséance,* or precedency. Precedency determined the order in which ambassadors would be placed during ceremonies of entry and reception, often of other ambassadors making their first appearance at a foreign court. Behind the tradition used by the participating diplomats and states to justify their vision of the correct order of procedure lay seething contestations and innovations.[36] Quarrels of precedency were by no means new to the seventeenth century; one of the most drawn-out and astonishing struggles for precedency occurred between France and Spain at the Council of Trent (1545–63). The fight over ceremonial and wording contributed directly to the length of the council and threatened more than once to scuttle it entirely. But widespread investment in *préséance* took hold throughout Europe in the seventeenth century, as ambassadors were seen less as pseudo-angelic figures and more as agents protecting and defining their princes' interests.

The question of precedency had a way of bringing to light the tensions inherent in the diplomat's function and role. Already at the turn of the century, Alberico Gentili experienced difficulty in describing the diplomat's relation to the enforcement of precedency in a consistent manner. He notes that "ambassadors are accustomed (and properly) to insist with the utmost emphasis that no one else, unless some reason makes it imperative, shall have a more honorable place than they; they will not submit to anything of the kind." He goes on, however, to recommend that "sometimes even ambassadorial dignity ought not to be rated so high as to prejudice the consideration of the proper plan (the ambassador will estimate this according to his prudence) for the expeditious accomplishment of the mission."[37] Significant in this last sentence is the idea that responsibility for deciding when precedency should outweigh the successful outcome of the negotiation lies with the ambassador, not the sovereign. The essence of this trust in the diplomat resides, of course, in the question of whether prudence is a necessary quality of the diplomat or of the prince he represents. Answering this question by insisting upon the diplomat's unique qualities limits the ambassador's representational function, as he is employed precisely to accomplish what the sovereign will not or cannot accomplish himself. In the example of precedency, this favoring of the diplomat's peace-making skills over the particular interests of his prince becomes tangible and visible to all participating in and watching the ceremonies in question. We shall see that at the beginning of his embassy in London, d'Estrades himself adhered to this vision of the primacy of the diplomat in such decisions, to the strong displeasure of Louis XIV.

Evidence of the growing importance of precedency over the course of the seventeenth century can be found merely by contrasting the few pages that Gentili devotes to the subject with the book-length discussion of the topic written by the Englishman James Howell in 1664. Titled "Proedria-Basilike: A Discourse concerning the Precedency of Kings: Wherein the Reasons and Arguments of the Three Greatest Monarks of *Christendom* Who claim a several Right *Therunto,* are Faithfully Collected, and Rendered," Howell's work is more than two hundred pages long, and its careful examination of the rights of precedency of Spain, England, and France is worth considering here, especially since it represents a point of view other than Louis XIV's.[38] Howell's work begins with the trope, by now familiar, of the lack of any sufficient definitions of the ambassador, this time adding a bit of national pride to his own efforts: "But those Forreners who have discoursed therof do amuse the Reader with such general Notions, that the Breeding and Qualities which they require, as also the Monitions, Precepts and Instructions which they prescribe, may fit any other Minister of State, or Man of Business. But this discourse doth appropriate itself soley to the subject we undertake, *viz.* to the Function, Office, and Incumbency of an *Ambassador.*"[39] Howell then goes on to concede that the pope and the emperor are exempt from any possible controversies regarding precedency in that their institutional relation with God separates them from the rest of the European sovereigns. This exemption is admitted by all writers of the period, and therefore the battle for precedency between Spain and France chiefly concerned who should participate in ceremonies directly after the emperor. Yet it is worth noting that European monarchs were beginning to chafe at the empire's ceremonial superiority, since the emperor had lost much of his power by the seventeenth century and, as an elected ruler, was viewed by followers of Bodin as minimally sovereign in the states he supervised. The status of the electors' claims to sovereignty consituted one of the ongoing debates of the century, from the Thirty Years' War and the Treaty of Westphalia to Leibniz's rather fascinating defense of those princes' sovereign right to send ambassadors of their own to other princes. Speaking of the emperor, Howell himself notes that "Nevertheless, though in point of *Power* and Territories the *Emperor* be grown so weak and naked in comparison of what he was, yet in point of *Precedence* and Dignity he bears up still the same, being accounted the prime Potentat, and Prince paramount of *Christen-*

dome."[40] Unsurprisingly, Louis XIV bridled at the precedency accorded the emperor in European courts:

> Je ne vois donc pas, mon fils, par quelle raison des rois de France, rois hérédi-taires, et qui peuvent se vanter qu'il n'y a aujourd'hui dans le monde, sans exception, ni meilleure maison que la leur, ni monarchie aussi ancienne, ni puissance plus grande, ni autorité plus absolue, seraient inférieurs à ces princes électifs. Il ne faut pas dissimuler néanmoins que les papes, par une suite de ce qu'ils avaient fait, ont insensiblement donné dans la cour de Rome, la préséance aux ambassadeurs de l'Empereur sur tous les autres, et que la plupart des cours de la chrétienté ont imité cet exemple, sans que nos prédécesseurs aient fait effort pour l'empêcher; mais en toute autre chose, ils ont défendu leurs droits.[41]

> [I fail to see, therefore, my son, for what reason the kings of France, hereditary kings who can boast that there isn't either a better house, nor greater power, nor more absolute authority than theirs anywhere else in the world today, should rank below these elective princes. It cannot be denied, nevertheless, that the popes, as a consequence of what they had done, have gradually given prece-dence at the court of Rome to the ambassadors of the Emperor over all the oth-ers and that most of the courts in Christendom have imitated this example without our predecessors having made any effort to prevent it, but in every other respect they have defended their rights.][42]

The Sun King's decision to refer to himself as ruler over an empire in his cor-respondence with Turkey is justified by the practice of precedency in that country: "On trouve, dès le dixième siècle, des traités publics, où ils [the French] se nomment les premiers avant les empereurs avec qui ils traitent; et à la porte du Grand-Seigneur, nos ambassadeurs, et en dernier lieu, le mar-quis de Brèves, sous Henri le Grand, mon aïeul, n'ont pas seulement disputé, mais emporté la préséance sur ceux des empereurs" (There are public treaties from the tenth century in which they are named first before the emperors with whom they deal, and our ambassador at the Porte of the Grand Seigneur, and most recently the marquis de Brèves under Henry the Great, my grandfather, have not merely disputed but also won the precedence over those of the emper-ors).[43] This brief digression concerning the rights of precedency of the emperor shows how ceremony and history intersect. If Howell still concedes precedency to the emperor despite the events of the first half of the seventeenth century and the emperor's status as elected ruler, Louis XIV resists this persistence, but also without citing recent historical events. Rather, he emphasizes France's long-standing claim to the title of empire (dating to Charlemagne, whom he does not neglect to cite) as well as the pope's weakness in allowing the emperor to claim precedency, thereby obliging other states to do the same. These passages from the memoirs also demonstrate the essential importance that Louis XIV placed upon precedency as a ceremonial expression of his own state's historical continuity and superiority, yet, once again, it is worth noting that unlike Howell, Louis XIV, when discussing the emperor or even the pope, disassociates precedency and proximity to the divine.

Howell uses precedency to argue the merits of the English Crown in relation to the monarchies of France and Spain, the other two countries he considers. Several reasons are offered for English precedency. He explains that English monarchs were Christian four hundred years before Clovis and that England achieved independence from Rome long before the other kingdoms did. He also follows Gentili's anticlericalism in demonstrating that the English king, unlike the French and Spanish who recognize papal authority over their subjects in matters of religion, is the head of both church and state. In order for this interpretation to hold, of course, the role of Parliament in British government must be elided, and Howell notes that the people of England have absolutely no part of the king's sovereign power.[44] Further arguments for British precedency include the king's ability to cure scrofula; the existence of treaties that England signed before France; battles won by England, especially in France; and the length of the English royal bloodline. Dominance over the sea (hotly contested by the Dutch, who through Grotius argued that the sea was common to all nations) and over colonies are also marshaled in the English Crown's defense, as is the English role in establishing peace between François I and Charles V in the sixteenth century. In this wide range of evidence, Howell combines historical "proof" or argument rather seamlessly with considerations of the monarchy's distance (or lack thereof) from God. Such variety demonstrates that precedency is far from an obscure ceremonial detail. Rather, it is the outward expression of an entire national history and monarchy and an implicit argument for its merits above those of its neighbors, whether on the paper of a treaty or in the procession of a diplomatic entry. By arguing for English precedency, Howell is also arguing for renewed respect for a state with an extremely troubled recent history. One has the impression that if English precedency were accorded, the episode of Cromwell—as well as the lingering controls exercised by Parliament over the monarch—would disappear like a bad dream.

Of course, the growing significance of precedency is directly related to the acceptance of the idea that the ambassador represents the sovereign who sends him. Indeed, precedency without this representational role of the diplomat would lose all political meaning. Accordingly, then, Howell's treatise on precedency is followed in the same volume by a short "Discourse of Ambassadors." This discourse once again laments the failure of others, including de Vera, to adequately define the ambassador, stating that previous attempts at definition are not definitions at all but rather descriptions. These descriptions relate diplomatic function to the role of priests; they also follow the Italians in deriving the word *Ambasciatore* from either the word *Bascer*, meaning to report or declare, or *Ambo*, "because he is a Mediator twixt both parties."[45] Howell rejects these derivations largely because they do not adequately describe the relation between diplomat and sovereign, for "Ambassadors are the emissitious Eyes of a Prince, they are his ears and hands, they are his very understanding and reason, they are his breath and voice."[46] Howell breaks, however, with the idea that diplomats are used only because the king cannot be everywhere at once, an idea that, as we have seen, emphasizes the humanity of the prince. Rather, it is because the majesty of kings "hath bin rather a disadvantage than an advance to any great business, specially intreating of Capitulations of Peace" that "in Politiks tis a Principle, that in Colloquies for Pacification Princes shold not appeer in person, but be represented by their Ambassadors and Commissaries."[47] This slight departure from diplomatic commonplace can be attributed to Howell's main goal, which is to elevate not the ambassador but the monarchy that he represents. He expresses this concept directly by stating that "In the present Prince ther is real Majesty, in an Ambassador only a representative; In the Prince ther is the truth of the thing, in an Ambassador the effigies or shadow: Now as the shadow yeelds to the light, so an Ambassador must yeeld to a Prince."[48] In the issue of precedence, where an injury done to an ambassador is significant not for the diplomat's misfortune or insult but rather for the injury to the king he represents, the diplomatic role is meaningful only in service and in relation to the sovereigns who send and receive. It is important to note that Wicquefort, who concentrates almost solely on the virtues and attributes of the ambassador and not the sovereign, almost never discusses precedence, pointing instead to the puzzle of attributing rank to monarchs whose sovereignty by its very nature does not admit any superiority to itself. Not only does the Protestant Wicquefort challenge the right of the pope's nuncios to claim precedence on the grounds that their representative and political capacity is temporal rather than spiritual,[49] he also states that "Aujourdhuy il y a competence entre tous les Rois, parce qu'estant tous Souverains, ils jugent que leur rang ne doit point estre reglé par leur puissance, qui est bien plus grande & plus absolue chez les uns que chez les autres, mais par la seule Souveraineté, qui n'admet point de comparatif" (Today there is competition between all kings, since, being all sovereigns, they judge that their rank should not be determined by their strength, which is indeed greater among some than among others, but rather by sovereignty alone, which admits no comparison).[50]

Such skepticism regarding the ultimate usefulness and grounding of *préséance* marks once again the implicit incompatibility of sovereignty and diplomatic practice. In theory, each sovereign is fully sovereign, and therefore no rank is possible. Howell's lengthy historical justifications for British rights to precedency clash with the timeless plenitude of sovereignty as articulated by Bodin. Yet in practice, of course, all sovereigns cannot sign a treaty at the same time, nor can they all appear simultaneously in a procession. The French argument for precedency was therefore based upon a tradition that, in fact, each state interpreted in its own way but also upon the status of the French monarch as *more* sovereign than his contemporaries, and this status was, in turn, based at least in part upon the direct, unmediated relation between the king and God.[51] Acquiring internationally recognized precedency over all other monarchs would therefore be both the cause and the effect of the model of divine right kingship so carefully elaborated by the theorists I discuss in chapter 1, uniting, in an important sense, theory and practice for the greater glory of Louis XIV.

The young Louis XIV sent d'Estrades into a contentious situation, since he was in the English court at the same time as the Spanish ambassador, Watteville, and conflict of precedency upon the arrival of other diplomats was inevitable.[52] Already in the instructions to the diplomat, Louis XIV's staff (probably Lionne) emphasizes the importance of keeping the order of precedency intact. D'Estrades is reminded that only the emperor's ambassador is allowed to precede that of the French king. Such instructions proved prescient, for only one week after announcing to d'Estrades his intention to handle diplomatic correspondence personally, Louis XIV wrote to protest his diplomat's handling of the Venetian ambassadors' official entry to the British court. He notes that he was "fort touché" by two details of d'Estrades's last report. First, the king of England "semble avoir voulu decider une entiere egalité entre moy et mon frere le Roy d'Espagne, quoy qu'il ne peust ignorer par combien de raisons la preeminence m'appartient, et que j'en suis de tout temps en possession en tous lieux" (seems to have wanted to establish an entire equality between myself and my brother the King of Spain, even though he cannot be ignorant of the many reasons for which preeminence belongs to me, nor of the fact that I possess it everywhere at all times). The second objection is to d'Estrades's conduct: "que vous ayez deferé a ce qu'il vous a envoyé dire n'ayant mesme esté qu'une priere de sa part de n'envoyer pas vos carosses, veu que quand mesme ç'auroit esté un ordre expres comme il luy est libre de les donner tels qu'il veut dans son estat, vous auriez deu luy respondre que vous n'en recevez que de moy" (that you deferred to what he told you, even though it was only a request on his part to not send your carriages; although it was an express order of the sort that he is free to give in his state, you should have responded that you receive orders only from me).[53] This letter demonstrates the close relation between arguments of precedency and the changing status of the ambassador as personal representative of his sovereign. Again, we should recall that d'Estrades, having practiced diplomacy since the 1630s in a variety of situations, would have been slow to understand the implications of the king's decision to take diplomacy personally, as it were. Louis XIV therefore reminds him that under no circumstances is he to receive orders from the sovereign in whose court he resides; for d'Estrades, who considered entering into the service of William of Orange only twenty years before, this would have been a fault that he would have been unaware of committing. D'Estrades must eschew the niceties of international convention in order to pursue and defend the interests of the king, which are the only interests he represents. Indeed, the extent to which personal interest and international agreement are increasingly entering into conflict during the first years of Louis XIV's reign is indicated by a sentence occurring later in the same letter, where the monarch states baldly that "Je vous diray . . . qu'autre chose est mon Interest que je connois fort bien et peut estre mon desir, et autre chose s'en expliquer et y agir ayant les mains liées par un traité que mon honneur ny ma foy ne me permettent pas de violer en rien" (I will tell you. . . . that my interest, which I am very well aware of, is one thing, and that explaining it and having my hands bound by a treaty which my honor and faith do not allow me to violate is quite another).[54]

This tense atmosphere, at the court of a "Royauté qui a peine s'establit,"[55] foreshadowed the violence that would occur on September 30, 1661, on the occasion of the Swedish ambassador's official entry into London. Having been notified of the ambassador's arrival, d'Estrades could not refrain from attending the ceremony, especially without assurances that Spain would not do the same. D'Estrades therefore entered the procession protected by two hundred Frenchmen and sixty people from his entourage as well as by the troops of Charles II, the English king. Despite these precautions, d'Estrades was attacked by a group of "batteliers bouchers et autres bourgeois et quantité d'Irlandois le tout en nombre de plus de Deux mil hommes meslez avec les gens de Watteville" (watermen, butchers and other bourgeois as well as a quantity of Irishmen, all numbering more than two thousand men mixed with Watteville's men),[56] whom the Spanish ambassador had hired for the occasion. In the ensuing violence and confusion, d'Estrades's carriage was disabled, and Watteville advanced ahead of him in the position of precedency. D'Estrades would inform the king that six of his entourage were killed and thirty-three wounded, including his own son. The only recently restored Charles II's weak control over his subjects contributed to the disorder, as the French continued to be harassed even after the street fight was over.

The swift reaction of Louis XIV demonstrates both his anger and his conviction that the incident in London offered him an opportunity to finally demonstrate his power to the rest of a still skeptical world. Both reactions rest upon his opinion, expressed earlier, that his ambassadors represented his person and that an injury done to the ambassador was one done to himself. His letter to d'Estrades immediately after the events threatens the king of England, saying that if justice is not forthcoming, he will have to suspect that Charles II himself was behind the attack, using it as an opportunity to sow discord among the French and Spanish. Of course, the irony of this threat consisted in the fact that the English king's control over his subjects and ministers was still extremely weak; proving that the king wanted to prevent the altercation, but was unable to do so, would also make Louis XIV's point of monarchical superiority. The same strategy was used with regard to the Spanish; a contemporary manuscript notes that the French ambassador to Spain was told to transmit that "sad. Majesté ne pouvoit prendre l'action du Baron de Bateville que pour un attentat entrepris de son pur caprice sans les ordres du Roy son Maitre et contre son intention au prejudice de cette possession puisque ses autres ministres ne disputoient rien a Rome ny a Venise a ceux de sa Majesté et ne leur avoient jamais rien contesté en Angleterre, qu'a Munster mesme qui estoit un theatre bien plus celebre" (his Majesty could only interpret the Baron of Bateville's action as an attempt committed on pure whim without the orders of the king his master and against his intention to the prejudice of this possession since his other ministers do not dispute his Majesty's ministers' position in Rome or Venice and have never contested their position in England or even in Münster, which was an even greater theater).[57] Again, either the king of Spain admits that the action was deliberate, thereby entering into a messy argument over the historical justifications for precedency (which is, in fact, what happened), or he disavows his envoy's actions, thereby proving his weakness just as effectively. Louis XIV accompanied this declaration with a demand that Watteville be recalled from London while also asking the Spanish ambassador to France to leave the court immediately. As for d'Estrades himself, the rapidly escalating situation led to the seasoned diplomat's intense discomfort, and he asked to be allowed to leave England and its hostile atmosphere, perhaps not comprehending that his role had shifted from negotiator to stand-in for the injured king. To this request, Louis XIV responds that the d'Estrades's departure would only give credence to the rumors being spread by Watteville, which stated that the French king had decided that the recall of both ambassadors would be a satisfying resolution to the conflict. It would also, as the king points out, put Louis XIV's sovereign power to choose his own representatives in doubt.[58]

Following close upon the heels of the London violence, another diplomatic incident marked Louis XIV's conviction of his superiority to his English counterpart, when his ships refused to salute English ships in the Channel. Louis XIV's ensuing letter to d'Estrades reveals his goals in provoking diplomatic incidents with France and Spain even better than the corresponding passages in his memoirs:

> Ce que Jay remarqué dans toute la teneur de vostre depesche cest que le Roy mon frere ny ceux dont je prend conseil ne me connoissent pas encore bien quand Ilz prennent avec moy des voyes de hauteur et d'une certaine fermeté qui sent la menace. Je ne cognois puissance sous le Ciel qui soit capable de me faire advancer un pas par un chemin de cette sorte. Et il me peut bien arriver du mal, mais non pas une impression de crainte. Je pensois avoir gaigné dans le monde qu'on eust un peu meilleure opinion de moy, mais je me console en ce que peut estre n'est ce qu'a Londres qu'on fait de si faux jugements. Cest a moy a faire par ma conduite qu'ils ne demeurent pas longtemps en de semblables erreurs.[59]

> [I have noted in the tone of your dispatch that neither the king my brother nor those who advise me do not know me well when they treat me with a certain haughtiness and firmness that seems threatening. I do not know of any power under the heavens that would be able to influence me in this manner. Misfortune may befall me, but not an impression of fear. I thought that I had obtained a better reputation in the world, but I console myself by thinking that perhaps it is only in London that such false judgments are made. It is up to me, through my actions, to make sure that they do not remain in such error for long.]

Left, then, to defend the ship-saluting scandal to the king of England, d'Estrades dutifully repeated Louis XIV's arguments for naval superiority at the British court, provoking the ire—seemingly superficial—of Charles II.

Yet early in 1662, in the midst of lengthy diplomatic wranglings with Spain, which made the mistake of agreeing too quickly to not participate in diplomatic ceremonies at which France was present, provoking Louis XIV to hold out hope for a complete cession of precedency to France, d'Estrades's wife, still back in France, passed away. The letters exchanged between the diplomat and Louis XIV during this period, seemingly far removed from the affairs that d'Estrades was negotiating, demonstrate the difficult situation of the ambassador whose private life was eclipsed by his representational capacity. Again, it must be recalled that d'Estrades had been serving France as a diplomat since the late 1630s and could therefore expect some leniency in the case of a personal emergency. His plea to Louis XIV for his return to France is poignant:

Sire, Dans l'indisposition et l'affliction ou je suis je ne me trouve gueres capable de la bonne conduite qu'il faut tenir dans les affaires de V.M. Le Zele pourtant que j'ay pour son service me fera faire tous les efforts possibles afin qu'il ne recoive aucun prejudice entre mes mains, et l'honneur que V.M. fait de me tesmoigner avec tant de bonté quelle est touchée de ma perte adoucit bien un peu ma douleur mais elle reste encore si forte que je la supplie tres humblement de luy imputer toutes les fautes que je pourray commettre a l'advenir dans le cours de ma negociation et mesme dans le compte que je luy rendray de l'estat ou elle se trouve a present. . . . Je supplie tres humblement V.M. de trouver bon que je m'en aille a Paris, et que pour raisons de m'en accorder la permission je luy represente cent obligations de conscience qui le veulent pour satisfaire aux legs pieux et autres dispositions que ma femme a faites en mourant, et pour regler aussy les affaires d'une famille qui se trouve dans la derniere desolation.[60]

[Sire, In my indisposition and affliction I do not think I am able to maintain the good conduct necessary for Your Majesty's affairs. The zeal that I have for your service will ensure that your affairs will not suffer in my hands, and the honor that Your Majesty gives me in being touched by my loss lessens my pain but it is still so strong that I humbly beg you to attribute to it any faults that I may make in the present negotiations as well as in my reports on its status. . . . I humbly beg Your Majesty to permit me to go to Paris, and to justify my request I cite hundreds of obligations of conscience that force me to satisfy the stipulations of my wife's testament and to take care of my afflicted family's affairs.]

The letters indicate that d'Estrades was not allowed to leave England until the beginning of April 1662; by August of the same year he was back in service, first to Holland and then to oversee the French reacquisition of Dunkirk, a town that d'Estrades had governed before it was ceded to the English under Mazarin.

In the meantime, however, Louis XIV was pursuing the political opportunity afforded him by the Spaniards' rash actions. In the memoir to d'Estrades written in November of 1661, he informs the diplomat that he has obtained the recall of Watteville from London and that the Spanish have even offered to follow Louis XIV's suggestions for punishment after the ambassador's return to Spain. The significance of the recall is not lost on the French king, who rightly sees the Spanish admission of guilt as a liability for the Spanish

monarch himself. The following observation makes sense only if one sub-
scribes to the idea that the ambassador and the sovereign employing him are,
in a sense, one and the same:

Quoy que dans les offres et propositions que les Espagnols font il y ait abon-
damment dequoy se satisfaire, et mesme qu'il ait fallu que l'orgueil et la gravité
de la nation se soit bien abaissée pour desadvouer et chastier un Ambassadeur,
qui apres tout n'a fait que servir son Maistre et executer ses ordres, et pour se
condamner eux mesmes a ne pouvoir plus concourir en Angleterre a l'advenir
avec cette Couronne, en sorte que la plus part du monde tenoit cette affaire cy
pour tout a fait inaccommodable, parce qu'on ne pouvoit presumer qu'ils s'hu-
miliassent a desapprouver l'action de Bateville, et encore moins a passer con-
damnation pour l'avenir.[61]

[The Spanish offers and propositions contain much that is satisfying and the
pride and gravity of the Spanish nation must be quite lessened for them to dis-
avow and punish an Ambassador who after all was only executing his master's
orders, and to condemn themselves to never contest our preeminence in
England. For these reasons, most people assumed that this affair could not be
resolved, because it could never be presumed that they would humiliate themselves by disapproving Bateville's actions and even less that they would commit
themselves to observing our precedency in the future.]

Louis XIV goes on to state, however, that the recall and "humiliation" of Watteville is not enough, given the gravity of the insult to d'Estrades and thus to
himself.[62] Louis XIV persists in attempting to place responsibility for the incident upon the Spanish monarch, thereby conferring real effectiveness to the
representational doctrine of diplomacy. He stresses that he, not the king of
England, is behind the request for Watteville's recall; as the injured party,
Louis XIV can be the only agent of punishment. In the same memoir to
d'Estrades, Louis asks Batailler, a member of the embassy, to ensure that
Charles II does not write to Spain concerning the incident. By the English
king's not writing, Louis states, both monarchs will find a certain advantage:
"le Roy mon frere en ce qu'il s'espargnera la peine de faire une priere super-
flue dans des choses accordées, et qu'on ne laisseroit pas de luy faire valoir
comme une faveur, et moy en ce qu'il me laissera la victime qui doit estre sac-
rifiée a mon ressentiment, sans que les Espagnols puissent publier dans le
monde qu'ils ont revoqué le d. Bateville a la priere du Roy de la Grande Bre-
tagne, et non pas pour me satisfaire" (the king my brother will find his advantage in sparing himself the trouble of making a superfluous complaint in
things that are already resolved, and this will be considered as a favor, and I
will find my advantage in that he will let me have the victim that must be

sacrificed to my resentment, without the Spanish being able to publish to the world that they revoked Bateville because of the king of England's complaints, rather than for my satisfaction).[63]

This last passage summarizes nicely the issues of authorship involved in diplomatic representation. Precedency itself, as I have shown, is closely tied to the evolving idea of the ambassador as stand-in for the king himself. Although d'Estrades's qualities as a diplomat, especially his skill in writing dispatches, are repeatedly praised, his attributes as a private citizen are sacrificed to his representational role. In the myriad documents, instructions, letters, and dispatches that characterize diplomatic exchange, it is all too easy to forget the ultimate agent–the sovereign–behind the flow of written material. This situation should recall the one facing advocates of divine right monarchy, who must ensure that the hand of God is detectable in each of the monarch's actions. Diplomatic action, especially reprisals for injuries, must be seen as emanating not from Louis XIV's ministers but from the monarch himself. The French king's early understanding of the radical steps needed to secure this identification as diplomatic author cannot be underestimated, as Lionne himself points out, and indeed, he was almost certainly the only ruler in Europe to adopt personal diplomacy–the handling of correspondence, the choice of diplomats–in this manner and to this degree. In addition, as we have seen, much of Louis XIV's ranking of his fellow sovereigns–and consequently, of the appropriate rank of their diplomats–is based on this conception of royal authorship. Charles II's extremely limited control over his subjects and ministers, some of whom, as Louis was able to ascertain through the careful use of spies in London, were coconspirators with the Spanish in the London affair, marks him as an inferior ruler whose ambassadors, notwithstanding the later pleas of writers such as Howell, would therefore never be worthy to compete for precedency with those of France. Likewise, Louis XIV would insist, both in diplomatic documents and in his memoirs, upon the emperor's status as an elected prince in order to justify his opinion that the empire's representatives may possess precedency as a matter of custom (*de fait*) but that this privilege is all but empty *de droit*. This worldview based upon authorship leads, then, quite logically to the conclusion that the only monarch who can compete with Louis XIV is the king of Spain, rendering the eventual victory of the French in diplomatic disputes all the more precious. We can now begin to understand Louis XIV's exclamation in his memoirs that nothing more glorious had ever happened to the French monarchy.

This opinion followed Louis XIV's final revenge against the Spanish. As he stated above, the mere recall of Watteville and the closing of the French borders to traveling Spanish diplomats were not enough to satisfy him after the

London violence. The final act of this drama took place in Louis's own court, when the Count of Fuensaldagna appeared in order to announce that henceforth the French right of precedency in foreign courts would be ceded by the Spanish. Here, the text of Louis XIV's memoirs is worth citing at length:

> Le comte de Fuensaldagna, ambassadeur extraordinaire du Roi Catholique, se rendit au Louvre dans mon grand cabinet, où étaient déjà le nonce du pape, les ambassadeurs, résidents et envoyés de tous les princes qui en avaient alors auprès de moi, avec les personnes les plus considérables de mon Etat. Là, m'ayant premièrement présenté la lettre qui le déclarait ambassadeur, il m'en rendit aussitôt une seconde, en créance de ce qu'il me dirait sur cette affaire de la part du roi son maître. Ensuite il me déclara que Sa Majesté Catholique . . . lui avait aussi commandé de m'assurer qu'elle avait déjà envoyé ses ordres à tous ses ambassadeurs et ministres, tant en Angleterre qu'en toutes les autres cours où se pourraient présenter à l'avenir de pareilles difficultés, afin qu'ils s'abstinssent et ne concourussent point avec mes ambassadeurs et ministres, en toutes les fonctions et cérémonies publiques où mes ambassadeurs et ministres assisteraient.
>
> Je lui répondis que j'étais bien aise d'avoir entendu la déclaration qu'il m'avait faite de la part du roi son maître, parce qu'elle m'obligerait de continuer à bien vivre avec lui. Après quoi, cet ambassadeur s'étant retiré, j'adressai la parole au nonce du pape et à tous les ambassadeurs, résidents ou envoyés, qui étaient présents, et leur dis qu'ils avaient entendu la déclaration que l'ambassadeur d'Espagne m'avait faite, que je les priais de l'écrire à leurs maîtres, afin qu'ils sussent que le roi Catholique avait donné ordre à ses ambassadeurs de céder la préséance aux miens en toutes sortes d'occasions.[64]

[The count of Fuensaldaña, ambassador extraordinary of the Catholic King, came to my great chamber at the Louvre, where the papal nuncio and all the ambassadors, residents, and envoys at my court and the most important persons in my state were waiting. There, having first presented me with the letter that declared him ambassador, he immediately handed me a second one, authorizing what he would tell me regarding this matter on behalf of the King his master. Subsequently, he declared to me that His Catholic Majesty . . . had also commanded him to assure me that he had already sent orders to all his ambassadors and ministers, both in England and in all other courts where similar difficulties might arise in the future, to abstain from any competition with my ambassadors and ministers in all public ceremonies that my ambassadors and ministers might attend.

I replied that I was very pleased to hear his declaration on behalf of the King his master, because it would obligate me to continue to live on good terms with him. After which, this ambassador having withdrawn, I addressed the residents or envoys who were present and told them that they had heard the declaration of the Spanish ambassador and that I requested them to communicate it to their masters so that they might know that the Catholic King had issued orders for his ambassadors to cede the precedency to mine on every occasion.][65]

Louis XIV's victory over his closest rival, which followed long negotiations that extended even to the wording of the Spanish declaration (Louis objected to the text's placement of the Spanish ambassador's name before that of d'Estrades, stating that this amounted to a reseizure, however subtle, of precedency), was finally complete.[66]

DIPLOMATIC VICTORY OVER THE POPE: THE DUC DE CRÉQUY'S EMBASSY IN ROME

In 1662, almost exactly one year after the Comte d'Estrades's violent altercation over diplomatic precedency with the Spanish in London on the occasion of the Swedish ambassador's official entry into that city, Louis XIV appointed the Duc de Créquy to the position of French ambassador to Rome. By almost all accounts, this was a mistake. Not only were relations between Paris and Rome unusually tense, with the Spanish party enjoying unprecedented favor in the papal court, but the Duc de Créquy, a *noble d'épée* quick to anger, was particularly unsuited to engage in the delicate diplomatic negotiations needed to restore good relations between France and the pope.[67] In fact, whether the decision to send Créquy was a mistake depends on one's interpretation of the sincerity of Louis XIV's wishes to restore relations with the pontiff. The incidents surrounding d'Estrades's embassy the year before clarified Louis's desire to impose his importance on a Europe still skeptical of the young king's seriousness. Given the Sun King's long reign and many accomplishments, it is easy to forget the extent to which much of Europe failed to take Louis XIV seriously during the first years of his personal reign. The embassy in Rome would be Louis XIV's opportunity to capitalize on his diplomatic victory over the Spanish a year earlier, and this in the heart of diplomatic Europe.

Créquy was therefore sent into a situation even more contentious than that which had confronted d'Estrades a year earlier. Already in his first letter to Créquy, Louis XIV lays out his wish for satisfaction in a long-standing dispute with the new emperor, who had delayed in sending news of his election to the French court. The two leaders remained deadlocked over who should write to whom first, since sending the first letter was an implicit recognition of the other's superiority. Finally, the pope stepped in, and Louis XIV reluctantly agreed to write to the emperor. The king's words to Créquy are worth quoting here, since they reveal the extent to which he felt that he was sacrificing his authority by ceding: "J'ay gaigné sur moy mesme de complairre en cela a S Steté et luy ay accordé ce qu'il me demandoit. Quand vous ferez reflexion que ce que je viens de faire en cela est un relaschement d'une chose que j'avois long temps pretendue, et que vous considererez mesme ce seul mot de relaschement, vous me cognoissez assez pour juger qu'il ma fallu faire un grand effort sur moy mesme pour m'y laisser aller et notamment a l'esgard d'un autre Prince de dignité esgale a la mien" (I forced myself to please the pope in this matter and gave him what he asked. When you reflect upon the fact that what I have just done is to give in on something I have claimed for some time, and when you consider the very phrase "giving in," you know me well enough to judge that I had to make a great effort upon myself to do this and notably with regard to a prince whose dignity is equal to my own).[68]

Representative, then, of a king "jaloux de sa dignité," Créquy made his way to Rome, first refusing any welcoming ceremonies from Genoa as unworthy of his "caractère" (a refusal of which Lionne, and the king, approve), and then delaying his entry into Rome. On this last subject, the troubled nature of relations between Paris and Rome emerges in a letter sent by Lionne to Créquy: "Je tire bon augure que le Pape se soit laissé entendre que vous estiez trop long temps a faire vostre entrée, C'est signe qu'il a encore plus d'envie de vous voir que vous n'en avez de baiser sa mule" (I think that it is a good sign that the pope was heard to say that you were taking a long time to make your entry, it is a sign that he is more eager to see you than you are to kiss his slipper).[69] As might be expected in such an atmosphere, soon after Créquy's arrival the demands of maintaining the dignity of his representative character entered into conflict with the need for negotiation. The king writes to Créquy, "Je recognois aussi que c'est par le mesme motif du Zele de ma gloire que vous n'aviez point jusques la voulu entrer en aucun temperament sur la premiere visite qui vous est deue par les parens seculiers de sa Sainteté. Car au reste je vois fort bien qu'il vous seroit personnellement advantageux pour asseurer mieux le bon succez de vos negotiations et trouver moins de difficultez en toutes choses, que vous eussiez d'abord gaigné la bienveillance du Pape par quelque complaisance en une matiere qui doit fort le toucher" (I recognize as well that it is out of zeal for my glory that you have, up to this point, refused to concede in the matter of the first visit that the secular relatives of the pope owe you. But I also see that it would be personally advantageous for you, since it would lead to the success of your negotiations and to less difficulty in all matters, to win the pope's goodwill by agreeing to something that he regards as highly important).[70]

Further on in the letter, Louis XIV advises Créquy of his intent to follow the example of previous French kings by insisting that any graces that the pope wishes to accord the French king be channeled through the French ambassador rather than the papal *nonce* in Paris.

These preliminary details do much to establish Louis XIV's wish to uphold his authority through all possible means. They take on even greater significance given the historically contentious relation between the French kings and Rome. By insisting that diplomatic precedents be met and honored, Louis XIV is not merely asserting his wish to dominate the European diplomatic stage; in the context of negotiations with the pope, he is also asserting his independence from Rome. Each diplomatic success, each concession granted by the pope, reinforces the idea that the French king is not only the eldest son of the Catholic Church (le roi Très-Chrétien) but that his authority rests on a divine favor equal, if not superior, to that accorded the pontiff. In fact, the issue that the king alludes to above–the question of whether Créquy should visit the secular relations of the pope–occupies much of the first weeks of Créquy's stay in Rome and is quite significant in the context of French-Roman affairs. The pope's insistence that Créquy visit his relatives is read by Louis XIV as evidence of papal incursion beyond the ecclesiastic and into the temporal sphere of kings. Indeed, the argument that the pope's nephews and cousins should be regarded as a church equivalent of *princes du sang* reveals his desire to subjugate the princes of Europe on their own terrain.[71] Once again, Louis XIV is torn between the dignity due to him and the need to advance negotiations, and he repeatedly admonishes Créquy to humor the pope, "qui de son naturel s'arreste plus a ces petites circonstances de ceremonies qu'a des choses solides" (who, by his nature, is more preoccupied with these small ceremonial circumstances than with solid things).[72]

In spite of these recommendations of flexibility, which one assumes were carried out, the French ambassador remained subject to suspicion and even to the violation of his residence by papal officers. In July of 1662, Cardinal Imperiali, governor of Rome, carried out a search of a house near the French embassy while the latter building was empty. Although Rome was infamous (as was Madrid) for the *franchise de territoire* accorded foreign ambassadors, wherein each neighborhood was effectively viewed as outside the purview of local justice, Louis XIV's outrage at this incident (which Créquy almost certainly delighted in reporting) reveals the extent to which he viewed the aura of his authority and monarchy as encompassing not merely his personal representative but also the ambassador's physical residence and property. This detail would prove significant in the events that would take place at the end of August, but in the meantime it offered Louis XIV the opportunity to explain to his ambassador the superior nature of his own authority as opposed to that of the pope. In the letter that treats the violation of the diplomatic neighborhood by Cardinal Imperiali, Louis XIV moves from threats of retaliation–"je ne suis pas endurant et j'ay dequoy me faire respecter et par eux et par de plus puissans qu'eux" (I am not patient and I have what it takes to make them, and those more important than them, respect me)–to a fascinating distinction between papal and royal authority: "je trouverois bien facilement les moyens sans manquer au respect que je veux tousjours rendre au St. Siege, de distinguer la personne du Pape d'avec la Chaire ou Il est presentement mais je veux croire que je ne seray pas oblige d'en venir la" (I would find it quite easy, without damaging the respect that I owe to the papacy, to distinguish the person of the pope from the office he presently holds, but I hope that I will not need to go so far as that).[73] Later in the same letter, he elaborates this distinction further: "les partis de France et d'Espaigne lors qu'ils sont joints dans Rome pouvant estre facilement superieurs a celuy de la personne du Pape qui n'a qu'une puissance passagere laquelle finit avec sa vie, ce que je ne vous suggere pourtant que dans les cas d'une absolue et extreme necessité, vous recommandant au reste d'esviter toutes pareilles occasions autant qu'il sera en vostre pouvoir sans commettre ou prejudicier a ma dignité et a vostre honneur et sur tout que vous ayez tousjours la raison pour vous" (The Spanish and French factions, when they are joined in Rome, could easily be much more powerful than that of the papal person, whose temporary power ends with his life. I only suggest this to you in the case of a most extreme necessity, and otherwise recommend that you avoid such occasions as much as is possible without compromising my dignity or your honor, and that you always have reason on your side).[74] This sentiment, echoed by Lionne in a letter written on the same day–"les Roys ont les mains longues et leur puissance ne finit point avec leur vie" (Kings have long hands and their power does not end with their life)[75]–is significant in that it sheds new light on the applicability of Kantorowicz's model of "the king's two bodies" to the French monarch.

Both Louis and Lionne draw a sharp contrast between the power underlying the authority of kings and popes, a distinction that on the surface supports the model of the two bodies. As is well known, when the pope dies, the papal throne remains vacant until the cardinals have chosen a successor. Prodi and others[76] point out that this vacancy of power led imperceptibly to the strengthening of the College of Cardinals, especially during the early modern period. The college increasingly carried out the function assumed by the English Parliament, whereby authority would temporarily rest in that body until a new representative of singular power was installed. Papal authority thus began to move toward the model of the two bodies at the same time as the authority of the French monarch was moving away from it.[77] Indeed, if we look closely at Louis XIV's pronouncements, it would seem that the distinction that he and his ministers make between papal and royal authority signify his reluctance to have royal authority contained in that model.[78] In other words, when Louis XIV proclaims that the French king's power continues after his death, he seems here to be referring not to the overarching authority of sovereignty, or even the Crown, but to his own personal power as Louis XIV. While Louis XIV remained deeply ambivalent about his own predecessors' laws and edicts (we need only think of his 1685 decision to revoke his grandfather's Edit de Nantes), this language manifests the young king's reluctance to accept the temporary nature of his own authority that is also perceptible in the *Mémoires*, a project begun during this period. The carefully drawn difference between "le prince Alexandre Chigi" and "le pape Alexandre Septieme" that recurs throughout this diplomatic mission (and that strengthens after the events of August 20, 1662) implies that no similar separation may be made with regard to Louis XIV's royal person. The man and the king are one and the same, and their power is immortal; this doctrine, obviously unprovable, is made manifest by repeated reference to the inferior status of papal power.

Créquy therefore found himself in a paradoxical position, one alluded to by the theorists cited in the first section of this chapter. Representing a monarch who admitted no division of his power entailed a combination of obedience and independence. On the one hand, Créquy must obey his instructions; on the other, he was in fact chosen as ambassador partially for his ability to act not just as the king's mouthpiece but as an embodiment of royal authority (if not arrogance). Créquy's intransigence becomes a reflection of Louis XIV's own disinclination to cede any part of his authority, whether to the emperor, as earlier, or to the pope. Just as royal power was becoming godlike in its independence, rather than linked to the divine through a relation of dependence, the French diplomat's mission was not to present himself as a servile civil servant but as the dignified representative of Louis XIV's jealously constructed *caractère*.

The events of August 20, 1662, and their aftermath left no doubt as to Louis XIV's interpretation of diplomatic representation. On this day, members of Créquy's household got into a street fight with the Corsican guards charged by Cardinal Imperiali with policing the city. As I have already mentioned, Rome was well known for the application of *franchise de territoire* and the abuses that came with it. As a result, during this period, Rome resembled less a well-ordered city under the command of the pope and Cardinal Imperiali than a collection of quasi-independent states, each claiming inviolability and self-jurisdiction as extensions of their home state.[79] The French combatants thus logically sought refuge from the Corsicans in the diplomatic residence, or at least in its courtyard. The Corsicans' decision to pursue them into this courtyard, and to continue the fight on French territory, was therefore viewed as a direct violation of Créquy's diplomatic status, much like Cardinal Imperiali's search of an adjoining building a month earlier. To make matters worse, in the confusion of the fight, the carriage carrying the ambassador's wife was attacked as well.

Louis XIV's reaction to this incident was, of course, immediate outrage:

> Mon Cousin, le Courrier Marguin arriva hier icy et me rendit vos depesches du 21e par l'une desquelles j'ay appris avec l'estonnement et le ressentiment que vous pouvez vous imaginer, ce qui s'estoit passé le jour d'auparavant dans Rome. Le forfait de la milice du Pape contre vostre personne et vostre palais, contre la personne de ma Cousine la duchesse de Crequi et son carrosse, contre tous vos domestiques et tous les Francois qui ont esté rencontrez dans les rues, a des circonstances si atroces et si cruelles qu'il sera a jamais detesté par les nations mesme les plus barbares. Cest pourquoy bien que je sois l'offensé et d'une qualité d'offence qui n'a point eu de pareil exemple en aucun temps ny chez aucun peuple Je crois que le Pape a encore plus d'interest que moy quelle soit promptement reparée par un chastiment proportionné s'il s'en peut trouver d'assez grand pour l'énormité de cet assassinat.[80]

> [My cousin,[81] the Courier Marguin arrived here yesterday and gave me your dispatches of the 21st. In one of them I learned with the astonishment and the resentment that you can easily imagine what happened the day before in Rome. The acts of the papal militia against your person and your palace, against the person of my cousin the Duchess of Crequi and her carriage, against all of your servants and all of the Frenchmen they encountered in the streets, represent circumstances so atrocious and cruel that they will be forever hated by all nations, even barbaric ones. This is why even though I am the offended party and offended in a manner that has no example in any time or with any other people I believe that the Pope has even more interest than myself in punishing the offense appropriately, if he can find a punishment that equals the enormity of this assassination.]

Several ideas stand out in this missive. First, we should note the eventual replacement of the "vous" and "vostre" as objects of the offense by the royal "je," implying that the attack was not merely on the king's ambassador but, by extension, on the king himself. This is especially interesting given that Créquy himself was never under personal attack; rather, the attack on his wife and on the residence are interpreted as attacks on the diplomat (and therefore the king). If, on the one hand, the object of the attack is determined by a complex extension of representative relations (residence-wife-diplomat), on the other hand, responsibility for the attack should be laid at the feet of the pope himself (following the chain of *gardes corses*-Cardinal Imperiali-pope). Although Alexander VII would resist accepting responsibility for what was essentially a tawdry street fight gone out of control, Louis XIV would of course continue to insist upon the pope's agency in the affair. Also worth noting is Louis XIV's characterization of the events as "sans exemple." At this point, the French king was almost certainly anticipating a public humiliation of the pope similar to that imposed on Spain after the 1661 incidents involving d'Estrades in London. Indeed, one of the satisfactions demanded (and obtained, two years later, in the Treaty of Pisa) by Louis XIV was the elevation of a "piramide" commemorating the attack in Rome and declaring the Corsican guards unfit for police work. This event, like the concession of precedency by the Spanish through their ambassador Fuensaldagna a year earlier, was commemorated in the medallic history of Louis XIV's reign issued by the Académie des Inscriptions in 1702 and immortalized in the paintings decorating the *galerie des glaces* at Versailles.

The events of August 20 removed any need to recommend caution or compromise to the French ambassador. Créquy was immediately ordered to leave Rome (an order he did not follow right away), and several measures were taken to ensure that the offended Créquy be viewed as a direct representative of the offended Louis XIV: "Tout cela [les réparations que Louis XIV demande au Pape] doit dependre de vostre prudence et de vostre addresse a laquelle je suis resolu de remettre comm'il est bien juste pour vostre reputation, toute la Conduite de cette affaire et que l'accommodement s'il a a se faire ne passera par vos mains ou avec vostre direction si vous estes hors de Rome afin que ceux qui vous ont offensé soient obligez pour m'appaiser de recourir a vous mesme et ne trouvent point d'autre porte ouverte que la vostre pour avoir accez auprez de moy et se remettre en mes bonnes graces qu'ils ont quelque interest de desirer" (All of this depends on your prudence and your tact, which I have decided to depend upon as it suits your reputation. All matters regarding this affair and its resolution, if there is to be one, will pass through your hands or your direction alone, or not at all if you are outside of Rome, so that those who have offended you are obliged, to make peace with me, to have recourse to you and should not find any other door open other than your own to gain access to me and put themselves in my good graces, a desire that they know is in their best interest).[82]

Just as Louis XIV had sought to limit the king of England's participation in the resolution of his conflict with the Spanish in order to preserve total control and authorship over the events, any hint that Créquy's departure from Rome could be an expression of the displeasure of the pope, rather than that of Louis XIV himself, was to be avoided. By the end of the negotiations preceding the Treaty of Pisa, during which Louis XIV occupied Avignon and threatened the papal states with occupation by a French army, Louis XIV had established complete personal control over his diplomats:

> Ayant esprouvé par une experience que je fais depuis vingt mois que le secret est l'ame des affaires qui les fait le plus souvent reussir ou manquer selon qu'il est bien ou mal gardé j'ay cru que pour le bien de mon service je ne pouvois trop redoubler mes precautions sur cette matiere, et par ce motif je vous fais cette lettre a part pour vous dire la mesme chose que je mande en mesme temps a tous mes autres Ambassadeurs ou Ministres qui me servent au dehors, qui est que je ne desire pas qu'a l'advenir vous escriviez a quelque personne que ce soit ny de ma Court ny de la ville non pas mesme a mes Ministres, aucune chose de ce qui se passe dans les affaires ny mesme aucunes nouvelles si ce n'est les courantes et tout a fait publiques, mais seulement a moy seul sous l'enveloppe accoustumée que je vous ay ordonnée a vostre depart, et cependant que vous redoubliez vos soins et teniez la main que celuy ou ceux de vos secretaires a qui vous estes obligé de confier les affaires se gardent bien sous peine de mon indignation d'en rien mander jamais a quelque amy ou parent quils puissent avoir.[83]

[Having felt by the experience of the past twenty months that secrecy is the soul of affairs and that matters succeed or fail depending on whether the secret is kept, I have decided for the good of my service that I cannot make too many efforts in this direction, and for this reason I am writing this letter to you particularly to tell you the same thing I am sending to all of my other ambassadors and ministers who serve me abroad, which is that I do not want you to write affairs other than those which are well known to anyone in my court or in the city, nor to any of my ministers. Instead, address these matters to me alone in the accustomed envelope that I gave you when you left, and take special care that the secretaries to whom you are obliged to confide do not, under penalty of my indignation, communicate anything ever to any friend or relative that they may have.]

Echoing Lionne's letter cited at the beginning of this chapter, this declaration of absolute personal control over diplomacy demonstrates Louis XIV's ability to transform what could have been just a seventeenth-century *fait divers* into a show of power, all the more significant since it took place at the heart of papal territory. Indeed, by insisting upon the elevation of the pyramid, the removal of Cardinal Imperiali as governor of Rome (if not his actual exile), and the disbanding of the *gardes corses,* Louis XIV went well beyond his victory over Spain of the year before. He was also able to phrase his victory in terms that suggested that the pope was now subject to his benevolence and forgiveness rather than the other way around, no small feat given the long-standing hostility between the two powers. It is worth pointing out that

Louis's letter goes a long way toward preventing the development of any sort of independent diplomatic corps such as that which would exist during and after the negotiations at Utrecht in 1713.[84] With Créquy, and a little help from the *gardes corses,* Louis XIV was able to articulate a diplomatic model based simultaneously on absolute obedience and absolute independence, a model that the ambiguous reaction of both the pope and other countries showed to be truly unique in European international affairs at the time.

5

MEDIATION AND SEVENTEENTH-CENTURY

FRENCH THEATER

Seventeenth-century French theorists of sovereignty and diplomacy felt the urgent need to reconcile independence and mediation in order to shore up the legitimacy of state practices both at home and abroad. Their literary counterparts, however, often profited from the impossibility of fully reconciling these models by exploring the tension between them. Questions of authorship and influence—which can be viewed as another manifestation of what I have termed the crisis of mediation, as Louis XIV's *Mémoires* show so well—penetrated all areas and genres of French literature during this time, culminating in the *querelle des anciens et des modernes* later in the century. The seventeenth-century legitimization of authorship, while fascinating, exceeds the scope of this study.[1] Here, I propose a deeper analysis of the genre that had the most contact with the problem of mediation—theater. Not only do numerous formal aspects of the theater, from the attribution of authorship to the complex figure of the actor, speak directly to the issues discussed earlier in this book, but of all literary production of the century—including, arguably, history—theater enjoyed what was perhaps the most complex relation to political power.[2] Seventeenth-century French theater occupied a liminal position between the Crown, which subsidized its productions and protected its authors, and the public, which was itself fractured between *doctes* and more naive spectators. As such, it was uniquely placed to both defend and critique governmental activity, and critics still debate the possible hidden messages contained in works by the century's greatest authors. In this chapter, I suggest that consideration of the problem of mediation that rests at the center of both government and theater can allow us to better appreciate the complex and nuanced relation between spectacle and monarchical politics.[3] Insofar as its very essence consists in the same problem of mediation central to governmental authority and legitimacy, theater is able to provide a commentary on the very principles underlying the structure of the seventeenth-century French state. The problematic relation between author and actor that characterized the theater throughout this period in many ways mirrors the theoretical difficulties encountered by writers on sovereignty or diplomacy. A better acquaintance with these problems can equip the reader to recognize the importance of playwrights' explicit treatment of mediatory figures, such as the actor or the ambassador, and to appreciate such treatments' political and cultural significance.

THE POLITICAL SIGNIFICANCE OF THEATRICAL PRODUCTION

Before beginning my analysis of these issues, however, I would like to call attention to the profound alliance between seventeenth-century theater and diplomatic practice. With the significant exception of Marie-Claude Canova-Green,[4] few critics have recognized that theatrical productions played an integral role in the politics of the time. Plays were performed not merely for the king's personal enjoyment but often to send messages, more or less bluntly, to ambassadors visiting the country. These ambassadors were expected to attend the performance, and their seating at such events was carefully regulated according to the rules of *préséance*. As a result, the content of the ambassadorial guest list at performances was deeply significant to both the French spectators and to the diplomats themselves. While often overlooked by current critics, the international importance of government-sponsored plays is commonplace in treatises of the time, including that of the Abbé d'Aubignac. His *Pratique du théâtre* (1657) mentions theater's role in impressing foreign visitors *before* his consideration of its role in educating the domestic populace and providing distraction for a hard-working prince: "Aussi, quelles marques plus sensibles, & plus generales pourroit-on donner de la grandeur d'un Etat, que ces illustres divertissements? C'est par là que durant la paix on fait paroître qu'il a beaucoup de richesses superfluës, beaucoup d'hommes inutiles sans lui être à charge, beaucoup d'Esprits civilisez & fertiles en toutes sortes d'inventions, & beaucoup d'habiles Ouvriers pour executer les plus ingenieuses pensées" (Therefore, what more striking and general marks can one give of a state's grandeur than these illustrious spectacles? This is how, during peace, one conveys that there are many superfluous riches, many idle men who do not depend on the state, many cultivated minds fertile in all sorts of inventions, and many skilled workers to execute the most ingenious thoughts).[5] If the display of luxurious superfluity in peacetime is meant to convey the state's grandeur, during times of war this same display serves to excite a different kind of admiration: "les Atheniens aiant reçu dans le Theatre la nouvelle de la défaite entière de leur armée devant Syracuse, n'en voulurent pas interrompre les Jeux, & les Ambassadeurs étrangers qui assistoient à ce Spectacle, & qui considererent cette action, admirerent leur generosité plus difficile à vaincre que leur Republique" (the Athenians, having received in the theater the news of their army's complete defeat at Syracuse, did not want to interrupt the games, and the foreign ambassadors who were at the spectacle and who considered this action admired their generosity, which was more difficult to vanquish than their republic).[6] Such statements suggest that the presence of foreign visitors at plays is essential and that plays have a political significance quite apart from their actual content. The "patriotic" significance of theater is further signaled by Samuel Chappuzeau, who attested, in his Le théâtre françois (1674), to the profound link between good theater and a successful monarchy, adding that French theater enjoyed a special status in all of the many countries that he visited.[7]

Louis XIV unquestionably used theater, especially plays ordered for specific occasions, to convey political messages to ambassadors. The message often went beyond the conveyance of French sumptuousness and grandeur. The most famous occurrence of this practice was Louis XIV's demand that Molière provide a comedy with Turkish elements in order to repair the affronts that the Turkish ambassador had committed during his official reception and stay in France. I have argued elsewhere that the resultant play, Molière's *Bourgeois gentilhomme*, is in fact a very complex response to the official version of French-Turkish relations,[8] but the fact that actual diplomatic events inspired the play's composition indicates the extent to which Louis XIV enthusiastically used the stage to promote (or disguise) political messages and events.[9] I would even go so far as to suggest that the first version of *Tartuffe*, produced as part of the *Plaisirs de l'Isle Enchantée* festival in 1664, was not unrelated to the upcoming, and long-awaited, visit of the cardinal Chigi, who was set to arrive in Paris a few months later with an official apology for the events surrounding

Créquy two full years before. This close relation between international events or audiences and the plays' actual content was facilitated in these cases by Molière's quickness in composing plays on royal command; yet political messages were also conveyed to both an international and domestic audience through other performances, such as ballet.

AUTHORSHIP AND THE THEATER

Such circumstances of production raise the question of who receives credit for a play's conception and success. Should the king, who transmitted the idea to the playwright, be acknowledged as the work's inspiration and therefore as its ultimate author? In fact, many writers do just this by dedicating their (printed) play to nobility, to ministers, or to the king himself.[10] In the dedication accompanying *Horace*, Corneille asked Richelieu, "Et certes, MONSEIGNEUR, ce changement visible qu'on remarque en mes ouvrages depuis que j'ai l'honneur d'être à Votre Eminence, qu'est-ce autre chose qu'un effet des grandes idées qu'elle m'inspire quand elle daigne souffrir que je lui rende mes devoirs?" (And certainly, Monseignor, this visible change that can be seen in my works ever since I have had the honor to work for you, what else can it be than an effect of the great ideas that you inspire in me when you deign to receive my work?).[11] Likewise, Racine's carefully drawn parallel between Alexander the Great and Louis XIV in his dedication of *Alexandre le Grand* implies that credit for the play belongs ultimately with the monarch whose example outshines and underlies the plot.

Despite the authors' own frequent resentment regarding the requirement of placing admiring dedications before their printed works, these formulations are too easily dismissed as empty flattery. Although such tributes are certainly in part pleas for financial support, to see them *only* as such is to ignore the importance of mediation as a dominant trope in seventeenth-century France.[12] The interpretation of the dedication as self-interested promotion assumes that there is a preexisting notion of the author as autonomous agent, and, indeed, that complete authorship itself is possible for any entity other than God. I hope to have shown that this is not the case even for the monarch, who must frame his own activities in the context of his status as "the image of God on earth." Although, as Alain Viala has persuasively argued, the author was emerging during this period as a distinct social identity, this emergence—much like that of the "absolute" monarch—was by no means simple. Arbitrary creation, true originality, was universally condemned by authors and critics alike. The seventeenth-century author was, in many ways, merely one node in a vast network of influences, sources, and inspirations. Indeed, many of the *querelles* surrounding the theater during this time focused on the question of authorship.[13]

The troubled relation between authorship and the theater can be traced, like so many other issues in seventeenth-century literature, to Aristotle. Seventeenth-century theorists noted that the philosopher distinguished between epic and theater through the different roles of the author in each. D'Aubignac's summary of this distinction is typical:

> La plus notable différence, & qu'on peut nommer essentielle, du Poëme Epique, & du Dramatique, est que dans le premier le Poëte parle seul, les personnes qu'il introduit pour faire des recits ne parlans que par sa bouche; c'est lui qui dit que ces Gens-là faisoient tels discours, & non pas eux qui viennent pour les faire. Mais dans la Poësie Dramatique, il n'y a que les Personnes introduites par le Poëte, qui parlent, sans qu'il y prenne aucune part, & dans toute l'action Theatrale il ne paroît non plus que si les Acteurs étoient en verité ceux qu'ils representent, & qui n'avoient pas besoin de son ministere pour s'expliquer non plus que pour agir.[14]

> [The most notable difference, and the most essential one, between the Epic Poem and the Dramatic, is that in the first the poet speaks alone, since the characters he introduces to recount the action only speak through his mouth; it is the poet who says that these people made a certain speech, and not these people themselves who come to make it. But in Dramatic Poetry, only the characters introduced by the poet speak, without the poet taking any part, and in all theatrical action it does not seem either that if the actors are indeed those whom they represent they do not need the poet's ministry to explain themselves anymore than they need it to act.]

I have quoted d'Aubignac rather than Aristotle here not only because most other theorists use the same terms as d'Aubignac to characterize the difference between the two genres but also because these words are a fairly serious distortion of the actual content of the *Poetics*. Aristotle himself places difference of mode (the subject discussed by d'Aubignac above) as only one of three determinant factors for genre, the other two being difference of media and difference of objects. With regard to epic and tragedy, similar genres insofar as they both are "a sizeable *mimesis* in verse of noble personages,"[15] Aristotle notes that epic, unlike tragedy, is unaccompanied by music, is longer, and is "in narrative form." This last quality, however, does not seem to imply the necessary presence of the author at each page. Later in the *Poetics,* Aristotle complicates what in d'Aubignac appears to be a clear distinction when he states that "Homer especially deserves praise as the only epic poet to realize what the epic poet should do in his own person, that is, say as little as possible, since it is not in virtue of speaking in his own person that he is a maker of *mimesis.*"[16] This assertion implies that, ideally, neither the writer of tragedy nor the writer of epic should implicate himself directly in his work. Such authorial involvement breaks the spell of *mimesis,* which is the illusion that the characters themselves are speaking to the audience. According to Aristotle, pure authorial presence unmixed with direct discourse should only be found in song or dithyramb.

Seventeenth-century theorists' misreading of these categorizations draws a firm line between epic and tragedy *primarily* through the difference in the manner of representation, indeed, implying that it is the *only* difference. The reasons for this misreading, which include the changing relation between music and literature during this period, lie beyond the scope of this study. Yet I believe we can read into d'Aubignac and his contemporaries a certain fascination with the problem posed by authorship in the theater, a genre in which the author should seem as absent as possible. This fascination fits well with the period's larger concerns with mediation and first causes, including the role of the divine in an increasingly independent or mechanized universe.[17] The theory of authorship in theater would therefore become—much like the theory of sovereign kingship—a privileged locus in which certain notions concerning authority, legitimacy, and influence could be tested.

The Abbé d'Aubignac's *Pratique du théâtre* (1657) exemplified the problematic status of the theatrical writer in its content and also in its form and purpose. The title implies that the work is a guide for potential writers, laying down rules that, if followed, will lead to a successful work. Yet the work is simultaneously addressed to the spectator, who needs to be reminded (or even informed for the first time) of the skill involved in creating a successful play: "J'écris seulement pour faire connoître au Peuple, l'excellence de leur Art, & pour lui donner sujet de les admirer, en montrant combien il faut d'adresse, de suffisance, & de précautions pour achever des Ouvrages qui ne donnent à nos Comediens que la peine de les reciter, & qui ravissent de joie ceux qui les écoutent" (I am writing only to show the people the excellence of their art, and to give them cause to admire it by demonstrating how much skill, aptitude and precautions are needed to achieve the works that give our actors the only trouble of reciting them, and which overwhelm those who hear them with joy).[18] Although the public may think, due to the very nature of the spectacle and its powerful *mimesis,* that the actors themselves are the creators of their texts insofar as they embody their characters, behind all of this show is the author himself, who should not be forgotten even though his presence on the stage is prohibited.

But here d'Aubignac has reasoned himself into a difficult situation, since reminding the public of the author's presence in a play is tantamount to breaking theater's spell and undermining the constitutive mimetic power of the genre.[19] In his famous comparison of the theater to a painting, d'Aubignac states that there are two ways of seeing a play. One way is as the creation of the artist and a (willed) assemblage of colors and shadows, and the other is representational, containing "une chose qui est peinte" (a thing that is painted).[20] The problem is that these two ways of seeing cannot coexist simultaneously. Paying attention to one implies the destruction or forgetting of the other. Indeed, this very inability of the spectator to consider two aspects of the play simultaneously while under the illusion of the spectacle motivates d'Aubignac's discussion of the unities of time, place, and action. In the case of action, "il est certain que le Theatre n'est rien qu'une Image, & partant comme il est impossible de faire une seule image accomplie de deux originaux differens, il est impossible que deux Actions (j'entens principales) soient representées raisonnablement par une seule Piece de Theatre" (it is certain that the theater is nothing but an image, and just as it is impossible to make one perfect image from two different originals, it is impossible that two principal actions can be reasonably represented by just one play).[21] Likewise, in his consideration of the unity of place, d'Aubignac discards the idea that the same actor can play two different roles, since his voice alone will make the spectator suppose not that he is, in fact, representing another person but rather that he is the same person disguised.[22]

This insistence on unity, on the correspondence on all levels of the play of the singular to the singular, should remind us of Bodin's method of proving that monarchy is the only logical form of sovereignty. Similar issues arose in diplomatic theory under Louis XIV and the insistence that the king be represented by a single (French) ambassador rather than by committee (or, if several diplomats were used, that they be considered as one body). The singular can only be represented by the singular; there *must* be some resemblance between the various levels of representation in order for the transfer of identity, power, or believability to work. Yet as we have already seen in the case of the diplomat and as we shall see shortly in the case of the actor, the idea that resemblance should motivate representation can be quite dangerous, especially when, as in theater and diplomacy, the goal of the representation is to forget the absence of that which is represented.[23] Take, for example, d'Aubignac's statement that "Le Theatre est comme un Monde particulier, où tout est renfermé dans les notions & l'étenduë de l'action representée, & qui n'a point de communication avec le grand Monde, sinon autant qu'il s'y rencontre attaché par la connoissance que le Poëte en donne avec adresse" (The theater is like its own world, where everything is enclosed in the ideas and breadth of the represented action, and this world does not communicate with the larger world except if it is explicitly attached to it by the poet's art).[24] This formulation expresses the capacity of the representation to take on an independent life of its own, which it will do if it is successful. A foreign prince dealing with an ambassador should in some sense believe that he is in fact speaking to the king whom that ambassador represents. An audience at a play should, likewise, believe that they are genuinely witnessing real actions.

D'Aubignac's qualification in the above statement that the poet provides the only connection between the two worlds brings us back, however, to the central yet contradictory role of the theatrical author. For the theorist, the successful writer of plays is invisible, since "le genie du Theatre est tel, que d'ordinaire, ce qui ne paroît point, en est le plus grand art" (the genius of the theater is such that ordinarily what does not appear is the greatest art).[25] D'Aubignac therefore provides a rather extreme interpretation of Aristotle's ideas concerning theatrical mimesis. Although in seventeenth-century France many authors acted as assistant directors, supervising the actors and supplying advice on the interpretation of the text, d'Aubignac holds that this participation in the play's production is unnecessary, since in many cases the author is either in a location far from the theater or, in the case of the ancients, dead. While this admonition against authorial presence during rehearsals is understandable, d'Aubignac extends his desire to eliminate all trace of the author further by instructing the playwright, in the text of his work, to abstain from notes outside of the dialogue. Indeed, according to d'Aubignac, all information available to the spectator (and the reader) must come from the verbal interaction of the actors.

This hostility to the direct intervention of the authorial voice can be explained, as we have seen, by an equally extreme defense of mimesis, or rather of *vraisemblance*. *Vraisemblance* governs not only what takes place on the stage but even the choice of subject, and d'Aubignac's valorization of *vraisemblance* is at least partly responsible for what critics have found to be his almost disturbing modernity and corresponding hostility to the ancients. Seventeenth-century French playwrights cannot treat the same legends as the ancients, or at least not in the same way, since the seventeenth-century French spectator cannot share the pleasure of a republican Athenian in seeing kings brought low and would find such a plot unlikely. Historical truth is to be sacrificed for the sake of probability, since d'Aubignac, like many of his contemporaries, believed that drama shows acts not as they happened but as they *should* happen. Yet here, once again, strict interpretation of *vraisemblance* carries the danger of subjecting the play's creator to its laws. The author, banished from the actual stage in the name of *vraisemblance*, finds that the central elements of the plot he has set in motion begin, after a certain point, to take on a life of their own. The play begins to write itself: "voire même est-il certain que le Poëte est moins excusable pour une faute qu'il fait dans les Incidens de son Sujet avenus auparavant l'ouverture du Theatre, parce qu'il en est le Maître absolu; au lieu que souvent dans la suite des intrigues il y a quelques Evenemens qui contraignent les autres, & qui ne laissent pas l'Auteur si libre à faire tout ce qu'il voudroit" (indeed it is certain that the poet is less excusable for a fault made in the incidents of his subject that occurred before the opening of the play, because there he is the absolute master. Inside the play in the sequence of intrigues there are often a few events that determine the others and that do not leave the author as free to do everything that he would like).[26]

This conclusion, with its striking similarities to the thought of another resolute modernist and mechanist of the period, Descartes, threatens to bring down the central purpose of the treatise—that of enlightening the spectator/reader as to the immense effort and talent required to create a successful play. The possibility remains that some sort of *invraisemblable* event is necessary not only to signal the author's creative powers but also to keep the spectator's interest; it is indeed difficult to imagine repeated viewing of a play in which events follow their own internal, unsurprising logic. To his credit, d'Aubignac is aware of this difficulty. In the chapter titled "De la Préparation des Incidents" of the third book of the *Pratique*, d'Aubignac warns:

On pourroit peut-être s'imaginer que le Discours où nous allons entrer, ne seroit pas une instruction avantageuse au Poëte, mais plutôt au contraire une pratique capable de détruire tous les agrémens du Theatre. Car dira-t-on, s'il faut que les Incidens soient préparez long-temps auparavant qu'ils arrivent, sans doute ils seront prévenus; & partant ils ne seront plus surprenans, en quoi consiste toute leur grace, & ainsi le Spectateur n'en aura plus aucun plaisir, ni le Poëte aucune gloire. A cela je réponds qu'il y a bien de la difference entre prévenir un Incident, & le préparer; car l'Incident est prévenu lors qu'il est prévu, mais il ne doit pas être prévu encore qu'il soit préparé.[27]

[One could perhaps imagine that the discourse we are about to embark upon would not be an instruction advantageous to the poet, but rather a practice capable of destroying all agreements of the theater. For, one might say, if the incidents were prepared well before they happen, they will undoubtedly be expected, and therefore they will no longer be surprising, and the spectator will have no more pleasure and the poet will have no more glory. To this I respond that there is a great difference between expecting an incident and preparing it, for the incident is expected when it is foreseen, but it should not be foreseen even when it is prepared.]

The tension between the laws of poetic composition and regularity, on the one hand, and the spectator's pleasure and the poet's glory, on the other, could not be better expressed. In order to keep the two from working against each other, d'Aubignac must separate spectator and author in the sense that the writer's efforts to prepare the surprising incident must not be immediately noticed by the spectator, who mistakenly believes the incident to be new. The poet's art is expressed not through *coups de théâtre* resembling divine miracles but rather through the hidden preparation that the spectator/reader can discover through logic and reason (thereby deepening and extending his first pleasure): "Je sçai bien que le Theatre est une espece d'illusion, mais il faut tromper les Spectateurs en telle sorte, qu'ils ne s'imaginent pas l'être, encore qu'ils le sçachent; il ne faut pas tandis qu'on les trompe, que leur esprit le connoisse; mais seulement quand il y fait reflexion" (I know very well that the theater is a kind of illusion, but one must trick the spectators in such a way that they do not perceive that they are tricked, even if they know that they are; their minds must not know that they are being tricked while being tricked, but only afterwards, when they think about it).[28]

All of the qualifications and contradictions that d'Aubignac introduces regarding authorship are made necessary by his belief that the play is the *image* of real (however idealized) action. As a *made* object, the play's relation to its referent is infinitely complex, as is the proper status to be accorded to its maker. As we have seen, the spectator can be fooled into believing that the action on stage is really taking place. He can also take a rational, logical pleasure in contemplating the art through which this illusion is achieved. However, he cannot do both at the same time. The author, however, is in a much more difficult situation, since he must occupy a position placed precisely at the intersection of art and reality in order to write his play. In order for the play to succeed, to be believable, the author must share credit, as it were, with the model from which he works. Yet on the other hand, his art is *superior* to its model in that it is the fruit of rational thought and planning. What d'Aubignac implicitly demands from his author is precisely that which he identifies elsewhere as impossible–the *simultaneous* belonging to both worlds, the made and the given. This perhaps explains the sliding of the ostensible purpose of the treatise from that of advising potential writers to that of alerting the spectator to the skill involved in writing. No less than the divine right monarch or the diplomat, the author–situated at the confluence of two mutually exclusive models and forces–proves impossible to define.

D'Aubignac's unease with the figure of the theatrical writer is further evident in the inconsistency of his descriptions of that figure. Although he consistently identifies the author as the person who can do nothing more than establish the elements of his play at its outset, since once these elements are set in motion they will, in a certain sense, obey their own laws, in other places he singles out the playwright for great praise. This duality appears clearly in the following passage:

> Je sais bien que le Poëte en est le Maître, qu'il dispose l'ordre & l'oeconomie de sa piéce, comme il lui plaît, qu'il prend le temps, l'allonge & le racourcit à sa volonté, qu'il choisit le lieu tel que bon lui semble dans tout le monde, & que pour les intrigues il les invente, selon la force & l'adresse de son imagination: en un mot il change les matieres & leur donne des formes comme il le veut resoudre dans son conseil secret: mais il est vrai pourtant que toutes ces choses doivent être si bien ajustées, qu'elles semblent avoir eu d'elles-mêmes, la naissance, le progrez, & la fin qu'il leur donne. Et quoi qu'il en soit l'Auteur, il les doit manier si dextrement, qu'il ne paroisse pas seulement les avoir écrites.[29]

> [I know very well that the poet is the master of his play, that he orders it as he pleases, that he takes time and lengthens or shortens it at will, that he chooses whichever place pleases him out of the entire world, and that he invents intrigues according to the force and address of his imagination: in a word, he changes the material and gives it form as he resolves to do in his secret council: but it is nonetheless true that all of these things–their beginning, progress, and end–must be so well adjusted that they seem to happen by themselves. And although he is the author of them, he must treat them so adroitly that he does not even seem to have written them.]

The echoes in this passage of divine creation and even of political administration demonstrate the resonance of the problem of the theatrical author with that of the other figures discussed earlier. The author's absent presence verges on the great mysteries of church and state. On the one hand, the expectations of the spectators and the exigencies of probability significantly restrict the author's room for creation. On the other hand, the accomplished author is godlike and (by implication) kinglike. Unlike the spectator, who can only decipher events as they occur on stage, he sees everything all at once. Elsewhere, d'Aubignac alludes to this tension, without really trying to solve it, by listing the sources of the playwright's inspiration. First in order of mention are the subject or the content of the play; however, first in importance is the poet's imagination: "Ce n'est pas assez d'avoir ébranlé l'esprit des Spectateurs, mais il les faut enlever; & pour le faire, il en faut chercher la matiere, ou dans la grandeur du Sujet s'il la peut fournir; ou dans les divers motifs qui l'environnent; mais sur tout dans la force de l'imagination, qui doit s'échauffer, se presser, & se donner un travail égal à celui de l'enfantement, pour produire des choses dignes d'admiration. Ainsi fait Monsieur Corneille" (It is not enough to have shocked the spectators, but they must be transported, and to do this, one must find material either in the grandeur of the subject or in the diverse motives that surround it, but especially in the force of the imagination, which must excite itself and give itself work equal to that of childbirth to produce things deserving of admiration. This is what Monsieur Corneille does).[30]

D'Aubignac's invocation of Corneille in this context is far from coincidental. Throughout the *Pratique,* d'Aubignac praises Corneille's gifts as a writer to a point that, as in the passage above, Corneille's name becomes a kind of shorthand for authorial genius. This is not to say, however, that Corneille is easily integrated into d'Aubignac's theories of authorship and *vraisemblance.* As Georges Forestier argues, d'Aubignac's ideally invisible author is completely at odds with Corneille's elevation and celebration of the author's role.[31] In fact, Corneille's now-legendary efforts toward recognition of the author through titles, glory, or financial reward are proof enough that d'Aubignac's ideal of the self-effacing author could be—and was—challenged during the course of the century.

Indeed, exactly twenty years before the publication of d'Aubignac's *Pratique,* the quarrel that arose around Corneille's immensely successful play *Le Cid* (1637) amply illustrated the contentious nature of theatrical authorship in seventeenth-century France. Although critics of *Le Cid* professed to see faults in the play as soon as they saw it on the stage, the *querelle du Cid* began in earnest when a poem that Corneille had written to a friend became public. This playful work, titled *Excuse à Ariste,* was largely a lengthy excuse for the author's inability to write a song requested by his friend. In reality a fairly complex genealogy of inspiration in which the playwright ultimately credits his unforgettable first love for his poetic prowess,[32] the first part of the poem, in which Corneille states his intention of praising his own gifts while asserting that such self-praise is far from uncommon in his time, contained one line that ignited the fury of Corneille's contemporaries: "Je ne dois qu'à moy seul toute ma Renommée" (I owe my reputation only to myself).[33]

Disregarding the fact that the *Excuse* had been written before *Le Cid,* Corneille's contemporaries, led by the playwrights Mairet and Scudéry (who were further enraged by the poem's next lines, in which Corneille declares that he has no rivals), attacked. Although many critical accounts of the ensuing *querelle* focus on the competing opinions regarding the *vraisemblance* of the work's content, no less important were the various ideas of authorship and artistic autonomy expressed during the course of the year.[34] Mairet's initiation of the debate struck directly at the heart of Corneille's claim of authorship and was titled, pointedly, "L'Autheur du Vray Cid Espagnol à son Traducteur François, sur une Lettre en vers, qu'il a faict imprimer Intitulée (Excuse à Ariste) ou apres cens traits de vanité, il dit parlant de soymesme *Je ne doy qu'a moy seul toute ma Renommée*" (The Author of the True Spanish Cid to his French Translator, on a Letter in verse that he had printed, titled Excuse to Ariste, where after one hundred vain statements he says, speaking of himself, that *he owes his name only to himself*).[35] By pointing out that Corneille had not, in fact, created *Le Cid* but rather had adapted Guilhen de Castro's *Las Mocedades del Cid* (1618), itself only one of a long series of literary adaptations of the Spanish hero's life, Mairet emphasized that any merit that *Le Cid* might have came not from Corneille but rather from the Spanish original.

Georges de Scudéry did not waste time in seizing upon this line of attack. In his *Observations sur le Cid*, which would become the trigger for the Académie Française's intervention in the quarrel, he acknowledges the importance of "invention" for poetic creation all while asserting that the invention of *Le Cid* should be attributed to Guilhen de Castro, not the "French translator."[36] Worse yet, according to Scudéry, what contributions Corneille did make to the story are almost always objectionable. Like d'Aubignac later in the century, Scudéry uses *vraisemblance* to restrict the author's powers of creation, implying that breaks in verisimilitude should be attributed to the writer's problematic desire to celebrate himself over his text. Take, for example, Scudéry's criticism of the scene where Rodrigue announces that he found five hundred soldiers waiting to serve him against the Moorish invasion: "Et quoy que les bons Seigneurs (les 500) n'y songeassent pas, l'Autheur qui fait leur destinee, les a bien sceu forcer malgré qu'ils en eussent à s'assembler, et sçait luy seul, à quel usage on les doit mettre" [And although the good men (the five hundred) did not think of it, the Author who made their destiny knew how to force them to assemble in spite of themselves, and alone knows to what use to put them].[37] Such errors in judgment, combined with what Scudéry views as the false advertising for the play, in which Mondory, the posters, and the printing all present *Le Cid* as "purement de son traducteur,"[38] lead Scudéry to conclude that Corneille has usurped the title of author in a way that obscures the true source of his inspiration. Such usurpation, reinforced by the sentiments expressed in the infamous *Excuse*, is best described in political terms. The last lines of Scudéry's pamphlet read as follows: "J'estois obligé, de faire voir à l'Autheur du CID, qu'il se doit contenter de l'honneur, d'estre Citoyen d'une si belle Republique, sans s'imaginer mal à propos, qu'il en peut devenir le Tyran" (I was forced to show the author of *The Cid* that he should content himself to be the citizen of such a beautiful republic without imagining, out of turn, that he could become the tyrant of it).[39] The metaphor of tyranny demonstrates the close connection between the growing problem of authorship, especially in the theater, and the problem of sovereign legitimacy. Corneille's Bodin-like claim to absolute independence, despite the obvious presence of the Spanish play written less than thirty years before, is violently rejected by his contemporaries, who try to offer an alternative model of authorship that preserves the playwright's capacities for creation while ensuring his legitimacy.

As the rest of the quarrel demonstrates, however, this task is no less difficult than the similar one facing contemporary theorists of sovereignty. Scudéry's pamphlet was immediately countered by a *Deffense du Cid* (written, Gasté maintains, by Nicolas Faret), which pointed out that Scudéry's lengthy description of the play's faults should be directed not at the "translator" of the play, Corneille, but rather at the original story itself. In fact, Faret argues, given what Corneille had to work with, he should be accorded *more* glory than the "Author," since "il est beaucoup plus mal-aisé de traduire et de bien suivre l'esprit d'un Autheur qu'on fait parler en autre langue que de faire un ouvrage propre" (it is much harder to translate and to follow an author's thoughts well in another language than to write one's own work).[40] Corneille himself counters Scudéry by pointing out that Scudéry's attack is, in fact, no less presumptuous than Corneille's own claims to authorship: "Vous avez avancé des maximes de Theater de vostre seule auctorité, dont toutesfois quand elles seroient vrayes, vous ne pouriez tirer les consequences cornuës que vous en tirez" (You have advanced maxims of theater from your own authority. Even if they are true, you cannot deduct from them the twisted consequences that you do).[41] The charge of tyranny and misguided authority is therefore tossed back at Scudéry, revealing the ubiquity—despite *mondain* assertions to the contrary—of pretentions to authorship and authority that dared not speak their name (a point that Corneille had, in fact, made in the *Excuse à Ariste*).

Only one of the pamphlets in the *querelle* unambiguously defends authorial imagination. The anonymous author of the lengthy *Discours à Cliton sur les observations du Cid*[42] not only states that "je ne croy pas que nous soyons tenus de regler nos Poëmes sur les modelles des Grecs et des Latins, quand il nous vient quelque lumière qu'ils n'ont pas euë, ou quelque grace dont ils ont manqué" (I do not believe that we are obliged to model our poems on the models of the Greeks and Latins when we have had an insight that they did not have, or some grace which they did not possess),[43] he also rejects the "pre-tendüe Regle de vingt-quatre heures" (the so-called twenty-four hour rule). Resolutely *moderne* well before the *querelle des anciens et des modernes* erupted in the 1680s, the author seems not to have influenced the debate over *Le Cid* greatly, since his rather scandalous contributions are never referenced or even refuted by the other participants. His doctrine that "c'est une plus forte action d'entendement de produire quelque chose de soy, que d'admirer les inventions d'autruy, ou de les imiter" (it is a stronger action of understanding to produce something oneself than to admire or imitate the inventions of oth-ers)[44] seems to have fallen on deaf ears. It is worth remembering, while read-ing this pamphlet, that even *Le Cid*'s defenders (with the significant exception of Corneille himself) pointed out the immense talent needed for the transla-tion of others' works. Like d'Aubignac some years later, however, the author of the *Discours à Cliton* pairs his immense praise for the authorial role (and his modernity) with the requirement that the dramatic author, unlike the writer of epics, absent himself completely from his work. Decrying the ten-dency of playwrights to give in to their own vanity by placing their own words and thoughts in the mouths of the play's characters, the author of the *Discours* concludes that

> Asseurément comme il est permis au Poëte de faire des siennes, et de se don-ner carriere dans le Poëme Epique, il doit tellement observer le contraire dans le Dramatique, et se tenir tousjours si loing de la Scene, qu'au lieu de prester son esprit aux personnages qu'il y introduit, ou de les faire mouvoir comme avec des ressorts, par la voix et l'action naturelle des Comediens, il se doit entiere-ment oublier, se despoüiller de soy-mesme, transformer ses Acteurs en chacun de ceux qu'ils representent, et pour ainsi dire resusciter les morts en corps et en ame, plustost que de les inspiriter fantastiquement, et leur donner des ames et des mouvemens qu'ils n'ont jamais eus.[45]

> [Assuredly as the poet is allowed to carry on and give himself freedoms in the epic poem, he must observe the contrary in the dramatic poem, and hold him-self so far from the stage that instead of lending his mind to the characters he introduces there, or making them move like puppets, through the voice and the natural action of the actors he should forget himself entirely, transform his actors into the people they represent, and so to speak resuscitate the dead in soul and body instead of fantastically animating them and giving them souls and movements that they never had.]

The *Discours à Cliton* lacks much of the subtlety of d'Aubignac's treatise, pub-lished twenty years later, but its message is essentially the same.[46] On the one hand, both critics grant an almost unheard-of liberty to the author as to the choice of events to be portrayed and how to portray them. On the other hand, they demand a radical invisibility from the author that seems quite different from the attention that Corneille himself was seeking.

The Académie Française, in the *Sentiments* meant to put an end to the *querelle*, provided a lukewarm definition of the fields open (and closed) to authorial initiative: "Car si nous croyons que le Poète, comme maistre du temps, peut allonger ou accourcir celuy des actions qui composent son sujet, c'est tousjours à condition qu'il demeure dans les termes de la vray-semblance, et qu'il ne viole point le respect deu aux choses sacrées" (For if we believe that the poet, as master of time, can lengthen or shorten the actions that compose his subject, it is always on the condition that he remain within the bounds of verisimilitude, and that he does not violate the respect due to sacred things).[47] This equivocal answer reveals in itself the difficulty of defining authorship (a category very close to that of sovereign kingship) in seventeenth-century France. Could the author be bound by the laws of his own creation? Was his creativity restricted by the creations of his predecessors, and if so, how exactly could these predecessors themselves have legitimately created their own works? These questions alone should demonstrate that opening the category of the author to scrutiny—challenging the restrictions placed upon it that, to Corneille, obviously seemed to be quite arbitrary—began a series of searches for the origins of originality, as it were, that could only end in absurdity. Charles Perrault's playful assertion, in his *Parallèle des anciens et des modernes,* that the "creativity" and "invention" of the ancients was not merely just another instance of imitation but indeed was an imitation of animal activity—a conclusion supported, in his view, by evidence from the New World—represents the logical end to such persistent questioning.[48]

Much easier, therefore, is the assertion of absolute independence and self-generated originality; Corneille's "je ne dois qu'à moi seul toute ma renommée" and Louis XIV's apocryphal "l'état, c'est moi," bear more than a passing resemblance. Yet such proclamations are similar also in that their vehemence tends to mask the vulnerability of the positions of both author and king. Just as the monarch (increasingly, during the seventeenth century) governed through *intendants,* ministers, and ambassadors, the playwright, unlike his epic-writing counterpart, had to express himself through the intermediary figure of the actor. The question raised by the *querelle du Cid*—who, ultimately, is responsible for a play's success?—evokes the problem of preserving authorial voice despite its overwhelmingly mediated expression in the play. Corneille's naming of himself as his influence unleashed a fevered debate that revealed the sensitivity of the topic of authorship—and, concurrently, the mediation of meaning and authority—in seventeenth-century France. The amplitude of the stakes involved in this debate, as well as the similarities between it and ongoing difficulties in the characterization of legitimate sovereignty, are evident in Scudéry's reminder, in his letter to Balzac, that "Empidocles nomme les Poëtes des Dieux vivans entre les mortels, à cause de la perpetuelle communication qu'ils ont avec les idées" (Empedocles names poets gods living among mortals, because of their perpetual communication with ideas).[49] In addition, as the frequent comparisons between historians and poets during this period demonstrate,[50] literary theorists acknowledged the existence and even necessity of the poetic author but could not quite integrate him and his genius into a system that valued *vraisemblance,* legitimacy, and order. The *Lettre à *** sous le nom d'Ariste* veers wildly between accusing Corneille of wholesale plagiarism (pointing out that his *Médée* should in fact be attributed to Seneca) and overbearing authorial presence, since "l'humeur ville de cet autheur et la bassesse de son ame ne sont pas difficile à cognoistre dans les sentimens qu'il donne aux principaux personnages de ses Comédies" (the vile humor of this author and the lowliness of his soul are not difficult to perceive in the sentiments he gives to his plays' principal characters).[51]

ACTING AND MEDIATION IN SEVENTEENTH-CENTURY FRENCH THEATER

Yet if questioning the very possibility of theatrical authorship is a technique that can only turn against the critics themselves, most of whom were authors in their own right, attributing the play's success to factors other than the author's own work offered a less controversial, and more damaging, method of criticism. Mairet, as we have seen, began the quarrel by attributing any greatness *Le Cid* might possess to the Spanish source material, accusing Corneille of mere translation. Scudéry continues this line of critique but also goes further in suggesting that the play's positive reception by the audience is, in fact, due to the prowess of the actors: "Il est impossible que je sois atteint de ce vice (la jalousie), pour une chose où je remarque tant de deffaux, qui n'avoit de beautez, que celle que ces agreables trompeurs qui la representoient luy avoient prestées, et que Mondory, La Villiers, et leurs compagnons, n'estans pas dans le livre, comme sur le Theater, le Cid Imprimé, n'estoit plus le Cid que l'on a creu voir" (It is impossible that I could be accused of jealousy for something in which I see so many faults, where the only beauties are those which the pleasant tricksters who represented it gave it, and that since Mondory, La Villiers, and their companions, are not in the book but only on the stage, the printed Cid is no longer the Cid that one thought one saw).[52] This criticism marks a change of tactic from Scudéry's first contributions to the *querelle,* which followed Mairet's accusations of "translation" by presenting the simultaneous and paradoxical arguments that Corneille was a terrible author and that Corneille was not truly the author at all. Moreover, the praise that Scudéry accords to Mondory signals the changing perception of the actor in the period immediately preceding Louis XIII's decree of 1641 legitimizing their profession. More typical of the time was the sentiment expressed in the *Discours à Cliton* that the author no longer writes plays, "n'en pouvant gratifier que des comédiens, autant indignes du bien qu'on leur fait, qu'ils sont incapables de juger des pieces qu'on leur donne" (being only able to gratify the actors, who are as much unworthy of the good one does them as they are of judging the plays they are given). In fact, the writer continues, any glory to the actors takes away from that of the author: "j'aymerois mieux demeurer comme je suis, que de sousmettre mon esprit au leur, et adjuster mon travail à leur interest" (I prefer to stay as I am, than to submit my thought to theirs and to adjust my work to their interests).[53] Here, despite their seemingly opposite opinions concerning Corneille and *Le Cid,* the author of the *Discours* rejoins Scudéry by implying that attention paid to the actor detracts from the independence and creative skills of the author, and it would seem that this view was shared in part by Corneille himself, who states in the *Advertissement au Besançonnais Mairet,* "Criez tant qu'il vous plaira, et donnez aux Acteurs ce qui n'est deu qu'au Poëte" (Cry out as much as you like, and give the actors what is only due to the poet).[54]

The mixture of hostility and respect that characterized authors' opinions of the actor demonstrates that figure's fundamentally liminal nature throughout history, but especially in seventeenth-century France. The actor was very possibly even more controversial than the author, which perhaps explains the peculiar reticence of the pamphleteers in the *querelle,* who only briefly addressed the topic. It is, of course, possible that as playwrights themselves, they were unwilling to accord a large place to acting skill in a play's success. In a phenomenon quite similar to that concerning the relation between the king and his direct subordinates (and, indeed, God and the king), any talent attributed to the actor implies a disturbing shortcoming on the part of the author—a shortcoming that the actor, who is on stage and responding directly to the stimuli and difficulties surrounding him, is much better placed to combat and repair than his distant, if not absent, source. As a result, most treatises, including the pamphlets in the *querelle du Cid* and d'Aubignac's *Pratique,* advocate (and, to some extent, practice) the complete disappearance of the actor, whose prowess, even more than that of the author, consists in the audience's forgetting of his contribution to the play. The fears of playwrights that attention given to the actor will detract from their own glory seem to be borne out by the observations of those who only wrote about, rather than for, the theater. Samuel Chappuzeau, in his *Le théâtre françois* (1674), offers a considerable place to the actor's role in the play, so much so that the prioritization of the author is often lost. For example, Chappuzeau testifies to the existence of an "enchaînement si étroit de la Comedie avec le Poëte & le Comedien, qu'il est difficile de les separer, & qu'il faut toûjours les faire marcher ensemble" (the play is linked so tightly with the poet and the actor that it is difficult to separate them, and they must always be examined together).[55]

Yet even Chappuzeau is not above characterizing the actor as the merely material instrument of the author's genius. While d'Aubignac places the author on par with "les Decorateurs, les Toiles peintes, les Violons, les Spectateurs & autres semblables" (the decorators, the painted sets, the violins, the spectators and so forth),[56] Chappuzeau states that "l'invention du Poëte est l'ame qui fait mouvoir tout le Corps, & c'est de là principalement que le monde s'attend de tirer le plaisir qu'il va chercher au Théâtre" (the invention of the poet is the soul that makes the body move, and therein lies the pleasure that society expects when it goes to the theater).[57] Like the author whom d'Aubignac's treatise describes, the actor should aim for the disappearance of his personal self, only on an even more radical level, since the words he speaks as his character are not even his own. As d'Aubignac himself indicates, the ideal result is a total dispossession of the actor's own personality. "Ainsi Floridor & Beau-Château en ce qu'ils sont en eux-mêmes, ne doivent être considerez que comme Representans; & cet Horace & ce Cinna qu'ils representent, doivent être considerez à l'égard du Poëme comme véritables personnages: car ce sont eux que l'on suppose agir & parler & non pas ceux qui les representent, comme si Floridor & Beau-Château cessoient d'être en nature & se trouvoient transformez en ces Hommes, dont ils portent le nom & les interêts" (Therefore Floridor and Beau-Château in what they are in themselves should only be regarded as representatives, and this Horace and Cinna that they represent should be considered with respect to the poem like true characters: for it is they that we assume are acting and speaking, and not those that represent them, as if Floridor and Beau-Château ceased to be in nature and found themselves transformed into these men, whose names and interests they assume).[58] To do otherwise—to allow one's own persona to penetrate the character—is, in a very real sense, to betray the theatrical illusion.

Yet implicit in d'Aubignac's description of the actor is the idea that the transformation is never absolutely complete; indeed, only a fool unfamiliar with theatrical convention would think so.[59] Rather, much as for Le Moyne the sovereign's will disrupted the perfect correspondence between king and sun, for d'Aubignac what prevents complete conflation of the actor and his role is the actor's voice. In his treatment of the unity of place, d'Aubignac notes that one actor cannot perform two different roles in the same play, unless he is portraying a character who disguises himself as another character. The reason for this restriction is that even if the actor "change d'habits, de poil, & de visage" (changes clothes, appearance and face), his voice gives him away, thereby misleading the audience.[60] Likewise, earlier in the treatise, d'Aubignac admits that an actor can interrupt his performance to ask for silence "parce que l'on conçoit aisement en ces rencontres, que c'est Bellerose ou Mondory qui parle, & non pas un Dieu ou un Roi; sa voix, sa contenance, & le sujet present en donnent bien distinctement la connoissance" (because one easily imagines in these circumstances, that it is Bellerose or Mondory who is speaking, and not a God or a King; the actor's voice, his face, and the present subject are enough to convey this knowledge).[61]

Despite this presence of the voice as a sort of safeguard against total transformation of the actor into his role, or against total confusion of the spectator as to the reality of the action on stage, during the actual performance, these restrictions are lifted so that the illusion can become total. Immediately following his acknowledgment that an actor asking for silence is not disturbing to the spectator, since we know that it is the actor and not his character who is making the request, d'Aubignac explains how profound this transformation should be: "Mais quand un homme paroît à nos yeux avec le nom, l'habit, les paroles, le geste & les sentimens d'une autre personne qu'il represente, & qui porte des yeux à l'esprit une image toute autre que ce qu'il est, on ne le doit plus considerer, & il ne doit plus agir autrement, & son déguisement doit faire imaginer véritable ce qu'il represente" (But when a man appears to our eyes with the name, the clothing, the words, the gestures and the sentiments of another person whom he represents, and which convey to the eyes of the mind an entirely different image than what he is, one should no longer consider him, and he should not act in another way. His disguise should make us imagine as real that which he represents).[62] This must have been exactly what the theorists who found the comparison between the ambassador and the actor more useful than that between the diplomat and the angel had in mind—a sort of embodied trope that figures forth what is physically absent and that is capable of transmitting intact the absent figure's authority and even identity.

However, just as the actor and his role do not completely coincide, even in d'Aubignac, the actor and the ambassador are often strikingly different, and these differences further illustrate the difficulties inherent in seventeenth-century attempts to describe independence and mediated legitimacy simultaneously. As I have already noted, most seventeenth-century playwrights and theorists were loath to recognize the actor's skill as a factor in a given play's success. Although nearly all of these writers would have agreed on the identity of the best actors of the day, no one was entirely sure what to do with such a strange talent–a talent that consisted, ultimately, in making the audience forget one's existence (and thus talent). Unlike the figure of the diplomat or even the orator, to whom he was often compared, the actor was definitely not expected to react in an original manner or even to write his own words. Yet as a physical entity, a person in his own right, the actor was also profoundly different from inanimate means of representation, such as "décorations" or even language. If only through the distinctive nature of his voice, the actor always reminded the spectators that they were confronted with a thinking, feeling human being and not a mere literary construct or machine.

This strange passivity, as well as the seeming totality of the successful theatrical representation, provoked the anger and bewilderment of seventeenth-century moral critics of the theater. In viewing acting as only slightly less disturbing than, for example, demonic possession, these critics, too often dismissed as religious fanatics,[63] were merely entering a door left open by writers such as d'Aubignac, Scudéry, and Corneille. By refusing to accord a large place to acting talent in their accounts of poetic success, these authors implicitly advocated the conflation of actor and role, since talent and individual distinction are only needed to respond to unforeseen situations. Unlike the diplomat, whose presence at a foreign court necessarily implied a need to deal with the unexpected and contingent, the actor's part was entirely scripted (with the notable exception, of course, as d'Aubignac implicitly noted, of his own voice–the only aspect that remained beyond the control of the director or author).

The moral objections to theater, and, more precisely, to the actor, are therefore worth considering, as they suggest the consequences of a mediation that fails to maintain the proper distance between the source of the message or authority and the messenger himself.[64] This collapse should recall the Jesuit criticism of Galileo discussed in chapter 3, whereby the scientist was accused of fashioning himself as heaven's messenger (rather than the simple carrier of heaven's message). Is the fear of the actor merely a mark, as d'Aubignac stated and as Chaouche and Thirouin seem to imply, of theatrical naïveté–a fear that is not shared by people used to working for and attending the theater? Or does this fear speak to something more profound and rooted in the very structure of French society, including the monarchy?[65] A look at some of the better-known objectors to acting and theater will help to answer this question.

In his *Traité de la comédie*, Pierre Nicole opens his objections to the theater with his worry for the effect of acting on the souls of the actors themselves.

According to Nicole, it is impossible that the actor asked to embody certain passions and emotions can escape unscathed by this experience. Playing the part of, for example, a jealous lover will awaken the previous experience of such passions in the actor, or it will introduce them into an actor who had never even suspected their existence or, more important, their force. Nicole refuses the alternate view of theatrical representation, articulated by Montaigne and continued by Conti and most famously developed by Diderot, that the actor and the role can be viewed as separate and that acting is an art and skill in its own right. In a sense, Nicole's position is shared by the playwrights who vigorously denied any actorly contribution to a play's success. A closer look at Nicole's language in the *Traité* will further reveal the resonances of his position on the actor with a certain political conservatism, or belief in the real authority of those in power.

As Laurent Thirouin points out, the basis of Nicole's objection to the theater rests on his theory that ideas impress themselves on those who receive them.[66] Once an actor (or, by extension, a spectator) is marked by the ideas he has experienced in the theater, these marks appear no less real than the marks of nontheatrical ideas. Perhaps most troubling, the actor or spectator then moves from the position of receiver of such ideas to transmitter of them. The very persuasiveness of the theatrical illusion obscures (as d'Aubignac said that it should) the source of the impressions that become "real" sources in turn. In the Neoplatonist worldview of Nicole, the fact that even nontheatrical events, ideas, and passions are but distractions from the unique truth of the divine is precisely what makes the theater so dangerous. If everything is a potentially damaging illusion, then the theater loses its special and exceptional status and becomes remarkable solely for the force and concentration of the emotions and passions portrayed there. The difference between the temptations of life in this world and theater is one of degree, not kind; Nicole's world is structured along the lines of a smooth hierarchy, a fact that certainly contributes to his refusal of a clear distinction between actor and role. This hierarchy is expressed in passages such as the following: "ces esprits qui servent à Dieu de ministres ne sont pas stables, et il trouve des défauts dans ses Anges mêmes; à combien plus forte raison des âmes enfermées dans des corps, comme dans des maisons de boue, seront-elles sujettes à la corruption et au péché?" (these spirits that serve as ministers to God are not stable, and he finds faults even in his angels; what better reason is there that souls closed up in bodies, as if in muddy houses, would be subject to corruption and sin?).[67] By using the example of God's ministers, or angels, Nicole is not merely drawing an analogy between the terrestrial and the divine. Rather, through the *content* of his example, he is emphasizing the continual, unbroken process of mediation that flows from higher to lower, from more pure to more corrupted. This passage can be linked with one occurring near the end of the treatise: "Et comme [Dieu] est le principe de toutes nos bonnes oeuvres, et que la grâce par laquelle nous les faisons est le fruit de sa Croix, nous le devons remercier de toutes celles que son esprit nous fait faire" (And as God is the principle of all of our good works, and the grace through which we do them is the fruit of the Cross, we should thank him for all of the good actions that his spirit makes possible).[68] For Nicole, only God is capable of creation or authorship, even of the acts accomplished by that most independent of creatures, man. As divine will filters through the universe, it is diffused and diluted; the task of religion is to restore the original purity as much as possible.

In such a context, theater is particularly nefarious, given its professed tendency—the very tendency upon which its distinction from epic rests—to obscure its own authorship. The successful theatrical author is imperceptible in his work, just as the talented actor seems to disappear completely into his role, however temporarily. For critics such as Nicole and Bossuet, who could not admit the existence, however theoretical, of a morally acceptable theater, plays present fictional events—events made and arranged *by man*—as existing on the same level as the events overseen and perhaps ultimately precipitated by God. In addition, in a seeming admission of guilt, this creation seeks to hide its human source. The playwright and actor, in suffusing their creations with a presence impossible to locate or define, mock the relation of God to his creation. This mockery becomes more dangerous as it appears more attractive, and the spectator enjoying the play is, in such a context, idolatrous. Such idolatry should be distinguished from that identified by Tertullian in his own objection to theater, *De Spectaculis*. Tertullian's text wavers between condemning any worship of creature through the forgetting of its ultimate author (the idolatry described above and identified by Nicole) and idolatry as related to *content*, that is, the tracing of theater's roots to celebrations of pagan gods. This last aspect of idolatry was seized upon by theater's defenders, who used passages such as the following to prove that spectacle had changed considerably since its initial condemnation by the fathers of the Church: "For from the very beginning games were classed under two heads, sacred and funereal—in other words games in honor of heathen gods and of dead men. But, in the matter of idolatry, it makes no difference to us under what name and title they are given, seeing it comes in the long run to the same spirits—which we renounce. Suppose their games are in honour of dead men, suppose they are in honour of their gods, they pay exactly the same honour to their dead as to their gods;

on either side you have one and the same state of things, one and the same idolatry, one and the same renunciation of idolatry on our part."[69] Obviously, its proponents argued, seventeenth-century French theater was no longer commissioned to honor pagan gods or even the dead. Religious subjects could be, and were, represented on the stage (though not without controversy), and Richelieu himself had deemed French theater cleansed of the excesses and shocks to public morality of the previous century. Even Tertullian, the protheater side argued, would have to agree that the plays on the French stage, tamed by *bienséance,* were harmless for public morality and were clearly not idolatrous.

The result of such debates was not increased tolerance for theater but rather the development of a kind of *dialogue de sourds,* where each side argued from a position that was incomprehensible to the other. Each side based its reasoning upon a different aspect of the idolatry described by Tertullian in a quarrel that in several ways reinvoked the old Eucharistic arguments concerning essence and accident, with a bit of the temporal aspects of the *querelle des anciens et des modernes* thrown in. Writers such as Caffaro argued for a sort of temporal relativism typical of d'Aubignac, and later the *modernes,* in which the arguments against Roman and Greek theater were without foundation in seventeenth-century (Christian) France, stating that "Comme le temps qui change fait tout changer avec luy, les gens équitables doivent regarder les choses dans le temps où elles sont" (Since time, which changes, makes everything change with it, equitable persons should always look at things in the time in which they occur).[70] Against such arguments, antitheatrical writers such as Antoine Singlin argued for the intemporality of theater's immorality, basing their judgments on the very structure of the theatrical experience: "Comme les comédiens sont toujours infâmes, la comédie est toujours un mal" (since actors are always infamous, plays are always evil).[71]

Singlin's sentiment takes us back to the issue of the actor and also back to the role of writers' preoccupation with this figure in their antitheatrical sentiments. While those countering Nicole, Singlin, and Bossuet based their arguments upon the ultimate *irrelevance* of form to content, stating that one can easily be detached from the other, those writing against the theater refused any such distance, however implicit. Against those who saw the world as composed of discrete, separable moments and entities, whether in historical time or in theatrical performance, Nicole and Bossuet, among others, held fast to a world still governed by the smooth continuity of hierarchy, a world where entities—whether theatrical characters or the Holy Spirit itself—could infuse their recipients and alter them permanently. As Marc Fumaroli has implied, this is the worldview that led directly to the flowering of predication and rhetoric, which, in growing more powerful, grew more vulnerable to imitation, not unlike the menace of the counterfeit kings whom we find stalking seventeenth-century texts on sovereignty.[72] For writers who could not admit the impenetrability of the human subject–the possibility that the actor playing his role would be untouched by it after the performance (an idea that must have seemed like the height of hypocrisy if it was admitted as possible)–the theater unleashed a confusion of influences, passions, and agencies that could only sweep up author, actors, and spectators alike in a common tide of damnation. As Bossuet warns, "On se voit soi-même dans ceux qui nous paraissent comme transportés par de semblables objets. On devient bientôt un acteur secret dans la tragédie; on y joue sa propre passion; et la fiction au dehors est froide et sans agrément, si elle ne trouve au dedans une vérité qui lui réponde" (We see ourselves in those who appear to us as if transported by such objects. We soon become a secret actor in the tragedy; we play our own passion, and the exterior fiction is cold and unpleasant if it does not find in the interior a corresponding truth).[73]

If this potential interpenetration of passions and roles makes the theatrical experience dangerous, it is precisely because the positive aspects of society–the authority of the king, social cohesion, and the influence of predication–depend upon the prevalence and proper working of mediation as well. For seventeenth-century writers, accepting the arguments of theater's defenders would be admitting that mediation–the flow of authority and influence from person to person, ideally from God to man–was no longer an acceptable model of legitimacy and social order. Indeed, one can locate a confluence, which seems strange to us, between criticisms of the theater and defenses of divine right monarchy. Such a confluence by no means implies that writers who defended the theater or who argued that the actor and his role were quite separate entities were somehow guilty of lèse-majesté. However, among critics of theater, suspicion of acting and the idea that the monarch's authority is grounded, in a very real sense, in a transcendent force often went hand in hand. The example of the Jansenist Pierre Nicole is instructive. Unlike Pascal, Nicole never suggested that royal grandeur, or any grandeur for that matter, was merely due to appearance and the trappings of majesty. The following passage, with its emphasis on an almost physical impression of grandeur on its observers, strongly resembles the work of the Jesuit celebrator of monarchy, Le Moyne: "Ce n'est ni par leurs richesses, ni par leurs plaisirs, ni par leur pompe [que les grands sont dignes de respect]; c'est par la part qu'ils ont à la royauté de Dieu, que l'on doit honorer en leur personne selon la mesure qu'ils la possèdent. . . . Ainsi cette soumission ayant pour object une chose qui est vraiment digne de respect, elle ne doit pas seulement être extérieure et de pure cérémonie, mais elle doit aussi être intérieure, c'est-à-dire qu'elle doit enfermer la reconnaissance d'une supériorité et d'une grandeur réelle dans ceux qu'on honore" (It is not by their riches, nor their pleasures, nor their pomp that men of high rank are deserving of respect; it is through their participation in the royalty of God that we should honor their persons in proportion to their possession of this royalty. . . . Therefore this submission has for its object something truly deserving of respect; it should not be only exterior and made of ceremony, but also interior, that is to say that it should contain the recognition of real superiority and grandeur in those whom we honor).[74] The process through which the king's subjects acknowledge the real presence of divine qualities in the monarch resembles the process through which passions and ideas are impressed upon the spectator in the theater, a process that is the very source of Nicole's objection to theater. This real transference of qualities from one being to another is that which ensures the hierarchy of society and the constant contact, guarantor of legitimacy, between God and the king. Therefore, insofar as the theater evacuates the *reality* of grandeur, by asking the spectator to be impressed with the actor playing the king, it not only encourages idolatry but also threatens to bring down the very structure of society. Arguing that the actor and his role are far from contiguous, as theater's defenders did, does not relieve this threat. It merely introduces the frightening thought that majesty and grandeur may be achieved through special effects, with no essential link between signifier and signified.

Jean-François Senault's objection to theater is quite similar to that of Nicole and similarly lines up with his view of monarchy as based upon a real and constant connection between the king and God. In *Le monarque, ou les devoirs du souverain*, Senault rejects the argument that vice is punished and virtue rewarded in seventeenth-century French theater. Rather, he says, vice is so much more attractive than virtue, given man's predisposition to sin, that spectators cannot help being "impressed" more with vice than with virtue. Once again, the content argument *for* theater is opposed to the rigorist view that all theater, due to its form, is morally suspect. In this respect, it is interesting to note that Senault singles out theater as uniquely dangerous. Unlike Tertullian, who opposed almost all forms of public spectacle, Senault approves tournaments and other events "qui sont en usage depuis la naissance des monarchies" (that have been in use since the birth of monarchies)[75] as long as they do not overly impoverish the kingdom. The sense that spectacle as such is not dangerous but that theater represents a unique threat to society is a further demonstration that many objections to theater occur in the context of their writers' defenses of divine right monarchical theory.

In this context, the case of Bossuet is particularly compelling. The Gallican priest's *Politique tirée des propres paroles de l'Ecriture Sainte*, written in 1679 for the education of the dauphin, in many ways represents a distillation and intensification of the themes we have already seen in earlier treatises on the monarchy and its links to the divine. In many ways, the *Politique* is the culmination of the efforts of Le Bret, Senault, and Le Moyne to attach temporal government to divine intent.[76] Language such as that used in the following passage amply illustrates Bossuet's emphasis on an unbreakable, yet clear, link between God and the king: "Voyez un peuple immense réuni en une seule personne: voyez cette puissance sacrée, paternelle et absolue; voyez la raison secrète qui gouverne tout le corps de l'Etat, renfermée dans une seule tête; vous voyez l'image de Dieu dans les rois, et vous avez l'idée de la majesté royale. Dieu est la sainteté même, la bonté même, la puissance même, la raison même. En ces choses, est la majesté de Dieu. En l'image de ces choses, est la majesté du prince. . . . Je ne sais quoi de divin s'attache au prince" (See an immense people united in one person; see this sacred, paternal, and absolute power; see the secret reason that governs the entire body of the state, contained in one head; you see the image of God in the kings, and you have the idea of royal majesty. God is sainthood itself, goodness itself, power itself, reason itself. In these things is the majesty of God. In the image of these things is the majesty of the prince. . . . A certain divinity is attached to the prince).[77]

Yet as Bossuet implies by his language, this link is visible only to the outside observer, or spectator. Bossuet's king, like Le Moyne's, should never be able to observe himself in his role, thereby becoming seduced and impressed with his own prowess. As soon as the king abstracts himself from his duties in order to reflect upon his skills, he breaks the almost theatrical illusion upon which the legitimacy of his power rests, since he wrongly attributes his success to himself rather than to God. If the king is to regard himself exercising his functions at all, he should instead be stunned that a mere mortal has been entrusted with so immense a charge. The implications of this formulation for a monarch who had only recently abandoned the project of writing his own memoirs should be clear. Yet what is even more fascinating are the resonances of Bossuet's monarchical thought with the practice of theater. The king imbued with divine powers of understanding and governance very much resembles an actor whose role is only temporary. Once the play has finished, he returns to his "normal" status. Yet we immediately see that in order for the monarch's authority to be *real*, not only must the performance be perfect but the role must be internalized and assimilated as completely as possible.

Therefore, if this is how authority and legitimacy are transmitted in Bossuet's monarchical thought, it can hardly be surprising that he transfers this mechanism to the theater itself and, like Nicole, renders it the grounds for his objections. In his response to Caffaro, the Italian priest who wrote in defense of the theater, Bossuet describes a process of influence even more insidious than Nicole's model of impression. Like Nicole, Bossuet notes that theater is the most dangerous when the spectators believe it is morally accept-able, since "pendant qu'on est enchanté par la douceur de la mélodie ou étourdi par le merveilleux du spectacle, ces sentiments s'insinuent sans qu'on y pense, et gagnent le coeur sans être aperçus" (while we are enchanted by the sweetness of the melody or confused by the marvelous nature of the spec-tacle, these feelings insinuate themselves without our knowledge, and win our hearts without being perceived).[78] The penetrability of the human soul to outside elements leads Bossuet to follow Nicole in making the actor the cen-ter of his concerns. For him it is inconceivable that the actor skillfully play-ing his role is *not* affected by its content. To admit that the actor can coldly pick up and cast off the role given to him with absolutely no damage to his spiritual health would be to acknowledge, for example, the possibility that the human embodying divinely grounded monarchy is indistinguishable from his subjects, a notion that, despite Bossuet's repeated reminders to the king that he is a man like others, is explicitly rejected throughout the *Politique*. Moreover, this notion of indifference as to who performs certain roles flies in the face of actual theatrical practice. As metatheatrical plays often point out—from the *Comédie des comédiens* by N. Gougenot, the purported author of the *Discours à Cliton,* to Molière's own *Impromptu de Versailles*–the actors cho-sen to play specific parts generally have a certain affinity with them. Accord-ing to this model, which admits a certain interpenetration of actor and role, the individual man occupying the position of king–a position, as we have seen, more and more divorced from its historical and biological precedents and identified instead with will and independence–is fit to occupy this posi-tion in a way shared by none of his subjects. We have already seen, in the trea-tises of Le Bret and Senault, that the phantom of a counterfeit king and the accompanying need to explain why this man, and no other, occupies the posi-tion of monarchy grows directly out of the model of sovereignty posited by Bodin. And as we saw in Le Moyne, more and more writers and panegyrists would therefore take refuge in the formula, comfortingly vague, of a certain "je ne sais quoi," both unmistakable and indefinable, that distinguishes the king from his compatriots and even his blood relatives. Yet as I have pointed out earlier, the transformative contact between officeholder and office upon which this system rests has troubling implications for the diplomat, whose representative function is more or less temporary but who must fully occupy this function while employed. It is, I hope, no longer quite so surprising that defenders of the ambassador—those who argued for renewed attention to this pivotal political figure—used the actor as a model.

THE KING IN THEATER

This fundamental affinity between theatrical criticism and monarchical thought demonstrates that the link between seventeenth-century theater and French politics is quite involved and complex, in ways that often reach beyond the plays' explicit plots. Again, it would be highly simplistic and unfair to characterize those who argued that actor and role are separable as somehow guilty of lèse-majesté. Rather, I would argue that their acceptance of a gap between actor and role extends the emphasis on impenetrability and independence introduced into politics by Bodin and into physics through the revival of epicureanism, a doctrine whose implications for social (not just physical) order in the universe deeply troubled Le Moyne.[79] In such a world, authority and influence are almost impossible to imagine as universally efficient without extracting such forces from the universe that they govern. The worldview characterized by mediation was, in large part, constructed and revived to counter this conception. That theater is deeply involved in these questions in almost every aspect of its production from pen to stage made it the ideal vehicle for exploring, repairing, or revealing the contradictions inherent in seventeenth-century monarchical theory. Theater did this explicitly, through its subject matter, and implicitly, through its formal elements. From Jean-Marie Apostolidès to Hélène Merlin-Kajman, critics have provided insightful readings of the complex relation between seventeenth-century French theater and politics, including in their analyses some of the issues discussed here. It is clear, for example, that Corneille's repeated treatment of the status of Roman provinces or colonies bears directly on the topic of mediation, as the filtering of authority through the Roman Empire is called into question and problematized. It is also clear, as Richard Goodkin and Catherine Spencer have pointed out, that Racine's theater is uniquely preoccupied with figures of mediation and the middle.[80] Yet no study has explicitly addressed the two playwrights' presentation of the ambassador, a figure whose troubled mediation, since less protected by the mystery of state than the king, is an intensification of themes treated elsewhere and more obliquely. Before looking at the ambassador in Racine's *Andromaque* and Corneille's *Suréna*, however, I would like to revisit briefly the seventeenth-century play that bears perhaps the most directly on the question of the embodiment of the divine and the mediation of authority, Jean Rotrou's *Le Véritable Saint Genest*.

In 1645, at the height of his career, Jean Rotrou composed *Le Véritable Saint Genest*, taking up the story of the Roman actor who converted to Christianity on stage and who was subsequently martyred by the emperor Diocletian. The story was familiar to Rotrou's audience, either through Lope de Vega's treatment of the subject or, more certainly, through a French play on the same subject, Nicolas-Marc Desfontaines's *L'Illustre Comédien ou le Martyre de Saint Genest*, that was produced by Molière's rival troupe during the same year that Rotrou began writing his own version.[81] Often cited as a near-perfect example of baroque aesthetics, Rotrou's *Saint Genest* is, at the same time, perhaps more vulnerable than any other play of the period to misinterpretation. As John D. Lyons has pointed out, most modern readers simplify the play's content, professing to see a clear opposition between the framing plot–the presentation of a play to an imperial audience–and the internal play itself, which presents the story of Adrian, himself a well-known persecutor of Christians and acted by Genest, and which occasions the actor's conversion.[82] This separation has led to wildly different interpretations of the meaning of Genest's conversion as well as of the ultimate view of theater and its relation to Christian morality being proposed by Rotrou. Cynthia Osowiec Ruoff, for example, proposes a reading of the play that accentuates the fundamental creativity of Genest's performance, despite the character's repeated objections that he is only reading a role assigned to him by God and despite Rotrou's elision of the idea, present in Lope de Vega's Ginés, that the actor has actually written the play himself.[83]

Here, I would like to argue that the theme of mediation serves both to unite the two levels of the play and to counter allegations of Genest's fundamental creativity; only viewed through the perspective of an increasingly problematized mediation does *Le Véritable Saint Genest* become coherent and, indeed, comprehensible. The issue of mediation–not only its very existence, but also its mechanisms–is brought to the fore in the play's first moments, when Diocletian's daughter Valérie discusses her dream with her *confidente*, Camille. Even before Valérie's first words, Camille addresses her unseemly fear of this dream, arguing that such trepidation is out of place in her mistress: "A vous sur qui le Ciel, déployant ses trésors,/Mit un si digne esprit dans un si digne corps!" (To you, upon whom the heavens, distributing their treasures,/Placed such a worthy mind in such a worthy body!) (3–4). From the outset, then, the play announces the ideal of perfect mediation. The heavens have wisely originated the noble character of Valérie, placing this character in the appropriate bodily receptacle. The levels of origin and recipient are in perfect accord–perhaps, as we shall see, too perfect, as such perfection tends to obscure the relation of dependence that should characterize terrestrial objects in their relation to the divine. Valérie's account of her dream further accentuates the theme of privileged, unobstructed communication between the heavens and earth: "Le Ciel, comme il lui plaît, nous parle sans obstacle" (The heavens, when they please, speak to us without obstacle) (9). This assertion is supported by the events that follow; Valérie has dreamed that she will be married to a shepherd and, indeed, her father intends to unite her with Maximian, his coruler, who has just such a humble background.

Yet where the contemporary reader may perceive in Maximian a perfectly laudable instinct for self-advancement, in a world governed by hierarchy and divine will Maximian is monstrous. Unlike Valérie, whose character and body correspond, Maximian has rebelled against the humble place assigned to him and has become elevated to a position of coemperor. It is important to note here that Rotrou, whose title has been read as a reproach to Desfontaines's version of the story, breaks with his fellow playwright by insisting, at some length, upon the splitting of Diocletian's imperial power, while Desfontaines leaves Maximian out of the story entirely. As Valérie explains to Camille, her father's decision to include Maximian in his reign is deeply unnatural, as is his splitting of the empire itself in two, with Maximian and Constance governing the other part:

> Depuis Rome souffrit et ne réprouva pas
> Qu'il commît un Alcide au fardeau d'un Atlas,
> Qu'on vît sur l'univers deux têtes souveraines,
> Et que Maximian en partageât les rênes.
> Mais pourquoi pour un seul tant de maîtres divers,
> Et pourquoi quatre chefs au corps de l'univers?
> Le choix de Maximin et celui de Constance
> Etaient-ils à l'Etat de si grande importance
> Qu'il en dût recevoir beaucoup de fermeté,
> Et ne pût subsister sans leur autorité? (31–40)

> [Since Rome suffered and did not deny
> That it committed an Alcide to the burden of an Atlas,
> That we see in the universe two sovereign heads,
> And that Maximian shared the reins.
> But why for just one so many masters,
> And why four heads for the body of the universe?
> The choice of Maximian and that of Constance
> Were they of such importance to the state
> That it had to borrow such firmness from them
> And could not subsist without their authority?]

The importance of this aberrant governance cannot be overstated, although many critics leave it out of their readings entirely.[84] Against the ideal of perfect mediation put forth in the play's opening moments, Diocletian's entirely personal decision to redistribute his authority flies in the face of nearly every maxim of monarchical government—of the king as image of God on earth—that was being articulated at the time of the play's composition. I have shown how, following Bodin, most writers agreed that one of the fundamental signs of royal legitimacy was precisely its *singularity*, which mirrored that of God. These theorists were equally adamant in their insistence upon sovereignty's ultimate incommunicability, a principle obviously ignored by Diocletian. Diocletian appears here as the appropriate ruler for a pagan universe. The splitting of his reign is its own sort of legitimacy, in that it mirrors not the singularity of the Christian God but the multiplicity of pagan deities. Valérie correctly suspects that such multiplicity and division of functions obscures the one-to-one correspondence that validates both her own identity (the perfect character in a perfect body) and the meaning of her dream. Maximian's self-creation through his prowess in war therefore only reinforces the fundamental *disorder* of Diocletian's empire, where authority and legitimacy are without a clear and singular anchor. Camille's objection to Valérie's fears only confirms the seventeenth-century French audience's worst suspicions:

> Quand Dioclétian éleva votre mère
> Au degré le plus haut que l'univers révère,
> Son rang qu'il partageait n'en devint point plus bas,
> Et l'y faisant monter, il n'en descendit pas;
> Il put concilier son honneur et sa flamme,
> Et, choisi par les siens, se choisir une femme;
> Quelques associés qui règnent avec lui,
> Il est de ses Etats le plus solide appui:
> S'ils sont les matelots de cette grande flotte,
> Il en tient le timon, il en est le pilot,
> Et ne les associe à des emplois si hauts
> Que pour voir des Césars au rang de ses vassaux. (53–63)

> [When Diocletian elevated your mother
> To the highest degree revered by the universe
> The rank he shared did not become lower,
> And putting him there, he did not descend;
> He was able to reconcile his honor and his love,
> And, chosen by his people, chose a woman;
> Although his associates may reign with him,
> He is the most solid support of his states

If they are the sailors of this great flotilla,
He holds the rudder, he is its pilot,
And only associates them with such high offices
So he can see Caesars in the rank of his vassals.]

Here, we learn that Diocletian began his objectionable practice of splinter-
ing the empire not with his three associates but with the association of his
wife to the throne—a practice that flies in the face of French Salic Law, which
precludes women from governing in capacities other than that of regent. The
audience of 1645, living in just such a regency and faced with the increasing
ascendancy of Mazarin, may have been particularly sensitive to the critique
contained implicitly in these lines. Moreover, Camille's words emphasize the
unmediated nature of the emperor's power, insofar as *he* makes the decisions
in the state, going so far as to alter the fundamental singularity of imperial
rule. No divinity speaks to or through Diocletian, a fact made all the more
striking by the discussion that opens the play. These impressions are further
reinforced by Diocletian himself, who explains in his first speech how much
he owes to Maximian—"Je lui dois mon sang" (I owe him my blood) (117)—
adding, in his address to Maximian, "Et vous avez rendu mon pouvoir impuissant" (and you have made my power powerless) (123). Diocletian's later
elaboration of this theory of rule, whereby merit rather than birth or blood
endows the emperor with his power underscores his tyranny, and his listing
of examples of other rulers who have "fait de mêmes mains/des règles aux
troupeaux et des lois aux humains" (made with the same hands/rules for the
troops and laws for humans) (175–76) emphasize his vision of imperial rule
as a series of detached singularities rather than an unbroken continuation of
heredity, tradition, or divine legitimacy. Indeed, Rotrou's development of this
theme is so intricate and lengthy that the reader or spectator could well be
justified in viewing the main focus of the work not as (or not only as) Genest's rather spectacular conversion but as the elaboration of the tyrannical
nature of unmediated power.

For this issue of legitimacy and originality—of the power of men, unguided
by the divine, to *make their own laws*—colors seemingly unrelated events later
in the play. The conversation between Genest and Diocletian on the subject
of theatrical authorship in the fifth scene of the first act takes on political significance when read through the issue of tyranny. While Genest extols the talents of ancient authors, "[qui] font qu'ils vivent encor si beaux après mille
ans/Et dont l'estime enfin ne peut être effacé" (which make them so bril-
liantly alive after a thousand years/and whose esteem cannot be erased)
(268–69), Diocletian reveals that he prefers the attractions of surprise and

newness: "Mais ce que l'on a vu n'a plus la douce amorce/Ni le vif aiguillon dont la nouveauté force;/Et ce qui surprendra nos esprits et nos yeux,/Quoique moins achevé, nous divertira mieux" (But what we have seen does not have the sweet bite/nor the spike of newness/And what surprises our minds and our eyes/Although less finished, entertains us more) (273–76). As I have shown in the first section of this chapter, such an uncritical praise of the new falls directly in line with the larger question of the legitimacy of authorship, whether literary or political, that tormented writers in both fields. While Genest, in a passage often seen as Rotrou's tribute to Corneille, admits that there is one great man currently writing whose plays "ont acquis dans la scène un légitime bruit" (have acquired on the stage a legitimate reputation) (280), Valérie points out in turn that even his works are not pure inventions: "Mais les sujets [de ses pièces] enfin sont des sujets connus" (But the subjects of these plays are already known) (288).

Given the political overtones of the debate concerning artistic creation, it is not surprising that, unlike Lope de Vega, Rotrou never attributes the play that Genest and his troupe are going to perform for the emperor to Genest himself–its authorship is left deliberately vague. Indeed, in a manner recalling that of the *dédicaces* discussed earlier in this chapter, the fact that Maximian is responsible for the actions that will be portrayed in some sense renders *him* the author of its content–a suggestion that the coemperor, delighted to see himself as both spectator and actor, would be happy to entertain. Significantly, Genest and his troupe are never seen *creating* the dialogue that they are going to perform; rather, the second act opens (after the justly well-known scene between Genest and the *décorateur*) with Genest and, later, Marcelle rehearsing their roles. Rotrou's privileging of the rehearsal not only demonstrates the actorly process at work from behind the scenes but also places the actors firmly on the side of interpretation rather than artistic invention. Unlike several plays of the same period, which show the actor's aspirations to the coveted (and increasingly better-paid) status of playwright,[85] *Le Véritable Saint Genest* is careful to avoid any implication of newness or invention on the part of Genest and his troupe.

Instead, Genest's talent is in his gift for transformation, for exceptional imitation, to the point that, to his dismay, he begins to become his role. Yet the famous line that closes his expression of alarm at his own abilities, "Il s'agit d'imiter, et non de devenir" (It is about imitating, not becoming) (420), only concerns the part of the spectacle with which the actors are involved. The choice between imitating and becoming–a choice that in some sense resumes the dilemma of mediation expressed throughout this book, as kings pass from the image of God to godlike and as ambassadors vacillate between representing their monarch's will and embodying his sovereignty—leaves out a third term, that of creating or inventing. In this manner, Genest's fundamental and unique understanding of the actor's job as one of interpretation of a text already given and in place (Marcelle instead refers to the attention conferred upon her as an actress, thereby implying her partial responsibility for her success) predisposes him to conversion, as it implies that creation takes place elsewhere and, ultimately, is the province of God alone. Indeed, following the lines cited above, Genest sees the sky opening with flames and hears a voice that tells him "tu n'imiteras point en vain/ . . . /Et Dieu t'y prêtera la main" (you will not imitate in vain/ . . . /And God will help you) (422, 424). While most critics correctly point out that Genest attributes this voice to an artifice of theater, they leave out that his *initial* reaction to the voice is one of complete acceptance: "Qu'entends-je, juste Ciel, et par quelle merveille,/Pour me toucher le coeur, me frappes-tu l'oreille?/Souffle doux et sacré qui me viens enflammer,/Esprit saint et divin qui me viens animer" (What do I hear, and by what marvel,/Touching my heart, you strike my ear?/Sweet and sacred breath that inflames me/Holy and divine spirit that animates me) (425–28).[86] Genest goes on to present himself as the passive battleground of *dieux* and *Dieu*, gods and God—a presentation completely in accord, once again, with his vision of the actor's role in the play. In fact, when the *décorateur* comes to tell him that the court is arriving, Genest answers, "Allons. Tu m'as distrait d'un rôle glorieux/Que je représentais devant la cour des cieux" (Let's go. You have distracted me from a glorious role/That I was playing in front of the heavenly court) (447–48).

Such passivity is only accentuated and intensified when Genest begins playing Adrian, the martyr who very much understands his own life as that of a mere actor in a play written by God himself. Adrian repeatedly ascribes the events preceding his own conversion to divine causes: "Cette vigueur, peut-être, est un effort humain?/Non, non, cette vertu, Seigneur, vient de ta main/L'âme la puise au lieu de sa propre origine,/Et, comme les effets, la source en est divine" (Perhaps this vigor is a human effort?/No, no, this virtue, Lord, comes from Your hand/The soul drinks of it at its own source/And the effects and the source are both divine) (514–16). The frequent elaborations of this philosophy of passivity have the cumulative effect of rendering the divine cause of the actions in Adrian's story more *real*, at least to Genest and to the seventeenth-century spectator, than those of other "actors," most notably Maximian. While Maximian is the seeming direct cause of Adrian's martyrdom, Adrian persists in looking beyond him to the God whose will Maximian is involuntarily accomplishing. It should be clear that such denial of authorship and power to Maximian completely undercuts his satisfaction with his new identity as coemperor. Indeed, while Flavie offers Maximian as the example of self-transformation through human agency–"n'osez-vous songer/ Qu'avant qu'être empereur Maximin fut berger?" (haven't you thought/That before becoming emperor Maximian was a shepherd?) (634–35)–Adrian persists in following the "ferme propos" marked out for him through divine grace. The persistence of the political commentary inherent in Adrian's drama is underscored when, at the end of this scene, Valérie–who, as we have seen, doubts the legitimacy of her father's method of governing–significantly remarks, "L'intermède permet de féliciter [Genest on his role]/Et de voir les acteurs" (The intermission will allow us to congratulate Genest/And to see the actors) (669–70). Like Genest's initial response to the voice from the sky, this comment has been ignored by commentators of the text. Yet Valérie's statement reveals that unlike her father, who notes Genest's talent immediately, she is taken in by the spectacle to the extent that she has not "seen" the actors on stage; rather, she sees only their roles.

The play continues in this fashion, even after Genest's conversion. If Genest persists in viewing God as the sole author of worldly events–a vision to which, I hope to have shown, his excellence as an *actor* predisposes him–the other characters object that pagan gods, the emperor(s), and even Genest himself are responsible for the actions depicted. Significantly, however, the story of Adrian/Genest seems to have operated a change in Diocletian himself. In the second half of the surrounding play, Maximian vanishes, and Diocletian appears to have regained sole authority in the empire. Even more important, his language is no longer that of an emperor who views his authority as independent; rather, he ascribes his actions to the pagan gods:

> Les dieux, premiers auteurs des fortunes des hommes,
> Qui dedans nos Etats nous font ce que nous sommes,
> Et dont le plus grand roi n'est qu'un simple sujet,
> Y doivent être aussi notre premier objet;
> Et sachant qu'en effet ils nous ont mis sur terre
> Pour conserver leurs droits, pour régir leurs tonnerres,
> Et pour laisser enfin leur vengeance en nos mains,
> Nous devons sous leurs lois contenir les humains. (1635–42)

> [The gods, first authors of human fortune,
> Who, inside of our states, makes us what we are,
> And of whom the greatest king is only a mere subject,
> Should also be our first object,
> And knowing that in fact they placed us on earth
> To preserve their rights, to regulate their thunder,

And to leave their vengeance in our hands,
We should, under their laws, contain humans.]

Why this transformation? A cynical explanation would be that Diocletian is attempting to avoid responsibility for Genest's torture and death. Yet as I have shown, such a vision of divinely sanctioned authority strengthens Diocletian's role, since it would preclude the changes that he has introduced into imperial government. In the Christian logic of the play, Diocletian's new vision of his own power, legitimacy, and authority demonstrates that the conflict has passed from one between particular individuals into one between two opposed belief systems—a much larger conflict in which both Diocletian and Genest are mere actors. It should also be noted that from the moment of Genest's baptism and conversion, his martyrdom is foreordained, and Diocletian, like Pilate or Pharaoh, is now an instrument of the divine. The emperor realizes this; he merely errs in attributing his actions to pagan gods rather than the Christian God. The distance traveled by Diocletian in his understanding of power is manifested in the last lines of the play. Diocletian exclaims: "Ainsi reçoive un prompt et sévère supplice/Quiconque ose des dieux irriter la justice!" (May anyone daring to irritate divine justice/Receive a prompt and severe punishment!) (1743–44). Valérie, true to her rather uncanny perception of legitimacy and divine influence in this world, apologizes to Marcelle: "Vous voyez de quel soin je vous prêtais les mains;/Mais sa grâce n'est plus au pouvoir des humains" (You see with what care I tried to help you/But his grace is no longer in human hands) (1745–46). Finally, the last words of the play are spoken by Maximian, who, again, has been fairly silent during the fifth act. Maximian's words reveal his persistent error in attributing agency to human forces and thereby implicitly underscore the abiding illegitimacy of his role in the government. Speaking to Valérie, he states, "Ne plaignez point, Madame, un malheur volontaire,/Puisqu'il l'a pu franchir et s'être salutaire,/Et qu'il a bien voulu, par son impiété,/D'une feinte, en mourant, faire une vérité" (Do not bemoan a voluntary fate,/Since he could have avoided it and helped himself,/And he wanted, through his impiety,/To turn a feint into a truth by dying) (1747–50). Where Genest has repeatedly argued that he sees eternal life (and whereas Diocletian will be immortalized as the agent of Genest's martyrdom), Maximian, unsurprisingly, can only see death, since he remains contained by human time, untransformed by the collapse of opposites (birth and death, past and future) exemplified in Genest's conversion.

Le Véritable Saint Genest is therefore as much an exploration of political agency and legitimacy as the familiar story of the martyr. The theme of mediation and the complex relation among the political, the religious, and the theatrical brings the two halves, seemingly minimally related, of the play together nearly seamlessly. That this connection is rarely seen is a testament to a certain misunderstanding of the centrality of mediation in early modern France. Written and performed during Anne of Austria's regency, Rotrou's interpretation of this story is a near-perfect complement to contemporary reflections on sovereignty and legitimacy. The figure of Diocletian nicely emphasizes the conflicting forces bearing upon the ruler–the desire for innovation and authorship of laws or even the very form of government versus the pressing need to anchor authority firmly in the divine, a process that restricts capacity of action. The play reminds the public that the smooth mediation of authority from the divine through the ruler needs to be understood in a real, rather than figurative, sense. Such a vision of political order and hierarchy therefore implies, as we have seen in Nicole's and Bossuet's critiques of theater, the literal transformation of those through whom mediation passes. Genest's conversion, matched by a subtle, yet no less significant, alteration in Diocletian's politics, reassures the audience that the link between the transcendent and the material–when brought about by the true, singular, God–is substantial rather than the stuff of idle speculation.

THE ESSENTIAL DIPLOMAT: RACINE'S *ANDROMAQUE*

Yet Rotrou, in choosing to transmit this message through the familiar story of Genest's martyrdom, in some sense avoids (perhaps even as he points to) certain problems inherent in the seventeenth-century application of such a model. The final break between Diocletian and Maximian suggests the looming issue, deferred by the attention given to Genest, of governmental administration. Can the emperor choose the agents of his power, and does that choice involve transferring his (inalienable) power to that entity? If power is transferred, then the emperor/monarch sacrifices part of his uniqueness; if it is not, then the legitimacy of decisions made by the administrator can, justifiably, be called into question. On the eve of the Fronde (and during the years following the death of Richelieu), the question of ministerial delegation to persons outside of the king's family (and in the case of Mazarin, the king's own country) was a pressing one. As I have shown in previous chapters, as centralization of the French state proceeded apace, the legitimacy of the authority of those chosen to carry out the king's commands, whether *intendants*, ministers, or ambassadors, posed problems that were both theoretical and practical in nature.

I hope to have shown that in the panoply of multiplying governmental agents, the ambassador–and especially the ambassador as configured and imagined by Louis XIV—was unique in that his representational relation to his sovereign was more direct, immediate, and supported by ceremony than that of other officials. Unlike the priesthood, however, diplomatic representation was an office, not an order, and was therefore conferred upon its holder temporarily, although, as we have seen in Gentili's characterization of the diplomat as a mixed person and in Wicquefort's reluctance to consider himself an ex-ambassador, even in prison, the lines were never very clearly drawn. While Charles Loyseau attempted, early in the century, to draw clear lines and policy implications for this distinction, we have seen that theorists of the ambassador could not quite capture the nature of the diplomat's tremendous yet impermanent power. Significantly, they largely settled upon the figure of the actor, a figure whose status in seventeenth-century France was itself highly problematic. Yet this comparison, along with the singular diplomatic role of theatrical performance (where foreign ambassadors frequently attended royal representations of these plays) suggests that theater was a natural forum for authors to investigate the peculiar, and tragic, conundrum of diplomatic identity.

Racine's *Andromaque*, first performed in the queen's apartments by the Hôtel de Bourgogne theater troupe in 1667, was the playwright's first major success. As such, it announces and develops several themes that would be central to Racine's later production, not least the problem of mediation. Loosely adapted from Euripides' version of the same story, Racine's play concerns the tangled relationships between the children of Troy. Andromaque, widow of Hector and mother of his son, has been captured and brought to Epirus by Pyrrhus, the son of Achilles. Pyrrhus, although he has promised to marry Hermione, Helen's daughter with Ménélas, is in love with Andromaque. The play begins with the arrival in Epirus of Orestes, Agamemnon's son, who has been sent as the Greek ambassador to ask Pyrrhus to turn over Astyanax, Andromaque and Hector's son. Orestes' diplomatic task is doubled by his own interests, which largely consist of his love for Hermione.

As many critics have noted, the issue of whether the second generation of heroes can ever emulate their parents is central to the play. While Hermione bemoans her rejection at the hands of Pyrrhus as unworthy treatment of Helen's daughter, Pyrrhus himself holds out the vision of independence from Troy and its destruction, seeking to make a new start with Andromaque and Astyanax. What has gone nearly unnoticed in readings of this play, however, is the centrality of the language of place-taking, or *lieu-tenance,* in the characters' own descriptions of their problems and the relevance of this language to Orestes' status as ambassador.[87] The other characters' struggle either to distinguish themselves from the place set out for them by their fathers or, conversely, to occupy that space entirely occurs against the backdrop of Orestes' position, which should be understood in terms of seventeenth-century diplomatic theory as literally not his own. Read against the doctrines of representational diplomacy, then, the issues facing Orestes as well as the other characters can be seen as offering an oblique political commentary on the possibilities of mediation.

Racine's own authorial connection to these problems should be noted as well. In the two prefaces to the published versions of *Andromaque*, the playwright offers strikingly different versions of writerly authority. The first preface, which appeared in the editions of 1668 and 1673, emphasizes Racine's conformity to his ancient models (both Virgil's *Aeneid* and Euripides' own *Andromaque*): "Mais véritablement mes personnages sont si fameux dans l'Antiquité, que pour peu qu'on la connaisse, on verra fort bien que je les ai rendus tels que les anciens poètes nous les ont donnés. Aussi n'ai-je pas pensé qu'il me fût permis de rien changer à leurs moeurs" (But truly my characters are so well known in antiquity, that even those with a limited acquaintance of it will see that I have made them exactly as the ancient poets gave them to us. Consequently, I did not think that I was permitted to change anything in their character).[88] It is hard to imagine more self-effacing language; however, in the paragraphs that follow, Racine defends his portrayal of Pyrrhus, whose violence some of his contemporaries found shocking. Here, Racine professes that he is unable to change the rules of the theater in order to domesticate Pyrrhus's character and render him another Céladon—a reference to the popular character from Honoré d'Urfé's seventeenth-century French novel, *L'Astrée*. In proclaiming that Pyrrhus's ferocity and violence is, in fact, in keeping with the rules of theater (more specifically, with Aristotle's recommendation that the hero exhibit a "bonté médiocre"—neither entirely bad nor entirely good), Racine operates a tricky alignment between obedience and rebellion. We should remember that Pyrrhus is not just violent; he is the only character who seeks to abolish the rules governing the previous generations' antagonism. Asking the reader to accept that a rule-breaking character is in fact the very embodiment of the rules governing theater is much like announcing that the king is godlike precisely in his independence from the divine. Yet despite this rather sneaky assertion of room for initiative, Racine describes his own role as playwright in immensely passive terms.

This tone changes in the second preface, which accompanied the 1674 edition of the play. Here, Racine emphasizes instead the distance separating him from the ancients, in quite striking terms. Referring to Hermione's jealousy, which was absent from the *Aeneid* but dominant in Euripides' play, Racine states, "C'est presque la seule chose que j'emprunte ici de cet auteur. Car quoique ma tragédie porte le même nom que la sienne, le sujet en est pourtant très différent" (This is nearly the only thing that I have borrowed from this author. For although my tragedy has the same name as his, the plot is very different).[89] Faithfulness to the ancients, in this case regarding Andromaque's marital status (Euripides marries her to Pyrrhus, and the son in question is their child), is sacrificed to the standards of the seventeenth-century audience, who "ne croit point qu'elle doive aimer ni un autre mari, ni un autre fils" (does not think she should love a different husband, nor another son).[90] Racine defends this choice not merely in reference to the practices of previous French writers, such as Ronsard, who also alter history to serve the French monarchy and its purported origins in the Trojan War but also in the practice of the ancients, such as Euripides, who themselves innovated rather wildly. The tradition that Racine inherits is therefore transformed from one of imitation to one of invention. Like Corneille, who proclaims in the preface to *Héraclius* that he states his opinions "à la mode de M. de Montaigne, non pour bonnes, mais pour miennes" (in the style of Montaigne, that is not as good opinions, but as my own),[91] Racine paradoxically uses his predecessors to emphasize a tradition of freedom and invention. That such a tradition is not really a tradition at all—in the words of Louis XIV himself, "nous devons aux règles mêmes et aux exemples l'avantage de nous pouvoir passer des exemples et des règles" (we owe to the rules and examples themselves the advantage of being able to do without examples and rules)—is something that Racine recognizes in the following paragraph, where he states, "Je ne crois pas que j'eusse besoin de cet exemple d'Euripide pour justifier le peu de liberté que j'ai prise" (I do not think I need the example of Euripides to justify the few liberties I have taken).[92] What follows is an account of the argument that poets may change details of the story, as long as they do not change its subject; examples of such changes are Homer's overlooking of Achilles' vulnerability in his heel and the differing times of death of Jocasta in the Oedipus plays of Sophocles and Euripides. These examples partially obscure the fact that changing Andromaque's husband and therefore the father of the son in question completely alters the story, as Racine himself recognized earlier in the preface.

It may well be objected that the change in tone in the two prefaces is merely the mark of a playwright asserting his authorial independence as his career progresses. Certainly the Racine of 1674 has a respectability and reputation as an author that he lacked in 1668; *Andromaque* was his first real success. Yet the striking similarity between the two positions that Racine inhabits—that of faithful imitator of the ancients and that of *emulator* of them—and the near-impossibility for the diplomat to navigate between representation of his master and enactment of his master's judgment and authority leads me to believe that the centrality of Orestes in the play can be linked to the issues Racine faced while inventing his authorial identity and legitimacy. I believe that this is even more the case given the persistence, throughout *Andromaque,* of situations that are either explicitly or implicitly diplomatic in essence. By opening the play with the arrival of Orestes, ambassador to the Greeks, Racine calls the reader's attention to the questions surrounding both the very possibility of faithful representation or delegation and the problematic identity of those occupying the position of mediator—questions that are far from irrelevant to Racine's own quest for authorial status and legitimacy.

Indeed, the play opens not merely with the arrival of Orestes the Greek ambassador but also with a deeply significant rhyme: "Oui, puisque je retrouve un ami si fidèle,/Ma fortune va prendre une face nouvelle" (Yes, since I have found such a faithful friend,/My fate will take a new turn) (1–2). By rhyming "fidèle" with "nouvelle" in the opening couplet, Racine points to the fundamental contradiction in diplomatic (and authorial) identity, a contradiction that reaches far beyond Orestes' own dilemma—which we soon learn is whether to represent his own interests by taking away Hermione or those of the Greek kings by taking away Astyanax, Andromaque's son—and into the central problem of the play. As many critics have pointed out, Pyrrhus's insistence on keeping Astyanax, and the justification of his love for Andromaque, is based precisely upon his belief that it is possible to start over, to forget his father and the years of the Trojan War. Pyrrhus's rather optimistic position is often opposed to that of Andromaque, who insists that such forgetting is impossible or undesirable. My own analysis of mediation and diplomacy in *Andromaque* does not fundamentally challenge this interpretation; rather, I believe that it enriches it and demonstrates otherwise hidden connections between the play's events and its characters. What Racine presents elsewhere as an either/or proposition—Pyrrhus's desire to start over versus Andromaque's attachment to the past—is therefore evoked in close proximity to Orestes' first lines. Can "novelty" and "fidelity" ever be reconciled? This question is intimately linked to that of whether sovereignty can maintain its independence and its legitimacy as well as to that of diplomatic practice—whether the ambassador who innovates can maintain his link to his masters.

Orestes' mood in the first scene of the play would seem to indicate that a resolution of these mutually exclusive models of representation is impossible. Critics have noted the strange passivity of Orestes' opening lines to his friend Pylade; however, they have failed to note that such passivity is perfectly in line with his diplomatic status.[95] Orestes arrives on the scene not as himself but rather as the representative of a multitude of Greek kings, and Pylade does not fail to note the clash between the magnificence of his entourage and his despondency. As we soon learn, Orestes' melancholy is equally due to his persistent love for Hermione, who is engaged to Pyrrhus, and his active pursuit of the status of Greek ambassador was an effort to forget his feelings. This detail would seem to undermine the primacy of Orestes' identity as diplomat, but if we enlarge the problem of diplomacy to that of faithful representation and the efficacy of substitution, in fact it strengthens it. For as the Greeks' desire to control Astyanax demonstrates, the dominant problem of the play, for nearly all of its characters, is that of replacement. In becoming the Greeks' ambassador, Orestes is in fact substituting one role for another—that of diplomat for that of lovelorn suitor—and his consciousness that this replacement is imperfect places the entire enterprise of diplomatic representation in doubt.

Reinforcing Orestes' own consciousness of the impossibility of reconciling these competing roles is the seeming success of Andromaque in operating smooth substitutions when necessary. As Orestes reminds Pylade, Andromaque saved Astyanax by replacing him with another (nameless) child whom the Greeks killed instead: "J'apprends que pour ravir son enfant au supplice,/Andromaque trompa l'ingénieux Ulysse,/Tandis qu'un autre enfant arraché de ses bras,/Sous le nom de son fils fut conduit au trépas" (I have learned that to save her child from torture,/Andromaque tricked ingenious Ulysses/While another child, ripped from her arms,/Under her son's name was taken to his death) (73–76). By recounting this story, Orestes places the events at the origin of the current conflict under the sign of substitution and draws a parallel with his own situation at the start of the play itself. The choice of words, "sous le nom de son fils," strongly evokes diplomatic representation, as the ambassador always acts in the name of his sovereign(s). What is at stake here are two competing models of delegation. In order to save her son, the biological representative of his father, Andromaque deploys a nonbiological, nameless representative, whose success in carrying out his mission is marked precisely by his death. While it might seem inappropriate to ascribe diplomatic attributes to an infant, it should be noted that in some sense the infant—he who does not speak, the *in-fans*—is in fact the perfect ambassador, the zero degree, as it were, of pure representation. We should recall Racine's strange celebration of Bergeret before the Académie Française, wherein the diplomat's personal accomplishments disappeared behind the glory of the monarch. Moreover, d'Aubignac's suggestion that the actor's voice is the only aspect of his self that prevents complete conflation with his role (and de Vera's evocation of the diplomat imitating his monarch's voice) contribute to the understanding that the ultimate ambassador is silent. Orestes' dilemma, one faced by all those of the century writing on diplomacy, is that absolute diplomatic representation entails the disappearance of the mediator. Much like La Fontaine's animals as described by Louis Marin,[94] speaking in such a situation, however difficult, is essential for survival; yet it is precisely this speech, the assertion of a subject of enunciation, that undermines, with each word, the representative's diplomatic mission.

The resultant situation for Orestes is one of extreme ontological instability, an instability that ends, not surprisingly, with his insanity at the end of the play. Neither fully diplomat nor fully lover—Hermione beautifully manipulates his dual status by answering his pleas for love with a reminder of his official status—"Songez à tous les rois que vous représentez" (Think of all of the kings that you represent) (508)—Orestes is similarly caught between reason and unreason, between life and death. For although Pylade helpfully points out that by pursuing his official mission and insisting upon the return of Astyanax to Greece he can in fact irritate Pyrrhus and thereby attain Hermione for himself, even during his diplomatic reception he fails to fully incarnate the will of the Greeks. A close look at his speech to Pyrrhus reveals both the extent to which Orestes embroiders his instructions and the art with which Pyrrhus seeks to undermine any sort of substitution, diplomatic or biological. Orestes opens his discourse to Pyrrhus by clearing a space for his own speech: "Avant que tous les Grecs vous parlent par ma voix,/Souffrez que j'ose ici me flatter de leur choix,/Et qu'à vos yeux, Seigneur, je montre quelque joie/De voir le fils d'Achille, et le vainqueur de Troie (Before all of the Greeks speak to you with my voice,/Allow me here to flatter myself on their choice,/And to express some joy/Upon seeing the son of Achilles and the conqueror of Troy) (143–46). Seemingly innocuous, this opening asserts Orestes' personal identity in order to better eliminate that of Pyrrhus, who is merely identified as his father's son and who is reminded of his role in the Trojan War, a move calculated to excite the anger and pride of his interlocutor. After the following "Oui," Orestes begins to speak as the Greeks themselves, substituting the "nous" for his own "je" and thereby reinforcing the validity of the substitution argument. Just as he represents the Greeks, Pyrrhus represents his father—"le fils seul d'Achille a pu remplir sa place" (only the son of Achilles has been able to fill his place) (150)—and therefore Astyanax represents the danger of his own father, Hector. At the end of this speech, however, Orestes reverts to his own opinion: "Oserai-je, Seigneur, dire ce que je pense?" (Do I dare, Seigneur, say what I think?) (165). He uses this opportunity to imply that Pyrrhus is himself afraid of Astyanax and that even if he refuses to ascribe to the dynamics of substitution, he should be afraid for his own life. Pyrrhus's response demonstrates his own prowess in manipulating pronouns and is fully in line with his open refusal of substitution. If we remember that the sending and receiving of ambassadors during the seventeenth century was considered a mark of sovereignty, Pyrrhus's argument that he is himself a member of the Greek community amounts to a refusal to recognize Orestes' diplomatic mission. Pyrrhus therefore echoes Orestes' use of the *nous* to destabilize the diplomatic relation, pointing out to some extent that the very presence of Orestes as Greek diplomat is a recognition of the very independence the Greeks would seek to deny him.

This profound paradox—that diplomacy is simultaneously a recognition of the recipient's power and an effort to undermine that power to obtain the desired result, all operated through a mediator who himself has power only insofar as he remains dependent on orders from elsewhere—characterizes almost every interaction throughout the play. Pyrrhus's haughty reception of Orestes is partially undermined by his own subservience to Andromaque in the ensuing scenes. Here, it is his turn to cajole, persuade, and use the "nous" of community to obtain Andromaque's love. Andromaque's refusal of this community, her insistence that her "nous" can only be comprised of herself, Hector, and Astyanax, marks her hold on her own separate sovereignty.

In the second act, Hermione receives Orestes and uses her own hold upon him to transform him into her personal ambassador to Pyrrhus. Of course, before Orestes can represent Hermione's interests to Pyrrhus, the latter responds positively to Orestes' first oration and agrees to surrender Astyanax and marry Hermione. This result demonstrates Hermione's own problematic status in the play, since it is precisely what she asked Orestes to accomplish. Yet as she herself amply recognizes, she is not sovereign insofar as her presence in Epirus and her marriage to Pyrrhus were mandated by her father. Prefiguring the end of the play, where Pyrrhus dies but without Orestes having the opportunity to announce the source of this death as Hermione's will, here Hermione obtains what she wants but invisibly, since Orestes has no opportunity to speak on her behalf before Pyrrhus decides. Similarly, Orestes is left in the position of no longer knowing who, exactly, he represents—the Greeks or Hermione. Pyrrhus's belated recognition of Orestes' diplomatic status—at the marriage "vous y représentez tous les Grecs et son père/Puisqu'en vous Ménélas voit revivre son frère" (you represent all of the Greeks and her father/Since in you Menelas sees his brother come back to life) (620–21)—precedes his own deployment of Orestes as his *own* ambassador: "Voyez-la donc. Allez. Dites-lui que demain/J'attends, avec la paix, son coeur de votre main" (Go see her. Tell her that tomorrow, I await, with the peace, her heart from your hand) (622–23).

The variety of people deploying Orestes marks him not merely as ambassador of the Greeks but, in some sense, existentially a diplomat, whose identity depends completely on context. Unsurprisingly, after the scenes described above, Pylade tells Orestes "Je ne vous connais plus: vous n'êtes plus vous-même" (I no longer know you; you are no longer yourself) (710). This instability is worsened by the tenuous hold on sovereignty of those he is supposed to represent. In diplomatic terms, his instructions keep changing, since none of these characters are certain of what they want. What is advocated in one scene is revoked in the next, and therefore diplomacy becomes less a sign of strength than a symptom of weakness. Hence, Pyrrhus is able to describe his repudiation of his own diplomats' promise to Hermione–"Par mes ambassadeurs mon coeur vous fut promis" (Your heart was promised to me through my ambassadors) (1288)–as a mark of his independence and a further symptom of his general refusal of substitution and replacement. While Hermione sends Orestes to kill Pyrrhus, she herself retains doubts as to the efficacy of delegation. As she tells her *confidente* Cléone, "Je ne sais même encor, quoi qu'il m'ait pu promettre/Sur d'autres que sur moi si je dois m'en remettre. Pyrrhus n'est pas coupable à ses yeux comme aux miens,/Et je tiendrais mes coups bien plus sûrs que les siens" (I do not even know, whatever his promises,/If I should allow people other than myself to act for me./Pyrrhus is not guilty to Orestes' eyes as he is to mine, And I trust my blows more than his) (1257-60).

Orestes' transformation from ambassador of the Greeks to delegate for Hermione does more than merely mirror the innumerable replacements and substitutions in the play. By taking away the fundamental justification of diplomacy–the geographical distance between the countries whose affairs the ambassador must mediate–Racine exposes diplomatic representation as an impossible task. As each character searches for visibility in the eyes of the others as well as authorship of their own actions, delegation is less a mark of sovereignty than a recognition that representation is always imperfect. The idea that one person can take the place of another–the "fiction of representation" upon which the international order of the seventeenth century was based–is shown, through Orestes' struggle for recognition less as an ambassador than as himself (whatever that may mean), to be just as problematic as the idea, espoused by Pyrrhus, that anyone can make a completely fresh start outside of the domain of substitution. Because neither alternative offers fulfillment or perfection, the characters have no other choice than to oscillate between these models–between *fidèle* and *nouvelle*–alternately deploying representatives and repudiating them.

The connection between diplomacy and language itself is made painfully clear, as promises, like delegates, are proffered and revoked throughout the play. Yet just as theater itself spills beyond the domain of literature through the troubling presence of the actors—who, exactly, are they, and what do they feel?[95]—diplomacy differs from linguistic representation in the irreducible, opaque presence of the human figure at its core. Failed actions are therefore attributable, ironically, to Orestes, the one character whose will is rarely, if ever, presented as his own. As Cléone notes long before Hermione reproaches Orestes for killing Pyrrhus: "Je le plains: d'autant plus qu'auteur de son ennui/le coup qui l'a perdu n'est parti que de lui" (I feel sorry for him, all the more so because, as author of his troubles/the blow that undid him was his own) (835–36). This tragic mix of guilt and innocence, of notoriety and anonymity, is made manifest during the killing of Pyrrhus, where the multiplicity of Greeks who participate in the murder both mask Orestes' responsibility and underscore it, since they seem to incarnate the absent but multiple authority that sent him in the first place. Their presence once again renders Orestes' diplomatic identity meaningless, just as Hermione's repudiation of his act further leaves his function as delegate without a solid support. The ambassador without a master has, as Gentili and Wicquefort demonstrated, no clear identity—much like the actor without a play. In this sense, Orestes' insanity at the close of the play is deeply significant. At first "content" that he has found a fixed identity as an example of divine anger—"Jétais né pour servir d'exemple à ta colère/Pour être du malheur un modèle accompli./Hé bien! Je meurs content, et mon sort est rempli" (I was born to serve as example of your anger/to be a perfect model of unhappiness/Well then! I die happy, and my fate is accomplished) (1618–20)—Orestes soon finds himself plunged once again into instability and oblivion. Speaking to the Furies, he asks, "Pour qui sont ces serpents qui sifflent sur vos têtes?/A qui destinez-vous l'appareil qui vous suit?" (For whom are these serpents hissing on your heads?/For whom is the pomp that follows you?) (1638–39). Ever the diplomat, Orestes can never be certain that attention, whether love or vengeance, is directed at him. Insofar as attention is addressed to him, he has failed to fulfill his mission; insofar as it reaches beyond him, he becomes invisible, enveloped in an "éternelle nuit." Orestes' fate, his madness, is to occupy both of these roles at the same time.

Is it possible to read *Andromaque* as a political commentary on seventeenth-century France? Racine restricts the inability to use delegation successfully, to become fully sovereign in any meaningful way, to the Greek characters, who seem to be condemned from the outset since their state is governed not by a single, unified monarch but by a coalition of kings. If we recall the seventeenth-century French insistence upon singularity as a hallmark of sovereignty as well as Louis XIV's efforts to deny the status of ambassador to representatives of those states governed by multiple or elected figures, Orestes' ultimate failure is not particularly surprising. Against the Greek confusion Racine sets Andromaque and her son Astyanax, who seems victorious in his own silent mission to occupy the place of his father. His recognition by Pyrrhus as the new Trojan king sets in motion a string of successions that, as Racine reminds the reader in the preface, will ultimately lead to the French monarchy. Yet as the *Mémoires pour l'instruction du dauphin* demonstrate, the ideal of the plentitude of succession and of total representation is quite difficult to achieve in practice.

Racine's indirect explanation for how this ideal remains possible places its achievement in a potentially disturbing light. In both prefaces to *Andromaque,* Racine cites the scene in the third book of the *Aeneid* where Aeneas meets Andromaque. Although he edits the original Latin considerably, Racine takes great pains to preserve a telling detail–Andromaque is honoring Hector's *empty* tomb. Racine seems to be suggesting that full representation and substitution can only occur when the place that one is taking is vacant. In the context of the divine right monarchy articulated in seventeenth-century France, this would appear to confirm the darkest suspicions of those trying to prove the link between king and God–that at the moment when the *lieutenance* of the monarchy is its fullest, when the king becomes the image of God on earth, the divine model is emptied of its specificity and meaning. Likewise, in such a context, completely successful diplomatic representation–the embodiment of royal sovereignty by the ambassador–would render the kingly master irrelevant. As Racine's comments concerning Bergeret state, under a king such as Louis XIV, the diplomat has only to repeat his instructions–an ideal that the treatment of Orestes in *Andromaque* reveals as fraught with difficulty for the ambassador himself. The triumph of monarchy implies the tragedy of its instruments.

THE TRAGEDY OF PERFECT DIPLOMACY: CORNEILLE'S *SURÉNA*

The consequences of excellence in diplomacy–the idea that perfect representation eliminates the relevance of the model upon which it is based–form the basis of Pierre Corneille's *Suréna.* Written and performed in 1673, it is Corneille's last play, and indeed, if we continue the parallel between the ambassador and the actor, its exploration of the potential independence and superiority of these figures to their masters marks the end of theatrical possibility.[96] As the play opens, Eurydice, the daughter of Artabase, king of Armenia, is informing her *confidente* that she is in love. Since the states of Rome and Parthia were vying for her father's allegiance, they sent ambassadors to try to win him over. Eurydice has nothing but contempt for the Roman ambassador, who, as envoy of a powerful republic, despises kingship and holds out the possibility of subjugation of the Armenian state. The inclusion of this unsuccessful ambassador alongside Suréna, the ambassador of the Parthians, not only emphasizes Louis XIV's contemporaries' awareness of their monarch's disdain for envoys from nonmonarchical states; it also subtly underscores the right of embassy as a mark of sovereignty, setting in place the political puzzle that follows.

For Suréna, ambassador of Orode, the king of Parthia, makes an entirely different impression on the princess:

> [Suréna], par les devoirs d'un respect légitime,
> Vengeait le sceptre en nous de ce manque d'estime.
> L'amour s'en mêla même, et tout son entretien
> Sembla m'offrir son coeur, et demander le mien.
> Il l'obtint, et mes yeux, que charmait sa présence,
> Soudain avec les siens en firent confidence.
> Ces muets truchements surent lui révéler
> Ce que je me forçais à lui dissimuler,
> Et les mêmes regards qui m'expliquaient sa flamme
> S'instruisaient dans les miens du secret de mon âme.[97] (45–54)

> [Surena, through the duties of legitimate respect,
> Avenged our scepter for this lack of esteem.
> Even love was mixed in, and his entire speech
> Seemed to offer me his heart, and asked for mine.
> He obtained it, and my eyes, which his presence charmed,
> Suddenly shared their secret with his.
> These mute interpreters were able to reveal
> What I forced myself to hide from him
> And the same gaze which explained his love to me
> Instructed themselves, in my own gaze, on the secret of my soul.]

Eurydice's insistence on the silence in which their love was born and exchanged is highly significant. Falling in love with Orode's ambassador is in itself a recognition of the incompleteness of diplomatic representation, of the persistent opacity of its human instrument. While his official message comes from elsewhere and addresses itself not to Eurydice but rather to her father, the king, his mere presence and the silence of his gaze block the unbroken transmission of authority and subvert his mission. Suréna's situation with regard to Eurydice is the opposite of Orestes' position with regard to Hermione. The latter enjoys sporadic diplomatic success but, perhaps because of this very success, is too transparent and can never transcend his diplomatic status enough to be recognized *for himself.* Suréna, on the other hand, is by far too opaque, too physically present, for any accomplishment to be attributed to his king rather than to himself. As Pacorus, the king's son, tells Suréna (without knowing that he and Eurydice are in love), the danger of diplomatic representation is that its instrument can outshine the distant master: "Et par l'objet présent les sentiments émus/N'attendent pas toujours des Rois qu'on n'a point vus" (And feelings, moved by the present object/Do not always wait for kings never seen) (399–400).

Although Suréna's mission to Artabase fails and the Armenian king places himself under the authority of Rome, Orode goes on to win the battle, and Armenia (and its princess Eurydice) are placed at the mercy of the Parthians. Orode's wish is to marry Eurydice to his son, Pacorus; of course, she remains smitten with Orode's legal representative, Suréna. By placing Eurydice between the successor to the throne and the king's ambassador, Corneille offers a new spin on the question of status through birth or virtue that runs throughout his work, most notably in *Don Sanche d'Aragon*. He raises the implicit question of which figure most truly represents the king's authority and power—the son, who owes his position to the accidents of birth, or the diplomat, whose status is instituted through human law and culture. Suréna's rejection of the idea that his descendants could carry on his own glory only further underscores the contrast between the two systems of representation, biological and institutional. Adding to the problem of representing the monarch, the king himself does not appear until the third act, after both Suréna and Pacorus have appeared on stage and presented themselves to Eurydice. By beginning with those who represent the monarch and allowing them to make their impressions both on the princess and the audience, Corneille mirrors the larger political problem of whether the king remains visible through either figure or whether either system of mediation supports or undermines the monarchy.

When Orode finally appears, it is to complain of his relative invisibility. The first lines of the third act are spoken by Sillace, Orode's "autre lieutenant," a curious designation that emphasizes Orode's dilemma. With so many figures "holding his place," what exactly remains the place of the king? Furthermore, Sillace speaks in order to remark upon the curious impenetrability of Suréna, an impenetrability that corresponds to the opacity noted above. Orode explains to Sillace that the roles of king and representative have, in a sense, become reversed: "Il m'a rendu lui seul ce qu'on m'avait volé/Mon sceptre; . . . /Quand j'en pleurais la perte, il forçait des murailles,/Quand j'invoquais mes dieux, il gagnait des batailles (He alone gave me back what was taken from me,/My scepter; . . . /While I was crying for its loss, he was taking fortresses,/While I prayed to my gods, he was winning battles) (712–13,

716–17). The only means by which Orode may still control Suréna is through an arranged marriage to his daughter Mandane; of course, this solution is rendered immensely difficult since (in the words of the play itself) the "place" of Mandane, or, in the case of Eurydice, the "place" of Pacorus, is already occupied.

The ensuing drama turns, then, upon the fundamental incompatibility of political order and love–an incompatibility announced by the very failure of Suréna's diplomatic mission before the play even begins. As presented here, love, with its silence and its emphasis on the physical presence and corresponding attention to the person of the lover, is diametrically opposed to the ideal of mediation needed to successfully govern and legitimize the state. The passion with which Eurydice, Suréna, and Pacorus pursue the objects of their desire undermines the order that the (largely absent) king seeks to impose on the newly formed alliance of Armenia and Parthia. The extent to which love subverts mediation is perhaps nowhere better demonstrated than in Eurydice's response to Suréna's offer to die and let her live happily on the throne with Pacorus: "J'envisage ce trône et tous ses avantages,/Et je n'y vois partout, Seigneur, que vos ouvrages" (I imagine this throne and all of its advantages,/And I only see everywhere your handiwork) (1569–70). Here, Eurydice speaks the hidden scandal of the play–the scandal that Orode wishes to silence through the marriage of Suréna and his daughter–that Suréna, not the king, is the true author of Parthia's success. Orode himself reminds Suréna that while it may be true that he owes his throne to the diplomat-warrior, this truth must never be spoken:

> Suréna, j'aime à voir que votre gloire éclate,
> Tout ce que je vous dois, j'aime à le publier,
> Mais quand je m'en souviens, vous devez l'oublier.
> Si le ciel par vos mains m'a rendu cet Empire,
> Je sais vous épargner la peine de le dire. (906–10)

> [Surena, I like to see your glory manifest itself,
> Everything I owe you, I like to publish,
> But while I remember, you should forget.
> If the heavens restored to me this empire through your hands,
> I know how to spare you the trouble of saying it.]

Orode's effort to reconfigure the legitimacy of his rule–the *puissance de droit* rather than the *puissance de fait*–demonstrates the danger that the passion of Suréna and Eurydice poses to the very foundations of the monarchy. While Orode wishes to reestablish himself as author of his success by monopolizing the discourse proclaiming Suréna's heroic actions, he also alludes to the ultimate source of this success. In the lines above, Suréna is not portrayed as an isolated actor but rather as the instrument of the heavens, an observation that marks Orode's appeal to the principles of divine right sovereignty.

Yet Orode's vision of politics, while laudable, renders manifest the dangers that the seventeenth-century elaborators of divine right theory had foreseen. Only one link in the unbroken continuity between heaven and earth–the passive recipient of divine intent and the absent master condemned to act through his younger, more striking representatives–Orode dissolves into irrelevance, or at least into a position that utterly fails to command the hearts of his subjects (and the spectators). In the *examen* accompanying *Clitandre,* written for the 1660 publication of his works, Corneille had already provided a striking account of the disadvantages of presenting this kind of monarchy on stage. In this text, he explains that a king can appear on stage in one of three ways: as king, as man, and as judge. Kings respond to attacks on their throne or their life; men respond to their passions, without a direct danger for their states; and judges appear only to resolve the problems of others (such as the king in *Le Cid*). With regard to this last role, Corneille points out that "On ne peut désavouer qu'en cette dernière posture il remplit assez mal la dignité d'un si grand titre, n'ayant aucune part en l'action que celle qu'il y veut prendre pour d'autres, et demeurant bien éloigné de l'éclat des deux autres manières. Aussi on ne le donne jamais à représenter aux meilleurs acteurs, mais il faut qu'il se contente de passer par la bouche de ceux du second ou du troisième ordre" (We cannot deny that in this last posture the king fills the dignity of such a great role badly, having no other role in the action than that which he undertakes for others, and remaining far removed from the glory of the other roles. Therefore we never give this role to the best actors, but rather it should be enough that actors of second or third orders take this part).[98] Like Eurydice or Suréna, Corneille speaks the scandal of power here. The most legitimate king–one whose state is not in danger, who has conquered his own passions, and who appears as the recipient of divine authority and the instrument of its transmission to his (happy) people–is the least appealing and the most invisible on the stage. As the fears of counterfeiting in the theoretical texts discussed in the first chapter show, such a king can be "played" by almost anyone, an idea that the *Mémoires pour l'instruction du dauphin* seem written to counteract. *Suréna*, like *Andromaque*, explores the fissures and contradictions inherent in writings on monarchy and diplomacy. Corneille's play reveals that either the monarch is imperfect, and thus in a way more visible than the instruments of his power, or he is the perfect embodiment of authority and his diplomats outshine him.

In such a context, locating tyranny or even abuse of power in *Suréna* becomes problematic. Many critics view *Suréna* as an apology for private freedoms, a proof that state authority cannot and should not command the souls and hearts of its subjects; such readings have led readers to characterize the work as the most "racinian" of Corneille's plays.[99] Representative of this line of thought is Marc Fumaroli's argument that "le détachement des intérêts mondains, qui transfigure le couple de Suréna et d'Eurydice, l'humour noir avec lequel ils observent hors d'eux les jeux sinistres et sordides de la politique, ont pour corollaire l'amoureuse confiance, d'une transparence parfaite, qu'ils se font l'un à l'autre, figure profane de la confiance de l'âme en la loyauté de Dieu, préfiguration de l'union de l'âme à Dieu" (The detachment from worldly interests, which transfigures the couple of Surena and Eurydice, the black humor with which they observe the sinister and sordid political games around them, have as a corollary the loving confidence, of perfect transparency, that they have in each other, a profane figure of the confidence the soul takes in the loyalty of God, which is a prefiguration of the union of the soul with God).[100] Yet Eurydice's statement that when she looks at the throne she can only see Suréna's work, added to Suréna's own assertion that "mon vrai crime est ma gloire, et non pas mon amour" (my true crime is my glory, not my love) (1651), demonstrates that the two figures are keenly aware of the profoundly *political* nature of their passion. The love that Fumaroli describes as transparent is repeatedly described by Pacorus as an *obstacle* to the greater good of the state.[101] As neither Pacorus nor Orode is portrayed unsympathetically, this characterization is less a sinister advocacy of state involvement in private affairs and more a recognition of the fragility of the current political situation and of the profoundly public identities of both Eurydice and Suréna.

It should also be noted that Eurydice herself proudly claims a certain sovereignty over Suréna, a claim that places her as a direct threat to the king. In a move quite reminiscent of Hermione's attempts to shift Orestes' allegiances from the Greeks to herself (but complicated in Racine's play by the fact that the Greeks and Hermione overlap), Eurydice tells Suréna:

> Je veux que vous aimiez afin de m'obéir.
> Je veux que ce grand choix soit mon dernier ouvrage,
> Qu'il tienne lieu vers moi d'un éternel hommage,
> Que mon ordre le règle, et qu'on me voie enfin
> Reine de votre coeur et de votre destin,
> Que Mandane, en dépit de l'espoir qu'on lui donne,
> Ne pouvant s'élever jusqu'à votre personne,

Soit réduite à descendre à ces malheureux Rois
A qui, quand vous voudrez, vous donnerez des lois. (324–32)

(I want you to love me so that you obey me.
I want this great choice to be my legacy,
To serve as [literally, to hold the place of] an eternal homage to me.
I hope that my order will make it so, and that they will see me
As queen of your heart and of your destiny,
That Mandane, despite the hope she has been given,
Unable to attain your person
Should be reduced to descending towards those unhappy kings,
To whom you will be imposing laws at your pleasure.)

Eurydice's speech does not separate love and power but instead marks her desire to supersede royal authority with her own. The language of *lieutenance* clearly demonstrates her wish to transform Suréna from representative of Orode's authority into a symbol of their love; in such a context, as she explicitly remarks, she becomes a queen. Such an affair *is* political, as Pacorus and Orode themselves have noted throughout the play, since it subordinates political representation and mediation to the full moment and physical presence that characterizes amorous desire. Eurydice's reference to Suréna's abilities to subordinate kings to his will further denotes her consciousness that what she is proposing is the subversion of the very principles upholding political order. This love does not admit mediation or representation; as Eurydice notes later in the play, "Savez-vous qu'à Mandane envoyer ce que j'aime,/C'est de ma propre main m'assassiner moi-même?" (Do you know that sending the person I love to Mandane/Is tantamount to assassinating myself by my own hand?) (1705–6). Eurydice's passion for Suréna therefore points out the weakest aspect of governance through delegation, emphasizing the physicality and individuality—the irreplaceable nature—of its instruments.

If we read *Suréna* through the lens of mediation, then, it is love, not Orode's government, that is tyrannical. Eurydice herself notes this, saying that "L'amour rompt aisément le reste de sa chaîne,/Et tyran à son tour du devoir méprisé,/Il s'applaudit longtemps du joug qu'il a brisé" (Love easily breaks the rest of its chain,/and becoming tyrant over disdained duty,/it congratulates itself for a long time on its broken obligations) (1262–64). Further supporting this interpretation are the observations of Suréna's sister Palmis, who fully recognizes the public roles of her brother and Pacorus and who voices the necessity of subordinating the personal to the political. Indeed, by sacrificing her own sentiments for Pacorus—sentiments due as much to his status as prince as to any physical or moral virtues—she embodies the ideal subject.[102] Her observation to Pacorus is that "Je sais ce qu'à l'Etat ceux de votre naissance,/Tous maîtres qu'ils en sont, doivent d'obéissance:/Son intérêt chez eux l'emporte sur le leur,/Et du moment qu'il parle, il fait taire le coeur" (I know what those of your birth,/although masters, owe the state in obedience./The interests of the state supersede your own,/and from the moment the state speaks, you must silence your hearts) (609-12). This discourse matches Orode's own speech to Suréna, where he notes, "C'est bien traiter les Rois en personnes communes/Qu'attacher à leur rang ces gênes importunes" (What a nice way of equaling kings to commoners/by attaching such unwelcome concerns to their rank) (1025-26). By repeatedly exhorting Eurydice to compromise and send Suréna to Mandane—a sentiment accompanied by rather direct condemnations of Eurydice's own tyranny—Palmis shows that she understands the state and its mechanisms better than almost everyone else in the play.

Yet Palmis remains unheard, just as she remains unattached to any member of this state through marriage. Suréna meets his death in a manner that is a perfect illustration of the tension between love and tyranny and between politics and mediation that characterizes the entire play. Killed by three arrows launched by an unseen hand, Suréna falls on the square just outside of the palace. If the arrows symbolize the ideal of mediation—the authority that should pass through the state's agents with as few "obstacles" as possible—the invisibility of their source mirrors the quasi invisibility of Orode throughout the play. As I have demonstrated, the ruler basing his legitimacy upon mediation runs the risk of disappearing as agent, especially, one might add, in the context of a competing discourse—in this case, that of love—that emphasizes instead the opacity and presence of its own agents. Suréna, quite literally, is transformed into an obstacle; it is precisely this presence and opacity that leads to his death, rather than to his continued glory as servant of the state, as an agent through whom such arrows could pass. As Palmis herself notes in blaming Eurydice for the assassination (and as Orode himself laments earlier in the play), the affair between Eurydice and Suréna has forced the king into a tyranny of his own by pointing out the gaps covered over in the "fiction of representation" through which the state operates. Palmis's cries to the gods, who seem incapable of punishing Orode—"Que fais-tu du tonnerre,/Ciel, si tu daignes voir ce qu'on fait sur la terre,/Et pour qui gardes-tu tes carreaux embrasés,/Si de pareils tyrans n'en sont point écrasés?" (What are you doing with your thunder,/heaven, if you can see what we do on earth?/And for whom do you keep your burning bolts/if such tyrants are not punished?) (1721-24)— are a means of noting that the unbroken chain linking the heavens, the state,

the king, and his subjects is now open to doubt. Yet by refusing, unlike Eurydice, to die, Palmis demonstrates her continuing belief in this system by
accepting her status as instrument, albeit now an instrument of vengeance.

Suréna is thus not so much the most "racinian" of Corneille's plays as it is
the illustration of Corneille's conviction, expressed in the *Discours de l'utilité
et des parties du poème dramatique*, that love should not take center stage in
a tragedy: "Lorsqu'on met sur la scène un simple intrigue d'amour entre des
rois, et qu'ils ne courent aucun péril ni de leur vie ni de leur Etat, je ne crois
pas que, bien que les personnes soient illustres, l'action le soit assez pour
s'élever jusqu'à la tragédie. Sa dignité demande quelque grand intérêt d'Etat
ou quelque passion plus noble et plus mâle que l'amour, telles que sont l'ambition ou la vengeance, et veut donner à craindre des malheurs plus grands
que la perte d'une maîtresse" (When we portray on stage a simple love story
between kings, and these kings do not risk either their lives or their state, I do
not believe that, even though the characters are illustrious, the plot is dignified enough to be elevated as a tragedy. Tragic dignity demands a great interest of state or some more noble and male passion than love, such as ambition
or vengeance, and asks that we fear something more than the loss of a mistress).[103] As the playwright had implied earlier in *Cinna* (1640), love undermines not merely tragedy but also the very principles upholding the state. Yet
unlike *Cinna*, where Auguste's clemency sufficed to reestablish the government's authority over its subjects, *Suréna* offers no such hope. Quite possibly,
spectators and critics, distanced from the political upheavals of the first half
of the seventeenth century, lent their sympathies not to Orode and his son but
to Eurydice and Suréna, without seeing the tyranny of this couple's attraction.
The triumph of Racinian tragedy indeed marks the death of that of Corneille.

Yet I hope to have shown that both playwrights used the figure of the ambassador to more fully explore the problem of mediation that was indirectly
examined in their other works. *Suréna* is, in many ways, the mirror image of
Andromaque. In Racine's play, the characters cannot achieve the solidity
needed to command the full attention of others. Orestes' diaphanous nature,
his tragic betweenness, is merely an exaggerated example of the dilemma facing Hermione and Pyrrhus; Andromaque herself embraces her identity as
reaching beyond herself into the status of "wife of Hector" and "mother of
Astyanax"–she wishes for the invisibility that plagues Orestes. By evacuating
the question of political order and legitimacy from the play, or at least by
removing it to the "second plan" that Corneille himself assigns to love, Racine
presents the struggle for recognition in a tragic light, without noting that the
characters' status as themselves and more than themselves is essential to the
workings of the state. Perfect mediation is politically necessary but person-

ally tragic, and as long as the instruments of government are human, mediation is doomed to failure. Corneille offers much the same message, as he also exposes the contradictions inherent in the theoretical ideal of governmental mediation. Yet in *Suréna*, the problem is the opposite of that in *Andromaque;* apart from Orode and Palmis, the characters are *too* solid, and this solidity forms an obstacle to the smooth working of the state.

As both plays demonstrate, theater is uniquely positioned to explore the nuances and contradictions that the "fiction of representation," or the ideal of mediation, tries to cover over. The residual humanity and individuality of the actors who convey the author's message to the spectators—presumably never exactly in the same way twice—in itself affords the playwrights an intense experience of the advantages and disadvantages of this form of communication. Should we read the issues raised in *Suréna*—the frustration with the opacity of the human medium, only too apt to assert its independence from its sending authority—as a symptom of Corneille's own struggle to achieve recognition through, and perhaps despite, his theatrical productions? Does Corneille view himself as a counterpart to Orode, condemned to invisibility the more successful his actors-ambassadors are? And can Racine's embracing of the actor's inherent doubleness and betweenness be read as a reflection of his altogether more accepting view of antiquity and his sympathy for the actor's status and power? While both interpretations are certainly possible, for the purposes of this study it is enough to note that the two authors wrote against the backdrop of mediation all the while problematizing its possibilities in a way that official governmental texts or diplomatic practices could not. The impossibility of perfect mediation that both writers uncovered would only receive explicit theoretical attention in the final years of the seventeenth century and practical application in the eighteenth.

As Racine and Corneille demonstrate, the tension between the two competing, yet equally necessary, configurations of political power in seventeenth-century France persisted behind the veils shrouding the mystery of state, the "je ne sais quoi" of authority. "Fidèle" and "nouvelle" remained irreconcilable, but the fundamental incompatibility of sovereignty and legitimacy, of dependence and independence, remained hidden behind a fragile compromise wherein Louis XIV was held to embody both aspects of power perfectly. As long as it was agreed that the king's access to divinity was reserved for him alone, no one else could legitimately question his status as privileged mediator between heaven and earth. In addition, Louis XIV's seeming possession of godlike independence, force of will, and authority could be interpreted by sympathetic observers not as proof of the tenuousness (and ultimate meaninglessness) of his ties with the divine but rather as a further manifestation of his status as "the image of God on earth."

It goes without saying, however, that not all observers were as sympathetic as the French writers of panegyrics. Other states could not, of course, admit that France alone was the beneficiary of divine wisdom through its exceptional king, although the battles, early in Louis XIV's personal reign, for precedency and for the right to determine and define diplomatic language reveal the extent to which such an interpretation could be forced upon France's neighbors. Yet as James Howell's *Proedria Basilike* shows, challenges to French preeminence were quite often based upon the underlying assumptions set forth by the French; Howell follows French logic in bolstering the English claim to precedency by showing the privileged relation between the English king and the divine and England's relative independence with regard to Rome and by minimizing the status of the Parliament. The monarch's sovereignty is thereby defined and defended in terms that resemble those used across the Channel. In this context of French dominance, the work of Leibniz becomes significant. A frequent visitor to France and a friend of Bossuet, Leibniz offered scathing critiques of Louis XIV's policies, the most famous of which is his *Mars Christianissimus*. In this text, written in 1683, Leibniz attacks the very ideology of mediation and divine right monarchy upholding the French Crown. With ironic comments such as "it is thus for me to show at present that . . . there is no man today who has received from heaven, even from the antipodes, a greater power in temporal affairs than Louis XIV,"[1] Leibniz demonstrates that the location of the source of the French king's power in a sphere outside of human scrutiny contributes not to increased legitimacy but rather to the arbitrary cruelty of his actions. The logical conclusion of seeing, as the French do, the hand of God in Louis's victories is the liberation of their monarch from human laws and constraints: "the greatness of the King and of the French crown is above all other rights and oaths, of whatever character they may be."[2]

While the *Mars Christianissimus* exposes divine right monarchy to intense mockery, Leibniz distinguishes himself from other pamphleteers, such as Lisola, the author of the equally scathing *Bouclier d'Etat*, by elaborating, in the *Securitas publica interna et externa* (1670) and later, in his *Caesarini Furstenerii Tractatus de jure suprematus ad legationum Principum Germaniae* (1678), an alternative structure of governmental power. This model anticipates the Pan-European federalism that would, in part, result from the Treaty of Utrecht (1713) by envisioning a state as the product of several smaller entities, each of which can be said to possess certain attributes of sovereignty, such as the right to send and receive ambassadors.[3] In this manner, as Christiane Frémont argues, Leibniz's thoughts on sovereignty and the rights of the states comprising the empire mirror his efforts to rethink the physical world as a collection of monads, each possessing its own "will" and yet cohering with other monads as a result of mutual attraction and opposition. Leibniz's far-ranging interests further demonstrate the extent to which sovereignty and political order could be, and were, seen as linked to larger accounts of order in the universe; his efforts to reconcile the physical and political worlds recall the similar efforts of Le Moyne to redraw the actual sun to match its political symbolism.

Within France, the waning years of the seventeenth century were marked by the reemergence of Protestant critiques of royal power. Pierre Jurieu, writing from exile in Holland, furnished a series of writings that purported to demonstrate that God was not behind the French throne but rather behind its persecuted Protestant minority. In support of this thesis, Jurieu cited miracles that accompanied the execution of Protestant martyrs in his *Lettres pastorals adressées aux fidèles de France* (1686–87). He also provided "evidence" that the reign of Louis XIV bore certain similarities to the apocalypse in works such as the *Accomplissement des prophéties or Présages de la décadence des empires* (1686). Again, Jurieu's method of opposition consisted less in questioning the very link between divine will and human affairs than in asserting that divine will was attached not to the French monarchy but to the fate of the Huguenot minority. Pierre Bayle, on the other hand, rejected such interpretations outright by patiently arguing that the very terms of the debate needed to be changed if Protestant resistance was to avoid falling into the traps set for it by the Catholics.[4]

Within the terms laid out by this study, however, the shift in ways of thinking about royal power inside of France toward the end of the century is palpable in François de Callières's *De la manière de négocier avec les souverains*. I have already indicated that Callières's treatise is regarded as the essential expression of diplomatic theory under Louis XIV; it is often cited as the foundational text of modern diplomacy. Yet as Maurice Keens-Soper remarks, such readings, by abstracting Callières's diplomatic theory into a classical, ahistorical essence, neglect the context in and against which Callières was writing.[5] As Keens-Soper points out, Callières in fact breaks with the representational tradition evident in Wicquefort's writing: "Firmly but without commotion Callières redirects the centre of attention away from the ambassador as an officer of state, a legal and representative personality and a gentleman, and brings it to rest on the modalities of continuous diplomatic activity. It is a simple and yet telling adjustment in the angle of vision, from which he seldom departs. The move is one from exclusive focus on the actor to a view which brings the stage into the forefront of the picture."[6]

Keens-Soper's evaluation of Callières's context and innovations is valuable, but it neglects the tight link between diplomatic theory and theories of sovereignty and monarchical government. The evolution in diplomatic thought apparent in Callières was made possible by a changing view of kingship and sovereignty. No longer seen as the ambassador of the heavens imbued with special, if not mystical, authority, the king-administrator, like his diplomat, blends in with his peers, if not his subjects. Callières worked in diplomacy during the 1690s, a period when the legitimacy of the French government's policies, both domestic (with the Revocation of the Edict of Nantes, outlawing the exercise of the Protestant religion) and international (the wholesale destruction of the Palatinate and the pursuit of the Spanish succession) were under question as never before. It should also be remembered that Louis XIV, faced with an ever-shrinking pool of successors to the throne—the recurring deaths in the family could not have failed to remind observers of the inherent weaknesses in monarchical government, just as the strength and virility of Louis XIV's young person in the 1660s had led them to forget such drawbacks—decided, in 1714, to grant his legitimized bastard children access to the line of royal succession. This act followed the establishment, in 1694, of an intermediary rank especially for these children, which placed them between dukes and peers and the princes of the blood. Saint-Simon, in his *Mémoires sur les légitimés* (August 1720), decries this legitimization as follows: "L'habitude que les derniers exemples en ont formée a fait disparoistre l'ancienne jusqu'à l'oubli de la loy divine, de l'honnesteté publique et des dangers de l'Estat; et cette disposition a fait de si prodigieux progrès, qu'elle a attenté avec succès à la Couronne et y a porté ceux qui n'estant nés que pour l'oubli devant Dieu et devant les hommes, sont devenus un exemple effrayant de ce que peut l'affection et la puissance d'un Roy devenu de son vivant le père légitime ou naturel de toute sa race" (The habit that these last examples has formed has led to the forgetting of divine law, public honesty and the dangers of the state, and this way of thinking has made such prodigious progress that it has successfully damaged the crown and has led those who were born only to obscurity before God and men to become a frightening example of what can accomplish the affection and power of a king who has, during his lifetime, become the legitimate or natural father of his entire race).[7] The elevation of Louis XIV's children with Madame de Montespan provides an acute example of how undue attention to the physicality of the royal person—as well as the effort to equate the mystery of royalty with that person, to collapse the king's two bodies—necessarily obfuscates the divine source of his authority. The direct result of this decision seems not so much to have been the communication of majesty to these children but rather the confirmation of the nagging suspicion that the king was as much a mere human as his subjects.[8] Saint-Simon's emphasis on the importance of the Salic law, which was obliterated by the 1714 decision, should be read in this context, since many commentators had seen the law as proof of the king's exemption from the rules of succession and heredity that governed the rest of the kingdom.

Callières's treatise, although written in the 1690s, was not published until 1716, a year after Louis XIV's death. Rather than an affirmation of the quasi-divine status of the ambassador who represents the godlike French king, *De la manière de négocier avec les souverains* is a testament to the near-anonymity of both diplomat and sovereign in the context of international relations. Callières begins by noting that France has neglected to cultivate diplomats, an unsurprising observation given the official opinion, prevalent during much of the reign, that ambassadors of such a great monarch needed merely to read their orders or instructions in order to succeed. The criticism of the current state of French diplomacy that follows is worth citing, since it alludes to several of the problems inherent in failing to recognize that entering into negotiations is, by definition, a certain abdication of absolute sovereignty—a recognition that the solar system contains more than one sun:

> Ces négociateurs novices s'enivrent d'ordinaire des honneurs qu'on rend en leur personne à la dignité des maîtres qu'ils représentent, semblables à cet âne de la fable, qui recevait pour lui tout l'encens qu'on brûlait devant la statue de la déesse qu'il portait. Cela arrive surtout à ceux qui sont employés par un grand prince, auprès d'un prince inférieur en puissance. . . . Ils ressemblent plutôt à des *hérauts d'armes* qu'à des ambassadeurs, dont le but principal doit être d'entretenir une bonne correspondance entre leur maître et les princes vers lesquels ils sont envoyés et qui ne doivent leur représenter sa puissance que comme un moyen de maintenir ou d'augmenter la leur, au lieu de s'en servir à les abaisser et à exciter leur ressentiment et leur jalousie.[9]

> [These novice negotiators let the honors that are given through their person to the dignity of the masters that they represent go to their head, like the donkey of the fable, who attributes to himself all of the incense burnt before the statue of the goddess that he carried. This happens above all to those who are employed by a great Prince to go to a Prince whose power is inferior. . . . They are more like war heralds than ambassadors, whose principal goal should be to establish and maintain a good relation between their master and the princes to whom they are sent, and who should not represent their master's power other than as a means to maintain or augment that of the princes to whom they are sent, instead of using this power to lower them or excite their resentment and jealousy.]

Callières's use of the fable of the icon-carrying donkey, newly revived by La Fontaine in his *Fables,* underscores the parallel between the diplomat (and by extension, the king) who attributes honor to himself rather than to the source of his authority and the problem of idolatry. Such diplomats are not ambassadors at all; they are military heralds, who do not arrive in a foreign court to negotiate but rather to impose their masters' authority. Indeed, the idea that one prince is palpably superior to all others and that he can set the language and terms of "negotiation"–the idea lying behind the diplomatic incidents of 1661 and 1662 discussed earlier–contradicts the very essence of diplomacy as defined by Callières. In one of his more famous quotations, Callières declares that "Il n'y a point d'état si puissant par lui-même, qui n'ait besoin d'alliés, pour resister aux forces des autres puissances ennemies ou jalouses de sa prospérité, lorsqu'elles s'unissent contre lui" (There is no state so powerful by itself that it does not need allies to resist the forces of other enemy powers, or of those jealous of its prosperity, once they are united against it).[10] The lessons of the War of the Spanish Succession, and perhaps also the Treaty of Utrecht, have made their mark on Callières's theory.[11]

If the princes in Europe, viewed together, have in a sense lost their absolute sovereignty–according to Callières, "il faut considérer que tous les états dont l'Europe est composée ont entre eux des liaisons et des commerces nécessaires qui font qu'on peut les regarder comme les membres d'une même république" (one must consider that all of the states which comprise Europe have, between them, so many connections and interactions that one can regard them as members of one same republic),[12] a sentiment that anticipates the abbé de Saint-Pierre's *Projet de paix perpetuelle*–then ambassadors can be viewed, in a sense, as having recaptured their past prominence. Although Callières is far from arguing that diplomats have a Christian mission of peace and that their authority therefore derives from a source independent of their sovereign, his endorsement of Richelieu's advocacy of continual negotiation creates a diplomatic corps in possession of a peculiar kind of independence. Such diplomats as those present during the negotiations at Utrecht have, as Lucien Bély has noted,[13] more in common with each other than with their respective masters; their task is to accomplish a peace that will, to a certain extent, be *imposed* on their states upon their return. This evolution is evident in Callières's version of the now-familiar comparison of the ambassador with the actor: "Un ambassadeur ressemble en quelque manière à un comédien, exposé sur le théâtre aux yeux du public pour y jouer de grands rôles. Comme son emploi l'élève au-dessus de sa condition et *l'égale en quelque sorte aux maîtres de la terre,* par le droit de représentation qui y est attaché et par le commerce particulier qu'il lui donne avec eux, il ne peut passer que pour un mauvais acteur s'il n'en sait pas soutenir la dignité, mais cette obligation est l'écueil contre lequel échouent plusieurs négociateurs, parce qu'ils ne savent pas précisément en quoi elle consiste" (An ambassador is somewhat like an actor, exposed on the stage to the eyes of the public to play great roles, just as his work elevates him above his condition and renders him *somewhat equal to the masters of the earth* through the right of representation that is attached to his person, and through the particular relations that this right gives him with them. If he does not know how to maintain the dignity of his charge, he will be regarded as a bad actor, but this obligation is the downfall of many negotiators, since they do not know precisely in what it consists).[14] Although Callières does attribute the diplomat's elevated status in part to his representational character, his addition to this reason is significant; the ambassador is in some sense equal to the masters of the earth by the particular, that is, individual, exchanges that he has with them. Callières's formulation thereby allows the diplomat's independence, his personal attributes and gifts, to subsist alongside his role as representative of his master. Callières's comment that most diplomats do not support the dignity of their charge well because they are unsure of its precise definition is also significant here. More than a mere remark upon the difficulties of consistently maintaining one's identity, it demonstrates that the relation between master and diplomat is forcibly the weak point of ambassadorial representation. In a puzzle that should be familiar to the reader at this point, the question is whether the diplomat should mimic the often imperious nature of his prince or work *outside* of this representational relationship in order to achieve a treaty or agreement satisfactory to all of the negotiating parties.

Callières's emphasis on the diplomat's personal attributes, which comprises the majority of his text, implies that a rare convergence of personal qualities is necessary for the successful ambassador. As a result, in passages such as the following, the emphasis is less on the prince's reputation and status than on that of his ambassador: "Quand bien même la fourberie ne serait pas aussi méprisable qu'elle l'est à tout esprit bien fait, un négociateur doit considérer qu'il aura plus d'une affaire à traiter dans le cours de sa vie, qu'il est de son intérêt d'établir sa réputation et qu'il doit la regarder comme un bien réel, puisqu'elle lui facilite dans la suite le succès de ses autres négociations et le fait recevoir avec estime et avec plaisir dans tous les pays où il est connu. Il faut donc qu'il établisse si bien l'opinion de la bonne foi de son maître et de la sienne propre qu'on ne doute jamais de ce qu'il promet" (Even if lying were not as worthy of disdain as it is to anyone of decency, a negotiator should consider that he will have more than one affair to treat during the course of his life, that it is in his interest to establish his reputation, and that he should regard this reputation as a real asset, since it facilitates the success of his other, later negotiations, and makes him welcome and esteemed in all of the countries where he is known. He must therefore establish his and his master's good faith so that no one ever doubts his promises).[15] The brusque separation at the end of this passage between the master and the diplomat's "own" reputation demonstrates the uncoupling of the representational relationship between the two. That the diplomat could even be envisaged separately from the power sending him would have been unthinkable for a Frenchman in the 1660s. It is tempting to see, in comments such as the one above, Callières's realization that the elderly king will not live forever and that the ambassador may have not just more negotiations to accomplish but also other masters to serve. Accordingly, his own reputation for truth-telling is paramount if he wishes to survive the transition.

Callières's picture of diplomacy as the continual and constant backdrop against which European affairs are played out is reinforced by his repeated allusions to the possible shortcomings of the sovereign whom the diplomat represents. Ambassadorial virtue is necessary given the propensity of rulers to fall prey to their own interests and passions: "les passions des princes et de leurs ministres commandent souvent à leurs intérêts" (the passions of princes and their ministers often govern their interests).[16] Again, such statements would have shocked readers only fifty years before; these readers would have been imbued with the doctrine that a prince subject to interest and passions is more a tyrant than a legitimate ruler. Although Callières approvingly cites French *préséance* as well as the practice of according such precedency to *all* members of the French delegation when there are more than one, since they can be said to form one body,[17] and although he also adheres to the logic through which the ambassador's residence can be said to be that of the prince himself and through which princes, not ambassadors, should be held liable for perceived faults, since the "ministre n'a été que l'executeur de ces ordres" (the minister was only the executor of those orders),[18] such endorsements of "the fiction of representation" are somewhat undermined by statements such as the following: "Quelque élevés que soient les princes, *ils sont hommes comme nous*, c'est-à-dire sujets aux même passions, mais outre celles qui leurs sont communes avec les autres hommes, l'opinion qu'ils ont de la grandeur et le pouvoir effectif qui est attaché à leur rang leur donnent des idées différentes de celles du commun des hommes" (However elevated princes are, *they are men like us*, which is to say subject to the same passions, but besides those that they have in common with other men, the opinion they have of their greatness and the effective power attached to their rank give them different ideas from those of common men).[19] Even though Callières is speaking of the princes to whom the diplomat is sent, his abolition of the distance between the prince and the diplomat is just as subversive as his earlier separation of the two figures. The collapse in hierarchy operated here undermines the notion that only other princes can understand or negotiate with sovereigns—an idea that clearly marks the diplomat as the mere servant of his master. If the prince is merely a man like others, the ambassador has plenty of room to assert his gifts and talents in an effort to comprehend (and perhaps even undermine) that prince's interests; the diplomat is promoted from mere representative to an operator in his own right. In this sense, the passage immediately following marks a complete revolution from de Vera's assertion that the ideal diplomat should attempt to imitate the tone of voice and dignified manner of the king who sends him: "Il faut donc que [l'ambassadeur] se dépouille en quelque sorte de ses propres sentiments pour se mettre en la place du prince avec qui il traite, qu'il se transforme pour ainsi dire en lui, qu'il entre dans ses opinions et dans ses inclinations et qu'il se dise à lui-même après l'avoir connu tel qu'il est: *Si j'étais en la place de ce prince avec le même pouvoir, les mêmes passions et les mêmes préjugés, quels effets produiraient en moi les choses que j'ai à lui représenter?*" (The ambassador must therefore shed his own sentiments in order to place himself in the position of the prince with whom he negotiates, he must transform himself, so to speak, into the prince, entering into his opinions and inclinations, and he must say to himself after knowing this prince, *if I were in the place of this prince with the same power, the same passions and the same prejudices, what effects would the things that I have to relate to him produce in me?*).[20]

The possibility of such identification with the prince to whom one is sent is significant for two reasons. First, it is predicated upon the abolition of the representational status of the diplomat. The ambassador no longer represents his king and only his king; his ability to penetrate the thoughts and interests of the prince in whose court he resides implies that he, in turn, and at least temporarily, casts aside his role as *lieutenant* of his own, absent, prince. Previously in the century—and indeed, as far back as Guicciardini—such a propensity to lose one's purpose and identity was viewed as the ultimate danger in diplomacy; this is why, in a decision that Callières cites neutrally, Louis XIV refused to recognize his own subjects as diplomats of other powers. For Callières to even imagine, not to mention recommend, such a practice marks to what extent the "fiction of representation" has been surpassed at the end of the seventeenth century. Liberated from the weighty clothing of his own master's *caractère*, Callières's protean diplomat—"qu'il soit comme le Protée de la fable" (he should be like the Proteus of the fable)[21]—operates by a set of rules that is distinct from those governing the sovereigns among whom he circulates. The parallel that I have been able to draw between sovereign legitimacy and diplomatic representation is no longer operable, save to mark a similar loss of the transcendental grounding of both parties' identity and authority.

The second reason that this remark is significant is that it further illustrates Callières's underlying conviction that the prince is merely a man, with interests and passions like other men. We should remind ourselves that the treatises on sovereignty written throughout the century had, as one of their main purposes, the goal of noting the incommensurable *distance* between the ruler and his subjects. Either through a privileged relation with the divine or through the fundamental incommunicability of sovereignty, the monarch was described as truly unique. His power was ultimately described as beyond the reach of logic. Callières's assertion that the diplomat may, through his own talents and efforts, place himself in the position of the prince reverses the idea that the initiative for diplomatic representation lies solely with the sending ruler. It also fulfills the worst nightmare of the treatises examined earlier, in that it collapses the distance between those occupying thrones and those sent to serve or observe them. This collapse is only made possible by abandoning the language of the divine source of kingly authority. Motivated not by transcendental legitimacy or essential *right* but rather by interest and passion, kingly decisions are open to influence and scrutiny. The success of the diplomat and of "modern diplomacy" that many historians locate with Callières and with the Treaty of Utrecht (1713) can be said to be the death of divine right kingship—a conclusion that even a quick reading of the treaty, and of the limitations and demands that it placed upon Louis XIV, supports.

Freed from its divine moorings, kingship and sovereignty were finally open to renewed debate and examination. Montesquieu's *Esprit des lois* (1748) certainly marks this transition, as does a lesser-known treatise by the Abbé de Saint-Pierre titled *Discours sur la polysynodie, où l'on démontre que la polysynodie, ou pluralité des Conseils, est la forme de ministère la plus avantageuse pour un roi, & pour son royaume* (1719). Saint-Pierre is better known for his *Projet pour rendre la paix perpetuelle en Europe,* published in 1713—the year of Utrecht and before Louis XIV's death in 1715. The *Projet* therefore cannot be said to be a full representation of Saint-Pierre's thought, since his arguments are tailored to render them palatable to a divine right monarch. The central premise of the *Discours sur la polysynodie* is, by contrast, radical.[22] It argues that the singular and unique status of the monarch is not a strength but rather a weakness, albeit a weakness that can (and should) be remedied by the institution of a counsel comprised of several persons. Granted, Saint-Pierre's discourse is somewhat based upon actual events, since the regent, Philippe d'Orléans, had established just such a polysynody while waiting for the king to achieve adulthood: "Je sais bien que cette merveilleuse forme de

Ministère n'a pour le present d'autre sûreté de sa durée, que la volonté de celui qui tient la place du Roi" (I know that this marvelous form of ministry has no other guarantee of lasting than the will of he who holds the place of the king).[23] This form of governance is opposed, throughout the discourse, to Louis XIV's method of governing with only a few powerful ministers, many of whom had descended from the powerful Le Tellier (Louvois) and Colbert families.

Yet the philosophical reasons for Saint-Pierre's approval of the regent's methods carry a weight that goes beyond the current circumstances. As the statement above, with its reference to "celui qui tient la place du Roi," implies, part of Saint-Pierre's project is the establishment of an immortal state that would transcend the interests and passions of the individuals who comprise it: "C'est que dans le *Visirat* [the means of governing through a few] les *Visirs* sont mortels, les hommes se succedent, mais les maximes ne se succedent point; au lieu que dans les Compagnies de la *Polysynodie* il se forme sans y penser certaines maximes, tant par l'évidence des raisons, que par le succès des expériences. . . . Elles se transmettent des vieux aux jeunes, & deviennent aussi durables que la Compagnie même" (The fact is that in a Visirat the Visirs are mortal, men succeed each other, but the maxims do not, while in the companies comprising polysynody certain maxims for themselves almost without reflection, as much through the evidence of the reasons as through the success of experience. . . . They are transmitted from the old to the young, and become as durable as the company itself).[24] Again, we find that, as with Callières, humanity and mortality are unqualified weaknesses to be surpassed and that this includes the humanity of the monarch himself. These weaknesses would have been evident to someone who had witnessed the last years of the extremely old Louis XIV as well as the first years on the throne of Louis XV. The deaths of the grand dauphin, Louis XIV's son and heir, in 1711 and of the Duc de Bourgogne, Louis XIV's grandson, the following year not only led the king to place his illegitimate children in line for the throne; they must also have impressed observers with the aleatory nature of monarchical succession. This succession would have seemed less a manifestation of the hand or intention of God and more a question of chance. Saint-Pierre therefore offers the following: "Ainsi le Régent a remedié habilement par l'art de la *Polysynodie* aux inconveniens fâcheux, où les Monarchies sont assujetties par la nature des Monarques. Car enfin les Rois *comme les autres hommes*, sont sujets aux imbecillitez d'un âge ou trop foible, ou trop affoibli; mais le Régent en conservant à l'Etat Monarchique tous les avantages qui lui sont propres, il lui a procuré encore un des principaux avantages de l'Etat Aristocratique, qui est de n'être point assujetti ni à aucune Minorité, ni à aucune Caducité" (Thus the Regent has skillfully remedied, through the art of polysynody, the unfortunate inconveniences that monarchies are subjected to by the nature of monarchs. For kings, *like other men,* are subject to the senilities and weaknesses either of too old or too young and age, but the Regent has not only conserved the advantages inherent in the monarchical state, he has also procured one of the principal advantages of the aristocratic state, which is not to be subjected to any minority nor any old age).[25] What the age–either too young or too old– of the manifestly human monarch does is render conceivable the separation of the monarchical state from the monarch himself. It should be recalled that similar explanations were offered for the necessity of ambassadors–the king is human and cannot be present in several places at the same time. Yet if we place Saint-Pierre's advocacy of polysynody against those earlier treatises, we see that the ideas of singularity, uniqueness, and incommunicability–so essential to those writings–have been abandoned. In Saint-Pierre's discourse, the king is best served not by the individual minister or ambassador, whose own singularity mirrors the king's authority, which in turn mirrors that of God. Rather, Saint-Pierre's monarch should be complemented by a system– aristocracy–that has little relation to kingship. This radical *difference* of the two systems is what will save the state. We are quite far here from Bodin's categorical rejection, rooted in his strong definition and description of the uniqueness of sovereignty, of any sort of mixed government.

Likewise, any ties between monarchy and divine will have been utterly abandoned. Government under polysynody is the affair of human individuals, who through their own efforts create an entity that surpasses them. Saint-Pierre's statement that if authority had been shared in France, "la race de *Clovis,* malgré le peu de mérite de ses Rois fainéans, seroit peut-être encore sur le Trône" (the race of Clovis, in spite of the feeble merit of its idle kings, would perhaps still be on the throne),[26] illustrates the fact that once history and government are seen to be essentially human affairs, the past becomes open to reinterpretation. For Saint-Pierre by no means sees polysynody falling away once the king reaches majority. Instead, a well-established multiple government can control the excesses of monarchical government: "Or n'est-il pas évident que si, en sortant de Minorité, [le Roi] eût trouvé dans son Royaume la *Polysynodie* bien établie, il n'eût jamais été poussé aux premières Guerres qu'il entreprit; & que par conséquent il n'auroit jamais été forcé de soûtenir les dernières; & qu'il auroit par sa réputation de Prince sage, moderé, pacifique, établi son Petit-Fils sur le Trône d'Espagne, sans que l'*Europe* en eût été allarmée?" (Is it not evident that if, leaving his minority, the king had found polysynody well established in his kingdom, he would not have been pushed to make his first wars, and consequently he would not have been forced to undertake the later wars, and, through his reputation as a wise, moderate, and peaceful king, he would have established his grandson on the Spanish throne without alarming all of Europe?).[27]

Saint-Pierre's *Discours* is only one example of the reexaminations of government and sovereignty (this last, however, a word that the author never uses) occurring after Louis XIV's death in 1715. The force field of mediation unifying God, king, ambassadors and ministers, and France, damaged during the last decades of the reign, evaporated with the disappearance of Louis XIV. Critical thought regarding government returned with a vengeance; the role of the state's members was less that of reading or interpreting the immutable (if only partially visible) truth of authority and legitimacy and more of articulating competing truths.[28] I have already alluded to Diderot's abandonment of the idea that actors embody, even partially, the roles they are asked to play. Such detachment and inviolability of self had previously been seen (albeit with strong reservations) as the unique property of the sovereign or, by extension, of God himself. The transference of sovereignty and the accompanying status of "image of God on earth" from the king to the people during the eighteenth century have been well analyzed.[29] I hope to have shown that the possibility of this transfer was foreseen early in the seventeenth century and was only held at bay through the painstaking elaboration of a theory of mediation that sought the almost miraculous reconciliation of sovereign independence with the dependence necessary for legitimacy. Understanding the efforts of those wishing to preserve the unique status of king, ambassador, and even actor allows us to better appreciate the efforts of the eighteenth century to abandon mediation altogether all while seeking an alternative to the rule of self-interest.

INTRODUCTION

1. See the introduction to Merlin-Kajman, *L'Absolutisme dans les lettres*.

2. For an overview of this process as it continued in the second half of the seventeenth century, see Bernard Tocanne's masterful study, *L'Idéé de nature en France*.

3. Malebranche, *Oeuvres*, 1:3.

4. Descartes, *Oeuvres philosophiques*, 1:634.

5. Ibid., 1:641.

6. To a large extent, this is my only objection to Merlin-Kajman's *L'Absolutisme dans les lettres*. While Merlin-Kajman provides a convincing and coherent illustration of Cornelian sovereignty as characterized by its independence and absolute singularity, she views this as a prefiguration of a social order in which the individuals comprising the state can preserve their selves while living together; in that sense, Racine's theater represents a regression of sorts. Yet by reading Corneille through the eventual victory of the discrete individual, Merlin-Kajman fails to fully appreciate the problems that his audience would have seen in extending sovereign selfhood beyond the king to his subjects; she also minimizes the tendency of Corneille's *souverains déliés* to instrumentalize others.

7. A helpful overview of theories concerning monarchy and tyranny in the years surrounding Henri IV's assassination can be found in Mousnier's *L'Assassinat d'Henri IV*.

8. Recent studies of divine-right kingship have emphasized its singularity to the seventeenth century and its dependence on the civil wars. See Guéry and Descimon, "Un Etat des temps modernes?", 183–356. As the writers state, "la monarchie d'Ancien Régime se constitua en un système *holiste* au sortir des guerres de religion. La pensée politique fit du roi la synthèse du pays, mettant au clair ce que les rituels et les actes donnaient à voir et à croire" (the monarchy of the Old Regime constituted itself as a holistic system after the wars of religion. Political thought set up the king as a synthesis of the country, making clear what the rituals and acts had rendered visible and believable) (239).

9. For an account of this resurgence as well as a helpful overview of its central premises, see Mercer, *Leibniz's Metaphysics,* especially chapter 5 (173–205).

10. See Jean Rohou's "La Rochefoucauld, témoin d'un tournant de la condition humaine" for an incisive overview of "intérêt" throughout the seventeenth century.

11. Bossuet, *Politique,* 73.

12. Ibid., 71.

13. Guillaume de Thieulloy makes this point quite effectively in his essay "Le Prince dans les traités d'éducation jansénistes," in Halévi, ed., *Le savoir du prince,* 261–93.

14. In addition to the excellent work of Robert Descimon, Alain Guéry, Joël Cornette, and Fanny Cosandey, I must also cite Marcel Gauchet's important work *Le désenchantement du monde.*

15. Bossuet, *Traité du libre arbitre,* chapter 4, cited in Truchet, *Politique de Bossuet,* 12. It is significant that this doctrine of the "two ends of the chain" occurs in Bossuet's treatment of the sticky issue of free will. Indeed, to a great extent, discussions of government during the seventeenth century mirror parallel debates over the respective roles of reason (legitimacy) and the will (sovereignty) in faculty psychology during the same period, and metaphors of state and governance are often deployed by philosophers treating this issue. For an overview of this debate, see Pink and Stone's *The Will and Human Action.*

16. Truchet, *Politique de Bossuet,* 13.

17. Joël Cornette, "Le Grand siècle absolutiste: Etat sacré, Etat de raison," in *La France de la monarchie absolue,* 21.

CHAPTER 1: WHAT IS A KING?

1. Budé, *De l'institution du prince,* 20.

2. Of course, this small quote is not enough to characterize Budé's rather complex attitude toward monarchical legislation. As Julian Franklin points out, in Budé's time the right of *parlement* to refuse to register laws was, to a certain extent, taken for granted, as were limits on the king's ability to make exceptions to his own laws. Franklin points to Budé's *Annotationes* to his *Digest,* where Budé draws a suggestive parallel between the French Parlement and the Roman Senate. See Franklin, *Jean Bodin and the Rise of Absolutist Theory,* 10. This sympathy for the *parlement* is consistent with Budé's praise of eloquence, as we shall see later in the chapter.

3. Several excellent studies have revised the opinion that the Reformation in France was, at large, a primarily political struggle between powerful noblemen and an increasingly centralized monarchy, arguing instead that religious issues were taken seriously by the participants and had a profound influence on early modern French statecraft. See Elwood's *The Body Broken,* Crouzet's *La nuit de la Saint-Barthélemy,* and Eire's *War against the Idols.* Recent works on the seventeenth-century French state have vehemently insisted upon the relevance of the religious wars to the emergence of divine-right monarchy. Guéry and Descimon note that "il n'est pas contestable que la division religieuse installait le doute dans le vieil édifice scolastique. Le catholicisme ne représentait plus ce principe d'union incontesté qui avait fait la force de l'ancienne chrétienté. L'Etat apparaissait dès lors comme un substitut nécessaire dont la sacralisation constituait un impératif" (it is incontestable that religious division had installed doubt in

the old scholastic edifice. Catholicism no longer represented the uncontested principle of union that had heretofore constituted the force of Christianity. The state appeared thereafter as a necessary substitute whose sacralization had become imperative) ("Un état des temps modernes?" 191).

4. References to the king's two bodies occur briefly in Apostolidès' *Le roi-machine,* Reiss's *The Meaning of Literature,* and repeatedly in Melzer and Norberg's *From the Royal to the Republican Body.* Although these works are not alone in citing Kantorowicz, often without comment, in reference to seventeenth-century French kingship, I have singled them out on the one hand because of their reflection of work occurring in the last twenty years and on the other because they are otherwise tremendously thoughtful. It is also well worth noting that Kantorowicz's work is undergoing sustained criticism by historians. See Monod's *The Power of Kings* for one such critique; Boureau's *Le simple corps du roi* is another, although I differ with his generally dismissive assessment of the efficacy of ideological constructs.

5. This absence should be evidence in itself that something else is preoccupying the writers of such treatises, yet Kantorowicz remains a very seductive model for the modern critic. Assaf, in his *La mort du roi* states that while "la séparation du corps physique et du corps politique est claire et explicite dans le système monarchique anglais et même consacrée par la loi, elle l'est bien moins dans la monarchie française, de sorte que certains auteurs la nient, ou du moins en minimisent l'importance. Nous maintenons cependant que la théologie politique française n'est pas monophysite" (separation of the physical and political bodies is clear and explicit in the English system of monarchy and even consecrated by law, this is less the case in French monarchy, and therefore certain authors deny it or at least minimize its importance. Nevertheless, we maintain that French political theology is not one-bodied) (11).

6. Fascinating in this respect is the contribution of the founder of the Oratory, Pierre de Bérulle, to the articulation of the relation between God and the king. If Bérulle saw the king as Christlike, his Christ was somewhat different from that of medieval theorists, at once submissive and sovereign, incorporating the recent theories of Bodin and Copernicus. See Morgain, *La théologie politique de Pierre de Bérulle.*

7. Marin, *Le portrait du roi,* 16.

8. See Rubin, *Corpus Christi,* for a description of the pre-Reformation importance of the Eucharist as a figure of mediation.

9. See Crouzet, *La nuit de la Saint-Barthélemy,* chapter 33, "Les réformés et le roi: Histoire d'un contentieux occulté," 468–83.

10. Garnett, *Vindiciae,* 27.

11. Ibid., 11.

12. The vehement emphasis on unity found in the writings of Pierre de Bérulle can be seen as a direct response to this challenge. See Morgain, *La théologie politique de Pierre de Bérulle.*

13. The passage in question is Samuel I, chapter 8, in which Samuel, distressed by Israel's request for a king and following God's advice, informs the people of the miseries in store for them because of their decision. This is perhaps the most damaging passage in the Bible to divine right theories of sovereignty—not least because of God's statement that "they have not rejected you, but they have rejected me from being king over them" (Samuel I 8:7)—and its interpretation becomes a key element in the attack upon, and defense of, the institution of kingship.

14. Garnet, *Vindiciae,* 28 (emphasis mine).

15. Bellarmino, *Response aux Principaux Articles,* 63. (Bellarmino cites page 69 of De Belloy's treatise).

16. Ibid., 66–67 (emphasis mine).

17. Ibid., 68.

18. Anonymous (CDSC), La Doctrine de Iesus-Christ Nostre Seigneur, 15.

19. Although the edition of the *Six livres* that I use here was published in 1580, before Bellarmino's opposition to the accession of Henri IV (Henri III died in 1589), it is clear, given the absence of an heir and Henri IV's marriage into the Valois family, that debate over the royal succession did not wait to begin until Henri III's death. Franklin, *Jean Bodin and the Rise of Absolutist Theory,* provides an insightful analysis of the *Six livres* as a logically flawed reaction to Protestant constitutionalism.

20. Budé, *De l'institution du prince,* 59–60.

21. Bodin, *Les six livres de la république,* 660.

22. Ibid., 69.

23. See Lyons's *Exemplum* and Hampton's *Writing from History* for accounts of the growing crisis in exemplarity occurring during this period.

24. Biblical examples are frequently employed in the *Six livres;* however, they are used less as an authoritative source on sovereignty than as illustrations of various aspects of its practices, which Bodin seeks to show are essentially the same over centuries, thereby bolstering his own attempt to reduce or distill the definition of sovereignty as much as possible.

25. Gérard Mairet makes a persuasive argument for Bodin's "atheism" in his various studies of the historical origins of sovereignty. See *Le principe de souveraineté* and *Les doctrines du pouvoir* as well as his excellent introduction to his edition of the *Six livres.*

26. Bodin, *Six livres,* 78.

27. This phrase was widely used in the seventeenth century, but particularly in reference to the king. See Bouhours, *Entretiens d'Ariste et d'Eugène,* 181.

28. Bodin, *Six livres,* 1.

29. Ibid., 122.

30. Of course, sovereignty as such was a pressing issue for others before Bodin, most notably in medieval efforts to recast the nature of papal power. See Wilks, *The Problem of Sovereignty in the Later Middle Ages.*

31. Bodin, *Six livres,* 122.

32. Ibid., 78.

33. Loyseau characterizes this property of sovereignty quite eloquently in his *Traité sur les seigneuries:* "Et comme la couronne ne peut estre, si son cercle n'est entier, aussi la souveraineté n'est point si quelque chose y défaut" (and just as the crown cannot be, if its circle is incomplete, neither can sovereignty exist if something is lacking in it) (2:2).

34. Bodin, *Six livres,* 124.

35. Ibid., 122.

36. Ibid.

37. Budé, *De l'institution du prince,* 155.

38. Bodin, *Six livres;* these figures are discussed on pp. 124–27.

39. Ibid., 128.

40. It should be noted that this argument makes manifest the inherent relativity of sovereignty that Bodin tries so hard to combat elsewhere by insisting that sovereignty depends only upon itself for its existence.

41. Bodin, *Six livres*, 951.

42. Ibid., 961–62.

43. Ibid., 211–12.

44. Bodin does make this argument, in a passage that is indexed "Dieu tenu de sa promesse" that can be found on page 153 of the 1580 edition.

45. Gérard Mairet, ed. *Six livres*, 10.

46. Bodin, *Six livres*, 289.

47. Ibid., 290.

48. Ibid., 307.

49. Hobbes, *Leviathan*, 130.

50. Le Bret, "De la souveraineté du roy," 1.

51. Bodin, *Six livres*, 1.

52. Roland Mousnier, in his authoritative *Les institutions de la France sous la monarchie absolue*, indicates the importance of the claims for superior power by the pope and the empire in forming French political doctrine, noting that "Les besoins de la défense contre l'étranger et l'influence du droit romain assurèrent le progrès de l'idée de souveraineté" (Both the needs for protection against foreigners and the influence of Roman law assured the progress of the idea of sovereignty) (1:511).

53. Le Bret, "De la souveraineté du roy," 3.

54. Ibid., 2.

55. For an account of this emergence of the "creative" king and its link to Bodin, see Guéry and Descimon, "Un Etat des temps modernes?", 215.

56. Le Bret, "De la souveraineté du roy," 11.

57. In fact, this problem of legal authorship touches upon the vexed issue of *lois fondamentales*, customary laws that undergird the kingdom but that cannot be viewed as invented by any human source. Historians still disagree about the number and status of these *lois*; Guéry and Descimon, "Un Etat des temps modernes?", 224, note that Mousnier counts the law of majority, discussed here, as one of five *lois fondamentales*, but there is significant evidence that in fact the *loi salique*, which excluded females from the royal line of succession (and itself is a sophisticated blend of historical expediency, law, and nature), was the only *loi fondamentale*. This is Cardin Le Bret's position; for more on the *loi salique*, see Colette Beaune, *Naissance de la nation France*.

58. Jean-Marie Apostolidès offers the suggestion that this inherent conservatism of even the most absolute monarch led to Louis XIV's irrelevance in *Le roi-machine*.

59. This is the heading for several chapters in the treatise. For example, "Qu'il n'apartient qu'au Roi de faire des Loix dans son Roïaume, de les changer, & les interpreter" (book one, chapter 9, p. 18) or "Qu'il n'apartient qu'au Roi de faire batre Monnoïe" (book 2, chapter 13, p. 74).

60. Le Bret, "De la souveraineté du roy," 80.

61. Ibid., 72.

62. Ibid., 128.

63. Ibid., 1.

64. Ibid., 181.

65. Ibid.

66. Ibid.

67. Ibid.

68. A brief account of the relationship between Richelieu and Le Bret, which was testier than this brief biography might imply, can be found in Picot's study of Le Bret. Picot's excellent work also finds Le Bret's position on sovereignty to be ambiguous, at best—an ambiguity that he also traces to the religious conflicts of the sixteenth century. Picot states: "De sa notion de souveraineté, Le Bret tire d'abord cette longue liste de 'tous les droits' qui constituent l'harmonieuse et puissante déduction d'une souveraineté entendue comme universelle, inhumaine et absolue. Puis comme Le Bret est aussi amené à insister sur les multiples règles, usages, statuts qui limitent et guident la puissance, l'adaptent à une forme précise du pouvoir: la monarchie française du début du XVIIe siècle, qui l'humanisent, qui la modèrent, on étudiera ensuite ce second aspect de son oeuvre. Ce n'est en effet que par cette double recherche que la conception de la 'Monarchie royale' de Le Bret prend tout son sens" (From his notion of sovereignty, Le Bret first pulls this long list of "all of the rights" that constitute the harmonious and powerful deduction of a sovereignty understood as universal, inhuman and absolute. Then, as Le Bret is led to insist upon the numerous rules, usages and statutes that limit and guide power, adapting it to a precise form of power: the French monarchy of the beginning of the seventeenth century, and humanizing and modernizing it, we will consider this second aspect of his work. It is only through this double approach that Le Bret's conception of "royal monarchy" takes on its full meaning) (91).

69. As Herbert H. Rowen states in his excellent book *The King's State,* "Sovereignty, the crown, was the gift of God: the theory of divine right was shifting its meaning from justification of royal authority to explanation of how it came to be in the hands of the reigning prince" (30).

70. Senault, *Le monarque,* 23–24.

71. Ibid., 41.

72. Ibid., 102.

73. The effort to insert the particularities of French rulers into divine, rather than human, history is presented in a much more lengthy and elaborate manner by Bossuet in his *Discours sur l'histoire universelle.*

74. As yet another example of the persistence of this view, see Assaf's *La mort du roi.* After citing the new Protestant perspective introduced into theories of sovereignty, Assaf remarks in a footnote, "Encore que cette perpective n'ait pas eu d'influence—on s'en doute—sur le siècle suivant" (Then again, this perspective had no influence, as we can easily imagine, on the following century) (35, note 32). This perspective may not have had vocal or elaborate articulation during the seventeenth century, but I would argue that it certainly had influence.

75. Senault, *Le monarque,* 117.

76. Senault refutes this interpretation of God's use of kings, but much later in his text: "Si [Dieu] employe les Anges ou les hommes dans la conduite du monde, ce n'est pas pour se

soulager, mais pour les associer à son Empire, & pour leur faire part de ce pouvoir absolu qu'il a sur les autres creatures" (If God employs angels or men in the conduct of the world, it is not in order to obtain relief for himself, but rather in order to associate them with his Empire, and have them share in the absolute power he has upon other creatures) (351). Why God wishes to share his absolute power—and here the contrast with Bodin's definition of sovereignty and its incommunicability is striking—remains unexplained.

77. Medieval representations of kingship often included this possibility; events such as famine or war were seen as proof of the king losing favor with God, and replacements were thereby authorized.

78. Ibid., 117–18.

79. Ibid., 121.

80. Ibid., 125.

81. Ibid., 127–28.

82. Indeed, Louis XIV, crowned by the Revocation of the Edict of Nantes in 1685, would spend most of his reign trying to eliminate the effects of religious division in the country. In the first years of his personal reign, he also disposed of all of Parlement's records dating from the years of the Fronde.

83. Le Moyne, *De l'art de regner,* iv.

84. Ibid., 258.

85. Ibid., 65.

86. Le Moyne, *De l'art des devises,* 193.

87. Ibid., 145.

88. Using the sun to describe the monarch was not new, although the theories of Copernicus gave this characterization new momentum. See, for example, Morgain, *La théologie politique de Pierre de Bérulle,* 374–77. Le Moyne's use of the sun, however, reaches new and, I believe, nuanced levels of political analysis.

89. Le Moyne, *De l'art de regner,* 26–27.

90. Ibid., 372.

91. One of the best explorations of this quality of the king's actions, and the difficulties encountered by those who had to describe such "miracles," is Louis Marin's analysis of Féli-bien's *Description sommaire du château de Versailles* (1673) in *Le portrait du roi,* 221–60. In many ways, however, such often hyperbolic formulations were, unsurprisingly, appropriations of eloquence from Parlement, an institution that, as Marc Fumaroli persuasively argues, was instrumental in establishing forms of expression at court and in the kingdom. See his *Age de l'Eloquence,* especially 551–68.

92. Ibid., 522.

93. Le Moyne's approach to the sunspots is quite similar to that found in a German emblem book published at around the same time, Johannes Kreihing's *Emblemata ethico-politica* (Antwerp, 1661). This book, and the larger issue of how the sunspots were treated in the arts during the seventeenth century, is discussed in Adriaan W. Vliegenthart, "Galileo's Sunspots."

94. Le Moyne, *De l'art de regner,* 99.

95. Ibid., 355.

96. Ibid., 401.

97. Ibid., 669.

98. See Lynn Sumida Joy's *Gassendi the Atomist.*

99. Pietro Redondi, *Galileo Heretic.* As Jean Dietz Moss states, Redondi's central thesis that the Jesuit Grassi, involved in a contentious debate at the time with Galileo concerning the nature of comets, had written the letter to the pope denouncing Galileo's atomism has been discounted by experts and historians of science, most notably Sergio Pagano, a paleographer and chief archivist of the Vatican's Secret Archives. Grassi did, however, warn of the dangers of atomism for Eucharistic doctrine in his 1626 *A Reckoning of Weights for the Balance and Small Scale,* and rumors of Galileo's atomism did circulate after the publication of the *Assayer.* See Moss, *Novelties in the Heavens,* 253–59.

100. Cordemoy, *Six discours sur la distinction & l'union du corps & de l'ame,* second discourse, 112–21.

CHAPTER 2: THE ABSOLUTE AUTHOR

1. Taken from Zoberman, *Les panégyriques du roi,* 103.

2. See Halévi, ed., *Le savoir du prince,* especially the introduction, for a thoughtful consideration of the questions inherent in royal education.

3. Zoberman, *Les panégyriques du roi,* 102.

4. Ibid., 102–3.

5. Ibid., 103.

6. *Recueil de plusieurs pieces d'éloquence et de poesie,* 27.

7. Ibid., 176–77.

8. Ibid., 186.

9. Louis XIV's ultimate authorship of the *Mémoires* was established by Paul Sonnino in his article "The Dating and Authorship of Louis XIV's *Mémoires.*"

10. This characterization is taken from Marc Fumaroli, "Les Mémoires au carrefour des genres en prose," in *La diplomatie de l'esprit,* 183–215. It should be noted that the royal memoirs fit none of the "types" identified by Fumaroli; obviously not an account of aristocratic debt, Louis XIV's *Mémoires* (unlike, to some extent, the *Basilikon Doron*) also resist the Augustinian effacement of self that became widespread in the genre after Arnauld d'Andilly's translation of the *Confessions* in 1650.

11. Moreover, insofar as the proliferation of memoirs can be read as a sign of the development of an independent interior self, they would implicitly challenge the king's command of his subjects (however much such desire for internal as well as external command was condemned as tyrannical throughout the century). For such a reading of seventeenth-century memoirs, see, for example, Nicolas Paige's *Being Interior.*

12. Louis XIV, *Mémoires pour l'instruction du dauphin,* 44; translation by Paul Sonnino, in his edition and translation of the memoirs, *Mémoires for the Instruction of the Dauphin,* 22.

13. Anon., *L'Ombre de Henri IV au Roi Louis XIII.*

14. For the fascinating history of this work, see Lacour-Gayet, *Un Utopiste inconnu.*

15. Lacour-Gayet, *L'Education politique de Louis XIV,* 75–76.

16. See Jenny Wormald, "*Basilikon Doron* and *The Trew Law of Free Monarchies.*"

17. James I, *Basilikon Doron*, 1–2.

18. Ibid., 52.

19. Le Bret, "*De la souveraineté du roy*," 19.

20. Kantorowicz's reticence regarding the application of his (in fact quite specific) theory to monarchies outside of England's is often overlooked, even though he states in the first chapter of the work, "to the English 'physiologic' concept of the King's Two Bodies the Continent did not offer an exact parallel—neither terminologically nor conceptually" (*King's Two Bodies*, 20).

21. This reading is summed up by Richard Lockwood in his "The 'I' of History in the *Mémoires* of Louis XIV*," which concludes that "The whole—the absolute King—exists prior, *préalablement*, and history merely represents its presence, fully recognizing its own fundamental lack, its inability to totalize, yet all the more empowered to perform an ideological function by pointing up that lack. The only possible writer of true history would be one coincident with the subject at the center of history, the King, and that historical text, any historical text, can then only be, like the *Mémoires*, in the end an autobiography" (564).

22. Charles Louis Dreyss, "Etude de la Composition des *Mémoires pour l'instruction du dauphin,*" 1:143.

23. Louis XIV, *Mémoires*, 66–67; translation, Sonnino, *Mémoires*, 43.

24. Louis XIV, *Mémoires*, 132; translation, Sonnino, *Mémoires*, 100.

25. Louis XIV, *Mémoires*, 150; translation, Sonnino, *Mémoires*, 123.

26. Louis XIV, *Mémoires*, 155; translation, Sonnino, *Mémoires*, 133.

27. Louis XIV, *Mémoires*, 132 (emphasis mine).

28. Sonnino, *Mémoires*, 99 (emphasis mine).

29. Louis XIV, *Mémoires*, 132; translation, Sonnino, *Mémoires*, 99.

30. See, for example, Pierre Zoberman's evocation of the "curieux phénomène, presque blasphématoire, d'assimilation entre le Roi et Dieu" in *Les panégyriques du roi*, 56.

31. Louis XIV, *Mémoires*, 82–83.

32. Sonnino, *Mémoires*, 57.

33. Charles Louis Dreyss's effort to recapture the very person of Louis XIV through the memoirs is evident throughout his study of their composition; he ends by comparing the text to a statue upon which many hands have worked. More recently, Simone Ackerman continues Dreyss's dream of visibility, in fairly similar language: "Sous le masque hautain, énigmatique, impassible du monarque, perce, dans les *Mémoires*, le visage—non de l'idole—mais de l'homme dont la précoce expérience du pouvoir lui dicte des maximes portant l'empreinte ineffaçable d'une civilisation à son zénith" (Under the haughty, enigmatic and impassible mask of the monarch shines, in the Memoirs, the face not of the idol, but of the man whose precocious experience of power dictates to him maxims bearing the ineffaceable mark of a civilization at its zenith), in "Réflexions sur les *Mémoires* de Louis XIV," 270. Both Dreyss and Ackerman thereby de-emphasize the textual nature of the *Mémoires*.

34. Marin, *Le portrait du roi*, especially "L'hostie royale: la médaille historique," 147–68.

35. Louis XIV, *Mémoires*, 213–14; translation, Sonnino, *Mémoires*, 224–25.

36. Louis XIV, *Mémoires*, 115.

37. Sonnino, *Mémoires*, 84–85.

38. Louis XIV, *Mémoires*, 43.

39. Ibid., 43.

40. Anon., *Receuil de plusieurs pièces*, 179.

41. Ibid., 28.

42. It would be fair to see the abruptness of the transitions between maxims and detailed description as a symptom of the more widespread crisis in exemplarity that other critics have shown characterizes this period. See the works of John Lyons and Timothy Hampton.

43. Louis XIV, *Mémoires*, 131.

44. Sonnino, *Mémoires*, 99.

45. Louis XIV, *Mémoires*, 162.

46. Most notably Kathryn A. Hoffman in her excellent *Society of Pleasures*, especially the first chapter, "Sun-Eye and Medusa-Head: Louis XIV's *Mémoires*," 13–39.

47. For more complete analyses of the evolution in monarchical conception and institutions, see the works of Sarah Hanley and Ralph Giesey.

48. Dreyss, "Etude," 227.

49. Louis XIV, *Mémoires*, 136–37; translation, Sonnino, *Mémoires*, 103.

50. Louis XIV, *Mémoires*, 137; translation, Sonnino, *Mémoires*, 104.

51. Louis XIV, *Mémoires*, 137.

52. Ibid., 43.

53. Sonnino, *Mémoires*, 21–22.

54. Louis XIV, *Mémoires*, 51.

55. Again, for an account of Louis XIV's role in the memoirs' composition, see Sonnino, "Dating and Authorship."

56. For information on the memoirs' authorship, see Dreyss's "Etude sur les Mémoires de Louis XIV" in his edition of the *Mémoires*, 1:1–251. This study has also been published as a separate text.

57. Bibliothèque National, Fr-MS 6732, fol. 122.

58. Ibid.

59. Ibid., fol. 132.

60. Ibid., fol. 136.

61. Ibid., fol. 179.

62. Louis XIV, *Mémoires*, 84.

63. Ibid., 150; translation, Sonnino, *Mémoires*, 122–23.

64. Bibliothèque National, Fr-MS 6732, fol. 183.

65. Ibid.

66. In volume 6734 of the manuscripts, this passage recurs with several changes. Here, "public" is replaced with "l'Etat" and then with "Royaume," replacements that indicate a certain malaise over how to characterize those over whom the king exercises his power.

67. Bibliothèque National, Fr-MS 6732, fol. 357.

68. Ibid., fol. 358.

69. This information is taken from Pierre Goubert's introduction to his edition of the memoirs, *Louis XIV: Mémoires pour l'instruction du dauphin*, 8–9.

CHAPTER 3: DEFINING THE DIPLOMAT

1. See, for example, Peter Burke's *Fabrication of Louis XIV,* Jean-Marie Apostolidès' *Le roi-machine,* and Jean-Pierre Néraudau's *L'Olympe du roi-soleil* as well as, of course, Louis Marin's *Le portrait du roi* for insightful comments on the creation and diffusion of the king's image.

2. Picavet's *Diplomatie française au temps de Louis XIV* and Blaga's *Evolution de la technique diplomatique* both document the important contributions that Louis XIV made to diplomatic practice.

3. Der Derian, *On Diplomacy.* In his introduction, Der Derian makes a strong case for a Foucauldian "genealogy" of diplomacy that would complement traditional, more teleological, accounts.

4. Indeed, Ragnar Numelin, in *The Beginnings of Diplomacy,* finds traces of fairly well-articulated diplomatic activity among the most remote tribes studied by anthropologists and extends his observations back in time to argue that diplomacy has always existed alongside any sort of community.

5. A useful survey of diplomatic treatises and the limitations of their methodology can be found in B. Behrens, "Treatises on the Ambassador." See also Daniel Ménager's *Diplomatie et théologie* for a more in-depth discussion of the linkage of diplomacy and religious imagery.

6. Again, I refer the reader to John D. Lyons's and Timothy Hampton's studies of the early modern crisis in exemplarity.

7. Leibniz, "Caesarinus Fürstenerius," in *Political Writings,* 111–20. See also Samuel Pufendorf's *The Present State of Germany.*

8. Difficulties, in fact, that led directly to many of Alberico Gentili's observations in *De legationibus libri tres,* discussed in detail later in this chapter.

9. I prefer the French expression to the Latin "*jus gentium*" or the English "law of nations," largely because the English introduces the problematic use of "nation" into a subject where it is not yet fully applicable. I prefer the French to the Latin only because it translates the frequent use of the French term throughout the treatises of the period and mirrors French dominance of seventeenth-century diplomacy.

10. Hotman, *L'Ambassadeur,* 1.

11. Abraham de Wicquefort, *L'Ambassadeur et ses fonctions,* 1:1.

12. Jean Barbeyrac, introduction to his translation of Cornelius Bynkershoek's *Traité du juge competent des ambassadeurs,* xvi. Wicquefort's own regret reads as follows: "Je sçais bien que tout ce que j'en pourray dire, ne fera pas une Science qui ait ses principes Mathématiques, ou qui soit fondée sur des raisons demonstratives, sur lesquelles on puisse faire des regles certaines et infallibles; mais aussy crois je pouvoir reduire tout mon discours à des maximes, où il se trouvera quelque chose de fort approchant d'une infallibilité morale" (I know well that everything that I could say on the subject would not constitute a Science with Mathematical principles or founded on demonstrative reasons upon which one could draw up certain and infallible rules; but I also believe that I can reduce my entire discourse to maxims, in which there is something approaching moral infallibility) (Abraham de Wicquefort, *L'Ambassadeur,* 1:2).

13. This idea of Callières as the ideal expression of ancien régime diplomacy and as the model for modern diplomatic theory has highly complex and often suspect origins. I will show

in the conclusion why I believe that Callières is far from the diplomacy *practiced* under Louis XIV; for an excellent discussion of the role of Callières in diplomatic history, see Keens-Soper, "François de Callières and Diplomatic Theory."

14. The full title, *De la manière de négocier avec les souverains: De l'utilité des négociations, du choix des ambassadeurs et des envoyés et des qualités nécessaires pour réussir dans ces emplois,* reintroduces the ambassador but arguably in reference to, and in the context of, the usefulness of the negotiations themselves.

15. See Mattingly, *Renaissance Diplomacy,* as well as the works of Corneliu Blaga and Camille-Georges Picavet.

16. De Vera, *Le parfait ambassadeur,* 29.

17. The Latin original reads, "Legatus, de quo institutus nobis est sermo, & *Orator* quandoq; & *Interpres,* & *Nuncius.*" Gentili, *De legationibus,* 2:5.

18. Ibid., 2:5.

19. Ibid., 2:6.

20. Ibid., 2:7.

21. Edward Rosen, "The Title of Galileo's *Sidereus nuncius.*"

22. Ibid., 288. The passage from Grassi is translated by Rosen.

23. Stillman Drake, "The Starry Messenger."

24. Gentili, *De legationibus,* 2:7.

25. James der Derian provides a brief yet incisive counterargument to those historians of diplomacy who would overlook the practice's "mythical origins," especially the sixteenth-century association of diplomacy with religion and angels, arguing that it is precisely this association that has led theorists to neglect the contributions of writers such as Gentili. See der Derian, *On Diplomacy,* 44–45.

26. Gentili, *De legationibus,* 2:11. This sly remark is then rejected, since "we see that it does not in any way constitute a hindrance to the going and coming of embassies." It is worth noting that Gentili's argument seems to reflect a commonplace in England regarding the inferiority of French claims to European preeminence; it is repeated in James Howell's *Proedria Basilike* (1664), which presents the claims of England, France, and Spain to diplomatic *préséance.*

27. "As an example of an envoy whose mission is in the name of one more sacred than the state, or to a more sacred person, or on more sacred business, I shall cite the case of one sent by a God or to a God on some sacred mission. Apostles, angels, and others of the kind have been sent by God" (Gentili, *De legationibus,* 9). Again, on this point, although Gentili is only briefly discussed, see Ménager, *Diplomatie et théologie.*

28. Further evidence of de Vera's influence is apparent in the frequent reappearance of several of his formulas, verbatim, in later treatises. The aforementioned *Proedria Basilike* quotes de Vera without acknowledging the source, and the apocryphal second volume of a later edition of Callières's *De la manière de négocier avec les souverains* consists almost entirely of passages from *Le parfait ambassadeur.* It is hard to believe that Callières himself would have approved of the inclusion of de Vera's text with his own, but the fact that certain of de Vera's statements lend themselves to a strict representative relation between prince and diplomat, to such an extent that they hardly seem out of place next to Callières's own work, reveals the profound ambivalence of de Vera's text.

29. This account of de Vera's limited relevance differs somewhat from that provided by Keens-Soper in "François de Callières and Diplomatic Theory." Keens-Soper describes the work, accurately enough, as another entry in the long line of texts assimilating the diplomat with the "honnête homme," and therefore of limited usefulness to the complexities—and specificities—of diplomacy.

30. De Vera, *Le parfait ambassadeur,* 29.

31. Ibid., 61.

32. Ibid., 31.

33. Without viewing the work of just two authors as representative of their country, it should be noted that the Spaniard Fernando de Galardi, in his response to Wicquefort's *Mémoires pour les ambassadeurs,* titled *Reflexions sur les Mémoires pour les ambassadeurs et response au ministre prisonnier,* spends much of his time defending the use of priests and monks in diplomatic service, and this in 1677. He finds particularly abhorrent the conduct of France during the *affaire Créquy,* which I discuss at length in chapter 4.

34. De Vera, *Le parfait ambassadeur,* 51.

35. Gentili, *De legationibus,* 2:64.

36. Wicquefort, *L'Ambassadeur,* 1:88–89.

37. François de Callières, *De la manière de négocier avec les souverains,* 189.

38. De Vera, *Le parfait ambassadeur,* 19–20.

39. "les Ambassadeurs ont été de tout tems & de toutes Nations si inviolablement respectés, que quand ils ont été offensés, la partie interessée a toûjours esperé que l'outrage en seroit vangé par la main de quelque Divinité, lors qu'il lui plairoit d'en tirer la satisfaction" (Ambassadors from every country have always been so inviolably respected that when they have been offended, the interested party has always hoped that the outrage would be avenged by the hand of some divinity, whenever it pleases him to exact his satisfaction) (ibid., 108–9).

40. Ibid., 123.

41. "Mais je crois que des Ordres si odieux ne viennent jamais gueres d'un Prince Catholique" (But I believe that such odious orders would never come from a Catholic prince) (ibid., 172).

42. Ibid., 266. The fundamental ambiguity of the ambassador is further revealed later in the treatise, where de Vera recommends the exact opposite: "il seroit requis que les Ambassadeurs s'habillassent à la mode de la Province où ils resident, & qu'ils laissassent la leur. Pour justifier combien il est necessaire que l'Ambassadeur qui va aupres un Prince, lui soit agreable en quelque maniere, & affectionné, sauf la fidelité qu'il doit à son Maître" (it would be required that ambassadors dress in the style of the province where they reside and that they abandon their own clothing. To justify how necessary it is that an ambassador who goes toward a prince be agreeable and likeable to him in some manner, excepting the loyalty that he owes his master) (489). Such remarks show de Vera once again to be a transitional figure; Guicciardini, in his *Ricordi,* takes it as given that the ambassador will almost inevitably form ties with the court to which he is sent. These issues will resurface in Louis XIV's refusal to use nonsubjects as ambassadors and in his dealings with d'Estrades, who had formed a close relationship with the Dutch stadtholder during his previous missions.

43. Ibid., 267.

44. Ibid., 319.

45. James der Derian argues something similar when he identifies diplomacy with alienation.

46. De Vera, *Le parfait ambassadeur,* 369.

47. Ibid., 471. This is an interesting forerunner of Wicquefort's assertion, which will be treated in chapter 4, that since all sovereigns are theoretically equal in power, precedency becomes difficult to determine.

48. Gentili, *De legationibus,* 2:62.

49. On this subject, see Adair, *The Exterritoriality of Ambassadors,* which does an admirable job of presenting the gap between diplomatic theory and practice during this period. Like other writers on the subject, however, he fails to note the ambiguities involved in characterizing the diplomat as "sacred." It should, of course, be noted that efforts to elevate and protect the diplomat were parallel to similar efforts, particularly in France, to establish the sacrality of the monarch himself.

50. For an insightful discussion of seventeenth-century French objections to the theater, see Thirouin, *L'Aveuglement salutaire.* Also useful on the subject of the actor's ambiguous identity in England, particularly as it intersected with religion and politics through the use of clothing, is Jones and Stallybrass, *Renaissance Clothing.* This last approach is particularly useful given the frequent references in France to the ambassador being clothed, or "revêtu" in his representative character.

51. Hotman, *L'Ambassadeur,* 61.

52. Gentili, *De legationibus,* 2:139.

53. Ibid., 174.

54. We shall see, in chapter 5, that the separability of actor and role was not, in fact, as taken for granted by certain critics of the theater as it seems to be by Gentili.

55. The phrase "et l'autre la sienne propre" was excluded from the 1709 edition of Lancelot's translation of the treatise but can be found in older versions.

56. De Vera, *Le parfait ambassadeur,* 276.

57. This distinction should be added to Gentili's carefully drawn difference between the interpreter, who is present but whose language we do not understand, and the ambassador, who represents someone alive but not present. Whether the ambassador continues to represent after his sovereign dies speaks to the issue of the identification of the prince and the state, raising once again the issue of the appropriateness of discussing "the king's two bodies" in the French context.

58. In the passage reproduced in the second edition, second volume, of Callières's *De la manière de négocier,* a significant change is made: here, the ambassador takes off the royal clothing when he exits the stage. This change in de Vera's wording greatly reduces the interest of the passage as well as its troubling ambiguity.

59. Galardi, in his attack on Wicquefort's *Mémoires,* justifies his work as able to enlighten the reader "sur tout ce que la passion du Ministre a generalement defiguré, l'infidelité dont il écrit n'étant pas moins grande que celle dont il a traité les choses qu'on luy avoit confiées" (on everything that the passion of the Minister has generally defigured, the infidelity with which he writes being no less than that with which he treated the things confided in him) (*Reflexions,* "au lecteur," n.p.). E. R. Adair offers the following: "Wicquefort, however, had in his own person

experienced the dangers to which ambassadors might be exposed, for, though by birth a Dutchman, he had resided in Holland as agent for the Duke of Luneburg and while there had been condemned to perpetual imprisonment for communicating Dutch secrets of state; he therefore gives very vigorous support to the view that an ambassador possesses full immunity no matter what his nationality may be, if he has been accepted in such capacity by the receiving state, for he represents the actual person of the sovereign who has sent him and who cannot be subject to a foreign jurisdiction; in addition, any such subjection on the part of an ambassador would so limit his freedom of action as to make it impossible for him to perform the duties of his embassy" (31).

60. Wicquefort, *L'Ambassadeur,* 1:5.

61. Ibid., 2:3.

62. "Les Princes, & les personnes de la premiere qualité aprés eux, donnent beaucoup de lustre à ces Ambassadeurs de ceremonies, & y sont plus propres que les plus habiles negociateurs, parce qu'ils representent plus naturellement le Souverain dans une Ambassade d'obedience, à un mariage, ou à un enterrement, où il y a quelque chose de plus éclatant & de moins solide, que dans la negociation" (ibid., 1:74–75).

63. Ibid., 2:5 (emphasis mine).

64. Ibid., 2:6.

65. Ibid., 2:6.

66. Ibid., 2:7.

67. Gentili, *De legationibus,* 164 (emphasis mine).

68. Wicquefort, *L'Ambassadeur,* 1:2. Compare this description to that given by James Howell, in the *Discourse of Ambassadors* contained in his *Proedria Basilike.* There, Howell takes extra care to make sure that the use of ambassadors is described in language that in no way affects the sovereignty of the sending prince, especially since the purpose of the larger treatise is, indeed, to establish precedency, which, as I show in chapter 4, is very closely tied to the representational model of diplomacy. "It is observed in all stories, and confirmed by multitude of examples, that the Interview and encounter of Kings hath bin rather a disadvantage than an advance to any great business, specially intreating Capitulations of Peace. Therfore in the Politiks tis a Principle, that in Colloquies for Pacification Princes should not appeer in person, but be represented by their Ambassadors and Commissaries" (182).

69. A thoughtful and complete discussion of these questions, in which theory is shown to lag considerably behind practice, can be found in E. R. Adair's study of early modern exterritoriality. Adair provides a clear picture of the complexities of exterritoriality as this concept accompanied the rise in use of resident ambassadors, with discussions of Grotius, Zouche, Wicquefort, and Bynkershoek.

70. Grotius's surprisingly brief remarks on the rights of diplomats are contained in chapter 18 of the second book of *De iure belli ac pacis.*

71. Grotius, *The Law of War and Peace,* 198.

72. Interestingly, and not insignificantly, Hotman shares Grotius's aversion to the resident ambassador, approvingly citing Henri IV's plan to expel them from his court and reminding the reader, as does Grotius, that this institution was unheard of in antiquity.

73. Hotman, *L'Ambassadeur,* 94.

74. Ibid., 101–2.

75. Ibid.

76. Ibid., 88.

77. Wicquefort, *L'Ambassadeur,* 2:415.

78. Ibid., 1:415.

79. Ibid., 1:420.

80. Ibid., 1:421 (emphasis mine).

81. Bynkershoek, *Traité du juge competent des ambassadeurs,* 23.

82. Ibid., 37.

83. Ibid., 40.

84. Ibid., 48.

85. Ibid., 87 (footnote).

86. Ibid., 118.

87. Hotman, *L'Ambassadeur,* 51.

88. On the herald, I have already cited Gentili's careful distinction of the ambassador from both the orator and the interpreter. Howell's phrasing seems appropriate here; he says of heralds that "they were strictly tied to the very same words that were dictated unto them" (*Proedria Basilike,* 182).

89. Gentili, *De legationibus,* 169.

90. Ibid., 170.

91. Ibid., 174.

92. Ibid., 180–81.

93. Ibid., 199.

94. Hotman, *L'Ambassadeur,* 70.

95. Ibid., 71.

96. Ibid.

97. Wicquefort, *L'Ambassadeur,* 2:103.

98. Ibid., 2:106.

99. Ibid., 2:109.

100. Ibid., 2:110.

101. Louis XIV asserts the uniqueness of this knowledge in the *Mémoires,* telling his son "ceux qui auront plus de talents et plus d'expérience que moi, n'auront pas régné, et régné en France; et je ne crains pas de vous dire que plus la place est élevée, plus elle a d'objets qu'on ne peut ni voir ni connaître qu'en l'occupant" (those that may, in the future, have more talent and experience than myself, will not have reigned, nor reigned in France; and I tell you that the more elevated the position, the more it has objects that can only be seen or known by occupying it) (Louis XIV, *Mémoires,* 43).

102. Rousseau de Chamoy, *De l'idée du parfait ambassadeur,* 38 (emphasis mine).

103. Ibid., 38–39.

104. Callières, *De la manière de négocier avec les souverains,* 177 (emphasis mine).

105. Bouhours, *Entretiens d'Ariste et d'Eugène,* 116.

106. Ibid., 118.

107. For useful background on Callières's career and other writings in relation to *De la manière de négocier,* see Alain Pekar Lempereur's preface to the 2002 Droz edition of the text, 7–50.

108. Cited in Camille-Georges Picavet, *La diplomatie française,* 64.

CHAPTER 4: REPRESENTING THE SUN

1. For more on the diplomacy of Louis XIV, see Picavet, *La diplomatie française au temps de Louis XIV.* Further discussion of Louis XIV's diplomatic practice can be found in Louis André, *Louis XIV et l'Europe.*

2. Letter from Lionne to the Comte d'Estrades, 5 August 1661, Archives du Ministère des Affaires Etrangères, Correspondance politique, Angleterre, vol. 76, fol. 203r.

3. Le Bret, "De la souveraineté du roy," 135–36.

4. Ibid., 136.

5. Ibid., 137.

6. The extent to which Richelieu's governance of the state was seen to be relatively unproblematic is evident in the pages of Silhon's *Le Ministre d'Estat* (1634). Well known and widely read at the time, often mentioned together with Guez de Balzac's *Le prince,* Silhon's work goes out of its way to praise the almost miraculous manifestation of virtue in Richelieu, in a language that often presents Louis XIII as a prince whose chief contribution to the kingdom was choosing such a glorious minister. The *Fronde* and its accompanying *Mazarinades* would problematize this role of principal minister, putting pressure on the monarchy to articulate a political vision in which power would be seen as emanating from the king alone, and, of course, Louis XIV responded with his famous declaration to do without such a figure after Mazarin's death in 1661 (on this subject, see Daniel Dessert, *1661: Le roi prend le pouvoir*). The change in royal ideology is indicated by a remark made by Fernando de Galardi in his *Traité politique,* which praises Richelieu's ability for dissimulation while noting that "il s'attribuait ce pouvoir absolu dont il depouilloit Louis XIII" (he attributed to himself the absolute power of which he deprived Louis XIII) (103).

7. Le Bret, "De la souveraineté du roy," 150.

8. Ibid., 151.

9. Senault, *Le monarque,* 351–52 (emphasis mine).

10. Ibid., 354.

11. Ibid., 365–66.

12. Bossuet's *Discours sur l'histoire universelle,* which in part "proves" the participation of the French monarch in a larger divine plan, can be viewed as a sophisticated attempt to provide just such a point of contact.

13. Senault, *Le monarque,* 378–80.

14. Ibid., 384.

15. Ibid., 383.

16. Le Moyne, *De l'art de règner,* 276.

17. Ibid., 312.

18. Ibid., 313–14.

19. Ibid., 524.

20. Ibid., 531.

21. Ibid., 560.

22. Ibid., 561.

23. Ibid., 533–34.

24. See Garrett Mattingly, *Renaissance Diplomacy.*

25. I say "justify rhetorically" because the ideal of a united Christian Europe had never been without fault lines or contradictions—witness the everlasting tension between the French kingdom and the Holy Roman Empire. These tensions, however, were able to be bridged through the exertions of legal apologists and presented as means to the ultimate end of peaceful unity, which remained the same. The outcry surrounding Richelieu's diplomatic relations with Protestant states, which were seen as evidence of his Machiavellian disregard for this unity, should prove my point that something fundamental changed in the years surrounding the end of the Thirty Years' War.

26. For a discussion of how this might be accomplished theoretically, see Grosrichard's *Structure du sérail.*

27. Bouhours, *Entretiens d'Ariste et d'Eugène,* 256–57.

28. See Ménager, *Diplomatie et théologie à la Renaissance.*

29. Jean Racine, *Oeuvres complètes,* 2:348.

30. Ibid., 348.

31. Ibid., 349.

32. Louis Marin, *Le portrait du roi,* 49–107.

33. The recounting of these events and their consequences occupies a full seven pages of Goubert's edition of the *Mémoires* (96–103).

34. Louis XIV, *Mémoires,* 102–3.

35. "Le roi ne reçoit plus de ses sujets en qualité de ministres des autres princes" (the king no longer receives his own subjects in the quality of ministers of other princes) (Callières, *De la manière de négocier,* 112).

36. In this respect, the issue of precedency resembles that of the lit de justice, insofar as the insistence on the institution's perpetuity in an unchanged form hid the very real changes taking place. See Sarah Hanley, *The Lit de Justice of the Kings of France.*

37. Gentili, *De legationibus,* 186–87.

38. It could also be argued that even though Howell argues for English precedency, he does so in language adopted from, and established by, the French; after all, the *Proedria* was written three years after the events in London in 1661 that contributed to establishing the importance of precedency on the international scene in a new, more urgent, way.

39. James Howell, *Proedria Basilike,* analysis, fourth section (unnumbered).

40. Ibid., 5.

41. Louis XIV, *Mémoires,* 76.

42. Sonnino, *Mémoires,* 51–52.

43. Louis XIV, *Mémoires,* 76–77; translation, Sonnino, *Mémoires,* 52.

44. Indeed, Louis XIV often implies that the significant role of Parliament in British government, especially, of course, after the beheading of Charles I, deprives the English king of any

claim of parity with either France or Spain. That Howell ends his defense of Britain's right to precedency with a plea to the House of Commons to give the king more money would only support the French interpretation of the British king's dependence on his people.

45. Howell, *A Discourse of Ambassadors* (follows *Proedria Basilike*), 179.

46. Ibid., 182.

47. Ibid.

48. Ibid., 187.

49. Wicquefort, *L'ambassadeur*, 1:287.

50. Ibid., 1:351.

51. Although Louis also cites the hereditary nature of the French Crown as support for his argument for precedency, heredity (again, nearly absent from the rest of the memoirs) is followed by references to the greatness of French power and the absoluteness of the king's authority. In a sense, therefore, Louis XIV is arguing less for recognition of the close *link* (and dependence) between the French monarchy and the divine than for recognition of the inherent similarity between the French king and God.

52. International experience in the Council of Trent and the negotiations at Münster that ended the Thirty Years' War had taught European monarchs that the best way to avoid counterproductive arguments of precedency was simply to avoid having the French and Spanish ambassadors at the same court or the same event. With the rise of residential diplomacy, however, this technique of avoidance was increasingly impossible, as the king of England would soon discover.

53. Louis XIV to d'Estrades, 13 August 1661, Archives du Ministère des Affaires Etrangères, Mémoires et Documents, Angleterre, vol. 27, fol. 9v.

54. Ibid., fol. 12v.

55. Louis XIV to d'Estrades, 24 September 1661, Archives du Ministère des Affaires Etrangères, Mémoires et Documents, Angleterre, vol. 27, fol. 22r.

56. D'Estrades to Louis XIV, 10 October 1661. Archives du Ministère des Affaires Etrangères, Mémoires et Documents, Angleterre, vol. 27, fol. 115.

57. Anon., *Relation de ce quy s'est passé entre les couronnes de France et d'Espagne,* 6.

58. Mémoire du Roi à Mr. le Comte d'Estrades, Archives du Ministère des Affaires Etrangères, Correspondance politique, Angleterre, vol. 76, fol. 256ff. Here, Louis XIV expresses his opinion that recalling d'Estrades would be wrong, "car au reste Elle a toute satisfaction de ses services, et le tient mesme aussi capable qu'aucun autre de ses sujets de continuer a luy en rendre de considerables" (for in fact his majesty is completely satisfied with his services and considers him to be as capable as anyone else of continuing to render his majesty considerable services).

59. Louis XIV to d'Estrades, 25 January 1662, Mémoires et Documents, Angleterre, vol. 27, fol. 48v.

60. D'Estrades to Louis XIV, February 1, 1662, Mémoires et Documents, Angleterre, vol. 27, fols. 134–36.

61. Mémoire du Roy a d'Estrades, November 1, 1661, Correspondence politique, Angleterre, 1661, supplément, vol. 76, fol. 260r.

62. The Newberry Library manuscript concerning these events contains a vivid picture of the atmosphere at Fontainebleau when the king decided not to accept the concessions made by the

Spanish but instead chose to hold out for full cession of precedency. See Anon., *Relation de ce quy s'est passé entre les couronnes de France et d'Espagne*, 40–41.

63. Lettre du Roy au Sr. Batailler, November 18, 1661, Archives du Ministère des Affaires Etrangères, Correspondence politique (Angleterre 1661), vol. 76, fols. 262–64.

64. Louis XIV, *Mémoires*, 101–2.

65. Sonnino, *Mémoires*, 74.

66. For the final negotiations, see Anon., *Relation de ce quy s'est passé entre les couronnes de France et d'Espagne*, 104–11.

67. These relations were particularly tense due to Mazarin's opposition to Alexander VII's election, and French influence at the papal court was at a very low point. See, on this subject as well as for more complete background of the Créquy affair, Charles de Moüy's exhaustive two-volume study, *Louis XIV et le Saint-Siège*.

68. Louis XIV to Créquy, 16 June 1662, Archives du Ministère des Affaires Etrangères, Correspondance Politique, Rome, vol. 151, fol. 38r.

69. Lionne to Créquy, 30 June 1662, Archives du Ministère des Affaires Etrangères, Correspondance Politique, Rome, vol. 151, fol. 51r.

70. Louis XIV to Créquy, 30 June 1662, Archives du Ministère des Affaires Etrangères, Correspondance Politique, Rome, vol. 151, fol. 53v.

71. For an excellent discussion of this conflict between the temporal and the ecclesiastic in the papacy, see Paolo Prodi, *The Papal Prince*.

72. Louis XIV to Créquy, 14 July 1662, Archives du Ministère des Affaires Etrangères, Correspondance Politique Rome, vol. 151, fol. 69v.

73. Louis XIV to Créquy, 28 July 1662, Archives du Ministère des Affaires Etrangères, Correspondance Politique Rome, vol. 151, fol. 82v.

74. Ibid., fol. 84v.

75. Ibid., fol. 85r.

76. See Agostino Paravicini-Bagliani, *The Pope's Body,* for further development of this theme.

77. Louis XIV's hostility to the Parlement of Paris after the Fronde is well documented; see also the discussions of changes in royal authority by Sarah Hanley, *The Lit de Justice;* Ralph Giesey, *Cérémonial et puissance souveraine;* and Kantorowicz, *The King's Two Bodies.*

78. I thank Helen Harrison for pointing out that the condemnation of Charles I of England in the name of the king (by Parliament) would have reinforced French ambivalence about separating the king's two bodies so strongly.

79. See E. R. Adair, *The Exterritoriality of Ambassadors,* for a (disapproving) discussion of this franchise in Spain and Rome.

80. Louis XIV to Créquy, 30 August 1662, Archives du Ministère des Affaires Etrangères, Correspondance Politique Rome, vol. 151, fol. 128.

81. As a duke, Créquy had a right to this title, just as other kings are called "brother" by Louis XIV.

82. Louis XIV to Créquy, 22 September 1662, Archives du Ministère des Affaires Etrangères, Correspondance Politique Rome, vol. 151, fol. 146 verso.

83. Louis XIV to Créquy, 3 November 1662, Archives du Ministère des Affaires Etrangères, Correspondance Politique Rome, vol. 151, fol. 227.

84. For a detailed discussion of these negotiations, see Lucien Bély's *Espions et ambassadeurs au temps de Louis XIV.*

CHAPTER 5: MEDIATION AND SEVENTEENTH-CENTURY FRENCH THEATER

1. For a useful survey of the emergence of authorship in the seventeenth century, see Viala's classic *La naissance de l'écrivain.*

2. A subtle consideration of the complex relation between writing and power is Jouhaud's *Pouvoirs de la littérature.*

3. I am, of course, far from the first critic to suggest a relation between seventeenth-century theater and politics. Interested readers should consult Jean-Marie Apostolidès, *Le Prince sacrifié.* Works that treat issues similar to those in this book include Murray, *Theatrical Legitimation,* which concentrates more on the role of the spectator than the roles of the author and actor, and Hermassi's excellent *Polity and Theater in Historical Perspective,* which does not look at seventeenth-century French theater but has pertinent observations on the tragedies of Shakespeare. Hélène Merlin-Kajman offers a reading of the content of several of the century's most noted plays, including many by Corneille, that dovetails nicely with my own study. Her work, *L'Absolutisme dans les lettres,* reads these plays through the prism of the conflict between private and public afflicting all levels of French monarchical society. Her readings, while much less centered on the king than my own, can and should be read in conjunction with my own work.

4. See Canova-Green, *La politique-spectacle au grand siècle.*

5. D'Aubignac, *La pratique du théâtre,* 2.

6. Ibid., 3.

7. Chappuzeau, *Le théâtre françois.*

8. McClure, "Une parfaite et sincère bonne correspondance et amitié."

9. Louis XIV's taste for spectacle is quite evident throughout the *Mémoires,* and especially in the description of the Spanish ambassador's cession of precedency cited at length in chapter 4.

10. The history of dedication is complex and much more fraught with tension and contradiction than I indicate here. For an excellent discussion of the issues involved with dedication, see Chartier, *Forms and Meanings,* especially the chapter titled "Princely Patronage and the Economy of Dedication," 25–42. Chartier states that the dedication to the prince "is also a figure by means of which the prince seems himself praised as the primordial inspiration and the first author of the book that is being presented to him, as if the writer or the scholar were offering him a work that was in fact his own" (42).

11. Corneille, *Oeuvres complètes,* 247–48. For insightful readings of this dedication, see Kajman, *L'absolutisme dans les lettres,* 81–90, and Jouhaud, *Pouvoirs de la littérature,* 292–307.

12. Alain Viala offers an excellent analysis of dedications and their functions in *Naissance de l'écrivain.*

13. For a good account of the influence of this question on the *querelles* surrounding Molière, see Norman, *The Public Mirror.* Norman shows how Molière's contemporaries leveled the charge against the playwright that he "merely" observed existing models of behavior and thus could not be considered a true author. Another means of denigrating Molière's theater at the time was by accusing him of "merely" being an actor.

14. D'Aubignac, *Pratique du théâtre*, 45. René Rapin, some years later, offers a similar explanation of the difference between the two genres. According to Rapin, theater is governed by action and epic is governed by narration, although he does place Homer (whose authorship of the epics d'Aubignac doubted) at the root of all poetry. See Rapin, *Les reflexions sur la poétique*, 71.

15. Aristotle, *Poetics*, 57.

16. Ibid., 83.

17. Interesting discussions of these issues can be found in Docherty, *On Modern Authority*, and especially in Weimann, *Authority and Representation in Early Modern Discourse*, which connects the problem of authorship to the Reformation.

18. D'Aubignac, *Pratique du théâtre*, 14.

19. For a perceptive discussion of the paradox through which d'Aubignac "privileges the poet, player and spectator as key figures of theatrical practice, stresses the complexity of their roles and characters, and simultaneously effaces them from the scene of representation" (61), see Murray, "Non-Representation in *La Pratique du Théâtre*." Again, however, I feel that Murray neglects issues surrounding the author somewhat in his focus on the spectator.

20. D'Aubignac, *Pratique du théâtre*, 28.

21. Ibid., 72.

22. Ibid., 88–89.

23. For a provocative look at the stakes involved in the similarities and differences between representation and referent in d'Aubignac, see Franko, "Act and Voice in Neo-Classical Theatrical Theory." Significantly, Franko touches upon the problematic notion of the image as it is deployed in d'Aubignac's theory of theatrical illusion.

24. D'Aubignac, *Pratique du théâtre*, 122.

25. Ibid., 280.

26. Ibid., 208.

27. Ibid., 115.

28. Ibid., 192.

29. Ibid., 29.

30. Ibid., 306.

31. Forestier, "Illusion comique et illusion mimétique." As Forestier states, "Il aurait assurément fallu un singulier retournement de personnalité pour que le créateur de l'*Illusion comique* se soumette à un principe d'*effacement* de l'auteur dramatique tel que le préconisait d'Aubignac et tous les 'doctes' à travers lui" (A singular transformation of personality would have been needed for the creator of the *Illusion comique* to submit himself to the principle of self-effacement of the dramatic author advocated by d'Aubignac and the other "doctes" through him) (390).

32. Here, I believe that Armand Gasté's reading of the *Excuse* in the introduction to his volume of documents relating to the *querelle* is perfectly accurate. The *Excuse* and all other documents cited are from his edition, *La querelle du Cid*, originally published in 1898.

33. Gasté, *La querelle du Cid*, 64.

34. A noteworthy study of these questions both in *Le Cid* and in the *querelle* can be found in Judovitz, "La Querelle du *Cid*: Redefining Poetic Authority."

35. Gasté, *La querelle du Cid,* 67–68.

36. Ibid., 73.

37. Ibid., 92.

38. Ibid., 103.

39. Ibid., 111.

40. Ibid., 120.

41. Ibid., 148.

42. François Lasserre seems to have solved the puzzle of the *Discours'* attribution, according it to N. Gougenot, the author, interestingly, of *Comédie des comédiens.*

43. Gasté, *La querelle du Cid,* 251.

44. Ibid., 260.

45. Ibid., 265–66.

46. I am unaware of any documented connection between d'Aubignac and the author of this *Discours,* although it seems that the profound similarities between the two works suggest that d'Aubignac would have been quite familiar with this pamphlet.

47. Gasté, *La querelle du Cid,* 371.

48. Perrault, *Paralèlle des anciens et des modernes,* 73–75, 129–31.

49. Ibid., 460–61.

50. As one of the texts in the *querelle* states, "L'Historien et le Poëte sont differens autant qu'un nain d'un geant, un homme nud d'avec un autre qui est vestu à l'advantage. L'Historien est serré, précis, racourcy, lié et attaché aux actions, mouvemens et rencontres des personnes, et du temps duquel il deduit les avantures . . . Le Poëte n'en est pas de mesme, encores qu'il ne s'esloigne pas tout à fait du vray, il luy est permis de faire mille tours auparavant que de l'approcher" (The historian is as different from the poet as a dwarf is from a giant, and a naked man is from someone clothed to his advantage. The historian is limited, precise, abbreviated, tied and attached to actions, movements, and meetings between persons, as well as the time in which his adventures are set. The poet is not the same, and although he does not abandon the true altogether, he is allowed to make many detours before approaching it) ("Le Souhait du Cid en faveur de Scudéry," in Gasté, *La querelle du Cid,* 164). This passage demonstrates the difficulty in qualifying poetic genius, all the while asserting its fundamental connection to the "vray."

51. Ibid., 205.

52. Ibid., 215.

53. Ibid., 273.

54. Ibid., 325. The *Advertissement* is generally attributed to Corneille, although its authorship remains uncertain. Corneille had also composed, in 1633, an *Excusatio* addressed to the archbishop of Rouen in which he attributed a large part of his success to the talents of Mondory: "Mais du moins la scène est là: le geste, la diction nous viennent en aide, et Roscius (Mondory) peut compléter l'oeuvre imparfaite. Il relève au besoin ce qui languit; toute sa personne contribue au succès, et de là peut-être le feu de mes vers, de là leur grâce" [But at least the stage is there: the gestures and diction help us, and Roscius (Mondory) can complete an imperfect work. He picks up what is languishing when needed; his entire person contributes to the play's success, and from him, perhaps, come the fire and grace of my verse] (Gasté, *La*

querelle du Cid, 11, in note 2 from the preceding page). The quote is a translation from the original Latin, which is also reproduced in the note. Corneille's attitude toward actors remained conflicted, however, not least in his ongoing efforts to gain control of his texts from the troupes who played them.

55. Chappuzeau, *Le théâtre françois,* 19.

56. D'Aubignac, *La pratique du théâtre,* 36.

57. Chappuzeau, *Le théâtre françois,* 53.

58. D'Aubignac, *La pratique du théâtre,* 37.

59. In a move oddly prescient of Octave Mannoni's exposition of the significance of the phrase "je sais bien, mais quand-même," with regard to theatrical illusion—each theatrical presentation requires the projected existence of someone who takes the spectacle for literal reality—d'Aubignac offers the following: "Supposons qu'un homme de bon sens n'ait jamais vu le Theater, & qu'il n'en ait même jamais ouï parler, il est certain qu'il ne connoîtra pas si les Comédiens sont des Rois & des Princes veritables, ou s'ils n'en sont que des phantômes vivans, & quand il sçauroit que tout cela n'est qu'une feinte, & un déguisement, il ne seroit pas capable de juger des beautez ni des défauts de la Piéce" (Suppose a man of good sense had never seen a theater, and had never even heard of one; it is certain that he would not know if the actors were really kings and princes, or if they were only the living ghosts of them, and when he finds out that all of this is only a play and a disguise, he would be unable to judge the beauty or the faults of the play) (*La pratique du théâtre,* 68).

60. Ibid., 88.

61. Ibid., 41.

62. Ibid.

63. Sabine Chaouche, in an otherwise thorough and admirable study of acting and oratory in seventeenth-century France, dismisses those who believe that the actor is in fact in danger of disappearing into his character, although she acknowledges that the moralists were encouraged in these opinions by treatises such as d'Aubigac's. Referring to a passage from d'Aubignac, Chaouche notes, "Ces propos montrent que le comédien ne s'identifie jamais au personnage" (These statements demonstrate that the actor never identified himself with his character) (*L'Art du comédien,* 123). Moreover, a few pages earlier, she refers to the belief that an actor could become "contaminated" by his role as "cette opinion fallacieuse du public" (this fallacious opinion of the public) (120).

64. Both Laurent Thirouin and Marc Fumaroli have contributed immensely to a profound reexamination of the logic behind the religious objections to theater. Thirouin's study of the quarrel between moralists and playwrights, *L'Aveuglement salutaire,* is an indispensable work on this subject, and I take up some of Thirouin's observations here. Marc Fumaroli, rightly and amply cited by Thirouin, offers, in *Héros et orateurs,* the explanation, which I agree with entirely, that during the seventeenth-century the strong division between theater and liturgy (which he characterizes as "faire croire" and "foi") was eroding and that much religious opposition to the theater was motivated by this erosion. I do differ with Fumaroli on the reasons for this erosion. Also very much worth reading, and with a wider scope than Thirouin, is Henry Phillips, *The Theater and Its Critics in Seventeenth-Century France.* Phillips includes some insightful readings of the problematics of the actor in this period.

65. This latter position would seem to be that of Merlin-Kajman, who provides an insightful reading of attitudes toward actors, including the proficient Montdory, in her *L'Absolutisme dans les lettres,* especially chapter 4, "Les Altérations du visage" (102–41). For a fascinating look at the evolution in political and theatrical representation from the seventeenth to the eighteenth centuries in France, see also Friedland, *Political Actors.* Friedland notes that "the genealogy of theater and politics reveals a surprising conceptual identity between the two representative forms" (3).

66. See Thirouin's reading of the *Traité* in *L'Aveuglement salutaire,* especially chapter 4, "Anthropologie," 121–80.

67. Citations are taken from Pierre Nicole, *Traité de la comédie,* 44, in Thirouin's edition of this and other texts.

68. Ibid., 103.

69. See Tertullian, *De Spectaculis,* 249.

70. Caffaro, "Lettre d'un théologien . . . ," in Urbain and Levesque, eds., *L'Eglise et le théâtre,* 93–94. The Prince de Conti said something similar several years before in his *Traité de la comédie et des spectacles:* "Or il faut avouer de bonne foi que la Comédie moderne est exempte d'idolâtrie et de superstition" (one must admit, however, in all good faith that modern theater is exempt from idolatry and superstition) (Thirouin, *Traité de la comédie,* 212).

71. "Lettre à la Duchesse de Longueville," cited in Thirouin, *L'Aveuglement salutaire,* 77.

72. See Fumaroli, *Héros et orateurs.*

73. Bossuet, "Maximes et refléxions sur la comédie," in Urbain and Levesque, *L'Eglise et le théâtre,* 178.

74. Nicole, "De la grandeur," in *Oeuvres philosophiques,* 392.

75. Senault, *Le monarque, ou les devoirs du souverain,* 205.

76. For an overview of Bossuet's political thought, see Truchet, *Politique de Bossuet.*

77. Bossuet, *Politique tirée des propres paroles de l'Ecriture Sainte,* 179.

78. Urbain and Levesque, *L'Eglise et le théâtre,* 123.

79. Once again, I must cite Merlin-Kajman's *L'Absolutisme dans les lettres* for its highly refined discussion of the opening of this gap throughout the century.

80. See Goodkin's excellent *The Tragic Middle* as well as Catherine Spencer's *La tragédie du prince.*

81. Rotrou's play is much closer to that of Lope de Vega than to that of Desfontaines. For an account of these influences, see the dossier compiled by François Bonfils and Emmanuelle Hénin in *Le Véritable Saint Genest,* 122–32. Quotations from the play, identified by line numbers, are taken from this edition.

82. See John D. Lyons, "*Saint Genest* and the Uncertainty of Baroque Theatrical Experience." While my own conclusions about the play's meaning differ from those of Lyons, I agree with his assessment of the modern critic's fundamental inability to read the play correctly: "Because the baroque theater is unsettling, we locate a single rational or acceptable meaning and cling to it. We therefore become, as readers and scholars, accomplices of modern cultural institutions that we profess to question on political or philosophical grounds" (603).

83. "Je pense avoir très bien écrit tout ce passage," in *Le Véritable Saint Genest,* dossier, 129. See Ruoff, "L'Art du comédien: Imagination créatrice et diversité."

84. Two interesting exceptions are Jean-Pierre Cavaillé and Jean-Claude Vuillemin. Cavaillé, in "Les Trois Graces du comédien," presents what could be called a libertine reading of the play, wherein Genest's conversion is placed in doubt, ultimately asking "si, sous la grâce du héros Chrétien, ce n'est pas la grâce profane du comédien qui triomphe" (if, under the grace of the Christian hero, it is not in fact the profane grace of the actor that triumphs) (712). This interpretation would be possible if the two graces were seen, at the time, as incommensurable; I would like to argue that the vehemence of religious criticisms of the theater suggests that they are not. Vuillemin, in "Rôle de Dieu, rôle du prince," draws a direct parallel between the emperor in the play and the absolutist monarch: "cette dramaturgie est faite avant tout pour un spectateur unique et privilégié. Pour celui qui, à l'image de l'empereur Dioclétian, a relevé Dieu de ses functions en se faisant lui-même la source de toute magnificence et de toute munificence" (this dramaturgy is made above all for a unique and privileged spectator. For he who, in the image of the emperor Diocletian, has relieved God of his functions by rendering himself the source of all magnificence and munificence) (96). Interestingly, Vuillemin only cites Camille's *defense* of Diocletian in response to Valérie's criticisms, not the criticisms themselves, that, pronounced by a character who has the best claim to understand perfect mediation, need to be taken seriously.

85. Several of the plays in Georges Forestier's excellent collection of lesser-known plays within plays revolve around this theme, and Montfleury himself wrote several plays of his own, including *Le comédien poète,* which can be found in Forestier's collection. See Forestier, *Aspects du théâtre dans le théâtre.* Forestier's critical work on this topic, *L'esthétique de l'identité dans le théâtre français,* remains an indispensable reference.

86. Vuillemin, for example, states, in reference to this scene, that "D'abord émerveillé, l'acteur se reprend et croit à un canular, à une supercherie. . . . La logique sceptique du théâtre ne semble pouvoir générer que le doute" (Awestruck at first, the actor regains control and thinks it is a practical joke. The skeptical logic of theater seems incapable of generating anything other than doubt) (Cavaillé, "Les Trois Graces," 707).

87. While Reinhard Kuhn, in his excellent article "The Palace of Broken Words," notes that "*Andromaque* is the interplay of surrogates in which everyone acts by proxy" (342), he does not consider the diplomatic role of Orestes as, in a way, the epitome of that principle.

88. Racine, *Oeuvres complètes* 1:259.

89. Ibid., 1:261.

90. Ibid.

91. Corneille, *Oeuvres complètes,* 440.

92. Racine, *Oeuvres complètes,* 1:262.

93. Timothy J. Reiss notes, in "*Andromaque* and the Search for Unique Sovereignty," that "[Orestes'] final madness . . . is no more than the concluding confirmation of that indecision, of the blindness, incapacity for correct action that has marked him from the beginning. Ambassador of the Greeks, he has remained always incapable of distinguishing his own interests from those of his society, private passion from public reason of state" (38). This assessment of Orestes' failings changes somewhat if we realize that precisely because he is an ambassador, he is the instrument of a state and thereby, as we have seen in the case of d'Estrades, almost legally unable to lay claim to any private personhood whatsoever.

94. Louis Marin, *La parole mangée.*

95. An interesting exploration of this specificity of theater is offered by Gouhier in *L'essence du théâtre*. It is worth noting that Gouhier draws a parallel between the actor and the ambassador, only to reject the comparison: "L'ambassadeur n'est pas le souverain dont il est le représentant: il lui prête sa voix. L'acteur est l'empereur qu'il représente: il lui prête son être" (the ambassador is not the sovereign that he represents: he only lends him his voice. The actor is the emperor he represents: he lends him his very being) (14). I hope to have shown that seventeenth-century efforts to ascribe to the ambassador more than a simple role of orator made this comparison more apt than Gouhier realizes.

96. Of course, as Georges Forestier reminds us, there is no indication that Corneille himself viewed *Suréna* as his last play. See Forestier, "Corneille et la tragédie: hypothèses sur l'élaboration de *Suréna*."

97. Line numbers are taken from the Seuil (L'Intégrale) edition of Corneille's *Oeuvres complètes*.

98. Corneille, *Oeuvres complètes*, 53.

99. The idea of Orode as tyrant has been qualified by several critics, including Serge Doubrovsky, who writes that "la vraie tragédie n'est pas qu'Orode soit, à l'instar de Marcelle ou de Cléopâtre, un 'monstre' qui ait tort, mais un sage qui *a raison* de redouter Suréna" (the true tragedy is not that Orode is, like Marcelle or Cleopatra, a monster who is wrong, but rather a wise man who has reason to fear Suréna) (Doubrovsky, *Corneille et la dialectique du héros*, 454). Pierre Zoberman disagrees with Doubrovsky's view of the play as supremely balanced between Orode and Suréna: "Suréna est trop coupable, ou Orode trop justifié pour que la tragédie soit esthétiquement satisfaisante" (Suréna is too guilty, or Orode too justified for the tragedy to be aesthetically satisfying) (Zoberman, "*Suréna*: Le théâtre et son trouble," 149). Such disagreements, which continue to be vigorous, attest to the problematic nature of allocating blame to either Orode or Suréna.

100. Fumaroli, *Héros et orateurs*, p. 77.

101. Pacorus's descriptions of love as an obstacle recur throughout *Suréna*: "Qui connaît un obstacle au bonheur de l'Etat/Tant qu'il le tient caché commet un attentat" (Who knows of an obstacle to the happiness of the State/As long as he hides it, commits a crime) (1175) and "Un sujet qui se voit le rival de son maître,/Quelque étude qu'il perde à ne le point paraître,/Ne pousse aucun soupir sans faire un attentat,/Et d'un crime d'amour il en fait un d'Etat./Il a besoin de grâce, et surtout quand on l'aime/Jusqu'à se révolter contre le diadème,/Jusqu'à servir d'obstacle au bonheur général" (A subject who finds himself the rival of his master/ Whatever pains he takes to hide it/Cannot even sigh without commiting a crime/And of a crime of love he makes a crime against the state/He needs grace and especially when he is loved/So much that he rebels against the crown/So much that he becomes an obstacle to general happiness) (1329–35).

102. Georges Forestier makes the apt observation that of all the characters, Palmis is the only one to appear in all five acts, identifying her as "le lien entre tous les personages, et le porte-parole des arguments des uns après les autres" (the link between all of the characters, and the spokesperson for their arguments, one after another), who nonetheless remains fairly invisible to the other characters. "Corneille et la tragédie," 159.

103. Corneille, *Oeuvres complètes*, 824.

CONCLUSION

1. Leibniz, "Mars Christianissimus," in *Political Writings*, 125–26.

2. Ibid., 137.

3. For a concise and well-argued account of Leibniz's theories and their opposition to the French configuration of universal monarchy, see Christiane Frémont, "Leibniz: Le modèle européen contre la monarchie à la française," in Méchoulan and Cornette, eds., *L'Etat classique*, 161–78.

4. For a good survey of Bayle's place in seventeenth-century French political debate, see Sally L. Jenkinson's recent edition of selected articles from the *Dictionnaire historique et critique* in Pierre Bayle, *Political Writings*. Bayle's article on David is particularly useful as an illustration of Bayle's attempts to separate the political and the religious into nearly autonomous spheres.

5. Keens-Soper, "François de Callières and Diplomatic Theory."

6. Ibid., 501.

7. Saint-Simon, *Mémoires sur les légitimés*, 1.

8. Of course, Saint-Simon's hatred of illegitimacy bordered on the pathological; yet it remains true that the placement of the bastards in the line of succession to the throne constitutes a violation of the fundamental laws of the kingdom that the king swears to uphold at his *sacre*. For a more in-depth exploration of Saint-Simon's feelings toward illegitimacy, see Le Roy Ladurie, *Saint-Simon ou le système de la Cour*.

9. Callières, *De la manière de négocier*, 63–64.

10. Ibid., 68.

11. While Lempereur holds that one cannot locate any precise influence of the War of the Spanish Succession or the Treaty of Utrecht on Callières's text (which was completed around 1700), he recognizes that "délibérée ou non, la publication tardive de *De la manière de négocier* vient à l'heure, quand elle correspond à la passation des pouvoirs vers le régent Philippe d'Orléans, au moment où ce dernier écarte ses rivaux. . . . Callières se fait pourvoyeur de légitimité pour une politique alternative, en rupture avec le principe de la bride laissée sur le cou d'un Bossuet où le Roi Soleil, 'lieutenant' de dieu sur terre, n'a de compte à rendre qu'à dieu sur la manière de régler l'ordre autour de lui" (whether it was deliberate or not, the late publication of *De la manière* arrived right on time, when it corresponded to the transfer of power toward the regent, Philippe d'Orléans, at the very moment when he was eliminating his rivals. . . . Callières becomes the vehicle of legitimacy for an alternative politics that breaks with the principle of the reins left on the neck of a Bossuet, where the Sun King, "lieutenant" of God on earth has only to answer to God for his method of regulating the order that surrounds him) (Callieres, *De la manière de négocier*, 26).

12. Ibid., 67.

13. Lucien Bély, *Espions et ambassadeurs*. Bély's work is essential reading for those wishing to understand the complex negotiations behind the Treaty of Utrecht.

14. Callières, *De la manière de négocier*, 79 (emphasis mine).

15. Ibid., 86.

16. Ibid., 104.

17. Ibid., 139: "ils sont égaux en titres et composent le même corps d'ambassade qui ne se peut séparer" (they are equal in title and compose one diplomatic body that cannot be separated).

18. Ibid., 132.

19. Ibid., 155 (emphasis mine).

20. Ibid., 155.

21. Ibid., 94.

22. In fact, the work, published in Holland, was seen as an insult to the recently deceased Louis XIV and earned Saint-Pierre expulsion from the Académie Française.

23. Saint-Pierre, *Discours sur la polysynodie,* 3.

24. Ibid., 43–44.

25. Ibid., 79 (emphasis mine).

26. Ibid., 89.

27. Ibid., 100–101.

28. For a good analysis of the developments leading to the transitional period of the regency, where competing interests governed both law and literature without reference to an overarching universal truth, see Biet, *Droit et littérature sous l'ancien régime.*

29. See, for example, Van Kley's valuable book *The Religious Origins of the French Revolution* as well as Chartier's *Cultural Origins of the French Revolution.* For a compelling analysis of the transformation of theatrical theory, especially concerning actors, and its relation to new conceptions of government based on representation, see Friedland, *Political Actors.*

Ackerman, Simone. "Refléxions sur les *Mémoires* de Louis XIV." In *Actes de Columbus,* ed. Charles G. S. Williams, 259–70. Tübingen: Gunter Narr Verlag (Biblio 17), 1990.

Adair, E. D. *The Exterritoriality of Ambassadors in the Sixteenth and Seventeenth Centuries.* New York: Longmans, Green, 1929.

Agamben, Giorgio. *Homo Sacer: Sovereign Power and Bare Life,* trans. Daniel Heller-Roazen. Stanford: Stanford University Press, 1998.

André, Louis. *Louis XIV et l'Europe.* Paris: Michel, 1950.

Anon. [CDSC]. *La Doctrine de Iesus-Christ Nostre Seigneur: Et celle de Robert, Cardinal Bellarmin, Jesuite Touchant les Roys et Princes: Rapportée l'une à l'autre pour monstrer que ainsi que l'une est veritable, aussi l'autre est fausse & partant iustement condamnee par Arrest de Parlement du 26 de novembre, 1610.* 1611.

———. *L'Ombre de Henri IV au Roi Louis XIII.* 1615.

———. *Recueil de plusieurs pieces d'éloquences et de poésie présentées à l'Académie Françoise pour le prix de l'année M. DC. LXXVII.* Paris: Jean-Baptiste Coignard, 1695.

———. *Relation de ce quy s'est passé entre les couronnes de France et d'Espagne pour la preseance en toutes les Cours et autres Lieux que le Roy catholique a declaré appartenir a Sa Majesté tres chrestienne par la bouche de son Ambassadeur en presence de tous les ministres et Ambassadeurs des Potentats et Princes Souverains qui estoient pres de sa Majesté tres Chrestienne.* Newberry Library. Case MS 6A33.

Apostolides, Jean-Marie. *Le Prince sacrifié: Théâtre et politique au temps de Louis XIV.* Paris: Editions de Minuit, 1985.

———. *Le roi-machine: Spectacle et politique au temps de Louis XIV.* Paris: Editions de Minuit, 1981.

Archives du Ministère des Affaires Etrangères (Quai d'Orsay). *Correspondance politique, Angleterre 1661,* Vol. 76, *supplément.*

———. *Correspondance politique, Rome,* Vol. 151.

———. *Mémoires et documents, Fonds Angleterre,* Vol. 27.

Aristotle. "Poetics." In *Classical Literary Criticism,* ed. D. A. Russell and M. Winterbottom, 51–90. Oxford: Oxford University Press, 1989.

Assaf, Francis. *La mort du roi: Une thanatographie de Louis XIV.* Tübingen: Gunter Narr Verlag (Biblio 17), 1999.

Barrett, James. *Staged Narrative: Poetics and the Messenger in Greek Tragedy.* Berkeley: University of California Press, 2002.

Bayle, Pierre. *Political Writings,* ed. Sally L. Jenkinson. Cambridge: Cambridge University Press, 2000.

Beaune, Colette. *Naissance de la nation France.* Paris: Gallimard, 1985.

Behrens, B. "Treatises on the Ambassador Written in the Fifteenth and Sixteenth Centuries." *English Historical Review* 31 (1936): 616–37.

Bellarmino, Robert. *Response aux Principaux Articles et chapitres de l'Apologie du Belloy, faulsement & à faux tiltre inscrite Apologie Catholique, pour la succession de Henry Roy de Navarre à la couronne de France.* N.p.: 1588.

Bély, Lucien. *Espions et ambassadeurs au temps de Louis XIV.* Paris: Fayard, 1990.

———, ed. *L'Invention de la diplomatie: Moyen Age-Temps Modernes.* Paris: Presses Universitaires de France, 1998.

Besançon, Alain. *L'Image interdite.* Paris: Fayard, 1994.

Biagioli, Mario. *Galileo Courtier: The Practice of Science in the Culture of Absolutism.* Chicago: University of Chicago Press, 1993.

Biet, Christian. *Droit et literature sous l'ancien régime: Le jeu de la valeur et de la loi.* Paris: Honoré Champion, 2002.

Blaga, Corneliu S. *L'Evolution de la technique diplomatique au dix-huitième siècle.* Paris: Pedone, 1937.

Bloch, Marc. *Les rois thaumaturges: Étude sur le caractère surnaturel attribué à la puissance royale particulièrement en France et en Angleterre.* Paris: Armand Colin, 1961.

Blumenberg, Hans. *The Legitimacy of the Modern Age,* trans. Robert M. Wallace. Cambridge, Mass.: MIT Press, 1983.

Bodin, Jean. *Les six livres de la république.* Paris, 1580.

Bonney, Richard. *Political Change in France under Richelieu and Mazarin, 1624–1661.* New York: Oxford University Press, 1978.

———. *Society and Government in France under Richelieu and Mazarin, 1624–1661.* New York: St. Martin's, 1988.

Bossuet, Jacques Bénigne. *Discours sur l'histoire universelle.* Paris: Garnier-Flammarion, 1966.

———. *Œuvres.* Paris: Librairie Catholique Martin-Beaupré Frères, 1868.

———. *Politique tirée des propres paroles de l'Ecriture Sainte.* Geneva: Droz, 1967.

Bouhours, Dominique. *Entretiens d'Ariste et d'Eugène.* Paris: Honoré Champion, 2003.

Boureau, Alain. *Le simple corps du roi: L'impossible sacralité des souverains français XVe–XVIIIe siècle.* Paris: Les Editions de Paris, 1988.

Boursier, Nicole. "La loi et la règle." *Papers on French Seventeenth-Century Literature* 10(9) (1983): 651–71.

Budé, Guillaume. *De l'institution du prince.* Paris, 1547.

Burke, Peter. *The Fabrication of Louis XIV.* New Haven, Conn.: Yale University Press, 1992.

Busson, Henri. *La religion des classiques (1660–1685)*. Paris: Presses Universitaires de France, 1948.

Bynkershoek, Cornelius. *Traité du juge competent des ambassadeurs, tant pour le civil, que pour le criminel*, trans. Jean Barbeyrac. La Haye: Thomas Johnson, 1723.

Caffaro, Thomas. "Lettre d'un théologien illustre par sa qualité et par son mérite, consulté par l'auteur pour savoir si la Comédie peut être permise, ou doit être absolument défendue," in *L'Eglise et le théâtre*, ed. Ch. Urbain and E. Levesque, 67–119. Paris: Grasset, 1930.

Callières, François de. *De la manière de négocier avec les souverains*, ed. Alain Pekar Lempereur. Geneva: Droz, 2002.

Calvin, Jean. *Institution de la réligion chrétienne*, ed. Jean-Daniel Benoît. 5 vols. Paris: Vrin, 1957–63.

Canova-Green, Marie-Claude. *La politique-spectacle au grand siècle: Les rapports franco-anglais*. Paris: Papers on French Seventeenth-Century Literature (Biblio 17), 1993.

Cavaillé, Jean-Pierre. *Dis/simulations: Religion, morale et politique au XVIIe siècle*. Paris: Honoré Champion, 2002.

———. "Les Trois graces du comédien: Théâtre, politique et théologie dans *Le Véritable Saint Genest*." *French Review* 61(5) (1998): 703–14.

Chaouche, Sabine. *L'Art du comédien: Déclamation et jeu scénique en France à l'âge classique (1629–1680)*. Paris: Honoré Champion, 2001.

Chappuzeau, Samuel. *Le théâtre françois*. Paris: Jules Bonnassies, 1876.

Chartier, Roger. *The Cultural Origins of the French Revolution*, trans. Lydia G. Cochrane. Durham, N.C.: Duke University Press, 1991.

———. *Forms and Meanings: Texts, Performances, and Audiences from Codex to Computer*. Philadelphia: University of Pennsylvania Press, 1995.

Cordemoy, Géraud de. "Six discours sur la distinction & l'union du corps & de l'âme." In *Oeuvres philosophiques*, ed. Pierre Clair and François Girbal, 112–21. Paris: Presses Universitaires de France, 1968.

Corneille, Pierre. *Oeuvres complètes*. Paris: Seuil, 1963.

Cornette, Joël, ed. *La France de la monarchie absolue, 1610–1715*. Paris: Seuil, 1997.

Crouzet, Denis. *La nuit de la Saint-Barthélemy: Un rêve perdu de la renaissance*. Paris: Fayard, 1994.

D'Aubignac, François-Hédelin. *La pratique du théâtre*. Amsterdam: Jean Frédéric Bernard, 1715.

David, Marcel. *La souveraineté et les limites juridiques du pouvoir monarchique du IXe au XVe siècle*. Paris: Librairie Dalloz, 1954.

De Moüy, Charles. *Louis XIV et le Saint-Siège: L'Ambassade du Duc de Créqui (1662–1665)*. Paris: Hachette, 1893.

Der Derian, James. *On Diplomacy*. Oxford, UK: Basil Blackwell, 1987.

Descartes, René. *Oeuvres philosophiques*. Paris: Garnier Frères, 1963.

Dessert, Daniel. *1661: Le roi prend le pouvoir; naissance d'un mythe?* Paris: Editions Complexe, 2000.

De Vera Zuniga y Figueroa, Juan Antonio. *Le parfait ambassadeur*, trans. Lancelot. Leiden: Theodore Haak, 1709.

Docherty, Thomas. *On Modern Authority: The Theory and Condition of Writing, 1500 to the Present Day*. New York: St. Martin's, 1987.

Doubrovsky, Serge. *Corneille et la dialectique du héros*. Paris: Gallimard, 1963.

Drake, Stillman. "The Starry Messenger." *Isis* 49 (1958): 346–47.

Dreyss, Charles Louis. "Etude sur les mémoires de Louis XIV." In *Mémoires de Louis XIV pour l'instruction du dauphin*, 1:1251. Paris: Didier, 1860.

Dupuy, Pierre. *Instructions et lettres des rois tres-Chrestiens et de leurs ambassadeurs et autres actes concernant le Concile de Tente pris sur les originaux*. Paris: Cramoisy, 1654.

Eire, Carlos M. N. *War against the Idols: The Reformation of Worship from Erasmus to Calvin*. Cambridge: Cambridge University Press, 1986.

Elwood, Christopher. *The Body Broken: The Calvinist Doctrine of the Eucharist and the Symbolization of Power in Sixteenth-Century France*. Oxford: Oxford University Press, 1999.

Eslin, Jean-Claude. *Dieu et le pouvoir: Théologie et politique en occident*. Paris: Seuil, 1999.

Forestier, Georges, ed. *Aspects du théâtre dans le théâtre au XVIIe siècle: Recueil de pièces*. Toulouse: Université de Toulouse-Le Mirail, 1986.

——. "Corneille et la tragédie: Hypothèses sur l'élaboration de *Suréna*." *Littératures Classiques* 16 (1992): 141–68.

——. *Esthétique de l'identité dans le théâtre français, 1550–1680: Le déguisement et ses avatars*. Geneva: Droz, 1988.

——. "Illusion comique et illusion mimétique." *Papers on French Seventeenth-Century Literature* 11(21) (1984): 377–91.

Foucault, Michel. *Les mots et les choses*. Paris: Gallimard, 1966.

Franklin, Julian H. *Jean Bodin and the Rise of Absolutist Theory*. Cambridge: Cambridge University Press, 1973.

Franko, Mark. "Act and Voice in Neo-Classical Theatrical Theory: D'Aubignac's *Pratique* and Corneille's *Illusion*." *Romanic Review* 78(3) (1987): 311–26.

Frémont, Christiane. "Leibniz: Le modèle européen contre la monarchie à la française." In *L'Etat classique*, ed. Henri Méchoulan and Joël Cornette, 161–78. Paris: Vrin, 1986.

Friedland, Paul. *Political Actors: Representative Bodies and Theatricality in the Age of the French Revolution*. Ithaca, N.Y.: Cornell University Press, 2002.

Fumaroli, Marc. *L'âge de l'éloquence: Rhétorique et "res literaria," de la Renaissance au seuil de l'époque classique*. Geneva: Droz, 1980.

——. *La diplomatie de l'esprit: De Montaigne à La Fontaine*. Paris: Hermann, 1994.

——. *Héros et orateurs: Rhétorique et dramaturgie cornéliennes*. Geneva: Droz, 1996.

Galardi, Fernando de. *Reflexions sur les Mémoires pour les ambassadeurs et response au ministre prisonnier, avec d'Exemples curieux et d'importantes recherches*. Villefrance: Pierre Petit, 1677.

——. *Traité politique concernant l'importance du choix exact d'ambassadeurs habiles*. Cologne: Pierre de la Place, 1666.

Garnett, George, ed. and trans. *Vindiciae, Contra Tyrannos: Or, Concerning the Legitimate Power of a Prince over the People, and of the People over a Prince*. Cambridge: Cambridge University Press, 1994.

Gasté, Armand, ed. *La querelle du Cid*. Geneva: Slatkine Reprints, 1970.

Gauchet, Marcel. *Le désenchantement du monde: Une histoire politique de la religion.* Paris: Gallimard, 1985.

Gentili, Alberico. *De legationibus libri tres,* trans. Gordon J. Laing. New York: Oxford University Press, 1924.

Giesey, Ralph. *Cérémonial et puissance souveraine.* Paris: Armand Colin, 1987.

——. *The Royal Funeral Ceremony in Renaissance France.* Geneva: Droz, 1960.

Goodkin, Richard E. *The Tragic Middle: Racine, Aristotle, Euripides.* Madison: University of Wisconsin Press, 1991.

Goubert, Pierre, ed. *Louis XIV: Mémoires pour l'instruction du dauphin.* Paris: Imprimerie Nationale, 1992.

Gouhier, Henri. *L'essence du théâtre.* Paris: Vrin, 2002.

Grosrichard, Alain. *Structure du sérail: La fiction du despotisme asiatique dans l'Occident classique.* Paris: Seuil, 1979.

Grotius, Hugo. *The Law of War and Peace,* trans. Louise R. Loomis. Roslyn, N.Y.: Walter J. Black, 1949.

Guéry, Alain, and Robert Descimon. "Un Etat des temps modernes?" In *L'Etat et les pouvoirs,* ed. Jacques Le Goff, 183–356. Paris: Seuil, 1989.

Habertal, Moshe, and Avishai Margolit. *Idolatry,* trans. Naomi Goldblum. Cambridge: Harvard University Press, 1992.

Halévi, Ran, ed. *Le savoir du prince du moyen âge aux Lumières.* Paris: Fayard, 2002.

Hampton, Timothy. *Writing from History: The Rhetoric of Exemplarity in Renaissance Literature.* Ithaca, N.Y.: Cornell University Press, 1990.

Hanley, Sarah. *The Lit de Justice of the Kings of France: Constitutional Ideology in Legend, Ritual and Discourse.* Princeton, N.J.: Princeton University Press, 1983.

Hardin, Richard F. *Civil Idolatry: Desacralizing and Monarchy in Spenser, Shakespeare, and Milton.* Newark: University of Delaware Press, 1992.

Hermassi, Karen. *Polity and Theatre in Historical Perspective.* Berkeley: University of California Press, 1977.

Hobbes, Thomas. *Leviathan.* Cambridge: Cambridge University Press, 1996.

Hoffman, Kathryn A. *Society of Pleasures: Interdisciplinary Reading in Pleasure and Power during the Reign of Louis XIV.* New York: St. Martin's, 1997.

Hotman, Jean. *L'Ambassadeur.* Paris, 1603.

Howell, James. *Proedria Basilke.* London, 1664.

James VI and I. *King James VI and I: Political Writings,* ed. Johann P. Sommerville. Cambridge: Cambridge University Press, 1994.

Jones, Ann Rosalind, and Peter Stallybrass. *Renaissance Clothing and the Materials of Memory.* Cambridge: Cambridge University Press, 2000.

Jouhaud, Christian. *Les pouvoirs de la littérature: Histoire d'un paradoxe.* Paris: Gallimard, 2000.

Joy, Lynn Sumida. *Gassendi the Atomist.* Cambridge: Cambridge University Press, 1987.

Judovitz, Dalia. "La Querelle du *Cid*: Redefining Poetic Authority." *Papers on French Seventeenth-Century Literature* 16(31) (1989): 491–504.

Kantorowicz, Ernst. *The King's Two Bodies: A Study in Medieval Political Theology.* Princeton, N.J.: Princeton University Press, 1957.

Keens-Soper, Maurice. "François de Callières and Diplomatic Theory." *Historical Journal* 16(3) (1973): 485–508.

Kuhn, Reinhard. "The Palace of Broken Words: Reflections on Racine's *Andromaque*." *Romanic Review* 70 (1979): 336–45.

Lacour-Gayet, Georges. *L'Education politique de Louis XIV.* Paris: Hachette, 1923.

———. *Un Utopiste inconnu: Les codicilles de Louis XIII.* Paris: Emile Paul, 1903.

Lasserre, François. *N. Gougenot: La comédie des comédiens et le discours à Cliton.* Tübingen: Gunter Narr Verlag (Biblio 17), 2000.

Le Bret, Cardin. "De la souveraineté du roy." In *Les Oeuvres de Messire C. Le Bret.* Paris: Charles Osmont, 1689.

Leclerc, Gérard. *Histoire de l'autorité.* Paris: Presses Universitaires de France, 1996.

Leibniz. *Political Writings.* Trans. and ed. Patrick Riley. Cambridge: Cambridge University Press, 1988.

Le Moyne, Pierre. *De l'art de regner.* Paris: Cramoisy, 1665.

———. *De l'art des devises.* Paris: Cramoisy, 1666.

Lempereur, Alain Pekar. Introduction to Callières, *De la manière de négocier avec les souverains,* 7–50. Geneva: Droz, 2002.

Le Roy Ladurie, Emmanuel. *Saint-Simon ou le système de la Cour.* Paris: Fayard, 1997.

Lockwood, Richard. "The 'I' of History in the *Mémoires* of Louis XIV." *Papers on French Seventeenth-Century Literature* 14 (1987): 551–64.

Louis XIV. *Mémoires pour l'instruction du dauphin,* ed. Pierre Goubert. Paris: Imprimerie Nationale, 1992.

———. *Mémoires for the Instruction of the Dauphin,* trans. Paul Sonnino. New York: Free Press, 1970.

Loyseau, Charles. *Traité sur les seigneuries.* Paris, 1610.

Lyons, John D. *Exemplum: The Rhetoric of Example in Early Modern France and Italy.* Princeton, N.J.: Princeton University Press, 1989.

———. "Saint Genest and the Uncertainty of Baroque Theatrical Experience." *MLN* 109(4) (September 1994): 601–16.

Mairet, Gérard. *Le principe de souveraienté: Histoires et fondements du pouvoir moderne.* Paris: Gallimard, 1997.

———. *Les doctrines du pouvoir: La formation de la pensée politique.* Paris: Gallimard, 1978.

———. "Préface." In *Les six livres de la république.* Paris: Librairie Générale Française, 1993.

Malebranche, Nicolas. *Oeuvres.* Paris: Gallimard, 1979.

Marin, Louis. *La parole mangée et autres essais théologico-politiques.* Paris: Klincksieck, 1986.

———. *Le portrait du roi.* Paris: Editions de Minuit, 1981.

Mattingly, Garrett. *Renaissance Diplomacy.* London: Cape, 1955.

McClure, Ellen M. "Une Parfaite et sincère bonne correspondance et amitié: French-Turkish Trade and Artistic Exchange in Molière's *Bourgeois Gentilhomme*." *Romanic Review* 90(2) (1999): 155–66.

Méchoulan, Henri, and Joël Cornette, eds. *L'état classique: Regards sur la pensée politique de la France dans le second XVIIe siècle.* Paris: Vrin, 1996.

Melzer, Sara E., and Kathryn Norberg, eds. *From the Royal to the Republican Body: Incorporating the Political in Seventeenth- and Eighteenth-Century France.* Berkeley: University of California Press, 1998.

Ménager, Daniel. *Diplomatie et théologie à la Renaissance.* Paris: Presses Universitaires de France, 2001.

Mercer, Christia. *Leibniz's Metaphysics.* Cambridge: Cambridge University Press, 2001.

Merlat, Elie. *Du pouvoir absolu des souverains.* Cologne, 1685.

Merlin-Kajman, Hélène. *L'absolutisme dans les lettres et la théorie des deux corps: Passions et politique.* Paris: Honoré Champion, 2000.

Monod, Paul. *The Power of Kings: Monarchy and Religion in Europe, 1589–1715.* New Haven, Conn.: Yale University Press, 1999.

Morgain, Stéphane-Marie. *La théologie politique de Pierre de Bérulle (1598–1629).* Paris: Publisud, 2001.

Moss, Jean Dietz. *Novelties in the Heavens: Rhetoric and Science in the Copernican Controversy.* Chicago: University of Chicago Press, 1993.

Mousnier, Roland. *L'Assassinat d'Henri IV.* Paris: Gallimard, 1964.

———. *Les institutions de la France sous la monarchie absolue.* Paris: Presses Universitaires de France, 1974.

Murray, Timothy. "Non-Representation in *La Pratique du Théâtre.*" *Papers on French Seventeenth-Century Literature* 9(16) (1982): 57–74.

———. *Theatrical Legitimation: Allegories of Genius in Seventeenth-Century England and France.* Oxford: Oxford University Press, 1987.

Néraudau, Jean-Pierre. *L'Olympe du roi-soleil.* Paris: Société d'Édition Les Belles Lettres, 1986.

Nicole, Pierre. *Oeuvres philosophiques.* Paris: Hachette, 1845.

Numelin, Ragnar. *The Beginnings of Diplomacy.* London: Oxford University Press, 1950.

Norman, Larry. *The Public Mirror: Molière and the Social Commerce of Depiction.* Chicago: University of Chicago Press, 1999.

Paige, Nicolas. *Being Interior: Autobiography and the Contradictions of Modernity in Seventeenth-Century France.* Philadelphia: University of Pennsylvania Press, 2002.

Paravicini-Bagliani, Agostino. *The Pope's Body,* trans. David S. Peterson. Chicago: University of Chicago Press, 2000.

Perrault, Charles. *Parallèle des anciens et des modernes.* Munich: Eidos Verlag, 1964.

Phillips, Henry. *The Theatre and Its Critics in Seventeenth-Century France.* Oxford: Oxford University Press, 1980.

Picavet, Camille-Georges. *La diplomatie française au temps de Louis XIV (1661–1715): Institutions, moeurs et coutumes.* Paris: Félix Alcan, 1930.

Picot, Gilbert. *Cardin Le Bret (1558–1655) et la doctrine de la souveraineté.* Nancy: Société d'Impressions Typographiques, 1948.

Pink, Thomas, and M. W. F. Stone, eds. *The Will and Human Action: From Antiquity to the Present Day.* New York: Routledge, 2004.

Pintard, René. *Le libertinage erudite dans la première moitié du XVIIe siècle.* Geneva: Slatkine, 1983.

Pitkin, Hanna Fenichel. *The Concept of Representation.* Berkeley: University of California Press, 1967.

Pocock, J. G. A. *The Machiavellian Moment: Florentine political Thought and the Atlantic Republican Tradition.* Princeton, N.J.: Princeton University Press, 1975.

———. *Politics, Language and Time.* Chicago: University of Chicago Press, 1989.

Prodi, Paolo. *The Papal Prince: One Body and Two Souls; The Papal Monarchy in Early Modern Europe,* trans. Susan Haskins. Cambridge: Cambridge University Press, 1987.

Pufendorf, Samuel. *The Present State of Germany.* London, 1690.

Racine, Jean. *Oeuvres complètes.* 2 vol. Paris: Gallimard, 1966.

Rapin, René. *Les reflexions sur la poétique de ce temps et sur les ouvrages des poètes anciens et modernes.* Geneva: Droz, 1970.

Redondi, Pietro. *Galileo: Heretic,* trans. Raymond Rosenthal. Princeton, N.J.: Princeton University Press, 1987.

Reiss, Timothy J. "*Andromaque* and the Search for Unique Sovereignty." In *The Shape of Change,* ed. Anne L. Birberick and Russell Ganim, 23–51. Amsterdam: Rodopi, 2002.

———. *The Discourse of Modernism.* Ithaca, N.Y.: Cornell University Press, 1982.

———. *The Meaning of Literature.* Ithaca, N.Y.: Cornell University Press, 1992.

Rohou, Jean. "La Rochefoucauld, témoin d'un tournant de la condition humaine." *Littératures Classiques* 35 (January 1999): 7–35.

Rosen, Edward. "The Title of Galileo's *Sidereus nuncius.*" *Isis* 41 (1950): 287–89.

Rotrou, Jean. *Le Véritable Saint Genest.* Paris: Flammarion, 1999.

Rousseau de Chamoy. *De l'idée du parfait ambassadeur.* Paris: Pédone, 1912.

Rowen, Herbert H. *The King's State: Proprietary Dynasticism in Early Modern France.* New Brunswick, N.J.: Rutgers University Press, 1980.

Rubin, Miri. *Corpus Christi: The Eucharist in Late Medieval Culture.* Cambridge: Cambridge University Press, 1991.

Ruoff, Cynthia Osowiec. "L'Art du comédien: Imagination créatrice et diversité." In *Esthétique baroque et imagination créatrice,* ed. Marlies Kronegger, 205–18. Tübingen: Gunter Narr Verlag (Biblio 17), 1998.

Saint-Pierre, Abbé de. *Discours sur la polysynodie, où l'on démontre que la polysynodie, ou pluralité des conseils, est la forme de ministère la plus avantageuse pour un roi, & pour son royaume.* Amsterdam: Du Villard & Changuion, 1719.

Saint-Simon, Louis de. "Mémoires sur les légitimés." In *Pièces diverses,* ed. Jean de Bonnot, 1–177. Paris, 1967.

Senault, Jean-François. *Le monarque, ou les devoirs du souverain.* Paris: Pierre le Petit, 1662.

Serres, Michel. *Le Parasite.* Paris: Grasset, 1980.

Silhon. *Le Ministre d'Estat.* Paris, 1634.

Sonnino, Paul. "The Dating and Authorship of Louis XIV's *Mémoires.*" *French Historical Studies* (1964): 303–37.

———, trans. and ed. *Mémoires for the instruction of the Dauphin.* New York: Free Press, 1970.

Spencer, Catherine. *La tragédie du prince: Etude du personage médiateur dans le theater tragique de Racine.* Tübingen: Gunter Narr Verlag (Biblio 17), 1987.

Tertullian, *De Spectaculis,* trans. T. R. Glover. Cambridge: Harvard University Press, 1953.

Thirouin, Laurent. *L'aveuglement salutaire: Le réquisitoire contre le théâtre dans la France classique.* Paris: Honoré Champion, 1997.

———, ed. *Traité de la comédie et autres pièces d'un procès du théâtre.* Paris: Honoré Champion, 1998.

Tocanne, Bernard. *L'idée de la nature en France dans la seconde moitié du XVIIe siècle: Contribution à l'histoire de la pensée classique.* Paris: Klincksieck, 1978.

Truchet, Jacques. *Politique de Bossuet.* Paris: Armand Colin, 1966.

Urbain, Charles, and E. Levesque, eds. *L'Eglise et le théâtre.* Paris: Grasset, 1930.

Van Kley, Dale. *The Religious Origins of the French Revolution: From Calvin to the Civil Constitution.* New Haven, Conn.: Yale University Press, 1996.

Vera y Zuniga, Juan Antonio de. *Le parfait ambassadeur,* trans. Lancelot. Paris, 1640.

Viala, Alain. *La naissance de l'écrivain: Sociologie de la littérature à l'âge classique.* Paris: Editions de Minuit, 1985.

Vliegenthart, Adriaan W. "Galileo's Sunspots: Their Role in Seventeenth-Century Allegorical Thinking." *Physis: Rivista internazionale di storia della scienza* 7 (1965): 273–80.

Vuillemin, Jean-Claude. "Rôle de Dieu, rôle du prince: *Le Véritable Saint Genest* de Rotrou." *Littérature* 68 (1987): 86–101.

Weimann, Robert. *Authority and Representation in Early Modern Discourse.* Baltimore: Johns Hopkins University Press, 1996.

Wicquefort, Abraham de. *L'Ambassadeur et ses fonctions.* 2 vol. Cologne, 1690.

Wilks, Michael. *The Problem of Sovereignty in the Later Middle Ages.* Cambridge: Cambridge University Press, 1963.

Wormald, Jenny. "*Basilikon Doron* and *The Trew Law of Free Monarchies:* The Scottish Context and the English Translation." In *The Mental World of the Jacobean Court,* ed. Linda Levy Peck, 36–54. Cambridge: Cambridge University Press, 1991.

Zoberman, Pierre. *Les panégyriques du roi prononcés dans l'Académie Française.* Paris: Presses de l'Université de Paris-Sorbonne, 1991.

———. "*Suréna:* Le théâtre et son trouble." In *Actes de Baton Rouge,* ed. Selma A. Zebouni, 143–50. Tübingen: Gunter Narr Verlag (Biblio 17), 1986.

ambassador/ambassadorship *(continued)* "representation," 127–31, 230–31, 259–60; resident ambassadors, 108, 143, 279n72; sacred origins of, 111–19; in seventeenth-century sovereignty treatises, 104–5, 154–66; sixteenth-century association of with religion and angels, 276n25; the tragedy of perfect diplomacy in Corneille's *Suréna,* 240–49. See also *De la maniere de négocier avec les souverains;* Louis XIV, diplomacy under; mediation; *préséance*

Amien Marcellin (Ammianus Marcellinus), 45

André, Louis, 281n1

Andromaque (Euripides), 231, 232

Andromaque (Racine), 11, 230–40, 248–49; centrality of Orestes in, 234; connection between diplomacy and language in, 238–39; and the issue of second-generation heroes, 231; language of *lieutenance* (place-holding) in, 231–32; paradox of diplomacy in, 237–38; replacement as the dominant problem in, 235, 238; two prefaces to, 232–33, 240

"*Andromaque* and the Search for Unique Sovereignty" (Reiss), 290n93

Anne of Austria, 230

Apologie Catholique, pour la succession de Henry Roy de Navarre à la couronne de France (Belloy), 20

Apostolidès, Jean-Marie, 221, 269n58, 285n3

aristocracy, 31, 32, 262

Aristotle, 32, 232; on the possibility of mixed states, 31; on substance and accident, 66; on theater, 197–98, 200; on tyranny, 35

Assaf, Francis, 267n5, 270n74

Assayer (Galileo), 66, 109–10, 272n99

atomism, 272n99; as threat to the Catholic Church, 65–67

author/authorship, 196–97; difficulty of defining in seventeenth-century France, 208. *See also* theater, author-

ship and *Authority and Representation in Early Modern Discourse* (Weimann), 286n17

Balzac, Guez de, 281n6

Barbeyrac, Jean, 106–7, 137–38

Basilikon Doron (James VI and I), 75–77, 101

Bayle, Pierre, 253, 292n4

Beaune, Colette, 269n57

Beginnings of Diplomacy, The (Numelin), 275n4

Behrens, B., 275n5

Bellarmino, Robert, 7, 19–22, 30, 268n19

Belloy, Jean-Baptise de, 20

Bély, Lucien, 256, 292n13

Bergeret, Jean-Louis, 167–68

Bérulle, Pierre de, 37, 267nn6, 12

Biagioli, Mario, 110

Biet, Christian, 292n28

Blaga, Corneliu S., 275n2

Bodin, Jean, 4, 8, 37, 38, 41, 44, 52, 56, 65, 67, 76, 103, 107, 150, 220, 221, 224, 269nn40, 44; accusations of atheism against, 26, 36; on eloquence, 22–26; on *puissance*, 31; insistence upon the importance of definition, 25–30; on sovereignty, 4, 6, 26–30, 33–34, 38, 86, 128, 161, 176, 199, 262, 271n76; on tyranny, 35–36, 54

Boileau, Nicolas, 150

Bonfils, François, 289n81

Bossuet, Jacques-Bénigne, 5, 8, 72, 80, 121, 155, 164, 230, 270n73; on free will, 266n15; objections to the theater, 215, 216, 217, 219–20

Bouclier d'Etat (Lisola), 252

Bouhours, Dominique, 101, 150, 166–67

Bourgeois gentilhomme (Molière), 195

Brianville, Abbé de, 72

Budé, Guillaume, 13–14, 17, 22–26, 30, 56, 150; complex attitude toward monarchical legislation, 266n2; references to classical models, 25

Bussy-Rabutin, Roger de, 74

Bynkershoek, Cornelius, 133, 137–40

Caesar, Julius, 75

Caesarini Furstenerii Tractatus de jure suprematus ad legationum Principium Germaniae (Leibniz), 252

Caffaro, Thomas, 216, 220

Callières, François de, 107, 114, 127, 148–51, 170, 253–60; role of in diplomatic history, 275–76n13

Calvin, Jean, 15–17

Calvinism, 14, 16; challenge to the legitimacy of the monarchy, 17

Canova-Green, Marie-Claude, 194

Cardin Le Bret . . . (Picot), 270n68

Cassius, Stephanus, 139

Catholic League, 3, 15, 37, 144; criticism/condemnation of the monarchy, 51

Catholicism. *See* Roman Catholicism

Cavaillé, Jean-Pierre, 290n84

Cérémonial et puissance souveraine (Giesey), 284n77

Chaouche, Sabine, 213, 288n63

Chappuzeau, Samuel, 195, 211

Charlemagne, 173

Charles I (king of England), 282n44, 284n78

Charles II (king of England), 177–78, 179, 182

Charles V (king of England), 174

Charles V (king of France [Charles the Wise]), 41, 42

Chartier, Roger, 285n10, 293n29

Cinna (Corneille), 248

City of God, 14, 17, 117–18

City of God (Saint Augustine), 164

city of man, 14, 17, 117–18

Clitandre (Corneille), 244

Codicilles de Louis XIII . . . à son très cher fils aîne, 74

Colbert, Jean Baptiste, 74, 78

College of Cardinals, 187

Comédie des comédiens (Gougenot), 220, 287n42

Commentaries (Caesar), 75, 101

Concept of Representation, The (Pitkin), 5

Considérations sur les coups d'état (Naudé), 42

Conti, Prince de, 121, 214, 289n70

Copernicus, 271n88

Cordemoy, Géraud de, 67

Corneille, Pierre, 2, 11, 204–9, 210, 213, 233, 240–49, 251, 265n6, 287n54; attitude of toward actors, 288n54; repeated treatment of Roman provinces or colonies, 221

Cornette, Joël, 8

Corpus Christi (Rubin), 267n8

Council of Trent (1545–63), 20, 114, 117, 171, 283n52

Créquy, Charles, duc de: diplomatic incident surrounding, 10, 137, 157, 184–92, 277n33

Cultural Origins of the French Revolution, The (Chartier), 293n29

d'Andilly, Arnauld, 272n10

"Dating and Authorship of Louis XIV's *Memoirs*, The" (Sonnino), 272n9, 274n55

d'Aubignac, François-Hédelin, 10, 213, 214, 286n19, 288n59; on the distinction between epic and theater, 197; on the international importance of government sponsored plays, 194–95; on the theatrical writer, 198–204, 211–12

David, Marcel, 27

de Castro, Guilhen, 205

De iure belli ac pacis (Grotius), 279n70

De la manière de négocier avec les souverains (Callières), 107, 114, 148, 253–60; as the foundational text of modern diplomacy, 253; full title of, 276n14

De la recherche de la vérité (Malebranche), 2

De la souveraineté du roy (Le Bret), 37, 39, 154–57

De l'art de devises (Le Moyne), 59–67

De l'art de regner (Le Moyne), 37, 56–59, 161–63; Le Moyne's procedure in, 60–61

De legationibus (Polybius), 105

De legationibus libri tres (Gentili), 107

Giesey, Ralph, 274n47, 284n77

God: as *deus absconditus,* 42; perfection of, 29; relationship of to His creation, 2, 18; relationship of to kings, 14–15, 16, 20, 41, 162; unity of, 18–19. *See also* divine right theory; king/kingship, the king as the "image of God on earth"; Louis XIV, view of God

Goodkin, Richard, 221

Gougenot, N., 220, 287n42

Gouhier, Henri, 291n95

Grassi, Horatio, 109–10, 272n99

Grotius, Hugo, 105, 132–33, 174, 279nn70, 72

Guéry, Alain, 265n8, 266–67n3, 269nn55, 57

Guicciardini, Francesco, 259, 277n42

Habsburg Empire, splitting of, 105

Halévi, Ran, 272n2

Hampton, Timothy, 268n23, 274n42, 275n6

Hanley, Sarah, 274n47, 284n77

Harrison, Helen, 284n78

Hénin, Emmanuelle, 289n81

Henri III (king of France), 88, 268n19

Henri IV (king of France), 1, 3, 15, 20, 22, 88, 144, 268n19, 279n72

Héraclius (Corneille), 233

Hermassi, Karen, 285n3

Herodotus, 104

Héros et orateurs (Fumaroli), 288n64

Hobbes, Thomas, 36, 52

Homer, 104, 197–98, 233

honnête homme trope, 125, 127, 129, 277n29

Horace, 196

Hotman, François, 3

Hotman, Jean, 105, 107, 108, 119–20, 121, 134, 136, 141, 143–44, 144–45, 279n72

Howell, James, 172–76, 252, 276n26, 279n68, 280n88, 282n38, 283n44

"'I' of History in the *Mémoires* of Louis XIV, The" (Lockwood), 273n21

Iliad (Homer), 104

Impromptu de Versailles (Molière), 220

Institution de la réligion chrétienne (Calvin), 15, 16

ius gentium, 59, 134, 137, 275n9

James VI and I (king of England), 75–77, 80

je ne sais quoi, 8, 9, 54, 64, 67, 71–72, 77, 220, 251

Jean Bodin and the Rise of Absolutist Theory (Franklin), 266n2, 268n19

Jeannin, Pierre, 142, 144

Jenkinson, Sally L., 292n4

Joly, Claude, 72

Jones, Ann Rosalind, 278n50

Jouhaud, Christian, 285n2

Judovitz, Dalia, 286n34

Jurieu, Pierre, 253

Kantorowicz, Ernst, 2, 14, 77, 122, 273n20, 284n77; recent critiques of, 267nn4, 5

Keens-Soper, Maurice, 148, 253, 276n13, 277n29

king/kingship, 11, 31; ability of to institute laws, 41–42; alliance between monarchy and sovereignty, 32–33; the biblical origin of kingship, 19, 48–50, 267n13; and counterfeiting, 44–45, 54, 244; impact of the Protestant Reformation on, 14–15, 17; the king as the "image of God on earth," 8, 32–36, 45–46, 51, 219, 251; the king as *lieutenant* (place-holder) of God in the kingdom, 45–46; and the law, 44; medieval representations of, 271n77; as a punishment to man, 39; relation of to science, 65–66; as representative of the divine, 21, 37; and royal education, 69; singularity of royal legitimacy, 224; specificity of the king's marks, 44–45, 52; as subject to the authority of the pope, 19–22; subject/monarch difference, 36–38, 39, 260; tripartite model of, 56–57; and units of the state, 43–44. *See also* French monarchy, the

King's State, The (Rowen), 270n69
"king's two bodies" model, 2, 14, 15, 37,
    77, 103, 122, 187; application of to
    monarchies outside of England,
    273n20; recent critiques of, 267n4
Kreihing, Johannes, 271n93
Kuhn, Reinhard, 290n87

*La diplomatie française au temps de
    Louis XIV* (Picabet), 281n1
La Fontaine, Jean de, 236, 255
La mort du roi (Assaf), 267n5, 270n74
La naissance de l'écrivain (Viala),
    285nn1, 12
"La Querelle du *Cid*" (Judovitz), 286n34
La Rochefoucauld, François, duc de 5,
    72
"La Rochefoucauld . . ." (Rohou), 266n10
L'Absolutisme dans les lettres (Merlin-
    Kajman), 265n6, 285n3, 289nn65, 79
Lacour-Gayet, Georges, 75
L'Ambassadeur (J. Hotman), 107
L'Ambassadeur et ses fonctions (Wicque-
    fort), 107, 123–27; on the meaning of
    "representation," 127–31; as reflection
    of Wicquefort's personal situation,
    123–23
Lambert, Nicolas, 17
L'Art du comédien (Chaouche), 288n63
Las Mocedades del Cid (de Castro),
    205
L'Assasinat d'Henri IV (Mousnier), 265n7
Lasserre, François, 287n42
L'Astrée (d'Urfé), 232
"L'Autheur du Vray Cid Espagnol . . ."
    (Mairet), 205
L'aveuglement salutaire (Thirouin),
    278n50, 288n64
law: international system of, 105; *lois
    fondamentales,* 269n57
"law of nations," 275n9
Le Bret, Cardin, 4, 8, 31, 37–38, 51, 52,
    54, 55, 65, 66, 76, 77, 85, 119, 154–57,
    159–60, 159, 165, 220; minimization of
    the royal bloodline, 88; personal role
    in furthering the centralization of the

kingdom, 47; on the problem of royal
    acts/action, 41–43; relationship with
    Richelieu, 270n68; on sovereignty and
    fortune, 39–40, 63
Le Cid (Corneille), 204, 244; and the
    querelle du Cid, 11, 204–10, 286n32
Le comédien poète (Montfleury), 290n85
Le Ministre d'Estat (Silhon), 281n6
Le monarque, ou les devoirs du souverain
    (Senault), 37, 48–56, 157–61, 218; fun-
    damental tension in, 48
Le Moyne, Pierre, 8, 56–67, 77, 82,
    161–63, 164, 211, 220, 221; dismissal of
    sunspots and atoms, 63–67, 271n93;
    equation of king and God, 58–59; solar
    imagery in, 37–38, 64–65, 161, 163,
    165–66, 253, 271n88
Le parfait ambassadeur (de Vera), 107,
    111–13, 114–18, 122–23
Le portrait du roi (Marin), 15
Le prince (Balzac), 281n6
Le prince sacrifié (Apostolidès), 285n3
Le roi-machine (Apostolidès), 269n58
*Le savior du prince du moyen âge aux
    Lumières* (Halévi, ed.), 272n2
Le théâtre françois (Chappuzeau), 195,
    211
Le Véritable Saint Genest (Bonfils and
    Hénin), 289n81
Le Véritable Saint Genest (Rotrou),
    222–30; figure of Diocletian in, 230;
    focus on tyranny, 225–26; framing plot
    of, 222; importance of aberrant gover-
    nance arrangement in, 223–25; play
    within the play, 222; theme of media-
    tion in, 222–23, 229–30; tribute to
    Corneille in, 226
L'éducation politique de Louis XIV
    (Lacour-Gayet), 75
Leibniz, Gottfried Wilhelm, 105, 172,
    252–53
"Leibniz" (Frémont), 292n3
Leibniz's Metaphysics (Mercer), 266n9
Lempereur, Alain Pekar, 292n11
*Les institutions de la France sous la
    monarchie absolue* (Mousnier), 269n52

ment for the term "representation," 7; in Rotrou's *Le Véritable Saint Genest,* 222–23, 229–30; in seventeenth-century French theater, 10, 141, 209–21; and sovereignty, 11; system of outlined by Bellarmino, 20. *See also* ambassador/ambassadorship

Mémoires pour l'instruction du dauphin (Louis XIV), 9, 103, 153, 161, 165, 188, 193, 244; as articulation of the king's actions as his own, 77–82; as a collaborative writing effort, 72; comparison with James VI and I's *Basilikon Doron,* 75–77; establishment of authorship of, 272n9; failure to mention precursors or influences, 78–79; fate of, 101–2; importance of Colbert's notes and memoirs in the construction of, 74; *je* in, 77, 82, 90–92; Louis XIV's taste for spectacle in, 285n9; Louis XIV's view of his place in the kingdom and the world in, 84–85; manuscripts of, 92–102; *moi* in, 91–92; *nous* in, 85, 92; parallels with Julius Caesar's *Commentaries,* 75; as proof of Louis XIV's unique enjoyment of God's favors, 72–77; reception of, 68–71; recounting of the Comte d'Estrade incident in, 169, 182–84; replacement of the role of God by that of the king in, 81–82, 84, 97; resistance of to characterization, 272n10; role of the dauphin outlined in, 85–92; sources for, 72–77; succession and representation in, 240

memoirs, 74, 272n11; of *frondeurs,* 74

Mémoires sur les légitimés (Saint-Simon), 254

Ménager, Daniel, 275n5

Mercer, Christia, 266n9

Merlat, Elie, 17, 39

Merlin-Kajman, Hélène, 2, 221, 265n6, 285n3, 289nn65, 79

ministers, in seventeenth-century sovereignty treatises, 154–66

Molière, 195–96, 220; denigration of by his contemporaries, 285n13

monarchy. *See* king/kingship

Montaigne, Michel Eyquem de, 214

Montesquieu, Charles de Secondat, baron de 260

Montfleury, Zacharie Jacob, 290n85

Moss, Jean Dietz, 272n99

Mousnier, Roland, 265n7, 269n52

Murray, Timothy, 285n3, 286n19

"mystery of state." See *je ne sais quoi*

Naissance de la nation France (Beaune), 269n57

Naudé, Gabriel, 42

Neoplatonism, 4, 214

Nicole, Pierre, 121, 213–15, 216, 217–18, 220, 230

"Non-Representation in *La Pratique du Théâtre*" (Murray), 286n19

Norman, Larry, 285n13

Numelin, Ragnar, 275n4

nuncius, 109–10

Observations sur le Cid (Scudéry), 205–6

On Diplomacy (der Derian), 275n3

orator/oratory, comparison of orators with actors, 213

Oratory, the, 37

Ovid, 30

Pagano, Sergio, 272n99

"Palace of Broken Words, The" (Kuhn), 290n87

Palatinate, destruction of, 254

panegyrics, 67

Papal Prince, The (Prodi), 284n71

papacy, the: contentious relationship with the French monarchy, 22, 186; Louis XIV's diplomatic victory over, 184–92; medieval efforts to recast papal power, 268n30; papal authority, 19–22, 27, 187; papal succession, 187

Parallèle des anciens et des modernes (Perrault), 208

Pascal, Blaise, 7, 217

Peace of Westphalia (1648), 105, 117, 166, 172

Pellisson, Paul, 68–70, 72, 95–97

Périgny, 72, 92, 94–95

Perrault, Charles, 208
Philippe d'Orléans, 260
Phillips, Henry, 288n64
Philo Judaeus, 4, 38, 39
Picavet, Camille-Georges, 151, 275n2, 281n1
Picot, Gilbert, 270n68
piety, false, 54–55
Pink, Thomas, 266n15
Pitkin, Hanna Fenichel, 5, 6
Poetics (Aristotle), 197–98
Political Actors (Friedland), 289n65, 293n29
political authority: role of the people (citizenry) as source of, 5–6; seventeenth-century French theories of, 2
Politique tirée des propres paroles de l'Ecriture Sainte (Bossuet), 219–20
Polity and Theater in Historical Perspective (Hermassi), 285n3
Polybius, 105, 106
La pratique du théâtre (d'Aubignac), 194–95, 198–204, 210 (again, this may mean moving it to "L")
premier ministre, 160–61; Louis XIV's rejection of, 47, 74; problematization of the role of by the Fronde, 281n6; suspicion of, 157–58
préséance (precedency), 169–76, 182, 194, 258; avoidance of counterproductive arguments of, 283n52; English claim to, 174, 252; and the *lit de justice*, 282n36; Louis XIV's argument for, 283n51. *See also* d'Estrades, Godefroi, comte de
Prodi, Paolo, 284n71
Proedria Basilike (Howell), 172–76, 252, 276nn26, 28, 279n68, 282n38; arguments for English precedency in, 174
Projet de paix perpetuelle (Saint-Pierre), 256
Projet pour rendre la paix perpetuelle en Europe (Saint-Pierre), 260
Protestantism, 54; criticism/condemnation of the monarchy, 30, 51, 155, 253; doctrine of election/reprobation, 51; political threat posed by, 55–56, 67;

radical, 22, 37; reliance on/adherence to Scripture, 21, 50; and tradition, 42. *See also* Calvinism; Reformation, the
Public Mirror, The (Norman), 285n13
Pufendorf, Samuel, 105
puissance, 28–29; *puissance absolue*,, 28, 30–31; *puissance perpétuelle*, 29; *puissance publique*, 27; *puissance souveraine*, 27; slippage of the term in meaning to the person holding the power (the *souverain*), 27–29, 31, 48

querelle des anciens et des modernes, 193, 207, 216
querelle du Cid. *See Le Cid.*

Racine, Jean, 168–69, 221, 230–40, 248–49, 251, 265n6; celebration of Bergeret before the Académie Française, 167–68, 235
Rapin, René, 286n14
Ravaillac, François, 1, 22
"reason of state," 8
Reckoning of Weights for the Balance and Small Scale, A (Grassi), 272n99
Recueil des maximes veritables et importantes pour l'instruction du roi (Joly), 72
Redondi, Pietro, 66, 272n99
Réflexions sur les Mémoires . . . (Galardi), 277n33, 278n59
Reformation, the, 14–15, 17; in France, 266n3
Reiss, Timothy J., 22, 290n93
relazioni, 142, 143
Religious Origins of the French Revolution, The (Van Kley), 293n29
Renaissance Clothing and the Materials of Memory (Jones and Stallybrass), 278n50
représenter, 6
representation, 4–7; capacity of to take on a life of its own, 200; as an extension of mediation, 7; the "fiction of representation," 238, 249, 258, 259; and the language of self-interest, 5; what it is, 127–31

ELLEN MCCLURE is Associate Professor of French at the University of Illinois at Chicago. She received a Mellon Postdoctoral Fellowship at the Newberry Library in 2000–2001 and has written several articles on the intersection of seventeenth-century French theater and political theory.

THE HUMANITIES LABORATORY

The University of Illinois Press
is a founding member of the
Association of American University Presses.

Composed in 9/13 Walbaum
with Meta display
by BookComp, Inc.
Designed by Copenhaver Cumpston
Manufactured by Thomson-Shore, Inc.

University of Illinois Press
1325 South Oak Street
Champaign, IL 61820-6903
www.press.uillinois.edu